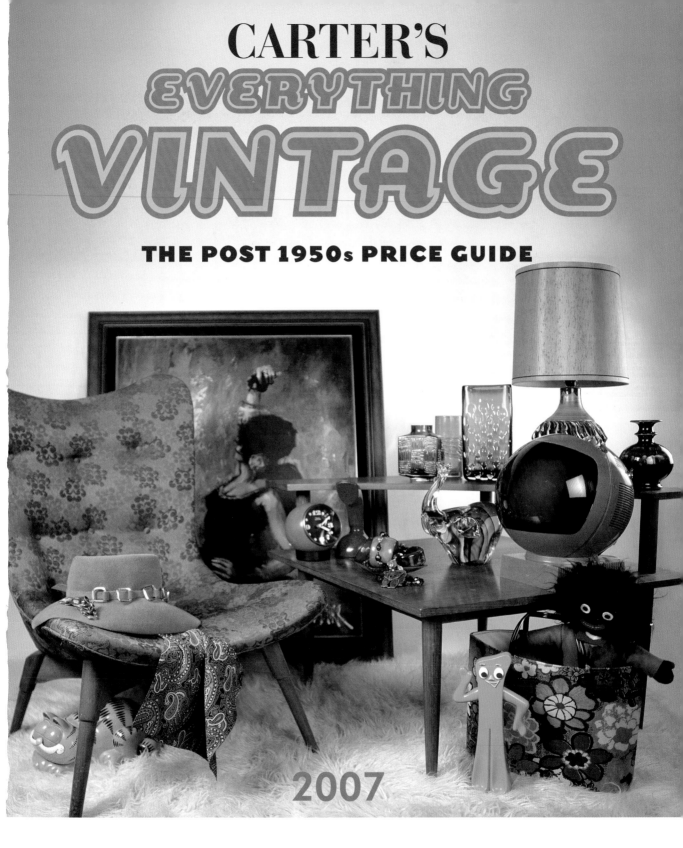

CARTER'S
EVERYTHING
VINTAGE

THE POST 1950s PRICE GUIDE

2007

2ND EDITION ~ PUBLISHED BY JOHN FURPHY PTY LTD

CARTER'S

EVERYTHING

VINTAGE

The Post 1950s Price Guide
2007
2nd Edition

CARTER'S Publications
The Most Comprehensive and Accurate Information

John Furphy Pty Ltd
Trading as
CARTER'S Antiques & Collectables Price Guide

PO Box 7246, BAULKHAM HILLS BC NSW 2153, AUSTRALIA
37/9 Hoyle Avenue, CASTLE HILL NSW 2154, AUSTRALIA

Toll Free Ph: 1800 670 630   Ph: + 61 2 8850 4600
Fax: + 61 2 8850 4100   ABN: 37 005 508 789
Email: info@carters.com.au   Web: www.carters.com.au

ISBN 1-876079-20-7

CONTENTS

ADVERTISER'S INDEX

ACKNOWLEDGEMENTS

The publishers would like to thank our staff, photographers, contributing dealers, designers, printers, friends, families and supporters whose contributions made this book a reality.

Joint Editors:	John Furphy Trent McVey
Publisher:	John Furphy Pty Ltd trading CARTER'S ANTIQUES & COLLECTABLES PRICE GUIDE 37/9 Hoyle Avenue Castle Hill NSW 2154 Australia ABN 37 005 508 789
Production Manager:	Susan Stafford–Hickson
Production Team Leader:	Leigh Holt
Production Team:	Rosalind Toombs, Nicola Ellis, Jill Vincent, Dylan Davies, Dane Gardiner, Amanda McVey, Vivienne Traynor, Jacqueline Madden, Peter Ellis, Linda Furphy, Sandie Chung, Stephen Ellis, Verusha Singh, Lauren Vincent, John Beggs
Additional Research Material Provided By:	Ian Pitt – Renniks Publications Pty Ltd
Photographers:	Chris Elfes (NSW, NZ, WA), Chris Maait (NSW, ACT), John Mildwaters (QLD), Len Weigh (VIC, SA), Matthew Abbott (NSW), Rick Merrie (VIC), Richard Parkinson (TAS), Tira Lewis (VIC, NZ)
Special thanks to:	Rick Milne
Page Design and Pre Press:	Colourscan Overseas Co Pte Ltd, Singapore
Cover Design:	Andrew Hogg Design Pty Ltd, Prahran VIC Australia
Cover Image:	Photographed at Chapel Street Bazaar, Prahran Victoria by Tira Lewis
Printers:	SNP Security Printing Pte Ltd, Singapore

INTRODUCTION

Our first edition confirmed the need for a publication such as *CARTER'S Everything Vintage*.

With *CARTER'S Everything Vintage* our aim is to cover all consumer items manufactured since the 1950s, that are available for sale on the secondary market. However, there is no single word in universal usage to describe this group of items.

We selected the word 'vintage' to cover these items, which all have some age, but are not antique. By itself, the word 'vintage' is often associated with motor vehicles or fashion, but our use of 'vintage' in our title is more encompassing.

Often the term 'collectables' is used to refer to this market segment, and indeed the largest group of items covered by this book would fall under the term 'collectables', which covers fields as diverse as ceramics, cereal toys, comics, CDs and records, badges and ephemera.

However, there are many groups of items we feature in *Everything Vintage* where the purchaser would not consider the items they are purchasing to be 'collectables' nor themselves to be collectors.

Purchasers of vintage clothing, for example, are hoping to make a fashion statement, as are those who purchase retro and Modern Design furniture. The items in these categories will be used on a day to day basis by the purchaser.

Similarly we have found that sales of *CARTER'S Everything Vintage* cover a wider spectrum than just 'collectors'. The first edition was popular with all age groupings, from the younger set who checked the latest fashions, to those of middle age, whose childhood memories were rekindled by the images of items they grew up with in the 1950s and 1960s.

Our feedback on the layout, index and table of contents was very positive so we have made no changes in those areas. We have expanded the number of dealers with items included, and have a much wider New Zealand coverage.

I hope you enjoy this second edition of *Everything Vintage*.

John Furphy,
Publisher.

FOREWORD

By Rick Milne

Rick Milne is a collectables dealer, radio personality, journalist and auctioneer. Rick lives in Melbourne and operates from the Camberwell Antique Centre. He writes a weekly sporting collectables column in the Melbourne 'Age', a column for the monthly newspaper 'Collectormania' and appears weekly on radio stations 3AW Melbourne, 2GB Sydney, 4BC Brisbane, Sport 927 Melbourne and the ABC Australia wide.

CONFESSIONS OF AN INCURABLE COLLECTOR

I'm at a party, twenty years ago. I'm telling someone that I collect pub signs, street directories and Marx Brothers film posters. Invariably, the response would be something like this: (incredulous look) "Why would anybody want to collect that old rubbish??." (End of discussion).

Fast-forward twenty years. At a party, I'm talking to someone about my recently acquired antique kitchen scales, or the sign from the Nhill railway station (my old home town) or the hood ornament off a 1938 Ford. Now, the reaction is more likely to be: (interested look) "A mate of mine has a set of kitchen scales. Tell you what, I loved Star Trek, and I've been thinking of collecting a bit of memorabilia. What's the best way to start?"

A BIG CHANGE

In just twenty years, the general population has become much more aware of the wide world of collectables. School children swap their Pokémon cards, their Dads and Mums have kept their school readers and favourite toys, their grandparents collect Murano glass, or Phantom comics.

I reckon the mass media: radio, television, newspapers and magazines have really pushed up the general interest in collecting and collectors. Now, even your next-door neighbour can talk with you about something they've seen or heard recently about collectables. It could be the selling of the memorabilia of a famous film star, or politician or a sporting figure.

I appear in a variety of media talking about or valuing collectables. All of them are commercial enterprises. If the interest isn't there, if the audience isn't increasing, I'd get the flick. It hasn't happened yet, in nearly nineteen years!

And I'm not the only one. There are many knowledgeable, enthusiastic dealers offering their expertise on radio, TV and in the print media on a regular basis.

WHY COLLECT?

Because we love it! I have a good friend who collects tea-bag labels (those little paper bits at the end of the string). He has limited means and has tended to live a rather solitary life. He's now in contact with people all round the world, and he has found a new lease on life, all for the most modest of financial outlays.

Ditto a fellow who collects cattle ear tags. His collecting passion has taken him all round the world, and he loves it!

There are thousands more heart-warming stories like these, the fellow who collects tractors, not Dinky and Matchbox toys, but the real thing! At last count, he had sixty, or Rebecca who collects anything and everything on actress Claudette Colbert or Bert Newton, who collects 1938 memorabilia, the year of his birth.

WHERE IS IT HEADING?

Onward and upward, collectables auctions are breaking records, the number of keen buyers increasing, lots of new and younger collectors are joining in. This is no idle observation. At our most recent People's Paraphernalia Auction, we had forty two first-time bidders. Many were under thirty years of age.

WHERE TO FIND?

The first and best place to go is your local antique centre. These days, their collective pencils have been sharpened, and they're keen to do business. I believe in the future of antique centres. I have stalls in two: Camberwell Antique Centre in Melbourne, and Southside Antique Centre in Brisbane. Call me old-fashioned, but I like to see, hold and inspect before I buy. Those antique centres still operating are staffed by good, reliable and trustworthy people. These days, there's no point in doing otherwise.

Secondly, go to the auctions. Listen, take notes and talk to other like-minded bidders. Most are free with their advice.

Thirdly, DEVOUR the information in this wonderful book.

Fourthly, and probably most important, collect what you enjoy, and enjoy what you collect.

Some 'serious' collectors occasionally lose sight of the main goal; to enjoy what they've collected. Don't be envious of your fellow collector who might have more than you. So their collection is bigger and better than yours. So what? As it happens, my three all-time favourite collectable items would be lucky to bring $100 all-up. But I love them! !

COLLECTING FOR INVESTMENT

Now and then, and mostly in the business press, there'll be an article about "collecting for investment". I can't think of a colder or more clinical reason to collect. I reckon you should collect from the heart. Don't take your lead from the business pages!

DISPLAY

You've gone to the trouble of collecting in a particular area. So use it, display it, look at it every day. Appreciate it. ENJOY it. Don't lock it away in a cupboard or (worse) put it in a bank vault.

THE FUTURE

Rosy. Don't listen to the doomsayers; good collectables are tootling along very nicely.

Enjoy this wonderful book. Read and learn. And enjoy.

CHAPEL STREET BAZAAR

80 Independent dealers • Open 7 days 10am – 6pm

Chapel Street Bazaar • 217-223 Chapel Street • Prahran VIC 3181
Tel: 03 9529 1727 • Fax: 03 9521 3174

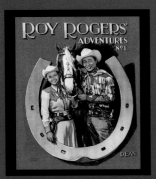

LM

yourlife
yourstyle

A 19TH CENTURY FRENCH ORMOLU CLOCK
Estimate: $ 2,800 - 3,000

Collectables

TRADER

AUSTRALASIA'S BIGGEST & BEST BI-MONTHLY ANTIQUES AND COLLECTABLES MAGAZINE

■ BOOK REVIEWS ■ EXHIBITIONS AROUND THE COUNTRY ■ COLLECTABLE FAIRS DIARY ■ COLLECTORS' CLUBS ■ TRADER SECTION

If you have a passion for anything collectable: from furniture to fine art; automobilia to art deco; comics to clocks; and anything imaginable in between, you'll find it in *Collectables Trader*.

The *Collectables Trader* is your up-to-date and authoritative source when buying, selling, keeping up on the latest prices or tracking down those extra-elusive items.

Subscribe now

For credit card orders call
02 9389 2919
or fax this coupon: 02 9387 7487 or mail to JQ Pty Ltd,
PO Box 324, Bondi Junction NSW Australia 1355

Subscribe for only ☐ $45 for 6 issues or ☐ $75 for 11 issues
including free delivery and save 16-24% off the cover price.

I enclose my ☐ cheque/money order payable to JQ Pty Ltd OR charge my credit card: $ _____

☐ Visa   ☐ Mastercard   ☐ American Express   ☐ Diners Club   ☐ Bankcard

☐☐☐☐   ☐☐☐☐   ☐☐☐☐   ☐☐☐☐

Cardholder Name:_____

Cardholder Signature:_____

Expiry Date_____/_____

*Prices for Australia. Overseas rates available on request

DELIVER TO

Name: _____

Address _____

_____ Postcode:_____

Daytime phone: (____)_____

Email: _____

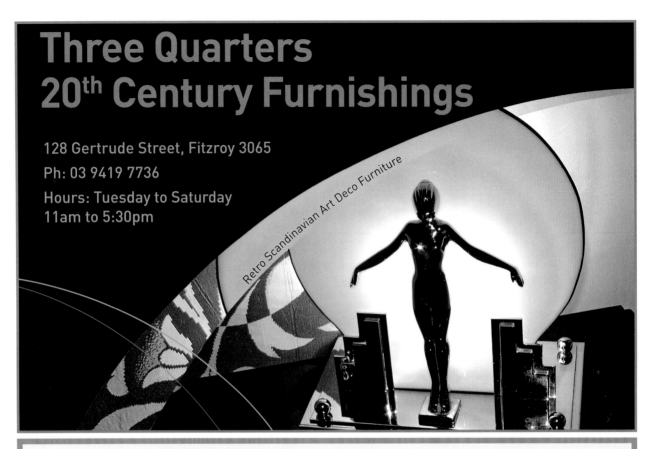
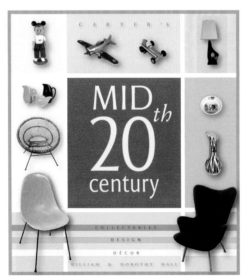

You've read the book now visit the dealers

To view antiques and collectables for sale, locate dealers for any area, or get fair details visit the Antiques & Art Australia site:

www.antique-art.com.au

The site contains thousands of items for sale from dealers located in Australia and New Zealand and are categorised, by dealer and item category.

Many of the dealers included in **CARTER'S** PRICE GUIDE showcase their items on this site.

If you find something you like, you correspond direct with dealer. There are no middlemen involved.

The Antiques & Art Australia domain is the largest, longest establshed and most comprehensive antiques and collectables site in Austalasia.

DEALERS: The Antiques & Art Australia site is sponsored by **CARTER'S** PRICE GUIDE enabling you to list your items free of charge.

To register, go to the site and click on the 'How to List' link on the front page.

'Brass Jim Beam' plaque, United States, c1970, 30cm wide, 17cm deep.

$110 - $130

The Bottom Drawer Antique Centre, VIC

'Tolley's Brandy' electric wall clock, 46cm high, 46cm wide, 9cm deep.

$430 - $470

Doug Up On Bourke, NSW

'Famous Reynella Wines', a mirror advertising the first South Australian winery established in 1838, taken over by Thomas Hardy and Sons in 1982, Australia, c1950, 110cm high, 91cm wide.

$2400 - $2600

How Bazaar, VIC

'Jim Beam', Model 'J' Duesenberg bottle, United States, 47cm long.

$175 - $195

Collectable Creations, QLD

'Jim Beam' decanter in the form of a 1978 corvette, United States, c1980, 10cm high, 38cm long.

$75 - $95

Glenelg Antique Centre, SA

'Baitz' liquor decanter bottle with a music box and moving dancers, Japan, c1950, 26cm high.

$55 - $75

Fat Helen's, VIC

'Jim Beam' decanter, commemorating the 11th anniversary of 'The Antique Trader', United States, c1968, 28cm high, 22cm wide.

$40 - $50

Glenelg Antique Centre, SA

'Gordon's Gin' tray, England, c1955, 22cm diam.

$15 - $25

Flaxton Barn, QLD

Jim Beam 'Tigers' decanter, Regal China, United States, c1977.

$100 - $120

Around The Grounds Football Memorabilia, VIC

'1969 Camaro SS Decanter', the body hand crafted by Royal China for Jim Beam, in its original box, United States, 9cm high, 12cm wide, 33cm long.

$220 - $260

Antique Revivals, VIC

'Jim Beam' whisky decanter in the form of a Mercedes Benz, with its original box, United States, c1974, 13cm wide, 33cm long.

$280 - $320

Settlers Store Antiques, NSW

Johnny Walker, figural advertising whisky bottle, England, c1950, 28cm high, 8cm wide, 8cm deep.

$135 - $155 **Parramatta Antique Centre, NSW**

Jim Beam fox figurine, 'Silver City Beamers 5th Birthday, 15th March 1987' Australia.

$65 - $85 **Alan's Collectables, NSW**

Vintage champagne bucket, France, c1960, 21cm high.

$90 - $110 **Kaleidoscope Antiques, VIC**

Advertising composition of a 'VAT 69' bottle, England, c1950.

$130 - $150 **Chapel Street Bazaar, VIC**

Musical cigarette dispenser, in the form of a 'Courvoisier' cognac bottle, Australia, c1965, 31cm high.

$35 - $45 **Atomic Pop, SA**

Wade, 'White Horse Scotch Whisky', horse shoe shaped ashtray, England, c1960, 20cm high, 19cm wide.

NZ$100 - $120 **Decollectables, New Zealand**

Carlton Ware, 'Gordons', triangular hand painted ashtray, England, c1960, 13.5cm wide, 12cm long.

NZ$92 - $112 **Decollectables, New Zealand**

'Vat 69' scotch whisky bottle shaped cigarette dispenser, Japan, c1970, 37.5cm high, 8.5cm diam.

NZ$55 - $75 **Right Up My Alley, New Zealand**

'Swan Lager' export radio in the shape of a beer can, Australia, c1970, 11.5cm long, 13cm diam.

$20 - $30 **Alan's Collectables, NSW**

'Tetley Ales' whisky water jug, c1960, 42cm high, 10cm diam.

$55 - $75 **Parramatta Antique Centre, NSW**

Three Ballarat labelled beer bottles, two for 'Ballarat Bitter' and one for 'Ballarat Invalid Stout', Australia, c1960, 28cm high, 7cm diam.

$40 - $50 **Lydiard Furniture & Antiques, VIC**

Haig Scotch Whisky water jug, by Carlton Ware, No. 2379, 'By Appointment to Her Majesty the Queen', England, c1955, 17.5cm high.

'Queen Anne Rare Scotch Whisky' water jug by Wade, England, 15cm high.

$60 - $80   **Journey to the Past Antiques & Collectables, QLD**

$85 - $105   **Sweet Slumber Antiques & Collectables, NSW**

'Johnny Walker Black Label' water jug, made by Moulin De Loups, France, 15cm high.

$595 - $695   **Kings Park Antiques & Collectables, SA**

Wade 'Hedges & Butler Royal Scotch' whisky water jug, England, c1970, 16cm high, 13cm wide.

$40 - $60   **Chapel Street Bazaar, VIC**

'Four Roses Bourbon' water jug by Arabia, Finland, c1960, 12cm high, 16cm wide.

$25 - $35   **Chapel Street Bazaar, VIC**

'Black Bottle' scotch whisky jug with a Castle Ceramics stamp to base, England, 16cm high.

$110 - $130   **Granny's Market Pty Ltd, VIC**

'Old Smuggler, Finest Scotch Whisky' water jug, c1960, 10cm high.

$20 - $30   **Dr Russell's Emporium, WA**

Royal Norfolk 'Old Smuggler Scotch Whisky' jug, in cream with gold trim, England, 17cm high, 17cm wide.

$305 - $345   **The Bizarre Bazaar, NSW**

Squat shaped, pillar box, red water jug with transfer print advertising 'Haig's Scotch Whisky', England, c1990, 18cm long.

$60 - $80   **Kenny's Antiques, VIC**

'Catto's Whisky' jug in pressed glass, England, c1950, 20cm high, 15cm diam.

$205 - $245   **Kings Park Antiques & Collectables, SA**

Coca-Cola bottle, unopened, Australia, c1970, 30cm high.

$25 - $35   **Castlemaine, VIC**

Unopened Coca-Cola advertising bottle, from the America's Cup 1987 in Fremantle WA, Australia, 20cm high.

$25 - $35   **Castlemaine, VIC**

Limited edition commemorative Coca-Cola bottle for the 'Royal Wedding', July 29, 1981, England.

$230 - $270   **The Glass Stopper, NSW**

Full and labelled 'Compound Beverage' Coca-Cola bottle, bottled in Auckland and dated 1964, New Zealand, 20cm high, 5cm diam.

NZ$15 - $25   **Peachgrove Antiques, New Zealand**

Millennium Coca-Cola bottles, each in their original cylinder, limited edition, Australia, c2000.

$280 - $320   **The Glass Stopper, NSW**

Coke 'Diamond' 12 oz. can, United States, c1960.

$185 - $205   **The Glass Stopper, NSW**

Coca-Cola dancing can with accompanying music, made by Musican, Taiwan, c1985, 17cm high.

$55 - $75   **Castlemaine, VIC**

Opened Coca-Cola can, Australia, c1985, 13cm high.

$5 - $15   **Castlemaine, VIC**

Coca-Cola cloth badge/patch, United States, c2000, 9.5cm long.

$5 - $15   **Modelcraft Miniatures, NSW**

Stainless steel Coca-Cola cooler with a tray situated underneath the lid for sandwiches etc, a handy cap catcher on the side and a drainage plug on the front, United States, c1950.

$1195 - $1395   **Retro Antiques, NSW**

Coke, AFL 1998 Grand Final 1st edition bottle, boxed and numbered, Australia.

$230 - $270

The Glass Stopper, NSW

Metal Coca-Cola bottle opener, Canada, c1950, 4.5cm long.

$15 - $25

Decorama, VIC

Metal Coca-Cola bottle key ring, United States, c1950, 4.5cm high.

$20 - $30

Decorama, VIC

Coca-Cola Olympic pin collector's set, including an official hat, vest, pin bag and pins, covering the period from the first Coca-Cola Olympic pin from Amsterdam 1928, to Atlanta, 1996, United States, c2000.

$160 - $180

model-cars.com.au, NSW

Parker brand Coca-Cola advertising pen, boxed and mint, c1960.

$40 - $50

The Glass Stopper, NSW

Coke advertising poster, framed, limited edition, Australia, c1980, 60cm high.

$90 - $110

The Glass Stopper, NSW

'Vendoriator, Dual 27' Coca-Cola dispensing machine, United States, c1950.

$4895 - $5095

Retro Antiques, NSW

Coke, Vendo 44 soda machine, produced between 1956 and 1959, United States.

$6675 - $7075

Retro Antiques, NSW

Timber crate in yellow with red lettering 'Drink Coca-Cola', 30cm wide, 47cm long.

$75 - $95

Treats & Treasures, NSW

Coca-Cola tin sign, Australia, 25cm high, 71cm long.

$115 - $135

The Nostalgia Factory, NSW

'Delicious Coca-Cola Refreshes You Best' enamel sign, 30cm high, 30cm wide.

$105 - $125

Lava Signs, SA

Coca-Cola shop sign, side mounted, with a fluorescent light, Australia, c1980, 52cm high, 74cm wide, 13cm deep.

$500 - $600

Calmar Trading, VIC

Flashing advertising sign for Coca-Cola, c1980, 46cm high, 40cm diam.

$415 - $455

The Glass Stopper, NSW

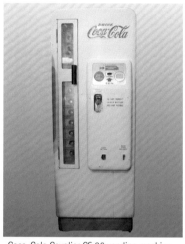

Coca-Cola Cavalier CS 96 vending machine, distinctive by its bold white appearance, Australia, c1957.

$4695 - $4895

Retro Antiques, NSW

'Drink Ice Cold Coca-Cola' enamel sign, 35.5cm high, 35.5cm wide.

$105 - $125

Lava Signs, SA

Fanta, Australian made 'Championship Genuine Russell Yo-Yo', issued by Coca-Cola, c1960, 5.8cm diam.

$45 - $65

Lucilles Interesting Collectables, NSW

Packaged Coca-Cola championship yo-yo, China, c2003.

$20 - $30

Modelcraft Miniatures, NSW

Coca-Cola yo-yo, Australia, c1958.

$230 - $270

Gardenvale Collectables, VIC

Display surf board for the 1997 'Coca-Cola surf classic', Australia, c1997.

$330 - $370

Terrace Collectables, NSW

Coca-Cola telephone in the form of a 'Coke' bottle, Hong Kong, c1985, 25cm high.

$75 - $95

The Mill Markets, VIC

Zippo lighter with advertising for Coca-Cola, United States.

$65 - $85

Paddington Antique Centre Pty Ltd, QLD

Black and white, plastic 'Spillers' flour shaker, in the form of a bowler hatted British gentleman, England, c1960, 22cm high.

$30 - $40

506070, NSW

St. George Bank plastic advertising sign, in the form of the St. George dragon, Australia, c1995, 43cm high.

$75 - $95

Old World Antiques (NSW), NSW

Advertising figure for 'Cadbury's Black Cat Chocolates', of plastic construction, Australia, c1960, 24cm high, 13cm long, 8cm deep.

$85 - $105

Dr Russell's Emporium, WA

Shop display head, Australia, c1950, 42cm high.

$275 - $315

Chapel Street Bazaar, VIC

Display box for 'Henri Wintermans' products, Holland, c1960, 30cm high, 37cm wide, 30cm long.

$150 - $170

J. R. & S.G. Isaac-Cole, NSW

'Sheffield Mini Sports Knife' display card, with one dozen pocket knives, England, c1950, 26cm high, 21cm wide.

$165 - $185

Chapel Street Bazaar, VIC

Plastic M&M's dispenser with a baseball theme, manufactured by Mars Inc, China, c1995, 20cm high.

$35 - $45

Chapel Street Bazaar, VIC

Light green, baseball themed 'M & M' dispenser, c1998, 20cm high.

$15 - $25

Dr Russell's Emporium, WA

Unopened box with an M&M basketballer dispenser, China, c1995, 21cm high, 7.5cm wide.

$15 - $25

Chapel Street Bazaar, VIC

Cardboard hat box by 'Crean', c1950, 30cm high, 36cm wide.

NZ$130 - $150

Collectamania, New Zealand

'The Stanmore' cardboard hat box, c1950, 25cm high, 33cm wide.

NZ$130 - $150

Collectamania, New Zealand

'Star' cardboard hat box, c1950, 29cm high, 36cm wide.

NZ$140 - $160

Collectamania, New Zealand

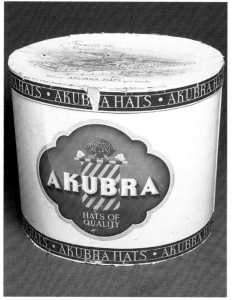

Cardboard 'Akubra' hat box, Australia, c1950.

$75 - $95

All In Good Time Antiques, SA

Cardboard 'Akubra' hat box, Australia, c1955, 31cm high, 37cm wide.

$100 - $120

369 Antiques, VIC

Pepsi Cola paper cup, United States, c1950, 9cm high.

$5 - $15

Decorama, VIC

Poster 'Ken Koala' kerb drill, issued by the Australian Road Safety Council, Australia, c1950, 75cm wide, 75cm long.

$230 - $270

369 Antiques, VIC

'Philips Model 100 Radioplayer' framed advertisement, Australia, c1950, 48cm wide, 73cm long.

$275 - $315

Ace Antiques & Collectables, VIC

'Holden Kingswood' original advertising/sales, soft cover, booklet type brochure, 16 pages, Australia, c1970, 28cm high, 21cm wide.

$45 - $65

Lucilles Interesting Collectables, NSW

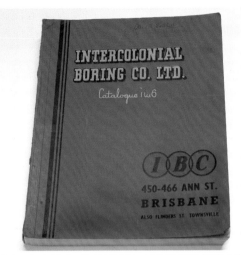

'Intercolonial Boring Co Ltd. Catalogue No. 6', 1952, lovely and well illustrated catalogue of engineering and farm equipment, 660 pages plus index, Australia.

$90 - $110

Yarra Valley Antique Centre, VIC

Ipana advertising poster, framed, limited edition, Australia, c1980, 60cm high, 40cm wide.

$90 - $110

The Glass Stopper, NSW

Motor oil company blotters, priced per item, Australia, c1955, 15cm long.

$25 - $35

Marsteen Collectables, VIC

Motor oil company blotters, priced per item, Australia, c1955, 8cm high, 14cm long.

$5 - $15

Marsteen Collectables, VIC

Advertisement for 'Stamina Youth's Sports Coats', Australia, c1955.

$15 - $25

The Nostalgia Factory, NSW

Paper 'Cadbury' show bag, Australia, c1960, 27cm high, 32cm wide.

$5 - $15

Terrace Collectables, NSW

'Saunders Christmas Gift' catalogue, 1954, Australia, 25cm high, 15cm wide.

$35 - $45

The Nostalgia Factory, NSW

Allens 'Golly', triangular sweet tin, Australia, c1960.

$105 - $125

**Jan James,
NSW**

Arnotts 'Don Bradman' biscuit tin, 450g net, Australia.

$30 - $40

**Treats & Treasures,
NSW**

Tin for Phoenix Biscuit Co P/L, Melbourne, Australia, c1955, 10cm high, 4cm wide, 29cm long.

$40 - $60

**Antipodes Antiques,
QLD**

Minties tin with 'Minties Moments' panels, Australia, 21cm high, 17cm diam.

$165 - $185

**Archers Antiques,
TAS**

'Webster's 8lb Family Assorted Biscuits' tin with paper labels and a hinged lid, from Brisbane, Australia, c1950, 17cm high, 23cm wide, 26cm long.

$45 - $65

**Possum's Treasures,
QLD**

Peak Freans horse racing biscuit tin, 'The Winner', with an inner tin, featuring different race horses, that is spun from the top and reveals the race winner in the front of the tin, the bottom still shows all biscuits, England, 14cm high, 17cm diam.

$130 - $150

**Baxter's Antiques,
QLD**

One gallon 'Castrol Upper Cylinder Lubricant' tin, Australia, c1960, 25cm high, 12cm wide, 17cm deep.

$20 - $30

**Chapel Street Bazaar,
VIC**

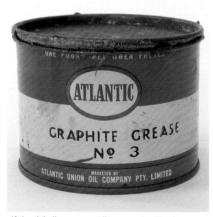

'Atlantic' oil company, 1lb grease tin, 'No 3', Australia, c1950, 9cm high, 12cm wide.

$40 - $50

**Wooden Pew Antiques,
VIC**

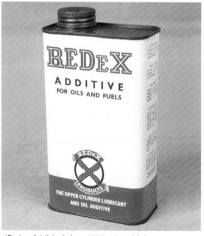

'Redex Additive' tin, c1950, 18cm high.

$25 - $35

**Dr Russell's Emporium,
WA**

TINS

Large 'Golden Fleece Dermolotion' hand cleanser tin, Australia, c1960, 35cm high, 23.5cm long, 23.5cm deep.

$165 - $185

Wooden Pew Antiques, VIC

Sample tin of 'Heinz Celery Soup', c1950, 4cm high.

$40 - $60

Stumpy Gully Antiques, VIC

'Chickube Chicken Broth Cubes' tin, England, c1948.

$15 - $25

The Nostalgia Factory, NSW

'Lucy Hinton Tobacco' tin, c1950, 8cm long.

$10 - $20

Chapel Street Bazaar, VIC

'Prince Albert Smoking Tobacco' tin, United States, c1950, 7cm high, 13cm diam.

$40 - $50

Southside Antiques Centre, QLD

'Shinola Shoe Polish' tin, United States, c1950, 7cm diam.

$25 - $35

Chapel Street Bazaar, VIC

'Finest Southland Honey, 2kg' tin by Glass Bros. Ltd., Gore, number 5, registered design, New Zealand, c1950, 13cm high, 13cm diam.

NZ$15 - $25

The Curiosity Shoppe, New Zealand

'Richard Hudnut, 'Three Flowers Dusting Powder' tin, United States, 7cm high,13cm diam.

$10 - $20

Baxter's Antiques, QLD

Old English 'Cinet' pot pourri tin, England.

$5 - $15

Flaxton Barn, QLD

Ensign Tea tins, No. 1 in red and blue, 33cm high, 24cm wide.

$75 - $95

Home Again, NSW

'Weeties' sand bucket, c1950, 15cm high.

$185 - $205

Antiques & Collectables On Moorabool, VIC

Empty 'Scanlens Comic Tattoo Gum' box featuring Felix the Cat, Australia, c1955, 20cm high.

$205 - $245

Decorama, VIC

Plastic 'Minties' truck, hollow with a screw-off cabin, c1950, 30cm long.

$245 - $285

How Bazaar, VIC

Box of ten multi-coloured, 'Oto Flashlight Lamps' by Osram, 40cm wide, 100cm long, 40cm deep.

NZ$10 - $20

Right Up My Alley, New Zealand

Advertising sample card for 'Columbia Gardener Tag Marking Pencil' with twelve pencils, Australia, c1950, 32cm high, 23cm wide.

$25 - $35

Terrace Collectables, NSW

Nestlé 'Winning Post' chocolates box 1/2 pound, printed underneath 'No. 238 Sydney', Australia, c1950, 8.5cm high, 14cm wide, 4cm long.

$10 - $20

Possum's Treasures, QLD

Pine two handled crate, painted and stencilled for 'Tenterfield Cordials, 10.62', Australia, c1962, 21.5cm high, 26cm wide, 41cm long.

$30 - $40

Possum's Treasures, QLD

'Dixon Carpet Shampoo' bottle with intact paper label and some original contents, made by 'Sharlands Laboratories, Morningside Auckland', New Zealand, c1950, 20cm high, 7cm wide, 7cm diam.

NZ$15 - $25

Peachgrove Antiques, New Zealand

'Rinso' washing powder box and powder, New Zealand, 20cm high, 19cm wide.

NZ$40 - $50

Hubbers Emporium, New Zealand

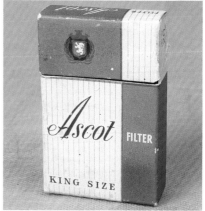

Packet of 'Ascot Filter, King Size' cigarettes, c1955, 8cm high.

$5 - $13

Dr Russell's Emporium, WA

Eveready 'Nine Lives Radio Batteries' enamel sign, 60cm high, 44cm wide.

$205 - $245

Lava Signs, SA

Enamel sign for 'Estrela' batteries, India, c1950, 39cm high, 27cm wide.

$275 - $315

Parramatta Antique Centre, NSW

'Eveready Flashlights & Batteries' enamel sign, 86cm high, 45.5cm wide.

$535 - $635

Lava Signs, SA

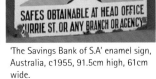

'The Savings Bank of S.A' enamel sign, Australia, c1955, 91.5cm high, 61cm wide.

$1450 - $1650

Lava Signs, SA

Cast iron C.B.A bank sign, c1950, 50cm high, 50cm wide.

$190 - $210

Home Again, NSW

Blue and white enamel street sign, Russia, c1950, 20cm high, 40cm long.

NZ$125 - $145

Country Antiques, New Zealand

'Carlton Brewery' advertising sign on thick cardboard, Australia, c1955, 55cm high, 73cm wide.

$255 - $295

Memorabilia on Parade, VIC

Reproduction sign for 'J. H. Abbott & Co Boots & Shoes, 1900', Australia, c2000, 15cm high, 20cm long.

$20 - $30

Woodside Bazaar, SA

Metal advertising sign for 'Betta Pies and Crumpets', Australia, c1950, 23cm wide, 30cm long.

$125 - $145

Decorama, VIC

'Cadbury's' cardboard, shop advertising sign, Australia, c1951, 41cm high, 34cm wide.

$20 - $30

J. R. & S.G. Isaac-Cole, NSW

'Fanta' tin sign with strong colours, Australia, c1970, 45cm high, 137cm wide.

$215 - $255

Wooden Pew Antiques, VIC

'Bears Honeydew Cigarettes' enamel sign, 44cm high, 31cm wide.

$125 - $145

Lava Signs, SA

Helena Rubinstein cardboard advertising sign for 'Colour Tint Rinses', Australia, c1950, 55cm wide, 90cm long.

$65 - $85

369 Antiques, VIC

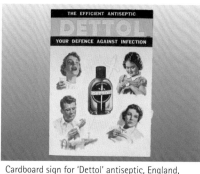

Cardboard sign for 'Dettol' antiseptic, England, c1953, 60cm wide, 90cm long.

$120 - $140

369 Antiques, VIC

Double sided enamel sign for 'Agfa' film, India, c1960, 43cm high, 76cm wide.

$245 - $285

Wooden Pew Antiques, VIC

'Wrigley's Spearmint' cardboard advertising sign, United States, c1960, 38cm high, 84cm wide.

$165 - $185

Kings Park Antiques & Collectables, SA

Reproduction 'Golden Fleece' enamel sign, Australia, 40cm high, 35cm wide.

$135 - $155

Unique & Antique, VIC

'His Master's Voice', gramophone nipper dog enamel sign, 43cm high, 58cm wide.

$395 - $435

Lava Signs, SA

Double sided 'Standard-Vacuum Oil Company Elephant Kerosene' enamel sign with a 5cm flange, 45.5cm high, 61cm wide.

$475 - $515

Lava Signs, SA

'Esso Elephant Kerosene', porcelain enamel sign, 60cm high, 30cm wide.

$185 - $205

Lava Signs, SA

Cardboard advertising sign for 'Christmas & New Year Special Holidays, Ansett Top 40 Holidays, 19 December 1980 – 31 January 1981', Australia, 38cm high.

$30 - $40

The Mill Markets, VIC

'Lloyd's Agency' insurance brass plaque mounted on timber, England, c1960, 38cm high, 33cm wide, 2.5cm deep.

$165 - $185

Wooden Pew Antiques, VIC

Small 'Castrol' enamel sign.

$85 - $105

Lava Signs, SA

Illuminated 'Caltex' sign, Australia, c1980, 68cm wide, 10cm deep.

$240 - $280

Wooden Pew Antiques, VIC

'Wakefield Castrol Motor Oils' circular enamel sign, Australia, c1950, 60cm high, 60cm wide.

$465 - $505

Lava Signs, SA

'Shell' enamel sign, 22cm high, 48cm wide.

$75 - $95

Lava Signs, SA

Hard plastic 'Ampol' petrol sign, Australia, c1970, 60cm high, 240cm long.

$185 - $205

The Bottom Drawer Antique Centre, VIC

Original 'Peters' ice cream cone advertising sign for milk bars, with bracket, Australia, c1960, 80cm high.

$800 - $900

Memorabilia on Parade, VIC

'Peters Keep the Good Things Coming', milk bar sign, Australia, c1970, 30cm wide,122cm long.

$200 - $240

Memorabilia on Parade, VIC

Tin advertising sign for 'Arrow Brand', Australia, c1950, 23cm high, 41cm wide.

NZ$70 - $90

Antiques & Curiosities, New Zealand

'Honer Mouth Organs' cardboard counter sign featuring Larry Adler, England, c1948, 20cm wide, 30cm long.

$50 - $70

369 Antiques, VIC

'Pelican Pens' enamel sign, Germany, 57cm high, 37cm wide.

$405 - $445

Lava Signs, SA

'Streets' original advertising light box, Australia, c1970, 90cm high, 70cm wide, 20cm deep.

$645 - $745

Memorabilia on Parade, VIC

'Omega' watches, convex enamel sign, Germany, c1950, 39cm high, 59cm wide.

$705 - $805

Lava Signs, SA

'Toyo Tyres' double sided enamel sign, 60cm high, 42cm wide.

$275 - $315

Lava Signs, SA

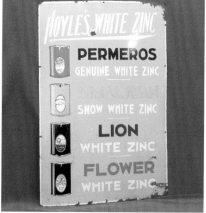

'Hoyle's White Zinc' enamel sign, 76cm high, 51cm wide.

$245 - $285

Lava Signs, SA

'Cherry Blossom Shoe Polish' lithographed tin sign, New Zealand, c1950, 70.5cm high, 44.5cm wide.

NZ$170 - $190

Peachgrove Antiques, New Zealand

'Tanqueray's' Gin sign painted on tin, England, c1950, 28cm high, 19cm wide.

$100 - $120

Chapel Street Bazaar, VIC

'Woodroofe's' tin advertising sign, Australia, c1960, 61cm high, 22cm wide.

$175 - $195

Kings Park Antiques & Collectables, SA

'Goodyear Authorised Dealer' enamel sign, 53cm high, 60cm wide.

$145 - $165

Lava Signs, SA

Begging dogs 'Always ask for 'Black and White' whisky' enamel sign, 36cm high, 36cm wide.

$135 - $155

Lava Signs, SA

Caltex water jug, Australia, c1950, 10cm high.

$80 - $100

The Junk Company, VIC

Perpetual calendars advertising 'Tucker Box Dog & Cat Food Co.', Australia, c1950, 7.5cm high, 5.5cm wide.

$15 - $25

Wooden Pew Antiques, VIC

Cloth calendar featuring a tattooed Maori Chief, made by 'Label Weavers Ltd' for their customers at Christmas, made and weaved the same form as the labels they produced for the clothing companies, New Zealand, c1980, 20cm wide, 71cm long.

NZ$100 - $120

Maxine's Collectibles, New Zealand

Rubik's cube, with Kodak logos on each face, c1980, 6cm high, 6cm wide.

$15 - $25

Marge's Antiques & Collectables, NSW

Pepsi Cola branded 'Esky', Australia, c1960, 40cm wide, 30cm deep.

$405 - $445

The Glass Stopper, NSW

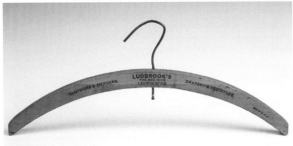

Wooden clothes hanger advertising 'Ludbrooks Clothiers & Mercers', Launceston, United States, c1950, 40cm long.

$65 - $85

Colonial Antiques & Tea House, WA

'McAlpins Flour' miniature advertising hat, made out of cardboard, Australia, c1955, 19cm diam.

$40 - $50

The Mill Markets, VIC

Astor radio advertising jewellery box for a man, by Goodwill Products and features a map of Australia and New Zealand on the lid, Australia, c1950, 2cm high, 10cm wide, 10cm long.

$20 - $30

369 Antiques, VIC

Glass 'Arnott's Biscuit' container, Australia, c1950, 30cm high.

$445 - $485

Chapel Street Bazaar, VIC

Advertising glass for 'Bushell's Cocoa' with children and fairies on the back, Australia, 10.5cm high.

$40 - $50

Baxter's Antiques, QLD

Pepsi square top machine from Fresno, California, United States, c1960.

$6095 - $6495

Retro Antiques, NSW

'Craven A' branded ashtray, in painted metal and chrome, England, c1950, 4.5cm high, 9cm wide.

$20 - $30

Yarra Valley Antique Centre, VIC

Alloy map of Australia, an advertising desk weight for 'Metalex', Australia, c1980, 5cm high, 7cm long.

$20 - $30

Ritzy Bits - ACT, ACT

Dulux advertising chair, for use in hardware or paint shops, Australia, c1950, 100cm high, 35cm wide, 35cm deep.

$355 - $395

The Mill Markets, VIC

Qantas airline bags, c1955.

$50 - $70

Home Again, NSW

Batman cola can, Australia, c1989, 13cm high.

$15 - $25

Castlemaine, VIC

Cream enamel ashtray for 'UMI' (United Metal Industries), Australia, c1950, 1cm high, 12.5cm diam.

$25 - $35

Possum's Treasures, QLD

Blue Pepsi 'Slider', lift the lid and you have icy cold drinks, also opens from the side with a crank handle to enable it to be loaded, United States, c1950.

$2895 - $3095

Retro Antiques, NSW

Pepsi-Cola ribbon badge, United States, c1960, 24cm long.

$40 - $60

Castlemaine, VIC

Souvenir matches for 'Luna Park', Sydney, Australia, c1960, 5cm high, 4cm wide.

$15 - $25

Southside Antiques Centre, QLD

ANIMATION CELS

'Rugrats' animation production cel with its matching original background and featuring Tommy, United States, c1990, 25cm high, 32cm long.

$85 - $105

Celamation, NSW

Animation production cel on a reproduced background featuring large images of 'Rainbow Brite and Friend', two cel setup, United States, c1980, 25cm high, 32cm long.

$85 - $105

Celamation, NSW

'Smurfs' animation production cel of Smurfette on a background, United States, c1980, 25cm high, 32cm long.

$70 - $90

Celamation, NSW

'She-ra Princess of Power' animation production cel, on a reproduced background, United States, c1980, 25cm high, 32cm long.

$80 - $100

Celamation, NSW

'Dilbert' animation production cel with a matching reproduced background, United States, c1990, 25cm high, 32cm long.

$90 - $110

Celamation, NSW

'Ritchie Rich' animation production cel, on a reproduced background, United States, c1990, 25cm high, 32cm long.

$70 - $90

Celamation, NSW

Animation production cel, on a reproduced non-matching background featuring a large centred image of Inuyasha, Japan, c2000, 21cm high, 25cm long.

$120 - $140

Celamation, NSW

Large centred animation production cel of 'Astroboy' on a hand painted, non-matching background, Japan, c1990, 21cm high, 25cm long.

$140 - $160

Celamation, NSW

'Dragonball GT' animation production cel, on a reproduced background and featuring Goku, Japan, c1990, 21cm high, 25cm long.

$120 - $140

Celamation, NSW

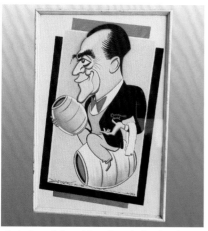

Caricature of the publican from the Brechnock Hotel, by Lionel Coventry, Australia, c1955, 68cm high, 46cm wide.

$245 - $285

Kings Park Antiques & Collectables, SA

Cedric Emanuel, 'Bourke Street Restoration, Woolloomooloo' 1980, pencil drawing, Australia, c1980, 22.7cm high, 29.2cm wide.

$1000 - $1200

Josef Lebovic Gallery, NSW

David Bromley oil painting, 'The Artist' on canvas, Australia, c2005, 61.5cm high, 48.5cm wide.

$5750 - $6150

C. V. Jones Antiques & Art Gallery, VIC

'Birds Leaving Lake Eyre' oil on board, 2004 by John Olsen, Australia, 148cm high, 124cm wide.

$115000 - $125000

Woollahra Times Art Gallery, NSW

Lance Solomon oil on board, 'Bush Outing', 1973, Australia, 70cm high, 64cm wide.

$6500 - $6900

Etching House, NSW

'Asphaltum' by Michael Johnson, oil on canvas, Australia, 152cm high, 122cm wide.

$37000 - $39000

Woollahra Times Art Gallery, NSW

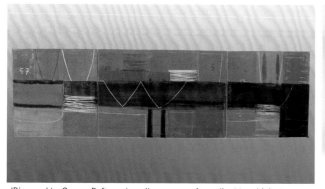

'Diaspora' by George Raftopoulos, oil on canvas, Australia, 80cm high, 282cm long.

$14000 - $15000

Woollahra Times Art Gallery, NSW

Signed Roy Henry Fluke abstract oil on board, titled 'Kings/Cross', Australia, c1960, 44cm high, 80cm wide.

$12000 - $13000

Nextonix, VIC

'The Waterhole - Cooroy' by Robert Dickerson, oil on board, Australia, 120cm high, 90cm wide.

$48000 - $50000   **Woollahra Times Art Gallery, NSW**

Oil painting by Sir Patrick Kilmgton, 1983 'Fire Away' painted in Queensland, provenance Dr Jim Cairns, Australia, c1983, 38cm high, 49cm wide.

$1400 - $1600   **Seagull Antiques, VIC**

David Boyd oil painting on canvas, titled 'Gathering Wildflowers', Australia, c1970, 53cm high, 63cm wide.

$20950 - $22950   **C. V. Jones Antiques & Art Gallery, VIC**

'Still Life' by Margaret Olley, oil on board, Australia, 60cm high, 74cm wide.

$44000 - $46000   **Woollahra Times Art Gallery, NSW**

'William Holden Show' by Maclean Edwards, oil on canvas, Australia, c2004, 150cm high, 150cm wide.

$29000 - $31000   **Woollahra Times Art Gallery, NSW**

'Europa Reaching for Wattle', oil on board by David Boyd, Australia, c1991, 45cm high, 36.5cm wide.

$16500 - $17500   **Woollahra Times Art Gallery, NSW**

Original oil beach scene, by Judith Roberts, Australia, c1960, 40cm high, 37cm wide.

$175 - $195   **Terrace Collectables, NSW**

Oil painting on board signed and dated 1978. Subject matter, The Hills of Wales, titled 'Wales', Australia, 67cm high, 66cm wide.

$4700 - $4900   **Nextonix, VIC**

Kasey Sealy oil on board 'View to North Head', Australia, c2000, 42cm high, 95cm wide.

$2550 - $2750   **Etching House, NSW**

Oil painting on board titled 'Hill Paddock' by John Eldershaw, Australia, c1960, 41cm high, 56cm wide.

$1375 - $1575   **Bathurst Street Antique Centre, TAS**

Garry Shead
'Checkmate'
collagraph,
Australia,
c2000,
102cm high,
126cm wide.

$6700 - $7100

Etching House,
NSW

Garry Shead
'Thirroul'
collagraph,
Australia,
c2000,
112cm high,
132cm wide.

$6700 - $7100

Etching House,
NSW

Garry
Shead,
'Epiphany',
an original
etching,
Australia,
c2000,
53cm high,
67cm wide.

$4900 - $5100

Etching House,
NSW

Jason
Benjamin
original
etcing,
'The
Clearing',
Australia,
c2003,
99cm high,
114cm wide.

$6700 - $7100

Etching House,
NSW

Van Cleef print, c1960, 55cm high, 46cm wide.

$40 - $50

Fat Helen's, VIC

'Autumn Leaves' pin-up girl print, by J. H. Lynch, in its original frame, England, c1960, 66cm high, 56cm long, 3cm deep.

$475 - $515

Dr Russell's Emporium, WA

J. H. Lynch print, 'Woodland Goddess', United Kingdom, c1965, 88cm high, 69cm wide.

$185 - $205

Atomic Pop, SA

Hard to find Tretchikoff print, 'Penny Whistlers', in original mount and frame, United States, c1960, 105cm wide.

$545 - $645

Collectors' Cottage Antiques, NSW

'East', an original print by Bjorn Wiinblad, from the series 'Points of the Compass'. This print possesses all the qualities we associate with Wiinblad's works. Rich vibrant colours, beautiful intricate borders and a state of lavish amusement, mounted and presented in a gilded frame, Denmark, c1970, 55cm high, 45cm wide.

$900 - $1000

Toowoomba Antiques Gallery, QLD

Facsimile etching of Norman Lindsay's 1920's etching, 'The C Sharp Minor Quartet', Australia, c1980, 44cm high, 31.5cm wide.

$2850 - $3050

Etching House, NSW

Framed print of a watercolour called 'Toucan Dreams', signed Carol Grigg and in an ebonised frame, 100cm high, 60cm wide.

$95 - $115

Born Frugal, VIC

Framed kitsch print, England, c1970, 84cm high, 63cm wide.

$115 - $135

Retro Active, VIC

Charles Blackman, 'Two Angels I', etching, limited edition of 60, Australia, c1990, 49.3cm high, 39.3cm wide.

$2430 - $2630

Gallery Savah, NSW

'Curtin of the Moon', John Coburn silkscreen print in its original frame, Australia, c1970, 42cm high, 72cm wide.

$2400 - $2600

Habitat Antiques, NSW

David Boyd, 'Sorting the Score', etching, limited edition of 60, Australia, c2000, 5cm high, 25cm wide.

$830 - $930

Gallery Savah, NSW

Sir Sidney Nolan lithograph, signed lower right, titled 'Mrs. Reardon at Glenrowan'. Features an unusual use of pink. Number 7 of 15, Australia, c1970, 50cm high, 66cm wide.

$6800 - $7200

Habitat Antiques, NSW

Arthur Boyd, 'Tosca & Scarpia', etching, from a limited edition of 60, Australia, c1990, 39cm high, 60cm wide.

$2650 - $2850

Gallery Savah, NSW

'The Daily Beast', a Leunig original etching, Australia, c1995, 41cm high, 49cm wide.

$2250 - $2450

Etching House, NSW

Original etching, 'Fish Dance' by Leunig, Australia, c2004, 30cm high, 23cm wide.

$550 - $650

Etching House, NSW

Weaver Hawkins (Raokin) 'Wrestling' linocut No. 6/10, Australia, c1961, 38.75cm high, 48.75cm wide.

$1150 - $1350

Barry Sherman Galleries, VIC

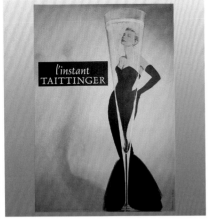

'Taittinger' by Anonymous, France, c1980, 168cm high, 116cm wide.

$1100 - $1300

Galerie Montmartre, VIC

Original lithograph tourism poster for Austria, designed by Fischer, Austria, c1956, 100cm high, 70cm wide.

$750 - $850

Vintage Posters Only, VIC

Lithograph advertising poster for Phillips, designed by Colin, France, c1955, 160cm high, 120cm wide.

$1150 - $1350

Vintage Posters Only, VIC

'Folies Bergere' by Aslan, France, c1970, 150cm high, 100cm wide.

$700 - $800

Galerie Montmartre, VIC

'Joker' print by Auriac, France, c1950, 120cm high, 160cm wide.

$1800 - $2000

Galerie Montmartre, VIC

Original lithographed tourism poster for Pamplona, designed by Polota, Spain, c1956, 100cm high, 70cm wide.

$750 - $850

Vintage Posters Only, VIC

Lithographed tourism poster for 'Spring in Switzerland', designed by Anon, Switzerland, c1960, 140cm high, 100cm wide.

$940 - $1040

Vintage Posters Only, VIC

Original lithographed poster for Foire de Paris, 1960, designed by Colin, France, 160cm high, 120cm wide.

$1100 - $1300

Vintage Posters Only, VIC

Original lithograph tourism poster for Spain, designed by Delpy, Spain, c1956, 100cm high, 70cm wide.

$750 - $850

Vintage Posters Only, VIC

'Marchal' by Jean Colin, France, c1952, 160cm high, 120cm wide.

$2100 - $2300   **Galerie Montmartre, VIC**

'Autol Motor Oil' print by Donald Brun, Switzerland, c1950, 128cm high, 90cm wide.

$950 - $1050   **Galerie Montmartre, VIC**

'Air France Orient Extreme' by Lucien Boucher, France, c1949, 50cm high, 31cm wide.

$1400 - $1600   **Galerie Montmartre, VIC**

'Formula 1' by Fix-Masseau, France, c1988, 100cm high, 62cm wide.

$500 - $600   **Galerie Montmartre, VIC**

'Orangina Café Table' by Bernard Villemot, France, c1970, 92cm high, 70cm wide.

$600 - $700   **Galerie Montmartre, VIC**

'Bally Blonde' by Bernard Villemot, France, c1982, 160cm high, 120cm wide.

$2400 - $2600   **Galerie Montmartre, VIC**

'Bally Lotus' by Bernard Villemot, France, c1973, 160cm high, 118cm wide.

$2100 - $2300   **Galerie Montmartre, VIC**

'Une Nuit' by Bernard Villemot, France, c1973, 100cm high, 62cm wide.

$950 - $1050   **Galerie Montmartre, VIC**

'Lido Grand Jeu' by Rene Gruau, France, c1973, 60cm high, 40cm wide.

$380 - $420   **Galerie Montmartre, VIC**

'Bic' By Raymond Savignac, France, c1978, 170cm high, 116cm wide.

$3900 - $4100   **Galerie Montmartre, VIC**

'Moutarde Bornibus' by Fore, France, c1954, 160cm high, 120cm wide.

$1500 - $1700   **Galerie Montmartre, VIC**

Poster 'Silly Willie Platypus' stop for the bus, issued by the Australian Road Safety Council, Australia, c1950, 75cm wide, 75cm long.

$230 - $270

369 Antiques, VIC

'Orangina Umbrellas' by Bernard Villemot, France, c1984, 160cm high, 234cm 'Orangina Umbrellas' by Bernard Villemot, France, c1984, 160cm high, 234cm long.

$3500 - $3700

Galerie Montmartre, VIC

'Philips Bikini Girl' by Fix-Masseau, France, c1960, 113cm high, 160cm wide.

$2500 - $2700

Galerie Montmartre, VIC

'Billecart Champagne' by Herve Morvan, France, c1959, 144cm high, 214cm wide.

$2900 - $3100

Galeri Montmartre, VIC

'Tricosteril' by Raymond Savignac, France, c1954, 117cm high, 158cm wide.

$3500 - $3700

Galerie Montmartre, VIC

'Vittel Delices' by Andre Roland, France, c1950, 114cm high, 155cm wide.

$2650 - $2850

Galerie Montmartre, VIC

Original poster, 'Peugeot', artist Vernier, France, c1960, 153cm high, 113cm wide.

$1300 - $1500

Galerie Montmartre, VIC

'Ameublement' print by Beric, France, c1950, 113cm high, 153cm wide.

$1100 - $1300

Galerie Montmartre, VIC

'Banania' by Herve Morvan, France, c1959, 160cm high, 120cm wide.

$2500 - $2700

Galerie Montmartre, VIC

'70's Girl' by Bernard Villemot, France, c1970, 160cm high, 120cm wide.

$1300 - $1500

Galerie Montmartre, VIC

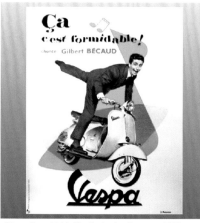

'Vespa Formidable' by Ambroise, France, c1955, 160cm high, 120cm wide.

$1400 - $1600

Galerie Montmartre, VIC

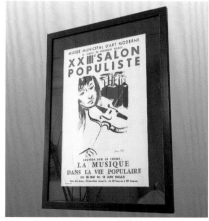

Advertising print for an art exhibition printed in Paris, France, c1962, 60cm high, 45cm wide.

$345 - $385

Le Contraste, VIC

Poster 'Swat That Fly' by Gwen Roberts, issued by the Department of Health, Melbourne, Australia, c1950, 60cm high, 45cm wide.

$190 - $210

369 Antiques, VIC

'Chanel' by Andy Warhol, United States, c1997, 170cm high, 117cm wide.

$700 - $800

Galerie Montmartre, VIC

Original lithographed tourism poster for San Sebastian, designed by Poza, Spain, c1956, 100cm high, 70cm wide.

$750 - $850

Vintage Posters Only, VIC

Original lithograph tourism poster for Salzburg, designed by Fischl, Austria, c1956.

$750 - $850

Vintage Posters Only, VIC

Original lithographed poster for Mon Soleil, designed by Robys, France, c1951, 160cm high, 120cm wide.

$1000 - $1200

Vintage Posters Only, VIC

'Tintin' by Raymond Savignac, France, c1980, 60cm high, 80cm wide.

$380 - $420

Galerie Montmartre, VIC

Original lithograph poster for Multzig, designed by Morvan, France, c1960, 160cm high, 120cm wide.

$1450 - $1650

Vintage Posters Only, VIC

Original lithograph tourism poster for Vovarlberg, designed by Horver, Austria, c1956, 100cm high, 70cm wide.

$750 - $850

Vintage Posters Only, VIC

Leach Barker, signed watercolour (1897 to 1967), Australia.

$175 - $195

Shenton Park Antiques, WA

Carrolup school aboriginal artwork, from south Western Australia of a uniquely portrayed landscape in exquisitely naive style, by G. Narkle, Australia, 43cm high.

$625 - $725

ShopAtNortham, WA

Maine – Le Hermitage by Donald Friend, watercolour and ink on paper, Australia, c1952, 29cm high, 46cm wide.

$11500 - $12500

Woollahra Times Art Gallery, NSW

'Sulphur Crested Cockatoo' etching watercolour in its original frame, edition number 5 of 25, Australia, c1977, 36cm high, 43cm wide.

$650 - $750

Habitat Antiques, NSW

Set of three, delicious, bright and clear, tiny watercolour landscapes, in cream/gold frames, signed 'H. H.', Australia, c1950, 14cm wide, 14cm long.

NZ$90 - $110

Waterfords of Mangaweka Village, New Zealand

Signed Bernard Hesling, rectangular, enamel in red 'The Quartet', c1974, 75cm high, 96cm wide.

$5300 - $5700

Capocchi, VIC

1978 'Pro Hart' catalogue, signed to the cover and inside with a dragonfly sketch, Australia, 23cm high, 19cm wide.

$330 - $370

McKays Mart, SA

'Cricketer and Sock Puppet' by McLean Edwards, watercolour on paper, Australia, 43.5cm high, 36cm wide.

$6300 - $6700

Woollahra Times Art Gallery, NSW

Signed original watercolour by Ben Abas; creator of the 'Dutch' comic strip, Australia, c1950.

$545 - $645

Colonial Antiques & Tea House, WA

Framed textured abstract painting by Joyce Donovan, Australia, c1970, 79cm high, 69cm wide.

$140 - $160

Retro Active, VIC

Copper wall art, Australia, c1970, 50cm diam.

$65 - $85

Atomic Pop, SA

Framed textured abstract painting by Joyce Donovan, Australia, c1970, 69cm high, 84cm wide.

$140 - $160

Retro Active, VIC

Bullfighter art work on painted foam, Australia, c1970.

$50 - $70

Atomic Pop, SA

Copper wall art, Australia, c1970, 53cm wide, 92cm long.

$100 - $120

Atomic Pop, SA

'Burning Flat at Tozers Gap', painted in 2003 with synthetic polymer and glaze on canvas by Samantha Hobson (1981-). This painting depicts the burning off-season at Lockhart River, Cape York. The ritual of burning off all the undergrowth after the wet season is crucial to good all year hunting and to the safety of the remote community. The danger and spectacle of this task is captured in Samantha's extraordinary images of the fires racing along the beaches and leaping into the skies of far north Queensland, Australia, 115cm high, 175cm wide.

$14500 - $15500

Lauraine Diggins Fine Art, VIC

Framed leaf painting of a pink rose painted on a pressed leaf, from the Pitcairn Islands made to sell as a tourist souvenir. An example of a form of souvenir ware made by the Pitcairn Islanders to sell to passing ships, New Zealand, c1950.

NZ$40 - $60

Casa Manana Antiques & Collectables, New Zealand

Mabel Lucie Attwell wall plaque, original Valette series, England, c1950, 31cm high, 20cm wide.

$45 - $65

Helen's On The Bay, QLD

Terracotta hand decorated wall plaque, of Madonna and child, Italy, c1950.

$1150 - $1350

Gallery Narcisse, NSW

Metal enamel wall sculpture signed, Australia, c1970, 180cm long, 60cm deep.

$1500 - $1700

Mondo Trasho, VIC

Signed John Campbell milk jug, with 'John Campbell' on the base and dated 1957 on the front, Australia, c1957, 7.5cm high, 6.5cm diam.

$140 - $160

Mac's Collectables, SA

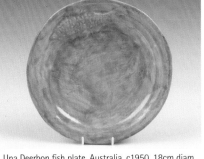

Una Deerbon fish plate, Australia, c1950, 18cm diam.

$275 - $315

Steven Sher Antiques, WA

Diana Pottery mixing bowl, in yellow with white polka dots, Australia, c1950, 10cm high, 16cm wide.

$115 - $135

Karlia Rose Garden Antiques & Collectables, VIC

Eight multi-coloured handled bowls, by Diana Pottery, Australia, c1954, 10cm diam.

$50 - $70

Step Back Antiques, VIC

Boxed set of Diana Ware ramekins, Australia, c1960, 27cm high, 40cm wide.

$115 - $135

Alltime Antiques & Bairnsdale Clocks, VIC

Ellis pottery platter, Australia, c1970, 24cm wide, 35cm long.

$85 - $105

Camberwell Antique Centre, VIC

Fowler Ware green ceramic bowl, size 12, Australia, c1950, 13cm high, 23cm diam.

$45 - $55

Step Back Antiques, VIC

Abstract Ellis Pottery sculpture of a woman, Australia, 23cm high.

$110 - $130

Victor Harbour Antiques - Mittagong, NSW

Diana Australia vase, decorated with hand painted Sturt Desert Peas, Australia, c1950, 26cm high, 16cm wide.

$255 - $295

Camberwell Antique Centre, VIC

'Nefertiti' stoneware decanter (J30) and stopper with cork, Australia, c1960, 25cm high, 12cm diam.

$35 - $45

Possum's Treasures, QLD

'H. McHugh Tasmania 63' vase in blue, Australia, 9cm high, 12cm diam.

$135 - $155

Bygone Beautys, NSW

MCP egg shaped vase with a textured exterior in an impressed MCP mark, Australia, c1959, 19.5cm high.

$65 - $85

frhapsody, WA

Disney 'Figaro' figurine, by MCP Sydney, Australia, c1950, 8.5cm high, 10cm long, 5.5cm deep.

$100 - $120

Southside Antiques Centre, QLD

Art Deco style vase by MCP, which can be wall mounted, Australia, c1950, 23cm high, 25cm wide.

$305 - $345

Vampt, NSW

'Donald' by Modern Ceramic Products, Sydney, with original paper sticker, Australia, c1950, 14cm high.

$165 - $185

Olsens Antiques, QLD

Signed Remued gumnut basket (#194/11), Australia, c1950, 21cm high, 26cm long.

$1000 - $1200

The Mill Markets, VIC

Pates Potteries, Sydney, fish shaped wall pocket vase, Australia, c1950, 13cm high, 19cm long, 5cm deep.

$45 - $65

Mockingbird Lane Antiques, NSW

Klytie Pate plate, embossed with a mythical horse in a teal green volcanic glaze with mulberry, the side incised 'Klytie Pate', Australia, 14cm diam.

$275 - $315

Jeremy's Australiana, VIC

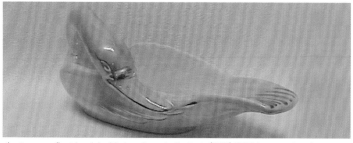

Lustre swan float bowl, by Modern Ceramic Products (MCP) 'P6H' impressed mark, c1962-1972, Australia, 17cm high, 45cm long.

$100 - $120

Olsens Antiques, QLD

Klytie Pate ribbed vase in the traditional style, in lovely light teal green and marked to the base 'Klytie Pate', Australia, 19.5cm high, 15cm wide.

$545 - $645

Jeremy's Australiana, VIC

William Ricketts Aboriginal bust of a young boy, Australia, c1950, 11cm high, 10cm wide.

$745 - $845

Hermitage Antiques - Geelong Wintergarden, VIC

Signed and hand painted bowl of an exotic bird by Tom Sanders, master potter from the 1950's and 1960's, and he often worked with John Perceval and Fred Williams, Australia, c1950, 12cm diam.

$255 - $295

Malvern Antique Market, VIC

Set of six Johnson duos with a Jessie Tait design ('Inca') on the cups, Australia, c1974, 7cm high.

$35 - $45

frhapsody, WA

Hand painted ceramic koala book ends, Australia, c1950, 10cm high, 18cm wide.

$55 - $75

Antiques & More At 24, SA

Daisy Ware eight setting dinner set with dinner plates, bread and butter plates, cups and saucers, soup bowls on bases, plates, goblets a large salad bowl and a large party plate, Australia, c1950.

$3400 - $3600

Antique Revivals, VIC

Grace Seccombe Taronga Zoo ceramic koala trough, Australia, c1950, 14cm long.

$225 - $265

The Junk Company, VIC

Grace Seccombe gumnut vase/bowl, Australia, c1950, 23cm long.

$330 - $370

Paddington Antique Centre Pty Ltd, QLD

Sylha (Sylvia Halpern) bowl with a matte white glaze and hand painted black rings, Australia, c1950, 6cm high, 25cm diam.

$80 - $100

Born Frugal, VIC

Pair of brown bowls with orange, white and blue trim, Australia, c1970, 6cm high, 14cm wide.

$20 - $30

Karlia Rose Garden Antiques & Collectables, VIC

Pair of bi-colour pottery dishes, each signed 'Janet Gray Australia', the interiors of the dishes with engraved fish designs, Australia, 11cm wide, 22cm long.

Born Frugal, VIC

$125 - $145

David and Hermia Boyd studio ceramic cup and saucer, signed to the base, Australia, c1955, 6cm high, 10cm diam.

$205 - $245

Malvern Antique Market, VIC

Carl Cooper cup and saucer with Aboriginal motifs, Australia, c1950.

$675 - $775

Hermitage Antiques - Geelong Wintergarden, VIC

Langdale serving dish, in black with orange, aqua and white artwork, Australia, c1960, 8cm high, 21cm wide.

$40 - $50

Karlia Rose Garden Antiques & Collectables, VIC

Pair of 'Helfire' jugs with crocodile formed handles, Australia, c1950, 11cm high, 14cm wide.

$215 - $255

Antique Curiosity Shop, QLD

Matt finished pottery figurine of a bikini girl, Australia, c1960, 28cm high, 24cm wide.

$190 - $210

The New Farm Antique Centre, QLD

Ceramic figurine of a koala in a tree, Japan, c1960, 10cm high.

$25 - $35

Shop 8 Mittagong Antiques Centre, NSW

Pair of ceramic horses with gold manes and tails, Australia, c1980, 18cm high, 28cm long.

$60 - $80

Chapel Street Bazaar, VIC

Beautifully modelled plump kookaburra figurine by Western Australian potter, Edwin Leech, mounted on a jarrah base and stamped with the potter's details, Australia, c1965, 21cm high, 15cm wide.

$430 - $470

ShopAtNortham, WA

Studio Pottery jug inscribed on the base 'Ellis '57', with a bright finish of green, white and ochre shades of drip glaze, Australia, 12cm high.

$40 - $50

Born Frugal, VIC

Jolliff jug with a raky glaze branch handle in purple, green, blue and copper, signed 'Jolliff, Handmade 1954', Australia, 14.5cm high, 7cm wide.

$1050 - $1250

Jeremy's Australiana, VIC

Robert Barron stoneware, single handed bottle, signed to the base. Robert Barron is a master potter and is represented in most state public art galleries, he has exhibited in many solo and group exhibitions in Australian and overseas, Australia, c1980, 27cm high, 16cm diam.

$375 - $415

Malvern Antique Market, VIC

CERAMICS

Ivory coloured pottery jug with its original box and signed, 'Breamore, Australian Made', Australia, c1970, 30cm high, 25cm diam.

$140 - $160
Towers Antiques & Collectables, NSW

Studio ceramic sculpture of an exotic bird, signed Stephen Benwell to the base. Stephen Benwell is one of Australia's leading ceramic artists and his work is represented in all state public art galleries and the National Gallery in Canberra. He has a high profile international profile and reputation, Australia, c1975, 14cm high.

$1500 - $1700
Malvern Antique Market, VIC

Ceramic piece signed Manuela Karolyi Sydney, Australia, c1950, 22cm high, 22cm wide.

$270 - $310
Retro Active, VIC

Flon studios, pig cocktail server, Australia, c1980, 6cm high, 8cm wide, 5cm deep.

$20 - $30
Antipodes Antiques, QLD

Rose Noble Maroochydore jug, Australia, c1950, 8cm high, 8cm long.

$35 - $45
Antipodes Antiques, QLD

David and Hermia Boyd pot with handle, signed to the base, Australia, c1950, 9cm high, 12cm diam.

$360 - $400
Malvern Antique Market, VIC

David Lyons pottery of a magpie, gum nuts and leaves dedicated to Oscar Louis Thomas Jones, signed David Lyons to the base, Australia, c2005, 21cm high.

$700 - $800
C. V. Jones Antiques & Art Gallery, VIC

Studio ceramic stoneware beaker, by master potter Alex Leckie, Australia, c1950, 18cm high, 9cm diam.

$460 - $500
Malvern Antique Market, VIC

Lucy Boyd 'Rabbit' decorated plate in white glaze with incised decorations, and 'Lucy Hatton Beck' to the back, Australia, 14cm diam.

$250 - $290
Jeremy's Australiana, VIC

Studio ceramic plate, by master potter Victoria Howlett, Australia, c1970, 24cm diam.

$345 - $385
Malvern Antique Market, VIC

Large Lucy Boyd plate with lovely flowing earthy glazes of brown and tans, incised to the base 'Lucy Hatton Beck', Australia, 25.3cm diam.

$350 - $390   **Jeremy's Australiana, VIC**

Gild edged cabinet plate, made by Melbourne based Rembrandt Pottery, with a large transfer print of an indigenous face, signed 'S. Hunter', Australia, c1960, 26cm diam.

$45 - $65   **Born Frugal, VIC**

Joyce Abbott, Aboriginal male portrait on a ceramic wall plaque, Australia, c1960, 21cm diam.

$100 - $120   **Rare Old Times Antiques & Collectables, SA**

Derbyshire lighthouse salt and pepper shakers with their original labels, Australia, c1950, 9cm high.

$55 - $75   **Antipodes Antiques, QLD**

Pair of ceramic Aboriginal wall silhouettes by Takacs Studios, Australia, c1950, 40cm wide.

$65 - $85   **Newport Temple Antiques, VIC**

Large ceramic owl umbrella stand, Australia, c1950.

$265 - $305   **The Junk Company, VIC**

Studio ceramic stoneware pot by master potter Van De Beth, Australia, c1970, 21cm high, 20cm diam.

$530 - $630   **Malvern Antique Market, VIC**

Pottery vase in 'Crescent Moon Pattern', signed by David Lyons to the base, Australia, c2005, 26cm high, 21cm wide.

$700 - $800   **C. V. Jones Antiques & Art Gallery, VIC**

Studio ceramic stoneware vessel by master Tasmanian potter Rynne Tanton. Rynne is represented in state public collections in Tasmania and Victoria, and in the National Gallery, Canberra, Australia, c1980, 24cm high, 20cm diam.

$530 - $630   **Malvern Antique Market, VIC**

Black and yellow striped ceramic vase, Australia, c1960, 22cm high, 27cm wide, 10cm deep.

$90 - $110   **506070, NSW**

A superb lizard vase with excellent detail, by E. A. Brown, Australia, 14cm high, 18cm wide.

$3150 - $3350   **Deco Down Under, WA**

Pottery vase with the original sticker on the base, Australia, c1950, 30cm high.

$40 - $50

How Bazaar, TAS

Studio ceramic vessel by master potter Andrew Cope who won the prestigious Fletcher Challenge ceramic award in the early 1990's, Australia, c1980, 13cm high.

$360 - $400

Malvern Antique Market, VIC

Studio ceramic stoneware vase, by master potter Victoria Howlett, Australia, c1970, 26cm high, 8cm diam.

$360 - $400

Malvern Antique Market, VIC

Studio ceramic, raku filled vessel by master potter Michael Chanter, this item comes with a numbered and signed certificate, Australia, c1984, 30cm high, 17cm diam.

$455 - $495

Malvern Antique Market, VIC

Fan shaped footed lustre vase with two original foil stickers, 'Raynham', Australia, c1950, 19.5cm high, 12cm wide, 38cm long.

$45 - $65

Possum's Treasures, QLD

Casey Ware swan vase, Australia, c1955, 13cm high, 18cm long.

$20 - $30

Antipodes Antiques, QLD

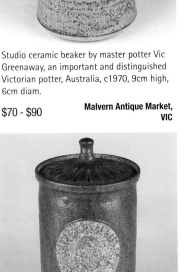

Studio ceramic beaker by master potter Vic Greenaway, an important and distinguished Victorian potter, Australia, c1970, 9cm high, 6cm diam.

$70 - $90

Malvern Antique Market, VIC

Studio ceramic lidded pot, by master potter Alex Leckie, Australia, c1950, 18cm high, 9cm deep.

$430 - $470

Malvern Antique Market, VIC

Large ceramic vase signed Greg Hamilton, Australia, c1980, 27cm high.

$85 - $105

Newport Temple Antiques, VIC

Five piece cruet set of kookaburra salt and pepper shakers with a gumnut lidded mustard pot, on a clover leaf tray and a ceramic original mustard spoon, Japan, c1950, 7cm high, 11cm wide, 13cm long.

$110 - $130

Isadora's Antiques, NSW

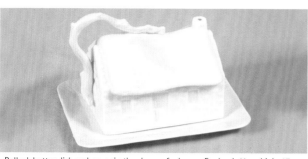

Belleek butter dish and cover in the shape of a house, England, 11cm high, 17cm wide, 13cm deep.

$275 - $315

Sherwood Bazaar, QLD

Aynsley twenty one piece tea set, includes six trios, sugar bowl, creamer and cake plate, all with pale green background and countryside scene, England, c1950, 7cm high, 8.5cm wide.

$375 - $415

Helen's On The Bay, QLD

Belleek teapot, England, 12cm high, 26cm wide, 15cm deep.

$430 - $470

Sherwood Bazaar, QLD

Belleek sugar bowl and cream jug, England, 8cm high.

$205 - $245

Sherwood Bazaar, QLD

Belleek jug with the sixth mark, produced from 1965-1980, Ireland, 15cm high.

NZ$255 - $295

Bonham's, New Zealand

Aynsley hand painted fruit plate, signed 'D. Jones', England, 2.5cm high, 26.5cm diam.

NZ$405 - $445

Country Charm Antiques, New Zealand

'Aynsley' heavily gilded fine bone china trio, England.

$45 - $65

Nicki's Collection, NSW

Aynsley comport, signed Bailey, England, c1980, 5cm high, 14cm diam.

NZ$145 - $165

Gales Antiques, New Zealand

Aynsley tea set of four trios with pattern of many different flowers, England, c1950, 6.5cm high, 8.5cm wide.

$145 - $165

Helen's On The Bay, QLD

Belleek vase in an ivory glaze, Ireland, c1950, 19cm high.

$230 - $270

Trinity Antiques, WA

Aynsley trio, floral design with gilt detail, England, c1950.

$55 - $75

Helen's On The Bay, QLD

BESWICK

Beswick 'Begging Dachshund', model No. 1461, in black and tan gloss, designed by Arthur Gredington, United Kingdom, 10cm high.

$135 - $155 **Glenelg Antique Centre, SA**

Beswick Doberman figurine, England, c1980, 15cm high, 17cm long.

$185 - $205 **Paddington Antique Centre Pty Ltd, QLD**

Very large Beswick 'Irish Setter' wall plaque, model No. 668, in production from 1938-1960, England, 26.7cm wide, 14cm deep.

NZ$515 - $615 **Country Charm Antiques, New Zealand**

Beswick figure of a Norfolk terrier with a matt glaze, England, c1990, 11cm high, 13cm long.

$70 - $90 **Yande Meannjin Antiques, QLD**

Beswick figure of Golden Retriever, with original sticker, England, c1970, 7cm high.

$115 - $135 **Palliaer Antiques, QLD**

Beswick figure of 'Duchess With Pie', England, c1979, 9.5cm high.

$945 - $1045 **Steven Sher Antiques, WA**

Beswick Collie, 'Lochinvar of Lady Park', designed by Arthur Gredinton, in golden brown and white gloss, England, c1961, 14.5cm high.

$230 - $270 **Neville Beechey Antiques, VIC**

Beswick figure of a Hereford calf, England, c1956, 8cm high.

$355 - $395 **Steven Sher Antiques, WA**

Beswick figure of a Hereford calf, England, c1957, 10cm high.

$330 - $370 **Steven Sher Antiques, WA**

Beswick bird, model No.991B, designed by Arthur Gredington issued 1973 - 1999, England, 7cm high.

$85 - $105 **Newlyn Antiques & Cottage Garden Nursery, VIC**

Beswick Grey Wagtail figurine, number 1041, England, c1980, 6cm high, 10.5cm wide.

$75 - $95 **Morrison Antiques & Collectables, NSW**

Beswick model of a blue tit, first version, model 992A, in production from 1943-1973, England, 6.5cm high.

NZ$135 - $155

John Varney, New Zealand

Large Beswick, winged eagle figure, England, c1960.

$545 - $645

Antiques & Heirlooms, WA

Set of three Beswick flying partridges, England, c1950, 26cm long.

$900 - $1000

Steven Sher Antiques, WA

Beswick 'British Blue Cat' (#1030) figurine, England, c1965, 16cm high.

$645 - $745

Sherwood Bazaar, QLD

Beswick figurine of a Siamese cat, in production from 1963-1989, England, 23cm high, 17cm wide, 11cm deep.

$355 - $395

Southside Antiques Centre, QLD

Beswick seal point, gloss cat figurine, produced from 1971 to 1989, England.

$115 - $135

Morrison Antiques & Collectables, NSW

Beswick grey shire horse figurine, England, c1949, 21cm high, 25cm wide.

NZ$455 - $495

Colonial Heritage Antiques Ltd, New Zealand

Beswick No.1484 Huntsman Horse, in Palomino Gloss, in production from 1957 to 1882, England, 17cm high, 23cm long.

$250 - $290

Kings Park Antiques & Collectables, SA

Beswick gloss dun mare, limited edition of 710 and Beswick gloss dun foal, limited edition of 730, a special commission in 1997, England.

$875 - $975

Julie Sandry, NSW

Beswick black gloss cantering shire horse figure, limited edition of 735 commissioned by the Beswick Collectors Club, England, c1996, 22cm high.

$550 - $650

Julie Sandry, NSW

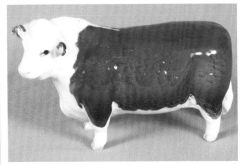

Beswick Hereford bull figurine, No. 1363, England, 12cm high, 20cm long.

$375 - $415

Sherwood Bazaar, QLD

Beswick farm animals 'Hereford Bull' model 1363A designed by Arthur Gredington, England, c1955, 108cm high.

$380 - $420

Newlyn Antiques & Cottage Garden Nursery, VIC

Gloss Beswick Limousin bull, limited edition of 653, England, c1998.

$1000 - $1200

Julie Sandry, NSW

Beswick farm animal 'Highland Cow' model No. 1740 designed by Arthur Gredington, issued 1961 - 1990, England, 13cm high.

$480 - $580

Newlyn Antiques & Cottage Garden Nursery, VIC

Beswick farm animal jersey bull 'Dunsley Coy Boy' model No, 1422 designed by Arthur Gredington, issued 1956 - 1997, England, 11.9cm high.

$330 - $370

Newlyn Antiques & Cottage Garden Nursery, VIC

Beswick farm animal Guernsey cow, model 1248B designed by Arthur Gredington, issued 1953 - 1989, England, 10.8cm high.

$355 - $395

Newlyn Antiques & Cottage Garden Nursery, VIC

Beswick model of 'Alice' from the Alice in Wonderland series, England, c1976, 12.5cm high.

NZ$475 - $515

John Varney, New Zealand

Beswick figure of an eagle, England, c1970, 20cm high, 15cm wide.

$280 - $320

The New Farm Antique Centre, QLD

Pair of Beswick penguins, England, c1970, 10cm high.

$480 - $520

The New Farm Antique Centre, QLD

Beswick set of eight Walt Disney figurines, including (clockwise from left) Rabbit, Tigger, Christopher Robin, Kanga, Owl, Eeyore, Piglet and Winnie the Pooh, England, c1970.

$2400 - $2600

Southside Antiques Centre, QLD

Beswick zebra, first version in tan and black, England, c1960, 18cm high.

$430 - $470   **Paddington Antique Centre Pty Ltd, QLD**

Beswick zebra (# 8450) by Arthur Gredington, discontinued 1969, England, c1960.

$475 - $515   **Antipodes Antiques, QLD**

Beswick butter dish in the shape of a loaf of bread, England, c1968, 10cm wide, 14.5cm long.

$65 - $85   **Camberwell Antique Centre, VIC**

Beswick figure of a trout, England, c1950, 17cm high.

$500 - $600   **Steven Sher Antiques, WA**

Beswick koala figurine, England, 9cm high.

$215 - $255   **Archers Antiques, TAS**

Beswick figure of a seal, designed by Colin Melbourne, England, c1955, 10cm high, 9cm long.

NZ$275 - $315   **Banks Peninsula Antiques, New Zealand**

Beswick (model No.755) mallard duck ashtray, in production 1939–1969, United Kingdom, 10cm high, 10cm diam.

$85 - $105   **Glenelg Antique Centre, SA**

Beswick wild animal lioness, model No.2097 issued 1967 – 1984, designed by Graham Tongue, England,14.6cm high.

$455 - $495   **Newlyn Antiques & Cottage Garden Nursery, VIC**

Beswick pheasant ashtray, England, c1950.

$75 - $95   **Tyabb Hay Shed, VIC**

Beswick 'Wild Animal', black puma on a rock, model No.1702, designed by Arthur Gredington, issued 1960 – 1983, England, 21.6cm high.

$750 - $850   **Newlyn Antiques & Cottage Garden Nursery, VIC**

Beswick Beatrix Potter, 'Mr Jeremy Fisher' figure, spotted leg variation, BP1 Gold backstamp, England, 7.5cm high.

$500 - $600   **Roundabout Antiques, QLD**

Beswick Beatrix Potter 'Old Mr. Brown' character jug, backstamp BP4, England.

$230 - $270   **Upwell Antiques, ACT**

Beswick Beatrix Potter 'Anna Maria' figure with a BP2 Gold backstamp, England, 7.5cm high.

$475 - $575   **Roundabout Antiques, QLD**

Beswick Beatrix Potter 'Pickles' figure, BP2, England, 11.5cm high.

$950 - $1050   **Roundabout Antiques, QLD**

Beswick Beatrix Potter's 'Tom Kitten', England, 9cm high, 5cm wide.

NZ$330 - $370   **Colonial Antiques, New Zealand**

Beswick Beatrix Potter 'Mrs Littlemouse', England, 8.5cm high, 6cm wide.

NZ$330 - $370   **Colonial Antiques, New Zealand**

Beswick 'Simpkin' Beatrix Potter figurine, modelled by Allan Maslankowski and in production from 1975-1983, England.

NZ$1000 - $1200   **Sue Todd Antiques Collectables, New Zealand**

Beswick Beatrix Potter 'Pigling Bland' figure, deep maroon jacket variation, BP2, England, 11cm high.

$700 - $800   **Roundabout Antiques, QLD**

Beswick 'Sir Isaac Newton' Beatrix Potter figurine, modelled by Graeme Tongue, in production 1973-1984, England.

NZ$1150 - $1350   **Sue Todd Antiques Collectables, New Zealand**

Beswick Beatrix Potter 'Ginger' figure, BP3b backstamp, England, 9.5cm high.

$875 - $975   **Roundabout Antiques, QLD**

Bisque figurine planter, Germany, 16cm high, 10cm wide, 18cm long.

$475 - $575

Rare Old Times Antiques & Collectables, SA

Bisque figurine of a New Zealand owl on a silver plated base, by Royal Hereford, Maori name - 'More Pork', New Zealand, 8cm high, 12.5cm wide.

NZ$275 - $315

Country Charm Antiques, New Zealand

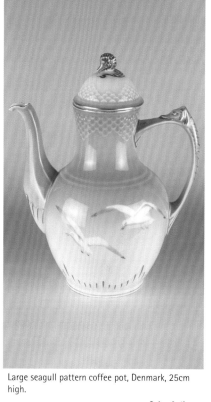

Large seagull pattern coffee pot, Denmark, 25cm high.

NZ$275 - $315

Gales Antiques, New Zealand

Royal Sphinx delfts ginger jar by Boch, Holland, c1980, 36cm high, 18cm diam.

$225 - $265

Chapel Street Bazaar, VIC

Spode blue and white plate, England, c1990, 26cm diam.

$55 - $75

Antipodes Antiques, QLD

Blue and white, six-box spice set, Japan, c1950, 8cm high, 17cm wide, 6cm deep.

$110 - $130

The Evandale Tinker, TAS

Blue Danube cup and saucer, Japan, c1985.

NZ$15 - $25

Colonial Antiques, New Zealand

Spode 'Italian' mug, England, c1990, 8.5cm high, 8cm diam.

$45 - $55

Antipodes Antiques, QLD

Royal Crown Derby blue and white cup and saucer, England.

NZ$40 - $50

Gales Antiques, New Zealand

Burleigh Ware 'Willow' pattern tea pot, England, c1950, 15cm high, 23cm long, 15cm deep.

$185 - $205

Antiques & Collectables Centre - Ballarat, VIC

Bossons 'Pancho' wall plaque, England, c1950, 17cm high, 15cm wide.

$70 - $90

Goodwood House Antiques, WA

Bossons 'Geisha' figurine, England, c1963, 33cm high.

$885 - $985   **Kings Park Antiques & Collectables, QLD**

Bossons 'Romany' wall figure, England, c1950, 26cm high, 24cm wide.

$200 - $240   **Goodwood House Antiques, WA**

Bossons 'Mikado' figurine, England, 36cm high.

$885 - $985   **Kings Park Antiques & Collectables, QLD**

Plaster wall plaque floral decoration made by Bossons, England, c1950.

$65 - $85   **Colonial Antiques & Tea House, WA**

Bosson's 'Sarie Gamp', England, c1960.

$55 - $75   **Chapel Street Bazaar, VIC**

Guy Boyd wall plate, black background with tea tree flowers, signed, Australia, c1960, 13cm wide.

$65 - $85   **Fat Helen's, VIC**

Guy Boyd vase with an aboriginal woman, Australia, c1950, 8cm high, 9cm diam.

NZ$85 - $105   **Maxine's Collectibles, New Zealand**

Guy Boyd display plate with a J.Fraser painted scene, Australia, c1960, 24.5cm diam.

$145 - $165   **Terrace Collectables, NSW**

Hand painted wall plate with an Aboriginal mother and child, by Guy Boyd, Australia, c1950, 15.5cm diam.

NZ$80 - $100   **Maxine's Collectibles, New Zealand**

Martin Boyd inscribed display plate, Australia, c1960, 17cm diam.

$135 - $155

Terrace Collectables, NSW

Signed Martin Boyd, hand painted pottery plaque, Australia, c1950, 19cm diam.

$370 - $410

Kollectik Pty Ltd, NSW

Martin Boyd hand painted plaque, Australia, c1950, 10.5cm diam.

$480 - $520

Kollectik Pty Ltd, NSW

Martin Boyd plate, featuring two ladies with parasols, Australia, c1950, 26cm diam.

$255 - $295

Goodwood House Antiques, WA

Martin Boyd cup, saucer and plate set, Australia, c1950, 8cm high, 19cm diam.

$45 - $65

Kookaburra Antiques, TAS

Martin Boyd wall plate with aboriginal designs, Australia, c1980, 26.5cm diam.

NZ$230 - $270

Maxine's Collectibles, New Zealand

Pottery jug depicting an Aboriginal, signed Martin Boyd, Australia, c1950, 20cm high, 9cm wide.

$545 - $645

Adornments, QLD

Martin Boyd dish, Australia, c1955, 26cm wide.

$205 - $245

Paddington Antique Centre Pty Ltd, QLD

Martin Boyd wall plate, 'Ophelia', Australia, c1950, 27cm diam.

NZ$230 - $270

Maxine's Collectibles, New Zealand

Martin Boyd 'Noah's Ark' bowl, c1950, 4.5cm deep, 15cm diam.

$115 - $135

Olsens Antiques, QLD

Set of four Martin Boyd bowls with the under plate all decorated with pink eucalyptus blossoms and leaves, Australia, c1950.

$330 - $370

River Emporium, NSW

BURLEIGH WARE & CARLTON WARE

Carlton Ware buttercup triple dish, Australian design, England, c1950, 22cm wide, 25cm long.

$75 - $95

Helen's On The Bay, QLD

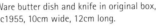

Carlton Ware butter dish and knife in original box, England, c1955, 10cm wide, 12cm long.

$125 - $145

Bygone Beautys, NSW

Carlton Ware 'Poppy' pattern platter, England, c1950, 25cm diam.

$100 - $120

Leven Antiques - Tasmania, TAS

Carlton Ware, Art Deco styled toast rack, England, c1955, 6cm high, 11cm long.

$85 - $105

Paddington Antique Centre Pty Ltd, QLD

Carlton Ware combination toast rack and jam and butter server, England, c1955, 10cm high, 17cm long.

$225 - $265

Antipodes Antiques, QLD

Carlton Ware lobster, 'Langouste' pattern serving plate, England, c1950.

$125 - $145

Antiques at Redbank, QLD

Carlton Ware 'Langouste' pattern egg plate, England, c1950, 31cm diam.

$110 - $130

Antiques at Redbank, QLD

Burleigh Ware 'Sairey Gamp' character jug, England, c1950, 12cm high.

$115 - $135

Antiques & Collectables Centre - Ballarat, VIC

Carlton Ware boat dish, England, c1950, 10cm high, 28cm long.

$90 - $110

Journey to the Past Antiques & Collectables, QLD

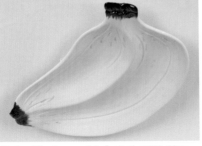

Carlton Ware banana dish, England, c1970, 28cm long.

$55 - $75

Out of the Ark, ACT

Carlton Ware foxglove 'Cottage Ware' dish, England, c1950, 18cm wide, 16.5cm long.

$30 - $40

Yande Meannjin Antiques, QLD

Carlton Ware jug, England, c1950.

$85 - $105

The Junk Company, VIC

Carlton Ware 'Rouge Royale' vase, England, c1960, 14cm high.

$255 - $295

Goodwood House Antiques, WA

Carlton Ware 'Rouge Royale' jug, England, c1960, 11cm high, 9cm wide.

$205 - $245

Goodwood House Antiques, WA

Carlton Ware lustre pottery walking ware, five piece tea set for two, made in 1973, England.

$430 - $470

Sherrill Grainger, NSW

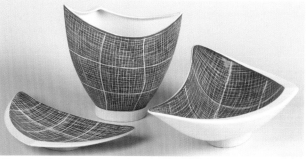

Three piece Carlton Ware hand painted vase, bowl and dish set, England, c1950.

$190 - $230

Vampt, NSW

Carlton Ware 'Walking Ware' tea pot with yellow shoes and blue and black socks, England, c1960, 18cm high, 18cm wide.

$330 - $370

Karlia Rose Garden Antiques & Collectables, VIC

Carlton Ware, 'Walking Ware' cup, England, c1973, 9cm high, 8cm wide.

$105 - $125

Karlia Rose Garden Antiques & Collectables, VIC

Carlton Ware 'Red Baron' teapot, England, 14cm high, 14cm wide, 21cm long.

NZ$545 - $645

Bulls Antiques & Collectables, New Zealand

Carlton Ware lobster jug and under dish, Australian design, England, c1950, 5cm high, 11cm wide, 19cm long.

$100 - $120

Helen's On The Bay, QLD

Carlton Ware 'Spring Time' chocolate mug and lid, England, c1950, 12cm high, 10cm diam.

$375 - $415

Camberwell Antique Centre, VIC

Carlton Ware sugar bowl, England, c1937.

$40 - $50

The Nostalgia Factory, NSW

Clarice Cliff 'Celtic Harvest' sauce boat with under dish, England, c1950, 11cm high.

$380 - $420

Antipodes Antiques, QLD

Limited edition 'Orange House' in The Bizarre World of Clarice Cliff, maximum of fifty firing days officially listed for trading on The Bradford Exchange, plate number 40P, stamped 'Wedgwood bone china, Made in England, 1994', England, 20cm diam.

$85 - $105

Decodence Collectables, VIC

Limited Edition 'Blue Lucerne' in The Bizarre World of Clarice Cliff. Maximum of fifty firing days, officially listed for trading on The Bradford Exchange, plate number 316Q, stamped 'Wedgwood Bone China, Made in England 1994', England, c1994, 20cm diam.

$85 - $105

Decodence Collectables, VIC

Clarice Cliff vase, England, c1950, 20cm high, 22cm wide.

$645 - $745

Goodwood House Antiques, WA

Clarice Cliff 'Celtic Harvest' teapot, England, c1950, 15cm high.

$545 - $645

Paddington Antique Centre Pty Ltd, QLD

'Rural Scenes' plate by Clarice Cliff, England, c1950, 27cm diam.

NZ$65 - $85

Memory Lane, New Zealand

Coalport 'Anne' figurine, England, c1990, 19cm high.

$135 - $155

Paddington Antique Centre Pty Ltd, QLD

Coalport set of six demi tasse, England, c1960.

$185 - $205

Goodwood House Antiques, WA

Bachelor tea set, made by Crown Works (Burslem) designed by Susie Cooper, England, c1950.

$1000 - $1200 **Eaglemont Antiques and Interiors, VIC**

Set of six Susie Cooper cups and saucers with the 'Strawberry' pattern, England.

$420 - $460 **Olsens Antiques, QLD**

Susie Cooper coffee set, with four coffee cans and saucers, a coffee pot and sugar bowl, produced from 1950 to 1966, England.

$240 - $280 **Robyn's Nest, VIC**

Set of six black and white, Susie Cooper coffee cups and saucers, England, c1965, 8.5cm high.

$290 - $330 **Avoca Beach Antiques, NSW**

Susie Cooper coffee set, consisting of a coffee pot, five coffee cans with matching saucers, stamped Susie Cooper bone china, England, England, c1950.

$300 - $340 **Decodence Collectables, VIC**

Suzie Cooper, lidded vegetable dish, made in 1959 with the 'Ferndown' pattern, England, 10cm high, 26cm diam.

$155 - $175 **Born Frugal, VIC**

Susie Cooper 'Carnation' coffee pot, creamer and sugar, pattern No. c2088, England, c1960, 20cm high, 10cm wide.

$225 - $265 **Woodside Bazaar, SA**

Susie Cooper 'Dresden Spray' lidded sugar bowl with a pink wash banding, Kestral shape, England, 7cm high.

$190 - $210 **Camberwell Antique Centre, VIC**

Susie Cooper coffee set, including six cups and saucers and the original box, England, c1960, 6.5cm high.

$155 - $175 **506070, NSW**

Susie Cooper coffee pot, teapot, cream jug and sugar bowl in the 'Apple Gay' pattern, made in her factory between 1950-1966, England.

$1150 - $1350 **The Best Antiques & Collectables, QLD**

CERAMICS

Crown Devon figure, 'Marina' painted and glazed cellulose, 'A Sutherland Figure', 17.5cm high.

$380 - $420 **Discovery Corner, QLD**

Crown Lynn earthenware, 'Metropolitan Series Ware' vase, New Zealand, 28cm high.

NZ$140 - $160 **Maxine's Collectibles, New Zealand**

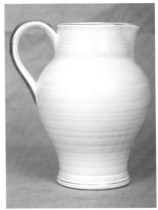

Crown Devon, green water jug with a gold handle, England, c1950, 24cm high.

$155 - $175 **Avoca Beach Antiques, NSW**

Crown Devon musical jug, decorated with the Irish jaunting car, muckross gates and the gap of Dunloe, plays the tune 'Killarney's Lakes and Fells', England.

NZ$475 - $515 **Tinakori Antiques, New Zealand**

Crown Devon 'Blue Royale' jug, England, c1950, 13cm high.

$115 - $135 **Yanda Aboriginal Art Melbourne, VIC**

Crown Devon 'Garden Path' dish, England, c1950, 17cm wide.

$40 - $50 **Yanda Aboriginal Art Melbourne, VIC**

Crown Lynn kiwi figurine, New Zealand, c1960, 9cm high, 12cm wide.

NZ$145 - $165 **Sue Todd Antiques Collectables, New Zealand**

Crown Lynn foal figurine, in production from 1948-1955, New Zealand, 18.5cm high.

NZ$230 - $270 **Antiques & Curiosities, New Zealand**

Crown Lynn pottery watering can, marked 'Crown Lynn' and numbered '215', New Zealand, c1956, 80cm wide, 17cm long, 10cm deep.

NZ$55 - $75 **Best Antiques & Collectables, New Zealand**

Crown Lynn Roydon, 'Tiny Tots Ware' mug (pattern number 100-884), New Zealand, c1960.

NZ$50 - $70 **Maxine's Collectibles, New Zealand**

Crown Lynn pottery bowl by Frank Carpay, marked 'Handwerk', New Zealand, c1960, 5cm high, 26cm diam.

NZ$900 - $1000

Trevor & Pam Plumbly, New Zealand

Crown Lynn child's bowl depicting the 'Old Woman Who Lived in the Shoe' No.83700, signed Norman Meredith, New Zealand, c1950, 18.5cm diam.

NZ$40 - $50

Fendalton Antiques, New Zealand

Crown Lynn 'Nursery Tales' bowl and mug, New Zealand, c1980, 8cm high, 8cm diam.

NZ$40 - $50

Maxine's Collectibles, New Zealand

Crown Lynn 'Bambi' figurine, New Zealand, c1955, 25.5cm high.

NZ$275 - $315

Antiques & Curiosities, New Zealand

Crown Lynn 'Blue Tango' cup and saucer, New Zealand.

NZ$15 - $25

Moa Extinct Stuff, New Zealand

Crown Lynn 'Ding Dong Dell' child's mug, New Zealand, c1950, 8cm high, 8cm diam.

NZ$40 - $50

Fendalton Antiques, New Zealand

Crown Lynn 'Fleurette' cup and saucer, New Zealand.

NZ$15 - $25

Moa Extinct Stuff, New Zealand

Pair of Crown Lynn cups and saucers featuing a kiwi motif, New Zealand.

NZ$60 - $80

Moa Extinct Stuff, New Zealand

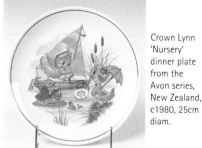

Crown Lynn 'Nursery' dinner plate from the Avon series, New Zealand, c1980, 25cm diam.

NZ$25 - $35

Maxine's Collectibles, New Zealand

Crown Lynn child's bread and butter plate, No. 83700, 'Oranges and Lemon', signed Norman Meredith, New Zealand, c1950, 17cm diam.

NZ$40 - $50

Fendalton Antiques, New Zealand

Crown Lynn plate, featuring a map of the Auckland CBD, New Zealand, c1970, 17cm diam.

NZ$10 - $20

Antiques & Curiosities, New Zealand

Blue Lovatt Langley Ware, Denby jug, England, c1950, 13cm high, 9cm diam.

$30 - $40

Baxter's Antiques, QLD

Brownie Downing nodding figure, Japan, c1950, 8cm high, 8cm long.

$115 - $135

Antipodes Antiques, QLD

Teapot, milk jug and lidded sugar bowl by Brownie Downing, Australia, c1950.

$155 - $175

Pedlars Antique Market, SA

Signed Brownie Downing display plate, Australia, c1960, 20.5cm diam.

$75 - $95

Newport Temple Antiques, VIC

Signed Brownie Downing display plate, Australia, c1960, 20.5cm diam.

$75 - $95

Newport Temple Antiques, VIC

Brownie Downing plate with transfers on ceramic, Australia, c1950, 10cm diam.

$30 - $40

Chapel Street Bazaar, VIC

Brownie Downing unsigned plate, featuring aboriginal girl's face, Australia, c1950, 2cm high, 20cm diam.

$40 - $50

Helen's On The Bay, QLD

Transfer on porcelain Brownie Downing plate, Australia, c1950, 10cm diam.

$30 - $40

Chapel Street Bazaar, VIC

Small Brownie Downing dish depicting young native Australian exercising artistic skill, Australia, c1950, 2cm high, 10.5cm diam.

$25 - $35

Lydiard Furniture & Antiques, VIC

Small Brownie Downing wall plate, Australia, c1950, 16cm diam.

NZ$35 - $45

Diane Akers, New Zealand

Brownie Downing serving dish, Australia, c1960, 15cm diam.

$160 - $180

Kings Park Antiques & Collectables, QLD

Brownie Downing egg cup decorated with an Aboriginal child, Australia, 4cm high, 11cm wide.

$115 - $135

Malvern Antique Market, VIC

Hand painted fruit bowl, Germany, c1950, 7cm high, 23cm diam.

$45 - $55

How Bazaar, TAS

Ceramic fruit bowl, style 209 20, with 'A' etched into the base, Germany, c1960, 21cm diam.

NZ$25 - $35

Mr Pickwicks, New Zealand

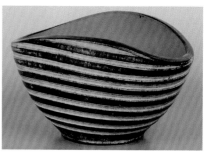

Pottery free form bowl, Germany, c1950, 10cm high, 19cm long, 15cm deep.

$85 - $105

Towers Antiques & Collectables, NSW

Pair of dark blue candle holders, designed by Cari Zalloni for Steuler, Germany, c1965, 12.5cm high.

$55 - $75

frhapsody, WA

Figural group depicting a young man playing a clarinet, the music for which he appears to be reading from, being on the exposed legs of a young lady. Designed by Raymond Peynet and produced by Rosenthal, Germany, c1950, 20cm high, 18cm wide, 12cm deep.

$1445 - $1645

Toowoomba Antiques Gallery, QLD

Alka Dresden nude figurine, Germany, c1960, 16cm high.

NZ$430 - $470

Bonham's, New Zealand

China figurine with a printed mark for the Rudolstadt Volkstodt factory, Germany, c1950, 36cm high.

$850 - $950   **Philip Cross Antiques, NSW**

Dresden Pompadour lady figurine, Germany, c1960, 10cm high, 7cm diam.

$210 - $250

Southside Antiques Centre, QLD

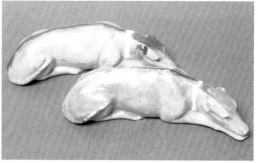

Pair of greyhound figurines, Germany, c1950, 12cm long.

$115 - $135

Trinity Antiques, WA

West German figure of a ballerina, Germany, 20cm high, 15cm long.

$125 - $145

Fyshwick Antique Centre, ACT

'Thomas' coffee pot, milk jug, sugar bowl and cups, Germany, c1960, 21cm high.

$110 - $130

Cool & Collected, SA

Puzzle jug with a ship motif and lithophane in the base, Germany, c1950, 19cm high.

$275 - $315

McLeod's Antiques, NSW

CERAMICS

Large Ruscha pottery plate signed 'G. S. Handmade No. 717/3', Germany, c1960, 36.5cm diam.

NZ$275 - $315

Maxine's Collectibles, New Zealand

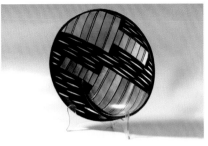

Hand painted 'Venezia' dish, painted with black stripes over colours, Germany, c1950, 28cm diam.

$170 - $190

Cool & Collected, SA

Hutschenreuther 'Pop Art' wall plate with amazing colours, Germany, c1970, 28.5cm diam.

NZ$230 - $270

Maxine's Collectibles, New Zealand

Pottery 'Pop Art' wall plaques with orange centres, Germany, c1970, 79cm long.

NZ$190 - $210

Maxine's Collectibles, New Zealand

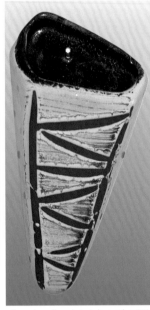

Ceramic wall pocket, style number 219 17, Germany, c1960, 9cm wide, 18cm long.

NZ$20 - $30

Mr Pickwicks, New Zealand

Ruscha mushroom wall plaque, Germany, c1970, 15.5cm high, 9cm wide.

NZ$190 - $210

Maxine's Collectibles, New Zealand

Platter, marked 'Made in Western Germany', with the maker's stamp, Germany, 28cm wide.

$50 - $70

Atomic Pop, SA

Set of five lidded beer steins with various scenes, and ranging in size from 14cm to 28cm high, Germany.

$375 - $415

Collectable Creations, QLD

Bone china dinner setting for eight, made by Bareuther, Bavaria, Germany, c1950.

$330 - $370

Retro Active, VIC

Handled vase by 'Eiwa' with a partial sticker and marks to the base, West Germany, c1961, 21cm high.

$40 - $50

frhapsody, WA

Blue handled vase with its original label, Germany, c1970, 12cm high.

$30 - $40

Dr Russell's Emporium, WA

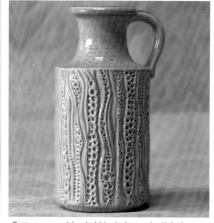

Pottery vase with a bubble design and a light brown glaze, Germany, c1970, 25cm high, 13cm diam.

$110 - $130

J. R. & S.G. Isaac-Cole, NSW

Small vase with '549-21' marked to the base and the original maker's label attached, 'Scheuzich Pottery', Germany, c1970, 23cm high.

$25 - $35

Atomic Pop, SA

Small vase with a handle, an impressed texture pattern and hand painting, Germany, c1965, 17cm high.

$25 - $35

frhapsody, WA

Pottery vase with a plant design on a spotted grey glaze, Germany, c1960, 30cm high, 15cm diam.

$190 - $210

J. R. & S.G. Isaac-Cole, NSW

Matte brown with orange, yellow and white drip glaze, 'Bay 6620' vase, Germany, c1970, 20cm high, 12cm diam.

$80 - $100

Possum's Treasures, QLD

Large ceramic vase, Germany, 37.5cm high, 19cm diam.

NZ$210 - $250

Right Up My Alley, New Zealand

Ceramic vase with urn style handles and a brown mottled glaze, West Germany, c1957, 41cm high, 39cm diam.

$190 - $210

Dr Russell's Emporium, WA

Medium size vase with '484-27' marked to the base, Germany, c1965, 29cm high.

$40 - $50

Atomic Pop, SA

CERAMICS

West German art vase, decorated with hieroglyphics, Germany, c1960, 31cm high, 21cm diam.

$135 - $155

Lydiard Furniture & Antiques, VIC

Large vase, with '7396-50' marked to the base, Germany, c1970, 51cm high.

$85 - $105

Atomic Pop, SA

Pottery vase with unusual colouring, West Germany, 19cm high, 10cm diam.

$65 - $85

Relic, QLD

Large vase with '268-51' marked to the base and the original maker's label attached, 'Scheuzich Pottery', Germany, c1970, 53cm high.

$55 - $75

Atomic Pop, SA

Pair of whimsical vases by Raymond Peynet, for Rosenthal, Germany, c1950, 18cm high, 7cm diam.

$600 - $700

Toowoomba Antiques Gallery, QLD

Pottery vase with '211-35' marked to the base, Germany, c1965, 37cm high.

$100 - $120

Atomic Pop, SA

Small pottery vase with '242-22' marked to the base, Germany, c1970, 24cm high.

$20 - $30

Atomic Pop, SA

Art pottery ceramic vase in blue, Germany, c1960, 19cm high, 10cm diam.

$60 - $80

Obsidian Antiques, NSW

Western German art pottery, matt glazed vase of unusual form, Germany, c1950, 40cm high.

NZ$185 - $205

Peachgrove Antiques, New Zealand

Large Scheurich floor vase with original stickers and banded patterns, West Germany, c1970, 35cm high.

$150 - $170

frhapsody, WA

Hummel figure group of 'Chick Girl', Germany, c1960, 10cm high, 8cm diam.

$380 - $420   **Glenelg Antique Centre, SA**

Goebel 'Monks' salt and pepper shakers, bee mark, Germany, c1950, 8cm high, 5cm wide.

$85 - $105   **Thompsons Country Collectables, NSW**

Goebel character mug of Friar Tuck, Germany, c1950, 14cm high.

$160 - $180   **Stumpy Gully Antiques, VIC**

Ceramic figures on wood based bookends, 'Good Friends' and 'She loves me, she loves me not', Germany, c1960, 13.5cm high, 19cm wide.

$305 - $345   **Maryborough Station Antique Emporium, VIC**

Hummel boy figurine, Germany, c1970, 14cm high, 5.5cm wide.

NZ$185 - $205   **Colonial Antiques, New Zealand**

Goebel bunny in egg, Germany, c1970, 6cm high, 6cm wide, 12cm long.

$30 - $40   **Antiques As Well, VIC**

Hummel hand painted 2nd Annual Plate 1972, Germany, 19cm diam.

NZ$205 - $245   **Gales Antiques, New Zealand**

Goebel swan in matt finish, Germany, c1970, 7cm high, 5cm long.

$100 - $120   **Newlyn Antiques & Cottage Garden Nursery, VIC**

Hummel 'The Little Gardener' figurine, No. 74, Germany, c1963, 10.5cm high, 5cm wide.

NZ$135 - $155   **Colonial Antiques, New Zealand**

M. I. Hummel by Goebel figure HUM#87, 'For Father' TMK3, in production 1958-1972, Germany, 14cm high.

$330 - $370   **Roundabout Antiques, QLD**

CERAMICS

Lladro cat figurine, Spain, c1981, 12cm high, 6cm wide, 12cm deep.

NZ$185 - $205

Amour Antiques & Collectables, New Zealand

Lladro duck group, Spain, c1980, 10cm high, 14cm wide.

$185 - $205

Goodwood House Antiques, WA

Lladro swan and baby figurine, Spain, c1980, 16cm high, 20cm wide.

$545 - $645

Goodwood House Antiques, WA

Lladro unicorn figurine, Spain, c1980, 23cm high, 20cm wide.

$455 - $495

Goodwood House Antiques, WA

Lladro figurine of a large fantail dove, Spain, 14cm high, 7cm wide, 19cm long.

$330 - $370

Patrick Colwell, NSW

Lladro, 'Nao' sitting girl figurine with a large hat, Spain, c1970, 29cm high.

$300 - $340

Lucilles Interesting Collectables, NSW

'Sad Clown' by Lladro with a wooden plinth, Spain, c1980, 26.5cm high, 21cm wide, 19.5cm deep.

NZ$785 - $885

Country Charm Antiques, New Zealand

Lladro seated mother with sleeping child figurine, Spain, c1997, 22cm high, 14cm wide, 24cm deep.

NZ$600 - $700

Amour Antiques & Collectables, New Zealand

Large Lladro 'Closing Scene' figurine, Spain, c1974, 23cm high, 35cm wide.

$800 - $900

Northumberland Antiques & Restorations, NSW

Lladro 'Nature's Bounty' figurine (1983-1995), Spain, 26cm high, 11cm wide.

NZ$275 - $315

Diane Akers, New Zealand

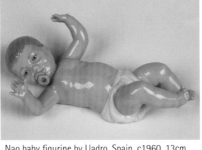

Nao baby figurine by Lladro, Spain, c1960, 13cm wide, 21cm long.

NZ$185 - $205

Diane Akers, New Zealand

Lladro clown figurine, Spain, c1980, 16cm high, 37cm long.

$745 - $845

Goodwood House Antiques, WA

Large Lladro man and lady figurine, Spain, 51cm high, 28cm long.

NZ$1195 - $1395

Amour Antiques & Collectables, New Zealand

Nao figurine of a boy by Lladro, Spain, c1984, 19.5cm high, 7cm wide.

NZ$125 - $145

Diane Akers, New Zealand

Lladro nuns figurine (DZIE), dated 1991, Spain, 33cm high, 12cm wide.

NZ$205 - $245

Diane Akers, New Zealand

Lladro clown with accordion figurine, introduced in 1969 and withdrawn 1993, Spain, 46cm high, 13cm wide, 20cm deep.

NZ$925 - $1025

Amour Antiques & Collectables, New Zealand

Lladro girl figurine with puppies, Spain, c1980, 21cm high, 16cm wide.

$525 - $625

Goodwood House Antiques, WA

Lladro bust 'Beauty in Bloom', limited edition (#985), Spain, c2002, 38cm high, 30cm wide, 23cm deep.

$1775 - $1975

Goodwood House Antiques, WA

Lladro figurine, 'Dancers', Spain, 30cm high, 39cm wide, 20cm deep.

$1560 - $1760

Patrick Colwell, NSW

Lladro figurine of a girl, Spain, 19cm high, 10cm wide, 5cm deep.

$255 - $295

Patrick Colwell, NSW

Lladro figurine of a young lady, 'Daisa' 1991, No. 525, Spain, 26.5cm high.

$330 - $370

Sweet Slumber Antiques & Collectables, NSW

Walter Moorcroft 'Anemones' vase, c1950, 11cm high, 14cm diam.

$950 - $1050

Philicia Antiques & Collectables, SA

Powder blue small dish with a Corinthian flower design, England, c1950, 35cm deep, 95cm diam.

$330 - $370

Old World Antiques, SA

Moorcroft 'Banksia' vase, England, c1990, 12cm high.

$945 - $1045

Steven Sher Antiques, WA

Moorcroft plate in the 'Arum Lily' design, in production 1959 - 1962, England, c1960, 23cm diam.

$1090 - $1290

Selkirk Antiques & Restorations, ACT

Moorcroft 'Leaves and Berries' flambe jug, signed Walter Moorcroft, England, c1950, 12cm high.

$2440 - $2640

Toowoomba Antiques Gallery, QLD

Moorcroft pottery plate, in the 'Oberon' pattern, England, c1993.

$675 - $775

The New Farm Antique Centre, QLD

Boxed Moorcroft 'Palmata' plate, England, c1999, 12cm diam.

$305 - $345

Morrison Antiques & Collectables, NSW

Moorcroft 'Clematis' vase, designed by William Moorcroft and executed by Walter Moorcroft, England, c1948, 11cm high.

Large Moorcroft hand painted vase, 'Bermuda Lily' stamped 'By Appointment-Potteries to the Late Queen Mary, W. Moorcroft', England, c1970, 36cm high.

$1700 - $1900

Hermitage Antiques - Geelong Wintergarden, VIC

NZ$1195 - $1395

Country Charm Antiques, New Zealand

Moorcroft vase in the 'Wattle' design, England, c1975, 30cm high, 6cm diam.

$1870 - $2070

Selkirk Antiques & Restorations, ACT

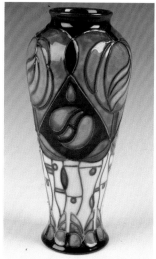

Moorcroft, Charles Macintosh tribute vase, England, c1995, 20cm high.

$745 - $845 **Steven Sher Antiques, WA**

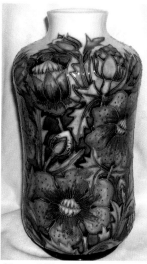

Moorcroft 'Pheasant's Eye' vase,19cm high.

$935 - $1035 **Noeline's Collectables, QLD**

Moorcroft vase, in the 'Oberon' pattern, England, c1993.

$675 - $775 **The New Farm Antique Centre, QLD**

William Moorcroft vase with flambe glaze and orchid decoration, England, c1948, 26cm high.

$4550 - $4750 **Yande Meannjin Antiques, QLD**

Moorcroft 'Hibiscus' flambe vase, by Walter Moorcroft, England, c1950, 9cm high.

$775 - $875 **Toowoomba Antiques Gallery, QLD**

Moorcroft blue on blue vase, England, c1999, 18cm high.

$1400 - $1600 **Morrison Antiques & Collectables, NSW**

Moorcroft 'Wine Magnolia' vase, England, c1991, 31cm high.

$1300 - $1500 **Morrison Antiques & Collectables, NSW**

Vase decorated with tall flowers, in deep crimson and lilac on green stems, England, c2002, 20cm high, 11cm wide.

$945 - $1045 **Maryborough Station Antique Emporium, VIC**

Boxed Moorcroft 'Claremont' enamel miniature, England, c1999, 2cm high, 5cm wide, 6.5cm long.

$585 - $685 **Morrison Antiques & Collectables, NSW**

Moorcroft limited edition vase, England, c2001, 28cm high.

$1250 - $1450 **Morrison Antiques & Collectables, NSW**

CERAMICS

Poole coffee set, England, c1960.

$65 - $85

Chapel Street Bazaar, VIC

Poole pottery bowl with a Truda Carter design, England, c1955.

$370 - $410

Centuries Past, NSW

Aegean Ware vase, by Poole Potteries, England, c1970, 40cm high, 13cm diam.

NZ$480 - $520

Bulls Antiques & Collectables, New Zealand

Multi coloured Poole pottery charger, United Kingdom, c1965, 50cm wide.

$540 - $640

Shenton Park Antiques, WA

Poole posy bowl, England, c1950, 7cm high, 21cm diam.

NZ$100 - $120

Ascot Collectables, New Zealand

Colourful, small plate, stamped 'Poole England 49', England, c1950, 13cm diam.

$110 - $130

Towers Antiques & Collectables, NSW

Poole pottery 'Aegean' pattern charger signed 'K. Ryall', England, c1960, 5.5cm high, 41cm diam.

NZ$800 - $900

Trevor & Pam Plumbly, New Zealand

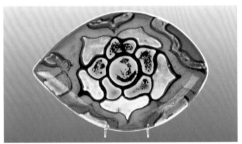

Poole tear shaped platter with a stylised geometric pattern, England, c1960, 29cm wide, 19.5cm deep.

NZ$85 - $105

Country Charm Antiques, New Zealand

Poole shell vase in blue (C96), England, c1960, 12.5cm high, 20cm wide.

NZ$45 - $65

Diane Akers, New Zealand

Aegean charger featuring trees and fences in silhouette, signed verso 'L. Elsden', c1970, 35cm diam.

$480 - $520

Timeless Treasures, WA

Poole studio plate, vividly coloured in reds and yellows, in an Art Deco or studio style, the base impressed with a diving dolphin, England, c1963, 26cm diam.

$165 - $185

Principal Antiques, SA

Contemporary designed, hand made Poole jar, hand decorated by Alfred Read with alternate vertical lines of stylized foliage and fronds, England, c1953.

$625 - $725 **The New Farm Antique Centre, QLD**

Delphi patterned plate, c1970.

$115 - $135 **Timeless Treasures, WA**

Poole Delphis studio plate, England, c1967, 27cm diam.

NZ$275 - $315 **Antiques & Curiosities, New Zealand**

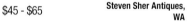

Poole vase with a red background, England, c1980, 10cm high.

$45 - $65 **Steven Sher Antiques, WA**

Poole pottery cylindrical vase, England, c1960, 23cm high, 12cm diam.

$260 - $300 **Beehive Old Wares & Collectables, VIC**

'Poole' biscuit barrel in pink and grey, England, c1950, 12cm high.

$115 - $135 **Antiques at Redbank, QLD**

Poole pottery circular pot with colourful decoration, England, c1960, 20cm diam.

$745 - $845 **The New Farm Antique Centre, QLD**

Poole pottery vase, England, c1955, 13cm high, 11cm diam.

$205 - $245 **Antiques & Collectables Centre - Ballarat, VIC**

CERAMICS

Royal Copenhagen faience pottery bowl, Denmark, c1950, 23cm diam.

$50 - $70

Mid Century Modern, SA

Royal Copenhagen lobster bowl, Denmark, 18cm diam.

$190 - $210

Bowerbird Antiques & Collectables, SA

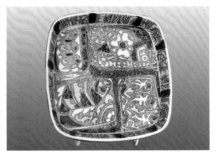

Royal Copenhagen faience fish-decorated bowl, c1960, 3.5cm high, 16.5cm long, 3.5cm deep.

$115 - $135

Pedlars Antique Market, SA

Royal Copenhagen lace edged comport, Denmark, 6cm high, 17cm diam.

NZ$255 - $295

Alexandra Antiques, New Zealand

Royal Copenhagen spaniel figurine, No. 2172, Denmark, c1960.

NZ$185 - $205

Colonial Antiques, New Zealand

Royal Copenhagen figure of a Polar Bear, Denmark, c1980, 33cm high, 15cm wide, 15cm deep.

$275 - $315

Southside Antiques Centre, QLD

Royal Copenhagen Siamese cat figurine, Denmark, c1960, 19.5cm high, 9cm wide.

NZ$275 - $315

Colonial Antiques, New Zealand

Royal Copenhagen rabbit figurine, No. 1019, Denmark, c1960, 9cm high, 8.5cm wide.

NZ$165 - $185

Colonial Antiques, New Zealand

Royal Copenhagen ceramic bear figurine, Denmark, c1950, 8cm high, 6cm wide, 6cm deep.

Royal Copenhagen bear figurine, Denmark, c1950, 7cm high, 9cm long, 6cm deep.

$115 - $135

b bold - 20th Century Furniture & Effects, VIC

$115 - $135

b bold - 20th Century Furniture & Effects, VIC

Royal Copenhagen farmer with scythe figurine, Denmark, c1960, 25cm high, 13cm wide, 11cm deep.

NZ$325 - $365

Colonial Antiques, New Zealand

Royal Copenhagen puppy figurine, Denmark, c1990, 7.5cm high, 8cm wide, 12cm long.

NZ$275 - $315

Diane Akers, New Zealand

Three Royal Copenhagen, faience pottery vases, priced per item, Denmark, c1950, 23cm high.

$150 - $170

Mid Century Modern, SA

Royal Copenhagen ceramic bear figurine, Denmark, c1950, 5cm high, 6cm wide, 3cm long.

$115 - $135   **b bold - 20th Century Furniture & Effects, VIC**

Royal Copenhagenm hand made and hand painted 'Faun with Rabbit' figurine.

$920 - $1020   **Ivanhoe Collectibles Corner, VIC**

Royal Copenhagen vase, Denmark, c1970, 26cm high, 16cm wide.

$1000 - $1200   **Goodwood House Antiques, WA**

Royal Copenhagen vase, featuring a megalithic stone burial site by the sea, Denmark, c1960, 17cm high, 11cm wide.

$255 - $295   **Bathurst Street Antique Centre, TAS**

Royal Copenhagen ceramic bear figurine, Denmark, c1950, 8cm high, 7cm wide.

$115 - $135   **b bold - 20th Century Furniture & Effects, VIC**

Royal Copenhagen white, brown and blue square vase, Denmark, c1950, 22cm high.

$370 - $410   **Vampt, NSW**

Royal Copenhagen faience series vase, signed and numbered to the base, Denmark, c1950, 30cm high.

$520 - $620   **Vampt, NSW**

Royal Copenhagen bird group, No. 402, Denmark, c1960, 13cm high, 10cm wide.

NZ$185 - $205   **Colonial Antiques, New Zealand**

CERAMICS

Royal Doulton Bunnykins 'Mr Bunnykins at the Easter Parade' DB51 and 'Mrs Bunnykins at the Easter Parade' DB52, produced in 1986 only for special events, England, 13cm high.

$3150 - $3350

Julie Sandry, NSW

Royal Doulton Bunnykins, 'Aussie Shearer' figurine, limited edition of 1000, England, c2005, 9cm high, 10cm wide.

$125 - $145

Morrison Antiques & Collectables, NSW

Royal Doulton Bunnikins bride and groom figurines, England, c1990, 11cm high.

$230 - $270

The Evandale Tinker, TAS

Royal Doulton Bunnykin figurine, 'Sydney', England, c1999, 11cm high.

$545 - $645

Morrison Antiques & Collectables, NSW

Royal Doulton Bunnykins figure DB5, 'Autumn Days', one of the original fifteen Bunnykins figures produced between 1972-1982. It was these first fifteen figures that started Bunnykins as one of the world's hottest collectables in the last ten years, England, 10cm high.

$430 - $470

Roundabout Antiques, QLD

Royal Doulton Bunnykins figure DB63, 'Bedtime Bunnykins', issued in 1987 only as a special colourway, England, 8cm high.

$480 - $520

Roundabout Antiques, QLD

'Tyrolean Dancer', Royal Doulton Bunnykins figurine, England, c2001, 13cm high.

$125 - $145

Morrison Antiques & Collectables, NSW

Royal Doulton Bunnykins figure DB59, 'Storytime Bunnykins'. This figure was issued in 1987 only as a special colourway figure for sale at special Doulton events, England, 7.5cm high.

$500 - $600

Roundabout Antiques, QLD

Royal Doulton Bunnykins 'Australian Federation' figurine, England, c2001, 12cm high.

$375 - $415

Morrison Antiques & Collectables, NSW

Royal Doulton 'Cliff Cornell' Toby jug, one of only 500 produced in 1956, England, 25cm high, 13cm wide, 15cm deep.

$1100 - $1300 **The Bottom Drawer Antique Centre, VIC**

Limited edition 'William Shakespeare' character jug, number 1281 of 3500, England, c1992, 18cm high, 23cm wide, 12cm deep.

NZ$475 - $515 **Memory Lane, New Zealand**

Royal Doulton 'Sam Weller' Toby jug D6265, England, c1950, 11cm high.

$380 - $420 **Upwell Antiques, ACT**

Royal Doulton character jug of 'Sir Henry Doulton', England, c1983.

$180 - $200 **Heartland Antiques & Art, NSW**

Large Royal Doulton character jug, 'Dick Whitington' (D6375), England, c1950, 16.5cm high.

$525 - $625 **Roundabout Antiques, QLD**

Royal Doulton Toby jug, Henry VIII, England, c1975, 10cm high.

$150 - $170 **Serendipity - Preston, VIC**

Royal Doulton small Toby jug, 'Old Charley' D6069, in production 1939-1960, England, 13cm high.

$410 - $450 **Roundabout Antiques, QLD**

Royal Doulton character jug of Field Marshall Montgomery, design number 6908, limited edition of 2500, England, c1992, 19cm high.

$320 - $360 **East West Collectables, NSW**

Royal Doulton 'Sir John Falstaff' Toby jug, designed by C. Noke, manufactured from 1939 to 1991, England, 22cm high, 12cm long, 14cm deep.

$425 - $465 **George Magasic Antiques & Collectables, QLD**

Royal Doulton miniature Toby jug, 'Mine Host' character, England, 6cm high, 9cm wide.

$115 - $135

Helen's On The Bay, QLD

Royal Doulton miniature jug 'tiny' size 'Saucy Gamp' in production, 1947-1960, England, 3.5cm high, 3.5cm wide.

$275 - $315

Turn O' The Century, QLD

Large Royal Doulton 'Alfred Hitchcock' character jug (D6987) pink curtain handle version, England, c1995, 19cm high.

$1750 - $1950

Roundabout Antiques, QLD

Royal Doulton 'Lumberjack' character jug, designed by M. Henk, in production from 1967-1983, England, 19cm high, 18cm long, 14cm deep.

$355 - $395

George Magasic Antiques & Collectables, QLD

Royal Doulton 'Groucho Marx' character jug, designed by S. Taylor, in production from 1984-1988, England, 17cm high, 17cm long, 16cm deep.

$475 - $515

George Magasic Antiques & Collectables, QLD

Large Royal Doulton 'The Phantom Of The Opera' character jug (D7017) limited edition of 2500, England, c1995, 18cm high.

$750 - $850

Roundabout Antiques, QLD

'John Doulton' character jug by Royal Doulton, England, c1980, 11cm high.

$180 - $200

Heartland Antiques & Art, NSW

Royal Doulton character jug, 'The Walrus and Carpenter', England, c1964, 6cm high, 6cm wide.

$175 - $195

Bowerbird Antiques & Collectables, SA

Royal Doulton large character jug, 'Friar Tuck' D6321, in production 1951-1960, England, 18cm high.

$550 - $650

Roundabout Antiques, QLD

Large Royal Doulton character jug of 'Winston Churchill', modelled by Stanley James Taylor, special edition for 1992, England, 16cm high.

$585 - $685

Malvern Antique Market, VIC

Royal Doulton character jug of Henry Cooper, from a limited edition of 9500, model no. D7050, England, c1997, 10cm high.

$185 - $205

East West Collectables, NSW

Royal Doulton bone china cocker spaniel figurine (HN 2517), England, 10cm high,12cm long.

NZ$225 - $265

Colonial Antiques, New Zealand

Royal Doulton Scottie dog figurine (HN 1016), England, 9cm high, 13cm long.

NZ$225 - $265

Colonial Antiques, New Zealand

Royal Doulton 'Images of Nature' series titled 'Freedom' this figurine features two otters, HN3528, England, c1983, 22cm high, 15cm wide, 24cm long.

$205 - $245

Principal Antiques, SA

Royal Doulton flambe tiger, England, c1980.

$2550 - $2750

Brisbane Antiques Pty Ltd, QLD

Royal Doulton 'Lion On Rock' figurine (HN2641), from the 'Prestige Series', designed by C. J. Noke, England, c1950, 26cm high, 48cm long.

$1395 - $1595

Roundabout Antiques, QLD

Pair of Royal Doulton sitting Persian cats, black and white cat HN999 in production 1930-1985 and white cat HN2539 in production 1940-1968, England, 13cm high.

$650 - $750

Julie Sandry, NSW

Royal Doulton horse 'The Winner' DA154B, gloss figurine on ceramic plinth in production 1991-1997, England, 20cm high, 27cm long.

$245 - $285

Julie Sandry, NSW

Handmade Royal Doulton figurine, 'Ideal Pony for a Nervous Child', (NT10) by Norman Thelwell, England, c2003.

NZ$175 - $195

Diane Akers, New Zealand

Handmade Royal Doulton figurine 'Body Brush' (NTZ) by Norman Thelwell, England, c2003, 13.5cm high, 10.5cm wide.

NZ$175 - $195

Diane Akers, New Zealand

Handmade and decorated Royal Doulton figurine 'He'll Find You', (NT 1Z) designed by Norman Thelwell, England, c2003, 11cm high, 10.5cm wide.

NZ$175 - $195

Diane Akers, New Zealand

Royal Doulton 'Grumpy' figurine, manufactured for the Walt Disney's 'Snow White'series, England, c2003, 9cm high.

$115 - $135   **Morrison Antiques & Collectables, NSW**

Royal Doulton Disney showcase, 'Snow White & The Seven Dwarfs', 'Dopey' figurine, England, c2001, 9cm high.

$115 - $135   **Morrison Antiques & Collectables, NSW**

Royal Doulton figurine 'Karen' model No. 2388, signed 'Peggy Davies', issued in 1982 and withdrawn in 1999, England, 20.3cm high.

NZ$595 - $695   **Country Charm Antiques, New Zealand**

Royal Doulton 'Gossips' figure, (HN2025) designed by L. Harradine, England, c1949, 14cm high.

$900 - $1000   **Roundabout Antiques, QLD**

Royal Doulton 'Delphine' figurine (HN 2136) in production 1954–1967, England, c1960, 19cm high.

$375 - $415

Antipodes Antiques, QLD

Royal Doulton figurine, 'Jester' designer Noke, in production from 1949 to present day, England, 25cm high.

NZ$1100 - $1300   **Sue Todd Antiques Collectables, New Zealand**

Royal Doulton 'Trotty Veck' figurine, England, 11cm high.

NZ$185 - $205   **Colonial Antiques, New Zealand**

'Good Day Sir'. Royal Doulton figurine, model No. H.N 2896 designed by W.K Harper, issued in 1986 and discontinued in 1989, England, 21.6cm high.

NZ$375 - $415   **Country Charm Antiques, New Zealand**

Royal Doulton 'Top of The Hill' figurine, registered design number 822821, England, 19cm high.

$305 - $345   **Heartland Antiques & Art, NSW**

Royal Doulton figurine, 'Thank You' (HN 2732), hand made and hand decorated, signed by Michael Doulton on a promotional trip to Australia in 1983, United Kingdom, c1982, 23cm high, 13cm diam.

$500 - $600   **Glenelg Antique Centre, SA**

Royal Doulton 'Uriah Heep' figurine, England, 11cm high, 3.5cm wide.

NZ$185 - $205   **Colonial Antiques, New Zealand**

Royal Doulton 'Jane Seymour' figurine (HN3349) from the 'Six Wives of Henry VIII' Series, limited edition of 9500, England, c1991, 23cm high.

$1150 - $1350   **Roundabout Antiques, QLD**

Royal Doulton 'Easter Day' figure, (HN2039) designed by L. Harradine, England, c1949, 18.5cm high.

$750 - $850   **Roundabout Antiques, QLD**

Royal Doulton 'Anne Boleyn' figurine (HN3232) from the 'Six Wives of Henry VIII' series, limited edition of 9500, England, c1990, 20.5cm high.

$900 - $1000   **Roundabout Antiques, QLD**

Royal Doulton figurine in production from 1936 to 1980, England, 20cm high.

$275 - $315   **Northumberland Antiques & Restorations, NSW**

Royal Doulton figurine, 'The Pied Piper' (HN 2102), England, c1953, 22cm high.

$375 - $415   **Steven Sher Antiques, WA**

Royal Doulton 'Lt. General Ulysses S. Grant' figurine (HN3403), limited edition of 5000, designed by R. Tabbenor, England, c1993, 30cm high.

$1550 - $1750   **Roundabout Antiques, QLD**

Royal Doulton figure, 'Edward VI' (HN 4263), number 265 of a limited edition of 5000, United Kingdom, c2000, 22cm high, 13cm diam.

$800 - $900

Glenelg Antique Centre, SA

Royal Doulton Henry VIII figure (HN3350) limited edition of 1991 figures, England, c1991, 24cm high.

$3250 - $3450

Roundabout Antiques, QLD

Royal Doulton 'Balloon Seller' mini figurine, HN2130, England, c1990, 10cm high.

$305 - $345

East West Collectables, NSW

Royal Doulton 'The Forest Glade Giselle' figurine, HN 2140, in production 1954 to 1965, England, 20cm high.

$625 - $725

East West Collectables, NSW

Royal Doulton 'Julia' figurine, England, c1974, 20cm high.

$285 - $325

Heartland Antiques & Art, NSW

Royal Doulton 'Diana' figurine, England, c1985, 20cm high.

$330 - $370

Heartland Antiques & Art, NSW

Royal Doulton 'Omar Khayyam' figurine HN2247, England, c1960, 15cm high.

$405 - $445

East West Collectables, NSW

Royal Doulton 'Suzette' figure (HN2026), designed by L. Harradine, England, c1949, 18.5cm high.

$645 - $745

Roundabout Antiques, QLD

Royal Doulton figurine HN1315, 'Old Balloon Seller', in production 1929-1998, designer L. Harradine, England, 18.5cm high.

$480 - $520

Roundabout Antiques, QLD

Royal Doulton Flambe figurine of Confucius, HN3314, in production 1990 to 1995, England, 23cm high.

$650 - $750   **East West Collectables, NSW**

'Blithe Morning' Royal Doulton figurine (No HIV 2065) released in 1950 and with drawn in 1973, designed by L. Harradine, England, 18.5cm high, 9cm diam.

NZ$545 - $645   **Country Charm Antiques, New Zealand**

Royal Doulton figure, 'The Balloon man' by L. Harradine HN1954 issued 1940-present, England.

$700 - $800   **Chilton's Antiques & Jewellery, NSW**

Royal Doulton 'Stiggins' figurine, England, 10cm high, 3.5cm wide.

NZ$185 - $205   **Colonial Antiques, New Zealand**

Royal Doulton figurine from the Enchantment collection, ' April shower' (HN 3024, United Kingdom, c1983, 13cm high.

$295 - $335   **Kings Park Antiques & Collectables, SA**

Royal Doulton 'Catherine Howard' figurine (HN3449) from the 'Six Wives of Henry VIII' Series, limited edition of 9500, England, c1992, 21cm high.

$950 - $1150   **Roundabout Antiques, QLD**

Royal Doulton 'Catherine of Aragon' figurine (HN3233) from the 'Six Wives of Henry VIII' series, limited edition of 9500, England, c1990, 16.5cm high.

$900 - $1000   **Roundabout Antiques, QLD**

Royal Doulton 'Field Marshall Montgomery' figurine (HN3405), limited edition of 1944, designed by R. Tabbenor, England, c1994, 29cm high.

$1550 - $1750   **Roundabout Antiques, QLD**

Royal Doulton 'The Helmsman' figure from the 'Sea Characters' series, in production 1970 - 1980, England, 24cm high, 13cm wide.

$695 - $795   **Thompsons Country Collectables, NSW**

Royal Doulton 'Carolyn' figurine (HN2112), England, c1950, 18cm high.

$600 - $700   **Roundabout Antiques, QLD**

Royal Doulton 'Winston S. Churchill' figurine (HN3433), limited edition of 5000, designed by A. Maslankowski, England, c1993, 30.5cm high.

$1150 - $1350   **Roundabout Antiques, QLD**

ROYAL DOULTON - FIGURINES

Royal Doulton figurine of 'The Potter', England, 18cm high, 15cm wide, 12cm deep.

$475 - $575　　**The New Farm Antique Centre, QLD**

Royal Doulton figurine 'The Flower Sellers Children' HN 1342, England, c1950, 21cm high, 18cm wide, 15cm deep.

$600 - $700　　**Lucilles Interesting Collectables, NSW**

Royal Doulton figurine, 'The Bridesmaid' (HN 2196) produced from 1960 to 1976, England, 14cm high.

$225 - $265　　**Paddington Antique Centre Pty Ltd, QLD**

Royal Doulton figurine, 'Hope', England, 20cm high.

$275 - $315　　**Northumberland Antiques & Restorations, NSW**

Royal Doulton 'Cynthia' figurine, England, c1990, 19cm high.

$255 - $295　　**Paddington Antique Centre Pty Ltd, QLD**

'Louise' Royal Doulton figurine, model No. H.N 3207, style two, designed by A. Hughes and signed 'Adrian Hughes', introduced 1990 and withdrawn 1995, England, 19.1cm high.

NZ$475 - $515　　**Country Charm Antiques, New Zealand**

Royal Doulton 'General Robert E. Lee' figurine (HN3403), limited edition of 5000, designed by R. Tabbenor, England, c1993, 29cm high.

$1550 - $1750　　**Roundabout Antiques, QLD**

Royal Doulton 'Calumet' figure (HN2068), designed by C. J. Noke, England, c1950, 16cm high.

$1000 - $1200　　**Roundabout Antiques, QLD**

Royal Doulton 'Catherine Parr' figurine (HN3450) from the 'Six Wives of Henry VIII' series, limited edition of 9500, England, c1992, 16cm high.

$950 - $1150　　**Roundabout Antiques, QLD**

Royal Doulton 'Anne of Cleves' figurine (HN3356) from the 'Six Wives of Henry VIII' Series, limited edition of 9500, England, c1991, 16cm high.

$1150 - $1350　　**Roundabout Antiques, QLD**

Royal Doulton figurine from the Enchantment collection, ' The Magpie Ring' (HN2978), United Kingdom, c1983, 22cm high.

$345 - $385　　**Kings Park Antiques & Collectables, SA**

Large Royal Doulton 'Pharaoh', flambe character jug, (D7028), limited edition of 1500, England, c1996, 20cm high.

$900 - $1000

Roundabout Antiques, QLD

Boxed Royal Doulton flambe egg and cup, No. 2278 of a limited edition of 3500, England, c1980.

$610 - $710

Selkirk Antiques & Restorations, ACT

Large Royal Doulton, 'Aladdins Genie' flambe character jug' (D6971), limited editionof 1500, England, c1994, 19cm high.

$800 - $900

Roundabout Antiques, QLD

Royal Doulton charger, England, c1950, 32cm diam.

$375 - $415

Louisa's Antiques, TAS

Royal Doulton 'Castles' Series 'Rochester Castle' plate, England, c1949, 27cm diam.

$165 - $185

Camberwell Antique Centre, VIC

Royal Doulton display plate, 'Poor Joe', England, 26cm diam.

$205 - $245

Eclectica, TAS

Royal Doulton bowl, 'Wild Rose' pattern 1940-59, England, c1950, 9cm high, 19cm diam.

$305 - $345

Wenlen Antiques, NSW

Royal Doulton 'Samarra' coffee set includes coffee pot, sugar bowl, creamer and six cups and saucers, England, c1970.

$85 - $105

Obsidian Antiques, NSW

Royal Doulton 'Merrywether' cup and saucer (D4650), England.

$85 - $105

Archers Antiques, TAS

Royal Doulton, 'Wynn' cup, saucer and plate (D5501), England.

$75 - $95

Archers Antiques, TAS

Royal Doulton Branewyn Ware vase, England, 19cm high, 23cm wide.

$425 - $465

The Bizarre Bazaar, NSW

Royal Doulton geisha cup, saucer and plate, pattern 'H1123', England.

$105 - $125

Archers Antiques, TAS

ROYAL WORCESTER

Pair of Royal Worcester Pheasants, limited edition of 500 by R. Van Ruckyvelot, with certificates, England, c1960, 36cm high, 48cm wide.

$9550 - $9950

Austiques Antiques & Collectables, NSW

Royal Worcester figure of a ballerina, England, c1980, 16cm high.

$475 - $515

Antiques & Collectables Centre - Ballarat, VIC

Royal Worcester pot pourri, hand painted with fruit by H. Ayrton, England, c1950.

$2700 - $2900

Brisbane Antiques Pty Ltd, QLD

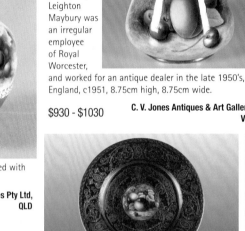

Royal Worcester vase, hand painted and signed by L. Maybury. Leighton Maybury was an irregular employee of Royal Worcester, and worked for an antique dealer in the late 1950's, England, c1951, 8.75cm high, 8.75cm wide.

$930 - $1030

C. V. Jones Antiques & Art Gallery, VIC

Royal Worcester vase, hand painted by M. Miller, who worked with Kitty Blake, England, c1954, 10cm high, 6.25cm wide.

$720 - $820

C. V. Jones Antiques & Art Gallery, VIC

Royal Worcester cabinet plate with fruit motif, hand painted and signed by James Austin, England, c1970, 27cm diam.

$925 - $1025

Hermitage Antiques - Geelong Wintergarden, VIC

Royal Worcester specimen plates with painted English birds, signed D. Jones. Priced per plate, England, c1950, 23cm diam.

$925 - $1025

Abbott's Antiques, NSW

Royal Worcester vase painted with highland cattle, signed Stinton.

NZ$5300 - $5700

Anthea's Antiques Ltd, New Zealand

Royal Worcester shell dish with the mark indicating a date of manufacture between 1944 and 1955, England, 10cm high, 18cm wide, 20cm long.

NZ$205 - $245

Bonham's, New Zealand

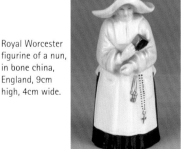

Royal Worcester figurine of a nun, in bone china, England, 9cm high, 4cm wide.

NZ$280 - $320

Deans Antiques, New Zealand

Shelley red and floral cup, saucer and plate, England, c1950.

$165 - $185

Roundabout Antiques, QLD

Shelley 'Primrose' cup and saucer, England, c1950.

$75 - $95

Yanda Aboriginal Art Melbourne, VIC

Shelley 'Georgian' trio, England, c1948.

$165 - $185

Roundabout Antiques, QLD

Shelley Dainty trio No. 2456, England, c1950.

$125 - $145

Antipodes Antiques, QLD

Shelley fifteen piece coffee set with a green colourway, 'Sheraton' pattern, M13290, England, c1950, 18cm high.

$525 - $625

Yande Meannjin Antiques, QLD

Set of six hand painted floral plates with green Shelley backstamp and signed William Barret to the base, England, c1955, 15cm diam.

$130 - $150

Ardeco Antiques & Collectables, WA

Shelley jelly mould, in the shape of an armadillo, England, 13cm high, 15cm wide, 22cm long.

NZ$255 - $295

Colonial Antiques, New Zealand

Shelley 'Harmony' vase, England, 12cm high.

$205 - $245

Paddington Antique Centre Pty Ltd, QLD

Shelley 'Jazz Circles' vase.

$310 - $350

Chelsea Antiques & Decortive Art Centre P/L, QLD

SylvaC poodle figurine (3110), England, c1950, 12.5cm high, 13cm long.

NZ$125 - $145

Diane Akers, New Zealand

SylvaC pug dog figurine, England, 12cm high, 13cm long.

$155 - $175

Sherwood Bazaar, QLD

SylvaC Collie Dog, reg. No. 1548, England, c1975, 14cm high, 19cm wide.

NZ$100 - $120

Country Charm Antiques, New Zealand

SylvaC dog named 'Toothache', England, 29cm high, 17cm wide, 18cm deep.

NZ$330 - $370

Maxine's Collectibles, New Zealand

Green SylvaC terrier dog, number 1578, England, c1980, 13cm high, 5cm wide.

NZ$135 - $155

Colonial Antiques, New Zealand

SylvaC vase with pink and green glaze, England, 11cm high, 8cm wide, 16cm long.

NZ$55 - $75

Strangely Familiar, New Zealand

Large SylvaC vase, c1950, 38cm high, 18cm wide.

NZ$245 - $285

Oxford Court Antiques Centre, New Zealand

Pixie vase (numbered 2275) and stamped SylvaC to the bottom, England, c1950.

$45 - $65

Dr Russell's Emporium, WA

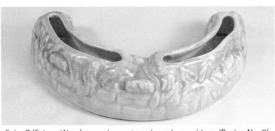

SylvaC (Falcon Ware) curved posy trough, early mould no, 'Burlee No. 2', England, c1950, 4cm high, 20cm wide, 4cm deep.

NZ$45 - $65

Anticus Antiques, New Zealand

SylvaC gnome (#87), 20cm high.

$275 - $315

Sherwood Bazaar, QLD

Wade teapot, milk jug and sugar bowl set, Ireland, c1960.

NZ$155 - $175

Diane Akers, New Zealand

Wade butter dish, England, c1950, 11cm high, 16cm long, 13cm deep.

$45 - $65

Antiques & Collectables Centre - Ballarat, VIC

Wade pin dish, England, 100cm diam.

$45 - $55

Cobweb Collectables, NSW

'Whimsies' miniatures by Wade, in original box, England, c1950.

$115 - $135

Goodwood House Antiques, WA

Hand painted Wade cabinet plate, England, c1960, 25cm diam.

$65 - $85

Antiques & Collectables Centre - Ballarat, VIC

Wade 'Nursery Rhymes' figure, 'Mary Had a Little Lamb', England, c1973, 7.5cm high, 4cm wide, 3.5cm deep.

$45 - $55

Antique General Store, NSW

Wade brown dog figurine, England, c1960, 6cm high, 7cm long.

$55 - $75

Cobweb Collectables, NSW

Wade 'Mrs Fluffy cat' figurine from the Noddy series, England, c1960, 6cm high, 4cm wide.

NZ$85 - $105

Diane Akers, New Zealand

Set of six harlequin colours trios, made by Wade, England, England, c1950.

$205 - $245

Retro Active, VIC

Limited edition Wade figure, 'The Hat Box Series', No.1 'Lady' with original miniature hat box, character from 'Lady And The Tramp', England, c1960, 3.7cm high.

$140 - $160

Camberwell Antique Centre, VIC

Wedgwood 'Kings and Queens of England' thimbles, forty one on a timber rack, England, c1980.

$500 - $600

Mentone Beach Antiques Centre, VIC

Wedgwood green and gold embossed set of six coffee cups and saucers, England, c1950.

$310 - $350

Avoca Beach Antiques, NSW

Wedgwood lilac Jasper Ware 'Seasons' bud vase, England, c1960, 12cm high, 7cm wide, 23cm diam.

$65 - $85

Fyshwick Antique Centre, ACT

Wedgwood Queens Ware Monteith bowl made for the 20th anniversary of The Wedgwood Club in 1953, England, 15cm high, 22cm wide, 33cm long.

$475 - $515

Mentone Beach Antiques Centre, VIC

Wedgwood pair of Scottie dogs, in the form of salt and pepper shakers, England.

$75 - $95

Camberwell Antique Centre, VIC

Wedgwood and Co. Ltd. 'Spinet' figure, England, c1948, 15cm high.

$375 - $415

Roundabout Antiques, QLD

Magnificent Wedgwood, pale blue Jasper Ware campagna shaped lidded urn, England, c1960, 29cm high, 18cm wide.

$950 - $1050

Fyshwick Antique Centre, ACT

Wedgwood jasperware dish, England, 15cm high, 11cm wide.

$30 - $40

Twice Around, NSW

Black Wedgwood figurine of Hercules, England, c1975, 29cm high.

$1025 - $1225

The Best Antiques & Collectables, QLD

Emu sculpture, realistically modelled as a pair of emus, one standing, the other seated, in high gloss metallic glazes in tones of green, ochre and charcoal, with impressed factory marks to the base 'Wembley Ware', Australia, c1953, 13.5cm diam.

$1350 - $1550

Hurnall's Antiques & Decorative Arts, VIC

Lizard decorated plate, in a green and orange lustre glaze with a life-like green gecko, marked to the base 'Wembley Ware', Australia, 26.5cm diam.

$545 - $645

Jeremy's Australiana, VIC

Wembley Ware figure of a frog, Australia, c1950, 15cm high.

$850 - $950

Steven Sher Antiques, WA

Wembley Ware crayfish plate, Australia, c1950, 27cm wide.

$115 - $135

Karlia Rose Garden Antiques & Collectables, VIC

Green lustre Wembley Ware lobster plate, Australia, c1950, 30cm high, 30cm wide.

$125 - $145

Serendipity Antiques - Newcastle, NSW

Wembley Ware eagle wall figurine, Australia, c1950.

$1900 - $2100

Steven Sher Antiques, WA

Wembley Ware 'Seagull' ashtray with a lustre glaze, Australia, c1950, 14.5cm high, 14cm wide, 12cm deep.

$75 - $95

Antique General Store, NSW

Wemblcy cockatoo wall vase, Australia, c1950, 4cm high.

$330 - $370

Shenton Park Antiques, WA

Large Wembley Ware trough, in white glaze with gumnuts and leaves depicted on the outside, Australia, 14cm high, 33cm wide, 12cm deep.

$645 - $745

Perth Antiques, WA

CERAMICS

Ceramic antelope by Dominique, France, c1950, 83cm high, 37cm wide, 63cm high.

$6300 - $6700

Geoffrey Hatty, VIC

Novelty cruet set in the shape of elephant carrying baskets of vegetables, Japan, c1950, 12cm high, 12cm long.

$75 - $95

Chapel Street Bazaar, VIC

Zsolnay spaniel dog, Hungary, c1960, 11cm high, 8cm wide.

$185 - $205

Helen's On The Bay, QLD

Bird in teal blue colours, Italy, c1960, 23cm high, 15.5cm wide, 15cm deep.

NZ$65 - $85

Maxine's Collectibles, New Zealand

Stylized figure of a bull, in lava glaze with iron horns, by Marcello Fantoni, Italy, c1960, 25cm long.

$500 - $600

Design Dilemas, VIC

Orange pottery horse, European, c1960, 26cm high, 28cm long.

$185 - $205

Victor Harbour Antiques - Mittagong, NSW

Herend porcelain rooster and hen figurines, Hungary, c1970, 24cm high, 18cm wide.

$1375 - $1575

Goodwood House Antiques, WA

Pierced ceramic pot pouri fish, 27cm high, 14cm wide.

$75 - $95 **Maryborough Station Antique Emporium, VIC**

Novelty cruet in the shape of a mother panda and babies, Germany, c1950, 10cm high.

$115 - $135 **Chapel Street Bazaar, VIC**

Signed Capodimonte figurine, numbered 1098, Italy, c1950, 28cm high, 34cm wide.

NZ$525 - $625 **Gregory's of Greerton, New Zealand**

Ceramica Franco Pozzi 'Gresline' bowl designed by Ambrogio Pozzi, with impressed mark and sticker, Italy, c1972, 20cm wide.

$110 - $130

frhapsody, WA

Terracotta bowl with enamel decoration, Italy, c1960, 38cm diam.

$80 - $100

Mid Century Modern, SA

Pair of Guido Gambone crackle glaze bowls in orange and green, Italy, c1960, 12cm diam.

$420 - $460

Design Dilemas, VIC

Seventeen piece coffee service by Thun, featuring red dots against white porcelain, Czechoslovakia, c1965.

$200 - $240

Design Dilemas, VIC

Set of six cups and saucers, sugar bowl, cream jug and coffee pot, made by Boch, Belgium, c1966, 23.75cm high.

$65 - $85

River Emporium, NSW

Eighteen piece setting for six, of black and white polka dot trios, Czechoslovakia.

$50 - $70

Newport Temple Antiques, VIC

White ceramic child and dog figurine, Czechoslovakia, c1950, 18cm high, 10cm wide, 18cm long.

$205 - $245 **Newport Temple Antiques, VIC**

White cockatoo figurine, Italy, c1950, 49cm high.

$225 - $265

Victor Harbour Antiques - Mittagong, NSW

Herend porcelain duck group, Hungary, c1970, 10cm wide.

$205 - $245

Goodwood House Antiques, WA

Metzler & Orloff Sealyham terrier with a circular Metzler & Orloff mark on the underside, stamped 'Germany' under one leg, Germany, c1950, 6.5cm high, 10cm long.

$275 - $315

Kilbarron Antiques and Collectables, VIC

Superb pierced jug style vase with gold leaf applied on the spout and handle, Italy, c1950, 35cm high.

$140 - $160   **Nicki's Collection, NSW**

Capodimonte flower pot with stand, Italy, c1950, 86cm high.

$280 - $320   **Nicki's Collection, NSW**

Funky teapot, European, c1970.

$65 - $85   **Vampt, NSW**

Stavargerflint hand painted vase, No. 14-219, 'Woman Watering the Flowers', Norway, 19cm high, 6cm diam.

NZ$110 - $130   **Maxine's Collectibles, New Zealand**

Herend hand painted three sectional divided plate, by Rothschild, Hungary, c1949, 19cm diam.

$135 - $155   **Helen's On The Bay, QLD**

Desmone plate, Italy, c1960, 37cm wide.

$175 - $195   **The Junk Company, VIC**

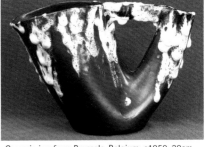

Ceramic jug from Brussels, Belgium, c1950, 20cm high, 25cm wide, 10cm deep.

$185 - $205   **Le Contraste, VIC**

Capodimonte jardinière, Italy, c1960, 26cm high, 19cm wide, 19cm deep.

$525 - $625   **Goodwood House Antiques, WA**

French lava glaze ceramic vases by Vallaurius, France, c1955, 30cm high.

$720 - $820   **Design Dilemas, VIC**

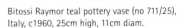

Bitossi Raymor teal pottery vase (no 711/25), Italy, c1960, 25cm high, 11cm diam.

NZ$185 - $205   **Maxine's Collectibles, New Zealand**

Bitossi hand built and decorated vase, featuring an impressed geometric design, Italy, c1960, 16cm high.

$40 - $50

Collectors' Cottage Antiques, NSW

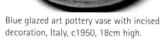

Blue glazed art pottery vase with incised decoration, Italy, c1950, 18cm high.

NZ$85 - $105

Peachgrove Antiques, New Zealand

Asymmetric vase with a geometric pattern, Italy, c1955, 19cm high, 14cm wide, 14cm deep.

$90 - $110

Chapel Street Bazaar, VIC

Danish ceramic green vase with bird motif, made by Knabstrip, Denmark, c1950, 40cm high, 25cm wide.

$275 - $315

Le Contraste, VIC

Signed pottery vase with masked dancers hand painted and scraffito techniques, France, c1950, 20cm high, 11cm wide.

$55 - $75

Retro Active, VIC

Fantoni style vase, of the 1950's Eames era, with stripes on yellow ground and hand decorated, Italy, 33cm high.

$30 - $40

Vintage Living, ACT

Ettore Sottsass 'Tigris' vase, for Memphis, Milano, Italy, c1980, 38cm high.

$2100 - $2300

Design Dilemas, VIC

Amphora enamelled vase with a bird design to the front and a band of flowers to the rear, impressed mark 'Amphora, Made in Czechoslovakia' and original 'Prouds Sydney' sticker, Czechoslovakia, c1950, 18cm high, 10cm wide.

$135 - $155

Thompsons Country Collectables, NSW

Ceramic decoration by Francesca Guerrier, France, c1990, 43cm high.

$11500 - $12500

Geoffrey Hatty, VIC

Unmarked Capodimonte flower encrusted tureen with under plate and ladle, Italy, 25cm high, 34cm wide.

$145 - $165

Bower Bird Art & Antiques, QLD

CERAMICS

Six ceramic designer coasters by Fornasetti Milano, Italy, c1950.

$490 - $590

Centuries Past, NSW

Rose decorated ceramic juicer, Czechoslovakia, 10cm high, 10cm diam.

$65 - $85

Antipodes Antiques, QLD

Jug and bowl set by Ditmar Ulrich, Czechoslovakia, 18cm high, 29cm diam.

$55 - $75

Baxter's Antiques, QLD

Floral motif Amphora vase, vibrant floral design on mottled deep blue ground, Czechoslovakia, c1950, 33cm high, 19cm diam.

$430 - $470

Toowoomba Antiques Gallery, QLD

An abstract design vase decorated with stick figures, numbered 'B.1591' to the base, Italy, c1950, 20.5cm high, 14.5cm wide.

NZ$140 - $160

Maxine's Collectibles, New Zealand

Art Deco ship vase, stamped 'Hand Painted', Czechoslovakia, c1950, 30cm high,13cm wide, 32.5cm long.

$130 - $150

Hamilton Street Antiques, VIC

Royal Stafford bone chine 'Blue Bird' sandwich tray, England.

$40 - $50

Laidley Old Wares, QLD

Pair modernist lava glaze vases, by Marcello Fantoni, Italy, c1960, 22cm high.

$1000 - $1200

Design Dilemas, VIC

Capodimonte coffee set, Italy, c1970.

$525 - $625

Goodwood House Antiques, WA

Royal Tudorware, Barker Brothers ironstone coffee set in the 'Springtime' pattern, comprising five cups and saucers, a coffee pot, sugar bowl and milk jug, England.

$140 - $160

frhapsody, WA

Three Hornsea bowls with kaleidoscope patterns, England, c1972, 15cm wide.

$50 - $70

frhapsody, WA

Midwinter Stylecraft classic shape gravy jug and stand with red and grey bands, England, c1960, 8.5cm high.

$55 - $75

frhapsody, WA

Stoneware dish by the famous British potter Takeshi Yasuda, England, 31cm high, 31cm wide.

$2400 - $2600

Chapel Street Bazaar, VIC

Parson Brown ash bowl, registered No. D5600.

$215 - $255

Eilisha's Shoppe, QLD

A seated cat by Parkinson, from a short lived English pottery, in production between 1952 – 1963, run by Richard and Susan Parkinson in Kent, England.

$380 - $420

Vintage Living, ACT

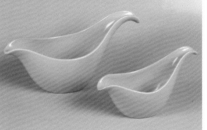

'Midwinter' Stylecraft sauce jug and a gravy jug with a semi matte glaze, England, c1950, 11cm high, 9cm wide, 22cm long, 6cm deep, 9cm diam.

$70 - $90

Born Frugal, VIC

Set of four side plates, made by Midwinter in the 'Stylecraft' pattern 'Saladware', design by Terence Conran, England, c1950, 10cm high, 20cm wide.

$275 - $315

Retro Active, VIC

Bretby 'Duckling' salt and pepper shakers, both with original stickers, England, c1950, 5cm high.

$45 - $65

Woodside Bazaar, SA

Derbyshire salt and pepper shakers, in the shape of pears, c1950, 7cm high.

$45 - $65

Shop 16, Southern Antique Centre, NSW

CERAMICS

Paragon trio in tapestry rose design, England, c1950, 7cm high, 8.5cm wide.

$55 - $75

Helen's On The Bay, QLD

Westminster Cottage Ware cup and saucer, England, c1950.

$40 - $50

Antiques & Collectables Centre - Ballarat, VIC

Paragon trio, golden emblem design, England, c1950, 8cm high, 7cm wide.

$55 - $75

Helen's On The Bay, QLD

Set of four 'Totem' design cups and saucers by Susan Williams-Ellis, Portmeirion pottery, England, c1960.

$90 - $110

Retro Active, VIC

J & G Meakin 'Domino' cup and saucer, England.

NZ$15 - $25

Moa Extinct Stuff, New Zealand

Set of six Brexton cups and plates, a TV set with South Pacific scenes thumb print handles, and the number '5765' on base, England, c1950.

$170 - $190

Regent Secondhand, VIC

Set of six Harlequin cups and saucers by Langley of England, c1950.

$55 - $75

The Botanic Ark, VIC

Thirty six piece Galaware dinner set, multi coloured, England, c1960.

$120 - $140

Regent Secondhand, VIC

Derbyshire owl salt and pepper shakers, c1950, 7cm high.

$65 - $85

Shop 16, Southern Antique Centre, NSW

Branksome coffee cups and saucers, in assorted colours. Priced per set, England, c1950.

NZ$25 - $35

Strangely Familiar, New Zealand

Jersey pottery figures of black musicians, England, c1960, 12cm high, 7cm wide, 12cm long, 7cm deep.

$115 - $135

Dr Russell's Emporium, WA

Westminster pottery Hanley, Staffordshire cottage shaped lidded jar, England, c1950, 10cm high, 9cm wide, 15cm long.

$85 - $105

Antiques at Redbank, QLD

Twenty piece Roslyn China tea set, in an Art Deco green, silver, and white striped pattern, including six trios, a sugar bowl and a cake plate, England, c1950.

$135 - $155

Newport Temple Antiques, VIC

Paragon cabinet plate of floral design with heavy gilding, England, c1953, 28cm diam.

$175 - $195

Helen's On The Bay, QLD

Ridgway home maker dinner plate in a red colourway, England, c1960, 26cm diam.

$185 - $205

Camberwell Antique Centre, VIC

Paragon cabinet plate, floral design with heavy gilding, England, c1953, 28cm diam.

$175 - $195

Helen's On The Bay, QLD

Two Johnson Brothers mid green jugs, England, c1950.

$60 - $80

Step Back Antiques, VIC

Three graduated Elijah Cotton Lord Nelson jugs in burgundy and white, England, c1950, 14cm high.

$90 - $110

Step Back Antiques, VIC

Character jug of a town crier by 'Sterling', England, c1975, 23cm high, 13cm wide.

$135 - $155

Glenelg Antique Centre, SA

A water or cordial set comprising of a jug and four beakers, by Lancaster & Sandland Ltd., England, c1950, 25cm high.

NZ$75 - $95

Anticus Antiques, New Zealand

Large Johnson Bros, genuine hand engraving, 'Haddon Hall' milk jug, England, c1960, 16cm high, 15.5cm deep, 10.5cm diam.

NZ$55 - $75

Country Charm Antiques, New Zealand

Set of six 'Domino' polka dot dinner plates, by T. G. Green, England, c1960, 25cm diam.

$170 - $190

Design Dilemas, VIC

CERAMICS

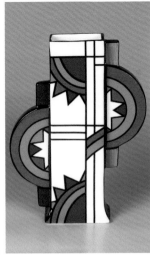

A rectangular section vase in the 'Jazz' pattern, from the Brian Wood Collection, England, c1998, 20cm high.

$115 - $135 **Decodence Collectables, VIC**

Vase hand painted by Amelia James, Homestead Cottage design, limited edition, England, c1990, 17cm high, 10cm diam.

$135 - $155 **Glenelg Antique Centre, SA**

Large wheel vase by Troika, Cornwall England with incised and raised decoration on both sides, monogrammed 'AB', England, c1970, 20cm diam.

$750 - $850 **Vintage Living, ACT**

One of a pair of mid-winter style craft, classic shape tureens with red and grey bands, England, c1960, 23.5cm wide.

$150 - $170 **frhapsody, WA**

Five piece 'Tea for Two' setting by Johnsons with pink tonings, c1950.

$85 - $105 **Den of Antiquities, VIC**

Prince Kensington red double decker bus teapot, 'The T. Potts Bus Co' marked on the base 'P & K Made in England', 17cm high, 22cm wide.

$140 - $160 **Bower Bird Art & Antiques, QLD**

Lingard novelty teapot, 'Old Lady Who Lived In The Shoe', England.

$170 - $190 **Squatters Antiques & Restorations, SA**

Empire 'Crinoline Lady' milk jug and sugar bowl, England, c1953, 8cm high.

$85 - $105 **Western District Antique Centre, VIC**

Hand decorated midwinter 'Stylecraft' jam and butter dish with a chrome plated toast rack, England, c1950, 11cm high, 10cm wide, 27cm long.

$60 - $80 **Born Frugal, VIC**

T.G. Green 'Patio Gingham' teapot and milk jug, England, c1950, 12cm high, 25cm wide.

$110 - $130 **The Botanic Ark, VIC**

Unusual candle holder and vase, in a pink and marble glaze, made by Shorter, England, c1950, 4cm high, 27.5cm wide, 16cm deep.

NZ$65 - $85 **Maxine's Collectibles, New Zealand**

Electric light house model with attached cottage, England, c1960, 50cm high, 45cm wide.

$330 - $370 **Hollywood Antiques, WA**

Pair of Derbyshire salt and pepper shakers in the form of angel fish, England, c1950, 3cm high, 3cm wide.

$40 - $60 **Fyshwick Antique Centre, ACT**

Westminster Pottery, 'Hanley Cottage' cheese dish, England, c1950, 11cm high, 17cm long.

$85 - $105 **Antiques at Redbank, QLD**

Vase by Snowdon, England, 21cm high.

$30 - $40 **Furniture Revisited, VIC**

Geometric lemonade set by Empire, the seven pieces with concentric orange and silver bands against a straw coloured body, England, c1930, 21cm high.

$420 - $460 **Design Dilemas, VIC**

Pie funnel, manufactured by Bristle Porcelain Ware, England, 7cm high.

$35 - $45 **Trinkets & Treasures, VIC**

Lancaster teapot stand, England, c1950, 25cm wide.

$175 - $195 **Paddington Antique Centre Pty Ltd, QLD**

Preserves dish by L & Sons Ltd., inscribed '976', and with a stainless steel lid, England, 8cm high, 9.5cm wide.

$45 - $65 **Baxter's Antiques, QLD**

Lancaster flour sifter, England, c1955, 12cm high.

$125 - $145 **Paddington Antique Centre Pty Ltd, QLD**

Set of six boxed ceramic coasters by Maw & Co, Stoke on Trent, England, c1970, 9cm diam.

$10 - $20 **Obsidian Antiques, NSW**

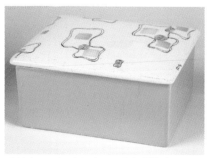

Lidded ceramic trinket box made by Midwinter, England, c1950, 5cm high, 12cm wide.

$40 - $50 **Shop 46, Centenary Antique Centre, NSW**

All over floral basket by Wood and Sons Burslem, England, c1950, 7cm high.

$85 - $105

Amour Antiques & Collectables, New Zealand

Royal Winton 'Balmoral', countess teapot, England, c1955, 12cm high.

$355 - $395

Paddington Antique Centre Pty Ltd, QLD

Empire Ware compote with a courting scene design on the front, gold handles and a pedestal base, England, c1950, 17cm high, 31cm wide.

$240 - $280

Journey to the Past Antiques & Collectables, QLD

Cotton Nelson Ware chintz 'Marina' dish, England, c1955, 4cm high, 12cm wide, 16cm long.

$40 - $60

Paddington Antique Centre Pty Ltd, QLD

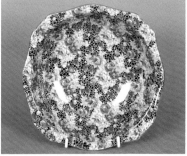

Royal Winton 'Hazel' bowl, England, 21cm diam.

$230 - $270

Camberwell Antique Centre, VIC

Salad bowl in the 'Hazel' pattern, c1950.

$480 - $580

Den of Antiquities, VIC

Royal Winton comport in the 'Sweet Pea' design, England, c1950, 7cm high, 15cm wide, 18cm long.

$190 - $210

Collectable Creations, QLD

Royal Winton all over floral rectangular dish, England, c1950, 3cm high, 11cm wide, 21cm long.

$55 - $75

Helen's On The Bay, QLD

Falcon Ware yellow 'abstract face' jug with gold trim, No. 486, England, c1950, 24cm high, 14.5cm wide, 9cm deep.

NZ$65 - $85

Maxine's Collectibles, New Zealand

Falcon Ware two-tier cottage comport, England, c1950, 26cm high, 24cm diam.

$115 - $135

Antiques & Collectables Centre - Ballarat, VIC

Goldscheider with Myott Son & Co. Staffordshire zebra foal 1946-1959, Marcel Goldscheider animal fancy, England, 19cm high, 11cm wide, 6cm deep.

$230 - $270

Retro Active, VIC

Hutschenreuther village scene porcelain serving platter, Germany, c1950.

$55 - $75

Cool & Collected, SA

Green majolica figurine cache pot, Japan, c1960, 18cm high, 10cm wide.

NZ$40 - $50

Bakelite Belle.com, New Zealand

Goldscheider wall mask, c1950, 10cm high.

$700 - $800

Armadale Antique Centre, VIC

Gouda vase No. 5218, Holland, 19cm high, 16cm wide, 16cm diam.

$280 - $320

Furniture Revisited, VIC

Fine quality Hutschenreuther porcelain figurine of a dancer, Germany, c1950, 23cm high.

NZ$475 - $515

Bonham's, New Zealand

Gouda Flora vase, with a crown mark (1271) and original Flora Plateel sticker, 'Petas' ,, Holland, 16cm high.

$115 - $135

Karlia Rose Garden Antiques & Collectables, VIC

Pair of Limoges handpainted steins, France, c1960, 21cm high, 17cm wide.

$500 - $600

Armadale Antique Centre, VIC

Limoges letter holder, in pink and green with gold relief, c1950.

$150 - $170

Tyabb Hay Shed, VIC

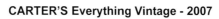

Maling plate, in blue 'Anemone' pattern, United Kingdom, c1951, 28cm wide.

$375 - $425

Shenton Park Antiques, WA

Maling blue-lustre glaze tennis set, England, c1950, 22cm long.

$65 - $85

Newport Temple Antiques, VIC

Maling Ware basket, 'Spring Time' pattern, green thumb print, England, c1950, 13cm high, 16cm wide, 25cm long.

$530 - $630

Mentone Beach Antiques Centre, VIC

Maling green thumbprint vase in the 'Maybloom' pattern, England, c1950, 21cm high, 11.5cm wide.

NZ$275 - $315

Bonham's, New Zealand

Maling trinket box, with the 'Anemone Rose' pattern, England, c1950, 10cm high, 12.5cm wide, 8cm deep.

$230 - $270

Southside Antiques Centre, QLD

Maling 'Spring Bouquet' bowl, England, c1950, 4cm high, 16cm diam.

NZ$185 - $205

Country Charm Antiques, New Zealand

Signed Charlotte Rhead 'Windblown Poppies' jug, England, c1950, 24cm high, 10cm wide.

NZ$600 - $700

Ascot Collectables, New Zealand

Set of four Mason's side plates, from the 'South Seas' series, England, c1950, 22cm wide, 12cm deep.

$90 - $110

Angel Cottage, QLD

Signed Charlotte Rhead vase, 'Windblown Poppies', England, c1950, 3cm high, 16cm diam.

NZ$240 - $280

Ascot Collectables, New Zealand

Signed Charlotte Rhead flared vase 'Windbown Poppies', England, c1950, 10cm high, 10cm wide.

NZ$360 - $400

Ascot Collectables, New Zealand

Three piece soup setting, by Thomas, a division of Rosenthal, Germany, c1969, 10cm wide.

$25 - $35

frhapsody, WA

Rosenthal 'Leones' art jug vase by Javier Mariscal, Germany, c1980, 13cm high, 14cm wide, 10cm deep.

NZ$180 - $200

Maxine's Collectables, New Zealand

Ceramic wall plaque, made by Rosenthal Studio-Linie with design by Peynet, Germany, c1950, 18.5cm high, 18.5cm wide.

$115 - $135

Retro Active, VIC

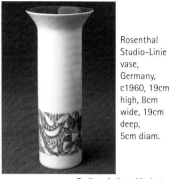

Rosenthal Studio-Linie vase, Germany, c1960, 19cm high, 8cm wide, 19cm deep, 5cm diam.

$75 - $95

Pedlars Antique Market, SA

Rosenthal Studio-Linie vase, Queensberry marble 'Erotic' vase, Germany, 13cm high, 13cm wide, 12cm deep.

NZ$115 - $135

Maxine's Collectibles, New Zealand

Royal Albert 'Prudence' trio, England, c1950.

$65 - $85

The Silky Oak Shop, QLD

Royal Albert trio, 'Kentish Rockery' pattern, England.

$85 - $105

Shop 5, Coliseum Antique Centre, NSW

Royal Albert trio, pink rose on yellow background, c1950.

$55 - $75

Southside Antiques Centre, QLD

Royal Albert 'Violetta' salt and pepper, England, c1980, 8cm high.

NZ$50 - $70

Gales Antiques, New Zealand

Royal Albert 'Lade Carlisle' gravy boat and stand, England, c1970.

$135 - $155

Northumberland Antiques & Restorations, NSW

Royal Albert 'Serena' soup bowl and saucer, England, c1950, 17cm wide.

NZ$135 - $155

Gales Antiques, New Zealand

Royal Albert 'Happy Birthday' first edition plate, signed A M Turner, England, c1970, 21cm diam.

NZ$50 - $70

Gales Antiques, New Zealand

Royal Albert 'Serena' six cup teapot, England, c1960, 12cm high, 18.5cm long.

NZ$445 - $485

Country Charm Antiques, New Zealand

Royal Albert rack plate with a robin, signed 'Reg Johnson', England, c1982, 21cm diam.

$65 - $85

Bowerbird Antiques & Collectables, SA

OTHER

Royal Doulton 'Marilyn' figurine, painted for Royal Crown Derby to show the Derby posies, England, c1985, 18.5cm high.

NZ$500 - $600

John Varney, New Zealand

Royal Crown Derby milk jug and sugar bowl, in their original box, England, c1963.

$175 - $195   **Journey to the Past Antiques & Collectables, QLD**

Large and impressive Royal Crown Derby display urn with the 'Imari' pattern, England, c1980, 42cm high, 15cm wide, 15cm diam.

$2850 - $3050   **Malvern Antique Market, VIC**

Royal Dux figurine of a bear with a double bass, c1960, 13cm high.

$115 - $135

Nana's Pearls, ACT

Royal Dux figure of an elephant, Czechoslovakia, c1970, 20cm long.

$85 - $105   **The Hall Attic, ACT**

Royal Dux ' Boy Fisherman' figurine with bronze, gold and green shades and a stone shade base, Czechoslovakia, c1950, 54cm high, 20cm wide.

NZ$950 - $1050   **Hubbers Emporium, New Zealand**

Figure of a Royal Dux cat in black and white, Czechoslovakia, 15cm high, 6cm wide, 30cm long.

$500 - $600   **Capocchi, VIC**

Royal Dux tiger figure, c1950, 7.5cm high, 19cm long.

$330 - $370   **Janda Antiques, NSW**

Royal Dux circus lion figurine, Czechoslovakia, c1980, 15cm high.

NZ$305 - $345   **Bonham's, New Zealand**

Royal Dux figure of a macaw, England, c1980, 20cm high, 40cm long.

$525 - $625   **Decodence Collectables, VIC**

Royal Dux gilt handled vase with a pierced neck and base and the original Royal Dux seal, Czechoslovakia, c1980, 27.5cm high.

NZ$265 - $305   **Bonham's, New Zealand**

Royal Winton pink petunia coffee pot, England, c1950.

$475 - $515   **Antiques & Heirlooms, WA**

Royal Winton cruet set on a tray, England, c1950, 7cm high, 11cm wide, 14cm long.

$100 - $120   **Helen's On The Bay, QLD**

Royal Winton pink petunia cup and saucer, England, c1960.

$165 - $185   **Antiques & Heirlooms, WA**

Royal Winton breakfast set in the 'Rose' pattern, England, c1950, 12.5cm high, 26cm diam.

$695 - $795   **Kookaburra Antiques, TAS**

Royal Winton six piece breakfast set in the 'Mulberry Petunia' pattern, England.

$945 - $1045   **Southside Antiques Centre, QLD**

Royal Winton pink petunia milk jug and sugar bowl, England, c1960.

$275 - $315   **Antiques & Heirlooms, WA**

Three piece Sadler tea service in bright green and gilt, England, c1950, 16cm high.

$305 - $345   **Northumberland Antiques & Restorations, NSW**

Sadler three piece tea set in aqua blue with gold relief, England, c1950.

$430 - $470   **Tyabb Hay Shed, VIC**

Shorter & Son platter decorated with flowers, c1950, 39cm long.

$55 - $75   **Timeless Treasures, WA**

Shell shaped vase by Shorter & Son in a lovely soft pastel coloured glaze, England, c1950, 12cm high, 12cm wide, 30cm long.

$40 - $50   **Woodside Bazaar, SA**

Shorter & Son Ltd. Stoke-on-Trent, green leaf design toast rack, England, 19.5cm wide.

$40 - $60   **Treats & Treasures, NSW**

CERAMICS

Spode china cabinet plate, with a hand painted castle scene and gilded highlights, c1950, 24cm wide.

$500 - $600

Philip Cross Antiques, NSW

Mack bird - 'Eagle Owl' one of a series of sixteen English birds by Robert and Joyce Mack of Staffordshire, England, c2000, 17cm high.

$210 - $250

Newlyn Antiques & Cottage Garden Nursery, VIC

Mack bird - 'Snowy Owl', one of series of sixteen English birds by Joyce and Robert Mack of Staffordshire, England, c2000, 13cm high.

$145 - $165

Newlyn Antiques & Cottage Garden Nursery, VIC

Mack bird - 'Song Thrush', one of a series of sixteen English birds by Robert and Joyce Mack of Staffordshire, England, c2000, 12cm high.

$140 - $160

Newlyn Antiques & Cottage Garden Nursery, VIC

Mack bird - 'Dartford Warbler', one of sixteen English birds by Robert and Joyce Mack of Staffordshire, England, c2000, 13cm high.

$80 - $100

Newlyn Antiques & Cottage Garden Nursery, VIC

Staffordshire model of a setter, hand painted, England, c1950, 16.25cm high.

$75 - $95

Newlyn Antiques & Cottage Garden Nursery, VIC

Pair of Royal Doulton Staffordshire dogs, England, c1980, 15cm high.

$455 - $495

Goodwood House Antiques, WA

Staffordshire fine bone china vase, of square shape with semi-circular 'handles', England, c2000, 19cm high.

$135 - $155

Decodence Collectables, VIC

Crown Staffordshire mallard, No. 25 of a limited edition of 250 hand painted by Peter Scott in 1975, England, 28cm high, 30cm wide.

$480 - $580

Newlyn Antiques & Cottage Garden Nursery, VIC

Torquay lidded mustard pot, 'Pass the Mustard', England, c1950, 6.5cm high, 6cm diam.

$115 - $135

Gumnut Antiques & Old Wares, NSW

Villeroy & Boch 'Amapola' pattern teapot, Germany, c1980, 18cm high.

$190 - $210   **Lucilles Interesting Collectables, NSW**

Villeroy and Boch 'Acapulco' cup and saucer, c1965, 6cm high, 7cm wide.

$25 - $35   **Out of the Ark, ACT**

Nymolte dish by Bjorn Wiinblad, No. 3028-1284, Denmark, 15cm diam.

NZ$110 - $130   **Maxine's Collectibles, New Zealand**

One from a selection of glass 'Nut Cracker' wall plates. Designed by Bjorn Wiinblad and produced by Rosenthal, Germany, c1970, 22cm high, 15cm wide.

$205 - $245   **Toowoomba Antiques Gallery, QLD**

Rosenthal 'Studio-Linie' coffee set for eight, includes a coffee pot sugar bowl, creamer and a small spoon plate, a total of twenty eight with quatre couleur gold decoration on the lids and plates, signed Bjorn Wiinblad, Germany, c1960.

$545 - $645   **Patinations, NSW**

Large 'Swan Lake' glass charger with all over decoration of swans and flowers, by Bjorn Wiinblad for Rosenthal, Germany, c1970, 4cm deep, 45cm diam.

$745 - $845   **Toowoomba Antiques Gallery, QLD**

'Year of the Dog' wall plate, limited edition of 3000 by Bjorn Wiinblad, Rosenthal, Germany, c1970, 28.5cm diam.

$375 - $415   **Toowoomba Antiques Gallery, QLD**

'Chinese Poetry' vase with a shaped top, sponge gilded background, bright enamel design and further gilding. Designed by Bjorn Wiinblad and produced by Rosenthal, Germany, c1970, 13cm high, 7.5cm wide, 5.5cm deep.

$545 - $645   **Toowoomba Antiques Gallery, QLD**

'Chinese Poetry' dish with a sponge gilded background and a couple afloat in a swan shaped boat, designed by Bjorn Wiinblad, produced by Rosenthal, Germany, c1975, 3.5cm high, 12.5cm wide, 12.5cm long.

$185 - $205   **Toowoomba Antiques Gallery, QLD**

Rosenthal bowl, designed by Bjorn Wiinblad, Germany, c1965, 25cm wide, 4cm deep.

NZ$375 - $415   **Banks Peninsula Antiques, New Zealand**

'Highland Cow' figurine (A5276) by the Border of Fine Arts, c2004, 10cm high, 17cm long.

NZ$85 - $105

Diane Akers, New Zealand

Green ceramic elephant, United States, c1950, 5cm high, 15cm long.

$120 - $140

Chapel Street Bazaar, VIC

Set of three ceramic cat figures in green, red and orange, c1970, 21cm high.

$50 - $70

Atomic Pop, SA

Slip cast china, gold and pink glaze gold fish, c1975, 8cm high, 7cm long, 5cm deep.

$40 - $50

Bowhows, NSW

Set of three ceramic wall elephants.

$85 - $105

Paddington Antique Centre Pty Ltd, QLD

Ceramic playful puppies, by Royal Copenhagen, Denmark, c1970, 6cm high.

$135 - $155

Glenelg Antique Centre, SA

Black ceramic bull figurine, c1970, 11cm high.

$20 - $30

Atomic Pop, SA

Art Deco ceramic style pelicans group, United States, c1950, 24cm high.

$430 - $470

Chapel Street Bazaar, VIC

Pair of ceramic abstract monkey figures, the bases signed 'Robyn', c1970.

$20 - $30

Atomic Pop, SA

Set of three flying wall bluebirds, marked 'Japan', the largest has 16cm wing span, Japan, c1950.

$230 - $270

Olsens Antiques, QLD

Pottery spaniel, Canada, c1980, 30cm high, 33cm long.

$85 - $105

Newport Temple Antiques, VIC

Lomonosoc white mink, Russia, c1970, 17.5cm high.

$475 - $515

The Best Antiques & Collectables, QLD

Large ceramic macaw, colourfully glazed with glass eyes and a realistic body, inscribed Delta '78, United States, c1978, 53cm high, 28cm wide.

$360 - $400

Principal Antiques, SA

Hereford Fine China Tui on a Kowhai branch. This Tui is part of 'The Riverland Collection', the base features yellow/gold kowhai flowers, New Zealand, c1970, 18cm high, 6cm wide, 12cm long, 8cm diam.

NZ$375 - $415

Country Charm Antiques, New Zealand

Pair of hand painted budgerigars on a branch with applied flowers, attributed to the Bridgwood Factory, England, c1950, 17cm high.

$265 - $305

Collectors' Cottage Antiques, NSW

Kitsch 'Jema' Dutch china lustre glass figure of a cat, Holland, c1950, 24cm high, 50cm long, 6cm deep.

$85 - $105

Cool & Collected, SA

Set of three graduated flying pheasant wall pockets with hand painted glaze.

$155 - $175

Born Frugal, VIC

'Swaledale Tup' cow figurine, (AV588), by The Border Fine Arts Pottery Company, c2004, 11cm high, 15cm long.

NZ$85 - $105

Diane Akers, New Zealand

Large Jena porcelain, blue glazed deer, Holland, c1950, 40cm high, 35cm long.

$500 - $600

Hollywood Antiques, WA

'Highland bull' figurine, by the Border Fine Arts Pottery Company (A5233), c2004, 12cm high, 17cm long.

NZ$100 - $120

Diane Akers, New Zealand

Set of three hand painted wall ducks, ranging in size from 12cm to 28cm wide, Japan, c1960.

$250 - $290

The Colonial Attic Antiques, VIC

Set of three hand painted wall swans, ranging in size from 10cm wide to 13cm wide, Japan, c1950.

$175 - $195

The Colonial Attic Antiques, VIC

Novelty 'Piggy' cookie jar with original cane handle, marked 'Made in Japan', c1950, 16cm high, 14cm diam.

$40 - $50

Northside Secondhand Furniture, QLD

Novelty cookie jar marked 'Made In Japan', c1960, 23cm high.

$55 - $75

Olsens Antiques, QLD

Novelty ceramic 'cat' biscuit barrel with a cane handle, Japan, c1958, 16cm high, 18cm wide.

$85 - $105

Beehive Old Wares & Collectables, VIC

O. C. Stephens bowl, New Zealand, c1950, 7.5cm high, 13cm wide.

NZ$135 - $155

Oxford Court Antiques Centre, New Zealand

Solholm pottery bowl, Denmark, c1950, 24cm wide, 40cm long.

$110 - $130

Mid Century Modern, SA

Solholm cutlery bowl, Denmark, c1950, 28cm wide, 38cm long.

$90 - $110

Mid Century Modern, SA

Striped green bowl with white glaze inside, c1965, 15cm diam.

$35 - $45

Bowhows, NSW

Buchan Stoneware 'Portobello Scotland' dish with fruit design, Scotland, c1970, 3.5cm high, 18cm wide, 18cm long.

NZ$40 - $50

Maxine's Collectibles, New Zealand

Black fruit bowl, c1950, 42cm high, 18cm wide.

$30 - $60

Rock N Rustic, SA

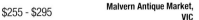

Argenta green bowl with silver inlay of a Marlin design, made by Gustavsberg, Sweden, c1960, 4cm high, 18cm diam.

$255 - $295

Malvern Antique Market, VIC

Ceramic green and black sugar bowl, Japan, c1960, 8cm high, 10cm diam.

$10 - $20

Newport Temple Antiques, VIC

Square shaped textured bowl by Grizelle, with crackle glaze inside and its original sticker, Japan, c1969, 9.5cm high, 16.5cm wide.

$40 - $50

frhapsody, WA

Faience bowl with polychrome decoration, by Stig Lindberg for Gustavsberg Fabriker, Sweden, Sweden, c1950, 22cm diam.

$255 - $295

Found Objects, VIC

O. C. Stephens bowl, New Zealand, c1950, 13cm high, 8cm wide, 22cm diam.

NZ$180 - $200

Oxford Court Antiques Centre, New Zealand

Gustavsberg 'Peanut Bowl', by Stig Lindberg, signed, Denmark, c1960, 15cm high, 32cm wide.

$550 - $650

Woollahra Decorative Arts Gallery, NSW

Five small, psychedelic patterned cups, Japan, c1969, 7.5cm high.

$20 - $30

frhapsody, WA

Regent shape coffee set designed in 1961 for Porsgrund by Tias Eckhoff, comprising six demitasse cups and saucers, milk jug and a coffee pot, with green anchor backstamps, Norway, c1962.

$280 - $320

frhapsody, WA

Novelty gnome salt and pepper shakers, marked 'Japan', Japan, c1950, 11cm high.

$30 - $40

Olsens Antiques, QLD

Wizard of Oz, queen and witch salt and pepper set, modelled as the 'Good Witch of the East' and 'Wicked Witch of the West', c1980, 10cm high.

$40 - $50

P. & N. Johnson, NSW

Novelty ceramic condiment set for salt, pepper, oil and vinegar in the shape of a nude lady, the underside marked 'Japan', Japan, c1950, 20cm long.

$135 - $155

Decorama, VIC

Figgilo flint 'Lotte' coffee pot, hand painted and silk screen printed, Norway, c1970, 22cm high, 17cm wide, 11cm diam.

$60 - $80

Antique General Store, NSW

Lidded ceramic bowl with a red apple design, Japan, c1950, 10cm high.

$40 - $50

Classic Vintage, NSW

Stavangeflint Turi design, 'August', set of six cups, saucers and plates, No. 2757, Norway, c1960.

NZ$60 - $80

Maxine's Collectibles, New Zealand

CERAMICS

Figure of a gnome holding a pick and basket, Japan, 29cm high, 7cm wide.

NZ$325 - $365 **Old & Past Antiques & Collectables, New Zealand**

Black lady head wall hanging, Japan, c1950, 20cm high, 10cm wide.

NZ$65 - $85 **Bakelite Belle.com, New Zealand**

Continental china figurine of a young girl with flowers, printed mark to the base, c1950, 13cm high.

$430 - $470 **Philip Cross Antiques, NSW**

Ceramic figurine of a New Zealand owl, by Royal Hereford, New Zealand, c1970, 11.5cm high, 4cm wide.

NZ$85 - $105 **Country Charm Antiques, New Zealand**

Pair of figurines of a boy and girl taking photographs, marked 'Made in Germany, No. 20883', Germany, 9cm high.

$120 - $140 **Yarra Valley Antique Centre, VIC**

Pair of ceramic African lady figures, c1950, 22cm high, 15cm deep.

$140 - $160 **Towers Antiques & Collectables, NSW**

Ceramic mouse figurine with a swivel head, Japan, c1960, 12cm high.

$40 - $50 **Classic Vintage, NSW**

Contemporary Spanish Galos porcelain figure, in gold and platinum, Spain, c1960, 14cm high, 14cm wide.

$85 - $105 **Helen's On The Bay, QLD**

Russian figurine of a mustachioed man with pipe and sabre, Russia, c1970, 23cm high.

$40 - $50 **Vintage Living, ACT**

Ceramic figure of a nude girl, Hungary, c1970, 22cm high, 14cm wide, 22cm long, 7cm deep.

$110 - $130 **Dr Russell's Emporium, WA**

Walt Disney Productions figure of 'Tramp', Japan, c1955, 16cm high, 10cm wide.

$55 - $75 **Thompsons Country Collectables, NSW**

Ceramic Mickey Mouse jug, Japan, c1950, 13cm high, 12cm wide.

NZ$115 - $135 **Right Up My Alley, New Zealand**

Picnic ware, part of a range 'Picnick' earthenware with printed decorations of vegetables and herbs painted in various colours, made by Rorstrand, designed by Marianne Westman in 1956, Sweden.

$155 - $175 **506070, NSW**

Kookaburra shaped ceramic jug, Japan, c1955, 13cm high.

$60 - $80

Paddington Antique Centre Pty Ltd, QLD

Lustre china novelty jug in the shape of a cow, Japan, c1950, 11cm high, 12cm wide.

$35 - $45

Nana's Pearls, ACT

Ken Castle pottery jug, New Zealand, 21.5cm high, 19cm diam.

NZ$275 - $315

Moa Extinct Stuff, New Zealand

Hanmer pottery lidded pot, New Zealand, c1970, 17cm high, 14cm diam.

NZ$65 - $85

Maxine's Collectibles, New Zealand

Ceramic breakfast set, in the form of a laden mule, Japan, c1970, 20cm long.

$30 - $40

The Hall Attic, ACT

Orange and brown ceramic jug, Holland, c1970, 18cm high.

$165 - $185

Victor Harbour Antiques - Mittagong, NSW

Cookie jar with dancing dogs on the front, Japan, c1960, 24cm high, 13cm diam.

$30 - $40

Woodside Bazaar, SA

Novelty 'Cookies' jar in the shape of a coffee grinder, Japan, c1975, 24cm high, 15cm diam.

$40 - $50

Woodside Bazaar, SA

'Mammy' biscuit jar, Japan, c1950, 21cm high, 21cm wide.

$255 - $295

Fat Helen's, VIC

'Sambo' cookie jar, Japan, c1950, 23cm high, 20cm wide.

$380 - $420

Chapel Street Bazaar, VIC

Ceramic 'Popeye' jug, Japan, c1950, 12cm high, 8.5cm wide.

NZ$55 - $75

Right Up My Alley, New Zealand

Cat biscuit barrel with a plastic coated cane handle, Japan, c1950, 18cm high.

$15 - $25

Chapel Street Bazaar, VIC

CERAMICS

Pair of ceramic cat wall plaques, c1960, 31cm high.

$40 - $50

**Fat Helen's,
VIC**

Unusual leaf shaped plate, Japan, c1960, 20cm wide, 25cm long.

$65 - $85

**Colonial Antiques & Tea House,
WA**

Graham Storm hand potted plaque with a floral pattern, New Zealand, c1965, 33cm diam.

NZ$140 - $160

**Colonial Heritage Antiques Ltd,
New Zealand**

Sugar bowl and plate with 'Made In Japan' stamped to the base, c1960, 6cm high, 13cm long.

$45 - $55

**Colonial Antiques & Tea House,
WA**

Temuka Potteries, Maori motif wall plaque by T. W Lovatt. The motif is on the front cover of Gail Henry's NZ pottery book, New Zealand, 11.5cm diam.

NZ$800 - $900

**Maxine's Collectibles,
New Zealand**

Small triangular pottery plate, c1960, 20cm high, 20cm wide.

$15 - $25

**Atomic Pop,
SA**

Palette plate with a 'red apple' design, Japan, c1950, 20cm high, 28cm long.

$40 - $50

**Classic Vintage,
NSW**

Stavengerfunt 'Thari' design dish, Norway, c1960, 13cm wide, 13cm long.

$50 - $70

**Retro Active,
VIC**

Stavengerfunt 'Thari' design dish, Norway, c1960, 13cm wide, 13cm long.

$50 - $70

**Retro Active,
VIC**

Risque pin-up plate, of a glamour girl, Japan, c1960, 10cm wide, 10cm long, 10cm diam.

$45 - $55

**Dr Russell's Emporium,
WA**

Square form 'Lotte' serving platter, Turi Design, Figgjo Factory, Norway, c1970, 4cm deep, 30cm diam.

$130 - $150

**Cool & Collected,
SA**

Signed pottery charger, decorated with an abstract fish, Sweden, c1970, 34cm wide.

$155 - $175

**Timeless Treasures,
WA**

Green windmill teapot, Japan, c1950, 11cm high, 13cm wide.

$40 - $50

Classic Vintage, NSW

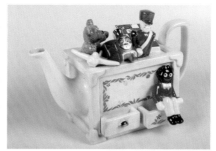

'Garden Mint' teapot, c1990, 25cm wide, 17.5cm deep.

$275 - $315

Jan James, NSW

Ceramic green teapot with a black lid, Japan, c1960, 13cm high, 22cm wide.

$25 - $35

Newport Temple Antiques, VIC

'Kelko' tea set, chocolate brown with white two tone tea cups, Japan, c1970, 6cm high, 5cm wide, 5cm diam.

$35 - $45

Bowhows, NSW

Turi design 'Market' three piece tea service, Norway, c1970, 18cm high, 19cm diam.

$115 - $135

Cool & Collected, SA

O. C. Stephens vase, New Zealand, c1950, 13cm high, 8cm wide.

NZ$110 - $130

Oxford Court Antiques Centre, New Zealand

Brilliantly coloured and mounted, decorative lidded ceramic urn with a plaque to the base which reads 'Christopher Sanders Lidded Vase II 1990', 97cm high, 30cm diam.

$2300 - $2500

Architectural Décor Australia, NSW

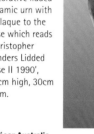

Brilliantly coloured and mounted, decorative, lidded ceramic urn with a plaque to the base which reads 'Christopher Sanders lidded vase 1990', 92cm high, 31cm diam.

$2300 - $2500

Architectural Décor Australia, NSW

Ernest Shufflebottom vase, hand potted, New Zealand, c1950, 18.5cm high, 13cm wide.

NZ$410 - $450

Oxford Court Antiques Centre, New Zealand

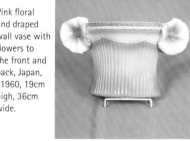

Pink floral and draped wall vase with flowers to the front and back, Japan, c1960, 19cm high, 36cm wide.

$65 - $85

Helen's On The Bay, QLD

Colourful pocket vase, depicting peaches on a tree, slip cast china, c1950, 12cm high, 13cm wide, 5cm deep.

$30 - $60

Born Frugal, VIC

Wall pocket vase inscribed, 'Lyn Dale, modelled by J. Moss', c1950, 20cm high, 13cm wide.

$115 - $135

Trinity Antiques, WA

OTHER

Upsala Ekeby vase, Sweden, c1960, 24cm high, 9cm diam.

$90 - $110

506070, NSW

Vase with an Aboriginal motif, Australia, c1950, 20cm high, 11cm diam.

$15 - $25

McKays Mart, SA

Vase with a green glaze, abstract design, signed, Sweden, 26cm high, 10cm diam.

NZ$140 - $160

Maxine's Collectibles, New Zealand

Ladyhead vase or pencil holder, in turquoise, United States, c1960.

$275 - $315

Antiques & Heirlooms, WA

Pair of green lady head vases, United States, c1950, 14cm high.

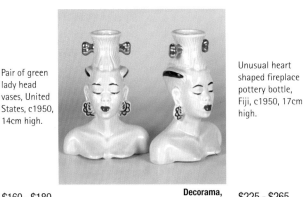

$160 - $180

Decorama, VIC

Negress wall vase, c1950, 45cm high.

$175 - $195

Shop 100, Antiques & Collectables - Hamilton, NSW

Biomorphic shaped vase with a drip glaze patterning, Japan, c1969, 16cm high.

$25 - $35

frhapsody, WA

Large ceramics face vase, hand painted with a pearl necklace, c1950, 18cm high, 10cm wide.

$185 - $205

Towers Antiques & Collectables, NSW

Unusual heart shaped fireplace pottery bottle, Fiji, c1950, 17cm high.

$225 - $265

Blue, green and yellow striped vase, c1960, 31cm high, 10cm diam.

$90 - $110

506070, NSW

Black lady vase with sequin earrings and a diamonte necklace, c1950, 25cm high, 16cm wide.

$85 - $105

Cobweb Collectables, NSW

Rose Cottage Antiques, ACT

Art Deco style pottery vase, 40cm high.

$50 - $70

Myriad Art, NSW

'Head' vase, Japan, c1950, 120cm high.

$135 - $155

Newport Temple Antiques, VIC

Black 'Harlem' vase, Sweden, c1960, 16.5cm high, 7cm diam.

NZ$115 - $135 **Maxine's Collectibles, New Zealand**

Rorstrand 'Sarek', hand made vase, Sweden, 17cm high, 8cm diam.

NZ$100 - $120 **Maxine's Collectibles, New Zealand**

Pottery vase by Carl Vendelbosch, made for the New Zealand Insurance Company (NZI), c1963, 38cm high, 16.5cm diam.

NZ$205 - $245 **Maxine's Collectibles, New Zealand**

Hanmer pottery, brown and cream vase, New Zealand, c1970, 26.5cm high, 13cm diam.

NZ$75 - $95 **Maxine's Collectibles, New Zealand**

Pottery Art vase, signed 'WJE', New Zealand, c1970, 10cm high, 22.5cm wide, 11cm deep.

NZ$115 - $135 **Maxine's Collectibles, New Zealand**

Uppsala-Ekeby vase (no 1500/1618), Sweden, 21.5cm high, 15cm diam.

NZ$140 - $160 **Maxine's Collectibles, New Zealand**

Temuka vase made for Farmers Trading Company, New Zealand, c1960, 8cm high, 8cm wide, 31cm long.

NZ$55 - $75 **Maxine's Collectibles, New Zealand**

Danico vase, No. 118, Denmark, c1950, 15cm high, 10cm diam.

NZ$115 - $135 **Maxine's Collectibles, New Zealand**

'Black Mammy' wall vase, Japan, c1950, 20cm high, 16cm wide.

$275 - $315 **Collectors' Cottage Antiques, NSW**

Solholm pottery vase, Denmark, c1950, 26cm high.

$140 - $160 **Mid Century Modern, SA**

Pottery vase by Barry Ball, dated 1987, Barry Hall is known for his abstract pottery and paintings, New Zealand, 22cm high, 17.5cm diam.

NZ$430 - $470 **Maxine's Collectibles, New Zealand**

OTHER

Large hand decorated vase by Danico with tubelined decoration of stylised oak leaves, Denmark, c1950, 40cm high.

$460 - $500   **Vintage Living, ACT**

Solholm pottery urn vase, Denmark, c1950, 57cm high.

$220 - $260   **Mid Century Modern, SA**

Gerald Hope pottery vase, New Zealand, c1980, 25cm high, 13cm diam.

NZ$55 - $75   **Maxine's Collectibles, New Zealand**

Rectangular studio pottery vase, Denmark, c1970, 21cm high.

$50 - $70   **Mid Century Modern, SA**

Four piece Lustreware egg cruet set, Japan, c1960, 14cm high, 11cm diam.

$45 - $55   **Woodside Bazaar, SA**

Pair of hand decorated terracotta vessels by Morach Pottery, Utrecht, Holland.

$185 - $205   **Found Objects, VIC**

Ian Firth wine set, New Zealand, c1970, 34cm high, 20cm wide.

NZ$240 - $280   **Oxford Court Antiques Centre, New Zealand**

Tableware range, 'Bla Eld' or 'Blue Fire', made by Rorstrand and designed by Bertha Bengston in 1949, Sweden, 25cm high.

$65 - $85   **506070, NSW**

Ladyhead vase or pencil holder with a frilled blue collar, United States, c1960.

$275 - $315   **Antiques & Heirlooms, WA**

Yellow ceramic elephant vase, by McCoy, United States, c1950, 16cm high, 15cm wide.

$70 - $90   **Chapel Street Bazaar, VIC**

Large Hanmer pottery lidded pot, New Zealand, c1970, 30cm high, 21cm diam.

NZ$115 - $135   **Maxine's Collectibles, New Zealand**

Peter Stitchbury wine set, New Zealand, c1970, 27cm high, 16cm wide.

NZ$185 - $205   **Oxford Court Antiques Centre, New Zealand**

Large Nicholas Branton pot, New Zealand, 49.5cm high, 35cm diam.

NZ$330 - $370

Moa Extinct Stuff, New Zealand

Walt Disney Mickey Mouse salt and pepper shakers, Japan, c1990, 7cm high, 4cm diam.

$20 - $30

Antipodes Antiques, QLD

Ceramic 'hatching chicken' salt and pepper shakers, Japan, c1960, 11cm high.

$30 - $40

Shop 8 Mittagong Antiques Centre, NSW

Apple shaped knife holder, Japan, c1950, 9cm high.

$55 - $75

Classic Vintage, NSW

Spoon rest with 'Love is the Best Cooking Ingredient', Japan, c1960, 23cm long.

$10 - $20

Shop 8 Mittagong Antiques Centre, NSW

'Holly Hobbie' egg coddler, inscribed 'Fill your world with happiness', Japan, c1960, 11cm high, 7cm wide.

$200 - $240

Helen's On The Bay, QLD

Pig biscuit barrel, milk jug, sugar bowl and salt and pepper shakers, Japan, c1950, 20cm high, 16cm diam.

$140 - $160

Heather Bell Antiques, VIC

'Bonzo' soap and toothbrush holder, stamped 'Made in Japan', c1950.

$230 - $270

Pearl Rose, VIC

Hand painted Titian Ware trout ornament with the water forming a dish, New Zealand, c1960, 11cm high, 9cm wide, 14cm long.

NZ$115 - $135

Colonial Heritage Antiques Ltd, New Zealand

Painted Edwardian cheese cover, 23cm deep.

$115 - $135

Paddington Antique Centre Pty Ltd, QLD

Lotte 'Turi' design large rectangular casserole lidded dish, Norway, c1960, 8cm high, 26cm wide, 37cm long.

$75 - $95

Helen's On The Bay, QLD

Figgjo, Kirsten decor casserole dish in the 'Annemarie' pattern, Norway, c1968.

$110 - $130

frhapsody, WA

Velvet jacket, c1970.

$65 - $85

Classic Vintage, NSW

Three piece pure wool men's, chocolate brown pinstriped suit with flared trousers and a small 32 inch waist, Australia, c1972.

$230 - $270

Clarence Park Bazaar, SA

'Stamina', light blue/grey double breasted, pin striped jacket, c1952.

$85 - $105

Classic Vintage, NSW

Grey cuffed pants suit, c1970.

$40 - $50

The Old Lolly Factory, NSW

Boat print body shirt, c1970.

$20 - $30

The Old Lolly Factory, NSW

Men's beige pinstriped polyester safari suit, size 36 inch waist, large, Australia.

$75 - $95

Clarence Park Bazaar, SA

Khaki wool suit, c1950.

$30 - $40

The Old Lolly Factory, NSW

Black pinstripe suit with cuffed and flared pants, c1970.

$45 - $65

The Old Lolly Factory, NSW

Men's mustard and white bowling shirt, small size.

$45 - $65

Clarence Park Bazaar, SA

Musk 'Le Coq Sportif' training T-shirt, size medium, Australia.

$30 - $40

Curve, VIC

Fornasetti silk tie, Italy, c1960.

$170 - $190

Malvern Antique Market, VIC

Fornasetti silk tie, Italy, c1960.

$170 - $190

Malvern Antique Market, VIC

Size 40 leather jacket with cloth arms, by Casablanca leather, 'LAB 84' badge on the front, New Zealand, c1984.

NZ$140 - $160

Shand's Emposium, New Zealand

'Burberry' men's silk raincoat, England.

$130 - $150

L.A. Design, NSW

Men's 'Austral' raccoon fur jacket, size 42, Australia, c1970.

$160 - $180

Curve, VIC

David Jones camel hair coat, England, c1960.

$140 - $160

L.A. Design, NSW

Maroon print velvet jacket, c1970.

$20 - $30

The Old Lolly Factory, NSW

Reproduction men's regency waistcoat of wool with a silk back, Australia, c1995.

$140 - $160

Christine McKenna, NSW

Men's jacket in wool plaid, c1970.

$20 - $30

The Old Lolly Factory, NSW

COSTUME & DRESSING ACCESSORIES

'Mayfair' paisley shirt, c1970.

$45 - $65

Classic Vintage, NSW

Polyester knit shirt, c1970.

$40 - $50

Classic Vintage, NSW

Yachtsman's terry towel shirt, c1970.

$55 - $75

Classic Vintage, NSW

Olive green check cuffed pants, c1970.

$20 - $30

The Old Lolly Factory, NSW

Men's corduroy, red decorated shirt by Jacques Tati, c1980.

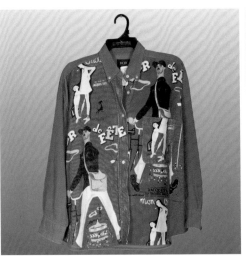

$8 - $18

The Old Lolly Factory, NSW

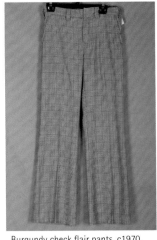

Burgundy check flair pants, c1970.

$20 - $30

The Old Lolly Factory, NSW

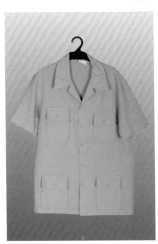

Blue safari jacket, c1970.

$20 - $30

The Old Lolly Factory, NSW

Cavalier polyester long sleeve shirt, c1960.

$45 - $65

Classic Vintage, NSW

Orange, navy print, long sleeve shirt, c1960.

$15 - $25

The Old Lolly Factory, NSW

Gold stripe lame shirt/tunic, c1960.

$15 - $25

The Old Lolly Factory, NSW

Medium brown, pure wool coat by iconic Australian fashion designer Prue Acton, size 14, Australia, c1970.

$185 - $205

OK WOW, ACT

Hand woven silk coat with belt, made for Peuan Thai Studio, Canberra, size 14-16, Thailand, c1960.

$140 - $160

OK WOW, ACT

Wool/mohair cape by 'Ben Nevis, Highland Exclusives' with wooden buttons, size small, Scotland, c1960.

$115 - $135

OK WOW, ACT

Tiger print on kangaroo fur coat, by Cornelius, size 10, Australia, c1970.

$645 - $745

OK WOW, ACT

Sanro overcoat, rayon with gold buttons and gold applique, size 8, Australia, c1960.

$110 - $130

Moustache Vintage Clothing, VIC

Ricky Reed overcoat in a red, white and blue hounds tooth pattern, size 10, Australia, c1965.

$85 - $105

Moustache Vintage Clothing, VIC

Prue Acton blazer with puffy sleeves, size 12, grey velveteen with polyester appliqué and grey velveteen covered buttons, Australia, c1980.

$110 - $130

Moustache Vintage Clothing, VIC

Brocade blazer with gold tapestry detail, 'Junior Dress Shop', United States, c1971.

$240 - $280

Gorgeous, VIC

Nylon full length floral housecoat, size 12-14 of printed nylon with rose and lilac motif, feature fitted collar, elbow length puff sleeves, frilled on pocket, fitted waist with belt, Ireland, c1948.

NZ$75 - $95

The Modern Miss, New Zealand

Silver pencil dress, size 10, boned bodice, plaited spaghetti straps, two pleats front and back, zip centre- back, silver lurex brocade with appliqué silver daisies, labelled 'Fenn Dill', New Zealand, c1955.

Coffee lace and chiffon cocktail dress, size 8 with a boned bodice, rusched straps, empire line band, all lined, and a zip to the centre back, just below knee length, labeled 'Robert Dorland' (probably London, made under license in New Zealand), c1950.

Brocade strapless dance/wedding dress with original stiffened petticoat and matching bolero jacket with zip, approx size 8, New Zealand, c1957.

NZ$275 - $315   **In Vogue Costumes & Collectables, New Zealand**

NZ$155 - $175   **The Modern Miss, New Zealand**

NZ$185 - $205   **The Modern Miss, New Zealand**

Brown glitter structured pencil dress, size 10 with a diagonal drape across the bodice and down the skirt, mid calf length, c1950.

Silk strapless mid calf length Chloe cocktail dress, France, c1983.

Black and white bustier dress with a ruffled skirt, size 8, United States, c1980.

Blue shot taffeta party dress, styled by Camille Lee of Melbourne, size 10, Australia, c1950.

$110 - $130   **Curve, VIC**

$75 - $95   **Moustache Vintage Clothing, VIC**

$155 - $175   **Circa Vintage Clothing, VIC**

NZ$190 - $210   **The Modern Miss, New Zealand**

Olive long dress, size 14-16 in shot olive taffeta with bronze beading, Empire line, drop beading, full length straight, two side splits below knee, sweetheart neckline and a 'Yule Gowns' label, New Zealand, c1960.

Red full length ball gown with a nylon tulle full skirt, fitted heavy lace bodice, pink pearls, sequins in flower centers, red satin lining, satin red ribbons on skirt bottom and a satin waist band, size 12, c1950.

Lavender nylon full length ball gown, size 10-12 with stole, boned fitted bodice, pin-tucked detail on bodice, very full skirt, fully lined, 'Siltex' garment label, centre zip and triple spaghetti straps, New Zealand, c1950.

NZ$190 - $210   **The Modern Miss, New Zealand**

NZ$230 - $270

NZ$255 - $295

The Modern Miss, New Zealand

The Modern Miss, New Zealand

Ladies full length silk nightie, decorated with pink and blue flowers, size 12, New Zealand, c1950.

NZ$45 - $65   **The Wooden Rose, New Zealand**

Pink floral rayon brocade full length ball gown with velvet flower trim by J. M. Martin of Melbourne, size 8, Australia, c1950.

$275 - $315   **Circa Vintage Clothing, VIC**

French guipure lace cocktail dress silk lined and trim, Australia, c1950.

$360 - $400   **L.A. Design, NSW**

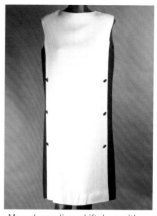

Monochrome linen shift dress with contrasting buttons, size 10, Australia, c1967.

$85 - $105   **Circa Vintage Clothing, VIC**

Essential little black dress, from Georges of Melbourne by Reece, in taffeta with stiffened pleated chiffon decoration on the bodice, Australia, c1980.

$550 - $650   **Seams Old Emporium, VIC**

Size 10-12 black mid calf length draped, Art Deco style inspired dress with Swarovski crystal motifs, long sleeves, asymmetrical draping, side split and an 'Inspirations - Paris' label, France, c1982.

NZ$175 - $195

The Modern Miss, New Zealand

Red satin two piece full length ball gown with black appliqué, empire line dress, spaghetti straps, two side splits below knee, fully stiffened, zip on the back, box top with lace, bead and plastic, floral motif appliqué, front and back and three coloured buttons centre back, c1960.

NZ$240 - $280   **The Modern Miss, New Zealand**

Hot pink spaghetti striped and sequin decoration dress, c1980.

$20 - $30   **The Old Lolly Factory, NSW**

Moss green jumpsuit with suede bust, gold piping and a suede belt with tassels, size 10, Australia, c1980.

$65 - $85   **Moustache Vintage Clothing, VIC**

Red 'Moschino' two piece metallic embroidered red denim suit, Italy, c1982.

$230 - $270   **Gorgeous, VIC**

Homemade pant suit, Australia, c1980.

$70 - $90   **Gorgeous, VIC**

CLOTHING - WOMEN'S

Chinese style cotton print long dress, size 12, Australia, c1970.

$55 - $75   **Clarence Park Bazaar, SA**

Electric blue chiffon cocktail dress, size 8, c1950.

$65 - $85   **Clarence Park Bazaar, SA**

Cotton button-through shift dress, size 14, Australia, c1960.

$45 - $65   **Clarence Park Bazaar, SA**

Lurex cocktail dress, size 12, Australia, c1960.

$65 - $85   **Clarence Park Bazaar, SA**

Black fringe dress styled for 'Carol Lea, Brisbane', with a bugle beaded collar and organza bodice with carnival diamante's, size 12-14, Australia, c1950, 49cm wide, 121cm long.

$85 - $105   **Northside Secondhand Furniture, QLD**

Silver wool dress with metallic sequins and heavy glass beading to the neck line, by Raoul Couture, Melbourne, with fabric by MacLennan and MacLennan, Ltd., Isle of Lewis, size 10-12, Australia, c1960.

$140 - $160

Long, strapless watermelon coloured evening gown, in nylon and tulle fabric, size 10, Australia, c1960.

$230 - $270   **OK WOW, ACT**

Clarence Park Bazaar, SA

'Youthcraft Reg' 50's party dress, size W (14) with raised black felt flowers and coloured sparkles on white rayon.

$150 - $170   **Decades of Fashion, VIC**

Long halter neck, polyester dress with an orange, white and red print, size 10.

$65 - $85   **Clarence Park Bazaar, SA**

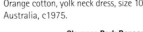

Orange cotton, yolk neck dress, size 10, Australia, c1975.

$65 - $85   **Clarence Park Bazaar, SA**

Yellow linen dress with a lacy overlay, size 8, Australia, c1960.

$75 - $95   **Clarence Park Bazaar, SA**

Full length lurex brocade dress, the bodice embellished with beads and crystals, hand made and fully lined, New Zealand, c1960.

NZ$55 - $75

The Wooden Rose, New Zealand

Black and white checkerboard mini dress, size 8, Australia, c1968.

$55 - $75

Clarence Park Bazaar, SA

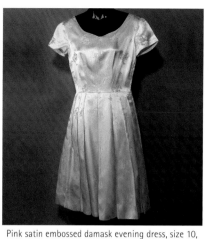

Pink satin embossed damask evening dress, size 10, Australia, c1952.

$110 - $130

Clarence Park Bazaar, SA

Lavender polyester go-go dress, size 10, Australia, c1968.

$110 - $130

Clarence Park Bazaar, SA

'Prue Acton' maxi 'ethnic' wool dress, Australia, c1970.

$140 - $160

Gorgeous, VIC

Two piece lightning bolt knit suit, England, c1970.

$90 - $110

Gorgeous, VIC

Swiss and French lace dress with inset sleeves, c1970.

$150 - $170

Gorgeous, VIC

Pink voile dress, with a short full skirt, c1950.

$20 - $30

The Old Lolly Factory, NSW

Ball gown of watermark taffeta with a bias cut skirt, c1950.

$155 - $175

Pymble Antiques - Linen & Retro, NSW

Navy blue chiffon, long evening dress, size 12, c1960.

$55 - $75

Clarence Park Bazaar, SA

Black floral cotton day dress, size 14, Australia, c1950.

$75 - $95

Clarence Park Bazaar, SA

Cream dragon print caftan, c1960.

$20 - $30   **The Old Lolly Factory, NSW**

Grey and cream satin brocade evening frock, size 8, Australia, c1955.

$175 - $195   **Circa Vintage Clothing, VIC**

Paisley shirt-waister ladies dress, cotton size 12-14, Australia, c1950.

$40 - $50   **Northside Secondhand Furniture, QLD**

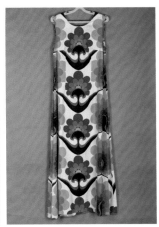

Cotton blue and purple long dress, c1960.

$15 - $25   **The Old Lolly Factory, NSW**

Three piece holiday wear of multicoloured bark cloth cotton skirt, shorts, and top set, size 8, Australia, c1955.

$205 - $245   **Circa Vintage Clothing, VIC**

Sky-blue mid calf length nylon dress, printed with a black and white floral pattern, with a drop waist, rusched centre panel, cap sleeves, square neck and a side zip, size 12, c1950.

NZ$165 - $185   **The Modern Miss, New Zealand**

Size 10-14, light pink night dress with buttons at the top for nursing babies, New Zealand, c1950.

NZ$30 - $40   **Middle Earth Antiques, New Zealand**

Sateen party dress, United States, c1950.

$280 - $320   **L.A. Design, NSW**

Green cotton caftan, free size, Thailand, c1970.

$55 - $75   **Clarence Park Bazaar, SA**

Long purple swirl pattern dress.

$15 - $25   **The Old Lolly Factory, NSW**

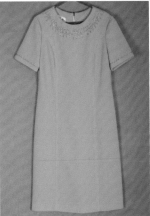

Short blue, chipdew dress with gold lace trim, c1960.

$15 - $25   **The Old Lolly Factory, NSW**

Two piece suit with a panelled skirt and top, with metallic printed stars, made by 'Body Map' London, made with cotton lycra, England, c1980.

$260 - $300

Gorgeous, VIC

Orange metallic dress, size 8 (approx), New Zealand, c1960.

NZ$85 - $105

In Vogue Costumes & Collectables, New Zealand

Diane Tre's dress, polyester georgette, ruched waistband, signature style puffed sleeves and tassels on the front collar, free size, United States, c1985.

$75 - $95

Moustache Vintage Clothing, VIC

Cotton cretonne day dress, Australia, c1950.

$230 - $270

L.A. Design, NSW

Reproduction 1875, two piece bustle, Australia, c1995.

$330 - $370

Christine McKenna, NSW

Pink lace and voile dress, c1960.

$20 - $30

The Old Lolly Factory, NSW

Chocolate brown velvet and gold embroidered caftan, c1970.

$20 - $30

The Old Lolly Factory, NSW

Blue and white floral dress, c1950.

$115 - $135

Classic Vintage, NSW

Raw silk ballerina length gown, c1950.

$85 - $105

Pymble Antiques - Linen & Retro, NSW

Reproduction of an 1835 day dress with imbecile sleeves, Australia, c2006.

$230 - $270

Christine McKenna, NSW

Pink crimplene and lace dress, c1960.

$15 - $25

The Old Lolly Factory, NSW

CLOTHING - WOMEN'S

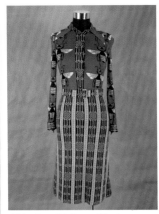

Polyester print dress with a bee design by Argos Dini, size 10–12, Italy, c1970.

$155 - $175

OK WOW, ACT

Yellow and white floral dress, c1950.

$85 - $105

Classic Vintage, NSW

Black cotton polyester bow dress, size 12, Australia, c1963.

$110 - $130

Clarence Park Bazaar, SA

Green tulle and moss green brocade satin ball gown, label 'I. M. Martin' with a tulle skirt and sash, bar feature, size 10, Australia, c1955.

$275 - $315

Shag, VIC

Chiffon pleated and waisted dress, in autumn tonings, c1980.

$10 - $20

The Old Lolly Factory, NSW

California country dress, rouched upper sheer cotton, checked, floor length, size 10–12, United States, c1970.

$65 - $85

Shappere, VIC

Psychedelic full length dress, size 12, Australia, c1970.

$80 - $100

Newport Temple Antiques, VIC

Pink chenille dressing gown, size 12, Australia, c1950.

$45 - $55

Newport Temple Antiques, VIC

Halter neck, button front long dress in sparkly polyester by 'Anda Fashions Melbourne' (size XXSW bust 32 in., waist 24 in., hips 34 in.), Australia, c1970.

$200 - $240

frhapsody, WA

Evening or cocktail dress once the property of Hollywood great June Allyson, by Beverley Hills designer Howard Shoupe, in tulle decorated with pearl lustre applique, United States, c1954.

$1000 - $1200

Seams Old Emporium, VIC

Embroidered dress with peasant inspired sleeves and collar, by St Tropez International Australia, black cotton, size 8, Australia, c1971.

$75 - $95

Gorgeous, VIC

Polyester body shirt, by iconic Australian fashion designer Prue Acton, featuring French language print, size 14, Australia, c1970.

$75 - $95

OK WOW, ACT

Original cotton printed blouse, featuring Spanish dancers and bars, size 12, Spain, c1950.

$25 - $35

Chapel Street Bazaar, VIC

Pink nylon shirt from the 'Clothing Company' with a tie front and fabric covered buttons, size 16, bust 38in., waist 30in., hips 40in., Australia, c1970, 70cm long.

$100 - $120

frhapsody, WA

Cotton size 10 print bikini by Rose Marie Reid, a Hickory product, Australia, c1950.

$140 - $160

OK WOW, ACT

Nylon bikini, by Jantzen, size 14, United States, c1960.

$120 - $140

OK WOW, ACT

Bri-nylon and lycra, two piece gingham pattern swimsuit by Miss Jantzen, size 36in. (approx size 8-10), Australia, c1967.

$110 - $130

frhapsody, WA

Pure silk print dress by Baker of Melbourne, size 8, Australia, c1950.

$140 - $160

OK WOW, ACT

Puppy knit U.S.A. acrylic 'Whimsey', United States, c1975.

$75 - $95

Gorgeous, VIC

'Watersun' cotton halter neck bathers with shirred back panel, size 36 (12-14), Australia, c1960.

$40 - $50

Womango, VIC

Purple bri-nylon ladies bathing suit by 'Ada of California', size 12, United States, c1958.

$75 - $95

Circa Vintage Clothing, VIC

COSTUME & DRESSING ACCESSORIES

Black ribbed wool coat with wrap over skirt and black rabbit collar, approximate size 10–12, label for 'Leon Cutler Model New York and Sydney, Pure New Wool', Australia, c1972.

$310 - $350

Circa Vintage Clothing, VIC

Nylon negligee set, England, c1960.

$65 - $85

Southern Antique Centre, NSW

Cotton lavender shirt dress with white buttons, flower motif, two inset pockets, elbow length sleeves with cuffs and two buttons and a 'Covergirl of New Zealand' label, size 8, New Zealand, c1950.

NZ$155 - $175

The Modern Miss, New Zealand

'Biba' jacquard jacket, England, c1970.

$330 - $370

L.A. Design, NSW

Black and white travel cape, Australia, c1960.

$200 - $240

L.A. Design, NSW

Black and white houndstooth cape, England, c1960.

$230 - $270

L.A. Design, NSW

Floral print velvet jacket by 'Fanny Adams', size 8, England, c1970.

$55 - $75

Curve, VIC

Lady's lined green check woollen coat, Australia, c1960.

$40 - $60

Newport Temple Antiques, VIC

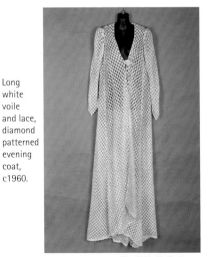

Long white voile and lace, diamond patterned evening coat, c1960.

$30 - $40

The Old Lolly Factory, NSW

Cream and brown frilled ankle length prairie dress, size XS, Australia, c1975.

$65 - $85   **Moustache Vintage Clothing, VIC**

Pure linen sun dress, with cotton daisy trim, size 12-14, Australia, c1950.

$100 - $120   **Circa Vintage Clothing, VIC**

Blue rayon day dress, size 8, Australia, c1940.

$75 - $95   **Clarence Park Bazaar, SA**

Pure wool dress by Tricosa, Paris, size 12-14, France, c1960.

$85 - $105   **OK WOW, ACT**

Pucci-style halter neck, with a lycra bustier top and black skirt, size 10, Australia.

$55 - $75   **Moustache Vintage Clothing, VIC**

Long dress with tie, in sparkly polyester by 'Maxine' (size XW, bust 40in, waist 32in., hip 42in.), Australia, c1970, 139cm long.

$175 - $195   **frhapsody, WA**

Nylon floral dress, size 10 (bust 90cm, hip 110cm), Australia, c1960, 90cm high, 110cm wide.

$45 - $65   **Northside Secondhand Furniture, QLD**

Long turquoise crimplene dress, with long pleated white sleeves, c1970.

$15 - $25   **The Old Lolly Factory, NSW**

Pale mauve, lace-over-taffeta long dress, c1970.

$15 - $25   **The Old Lolly Factory, NSW**

Turquoise dress with bronze sequin detail, c1970.

$20 - $30   **The Old Lolly Factory, NSW**

Pale blue nylon party dress, size 8, Australia, c1950.

$65 - $85   **Clarence Park Bazaar, SA**

COSTUME & DRESSING ACCESSORIES

Mid calf length, size 10 (old size 12), heavily printed cotton, abstract patterned frock in jade, orange and grey with short sleeves fitted bodice, three buttons to the front and labelled 'Crisp and Cool' for D.I.C, New Zealand, c1950.

NZ$140 - $160

The Modern Miss, New Zealand

Peach cotton blend day dress by 'Kortex', size 8, Australia, c1950.

$50 - $70

Curve, VIC

Olive knee length day dress, size 12 with a wide neckline, satin bias trim, three quarter sleeves, stiff cotton underskirt, slightly high waisted, and a centre back zip, 'Wendy – The Heart of Fashion' label, c1950.

NZ$155 - $175

The Modern Miss, New Zealand

'Sportshirt' yellow floral dress, Australia, c1950.

$85 - $105

Classic Vintage, NSW

Black and white wool dress with heart shaped buttons, size 10, Australia, c1970.

$75 - $95

Moustache Vintage Clothing, VIC

Cotton day dress, pink and white starburst print, size 10, Australia, c1950.

$65 - $85

Clarence Park Bazaar, SA

Purple and white dress, c1950.

$85 - $105

Classic Vintage, NSW

Home sewn colourful dress with gold appliqué and a bow belt, size 10, Australia.

$75 - $95

Moustache Vintage Clothing, VIC

Red ankle length dress with ruffled sleeves, size 8, Australia, c1960.

$85 - $105

Moustache Vintage Clothing, VIC

Cotton velveteen mini dress with covered buttons and ivory piping, size 8, Australia, c1975.

$65 - $85

Moustache Vintage Clothing, VIC

Merivale silk dress with a floral pattern, size 8, c1970.

$75 - $95

Moustache Vintage Clothing, VIC

Machine embroidered, long denim skirt, size 8-10, c1970.

$100 - $120   **OK WOW, ACT**

Pink cotton rock 'n' roll skirt, size 10.

$65 - $85   **Clarence Park Bazaar, SA**

Lady's green and red seersucker pants, c1970.

$15 - $25   **The Old Lolly Factory, NSW**

Original brown lace cocktail dress with a matching brown boa, Australia, c1950.

$75 - $95   **Southside Antiques Centre, QLD**

Pint taffeta frock in purple and pink, size 12 with a fitted bodice, princess line, V cross over neck, drop waist, tiered skirt, black velvet ribbon and a rose motif, New Zealand, c1950.

NZ$165 - $185   **The Modern Miss, New Zealand**

Mini dress with chiffon sleeves in a matching pattern, size 10, United States, c1970.

$55 - $75   **Moustache Vintage Clothing, VIC**

Pink and white pleated skirt dress, c1950.

$10 - $20   **The Old Lolly Factory, NSW**

Pink pleated dress with a lace bodice, size 12, Australia, c1950.

$40 - $60   **Newport Temple Antiques, VIC**

Cream striped leg warmers, c1980.

$5 - $13   **The Old Lolly Factory, NSW**

Blue, grey and cream leg warmers, c1980.

$5 - $15   **The Old Lolly Factory, NSW**

Yellow dress, size 10, Australia, c1950.

$45 - $65   **Newport Temple Antiques, VIC**

FURS

Cream imitation mink coat, c1970.

$40 - $50   **The Old Lolly Factory, NSW**

Nylon fur ladies coat, size 14, England, c1960.

$45 - $55   **Newport Temple Antiques, VIC**

Brown musquash fur coat, c1970.

$75 - $95   **The Old Lolly Factory, NSW**

White and brown lapin coat, c1970.

$45 - $65   **The Old Lolly Factory, NSW**

Fox fur coat.

$170 - $190   **The Old Lolly Factory, NSW**

Silver fake fur ladies jacket, size 14, Australia, c1950.

$15 - $25   **Newport Temple Antiques, VIC**

Red Fox cape with small hand pockets, Australia, c1950.

$250 - $290   **Patti K Temporary Interiors, VIC**

White rabbit fur cape, shaped and slightly fitted, longer at the back, France.

NZ$230 - $270   **In Vogue Costumes & Collectables, New Zealand**

Brown imitation seal skin coat, c1970.

$45 - $65   **The Old Lolly Factory, NSW**

Fake fur ladies coat, size 14, Australia, c1950.

$40 - $50   **Newport Temple Antiques, VIC**

Magid beaded handbag, Japan, 12cm high.

$230 - $270 — **Victor Harbour Antiques - Mittagong, NSW**

Gold Glomesh bag with a feature clasp with diamantes, snake chain and grosgrain tan lining, labelled 'Whiting and Davis', New Zealand, c1965, 12cm high, 19cm long.

NZ$85 - $105 — **The Modern Miss, New Zealand**

Gold tone mesh ladies purse with a diamante clasp, labelled with 'Made in USA, Duramesh', c1950, 14cm high, 19cm wide.

$55 - $75 — **Northumberland Antiques & Restorations, NSW**

Diamante evening purse with silver plate mounts and charm, c1950, 10cm high.

$85 - $105 — **Lancaster's Toowoomba Antique Centre, QLD**

Pastel beaded and sequined evening bag with a white satin lining, gold clasp and surround diamantes inserted in the catch, labelled 'A Product of Beverley Audair Ltd. Glen Innes, Auckland', New Zealand, c1960, 13cm high, 26cm long.

NZ$120 - $140 — **The Modern Miss, New Zealand**

'Glowmesh' evening bag by Glo International, Sydney, Australia, c1971.

$45 - $65 — **Patti K Temporary Interiors, VIC**

Stratton 'fitted' evening purse with compacts and lipstick, England, c1950.

$140 - $160 — **Malvern Antique Market, VIC**

Chunky chain and teak wood handled 'Oroton' purse/bag, Germany, c1969, 20cm long.

$110 - $130 — **Gorgeous, VIC**

Whiting and Davis, gold mesh evening bag, United States, c1970, 16cm high, 21cm wide.

NZ$100 - $120 — **Glenis Parker, New Zealand**

Oroton crystal diamante evening bag, in silver toned metal, c1970.

NZ$230 - $270 — **In Vogue Costumes & Collectables, New Zealand**

HANDBAGS & PURSES

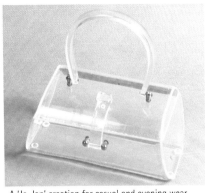

A 'Jo-Jan' creation for casual and evening wear, clear Lucite evening bag. Jo-Jan is a division of Nu Craft Industries, an early plastics manufacturer, United States, c1950, 10cm high, 10cm wide, 20cm long.

$140 - $160

Curve,
VIC

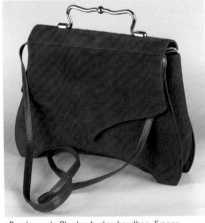

Purple suede Charles Jordan handbag, France, c1985, 22cm high.

$375 - $415

Chapel Street Bazaar,
VIC

Charles Kahn handbag with a Lucite handle, plastic over bullion embroidered satin and original comb and mirror inside, United States, c1955, 24cm high, 32cm wide.

$155 - $175

Chapel Street Bazaar,
VIC

'Clothfair' gold lame handbag, England, c1950, 13cm high, 27cm long.

$55 - $75

Classic Vintage,
NSW

Lucite box handbag with cut-out metal details, United States, c1950, 25cm high, 10.5cm wide, 19.5cm long.

$255 - $295

Retro Active,
VIC

Acrylic handbag, pearlised with coloured confetti with clear Lucite lid and handle, the lid decorated with diamantes to the top and sides, with 'Nelson Originals' label, United States, c1952, 24cm high, 24cm long, 11.5cm deep.

$770 - $870

Margo Richards Antiques,
NSW

Plastic weave and black patent leather handbag, United States, c1959, 9cm high, 23cm wide, 9cm deep.

$135 - $155

Chapel Street Bazaar,
VIC

Gold embroidered purse with the initial 'L', c1950, 12cm high, 22cm long.

$30 - $40

Classic Vintage,
NSW

White lucite handbag, United States, c1970.

$355 - $395

Victor Harbour Antiques -
Mittagong, NSW

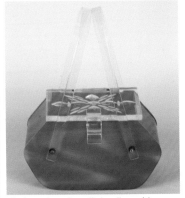

Amber coloured acrylic handbag with a clear Lucite carved lid and handles, United States, c1950, 22cm high, 10cm wide, 18.5cm long.

$400 - $440

Margo Richards Antiques,
NSW

Goanna skin evening bag, Australia, 10cm high, 8cm wide, 20cm long.

$100 - $120

Curve, VIC

Large leather and canvas handbag, Italy, c1970, 26cm high, 32cm wide.

$135 - $155

Chapel Street Bazaar, VIC

Immaculate sequin and felt decorated, hessian covered shopping bag, United States, c1960, 24cm high, 33cm wide.

$115 - $135

Chapel Street Bazaar, VIC

Linen and plastic collage handbag with a metal clasp, a picture of a horse and jockey on a mock newspaper background with inserts of velvet, beads and diamantes, all covered in clear plastic, c1960, 27cm high, 34cm long.

NZ$110 - $130

The Modern Miss, New Zealand

Crocodile skin handbag with original clasp and fittings, Australia, c1950, 27cm high, 24cm wide, 8cm deep.

$305 - $345

Eliza Jane Antiques, NSW

Basket purse with brown leather trim, Hong Kong, 15cm high, 12cm wide, 18cm long.

$55 - $75

Moustache Vintage Clothing, VIC

Box style handbag, decorated with twigs and leaves, United States, c1960, 24cm high, 18cm wide, 18cm long.

$150 - $170

Rosebud Antiques, NSW

'Cherie' brand vinyl handbag, c1980, 30cm long.

$55 - $75

Rosebud Antiques, NSW

Cowhide shoulder bag, Australia, c1975, 30cm high.

$50 - $70

Chapel Street Bazaar, VIC

Brown ostrich skin handbag, South Africa, c1960, 28cm high, 22cm long, 8cm deep.

$530 - $630

Rosebud Antiques, NSW

HANDBAGS & PURSES

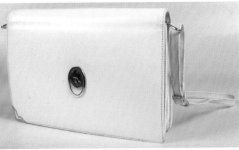

White leather Christian Dior handbag, stamped 'Made in France', c1970, 17cm high, 26cm long, 5cm deep.

$460 - $500

Rosebud Antiques, NSW

Vinyl mock crocodile print handbag with original internal and separate coin purse, England, c1948, 22cm high, 33cm wide.

$115 - $135

Chapel Street Bazaar, VIC

Cane handbag with a leather handle, Hong Kong, c1950, 18cm high, 22cm wide, 9cm deep.

$70 - $90

Dr Russell's Emporium, WA

Tooled leather handbag, Spain, c1950, 26cm high, 32cm wide.

$60 - $80

Chapel Street Bazaar, VIC

Velvet covered handbag with beaded decoration, United States, c1950, 30cm high, 30cm long, 7cm deep.

$135 - $155

Rosebud Antiques, NSW

A decoupage decorated box purse with quilted interior, United States, c1970, 15cm high, 23cm wide, 15cm deep.

$185 - $205

Rosebud Antiques, NSW

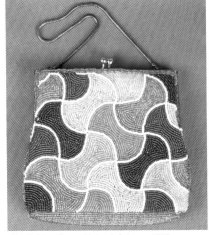

Beaded handbag with 'snake' strap, c1950.

$80 - $100

Circa Vintage Clothing, VIC

Tooled leather bag with a long shoulder strap and horse motif, United States, c1975, 20cm high, 8cm wide, 25cm long.

$55 - $75

Moustache Vintage Clothing, VIC

Crocodile skin clutch purse, c1970, 15cm high, 28cm long.

$430 - $470

Rosebud Antiques, NSW

White mesh shoulder bag with a silver plate clasp and trim and the original woven tag, 'Glomesh, made in Australia', c1979, 14cm wide, 23cm long, 4cm deep.

$25 - $35

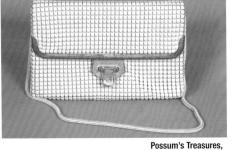

Possum's Treasures, QLD

Crochet beaded clutch purse, in unusual green colour, Italy, c1960, 13cm wide, 21cm long.

$40 - $60

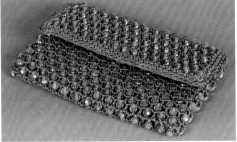

Shag, VIC

Burnt orange wool Trilby hat, Australia, c1970.

$40 - $50   **Clarence Park Bazaar, SA**

Straw hat with flower trim, England, c1950.

$80 - $100   **L.A. Design, NSW**

Ladies straw hat, Australia, c1960.

$40 - $50   **Clarence Park Bazaar, SA**

Brown felt hat with rust rose and chiffon trim, New Zealand.

NZ$40 - $60   **Country Charm Antiques, New Zealand**

Ladies hat with applied flowers, c1950.

$50 - $70   **Gumnut Antiques & Old Wares, NSW**

Cloche style hat, 'Dana-Marte original', United States, c1970.

$55 - $75   **Love Vintage, NSW**

Bow cocktail hat, France, c1950.

$85 - $105   **L.A. Design, NSW**

Grey coloured straw hat with satin trim, c1980.

$10 - $20   **The Old Lolly Factory, NSW**

Blue hat, c1950.

$15 - $25   **The Old Lolly Factory, NSW**

White netted cocktail hat, c1980.

$10 - $20   **The Old Lolly Factory, NSW**

COSTUME & DRESSING ACCESSORIES

Hat of champagne coloured organza, Australia, c1950, 23cm high, 25cm diam.

$55 - $75   **Northside Secondhand Furniture, QLD**

Black straw hat, c1950.

$8 - $18   **The Old Lolly Factory, NSW**

Men's checked woollen hat, Australia, c1950.

$25 - $35   **Clarence Park Bazaar, SA**

Stetson hat decorated with real pheasant wings, with manufacturer's label 'John B. Stetson Company three x Beaver', United States.

$185 - $205   **M J Durand, VIC**

Hat in lavender velvet with a purple feather trim, Australia, c1970, 10cm high, 22cm diam.

$40 - $50   **The New Farm Antique Centre, QLD**

Cream lace hat, c1960.

$8 - $18   **The Old Lolly Factory, NSW**

Mohair pillar-box hat, c1960.

$8 - $18   **The Old Lolly Factory, NSW**

Green felt 'pill box' hat, Australia, c1950, 8cm high, 18cm diam.

$55 - $75   **Northside Secondhand Furniture, QLD**

Black pill box with rose trim, New Zealand.

NZ$40 - $60   **Country Charm Antiques, New Zealand**

Pale blue picture hat with fabric floral trim, Australia, c1950.

$75 - $95   **Circa Vintage Clothing, VIC**

New 'Australian' green Akubra fur felt hat, marked 'McLeods Men's Store, Brisbane', Australia, c1960.

$80 - $100   **Baxter's Antiques, QLD**

Brown taffeta hat, c1950.

Yellow straw hat with eau-de-nil trim, plus full blown rose, c1950, 33cm wide.

NZ$50 - $70   **Country Charm Antiques, New Zealand**

$60 - $80   **OK WOW, ACT**

'Twiggy' lemon hat, c1960.

$10 - $20   **The Old Lolly Factory, NSW**

'Mr. Individual' cloche hat, c1960.

$185 - $205   **Classic Vintage, NSW**

Decorative hat made by Martina Exclusive Millinery, Prop. Gwen Holland, Australia, c1950.

$30 - $40   **Patti K Temporary Interiors, VIC**

Hand made purple and pink cotton organza ruched on bucrum hat, Australia, c1960, 15cm high, 18.5cm diam.

$40 - $50   **Possum's Treasures, QLD**

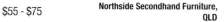

Black wool and feather hat, 'Huckel' brand, England, c1950, 13cm high, 18.5cm diam.

$55 - $75   **Northside Secondhand Furniture, QLD**

Cream floppy weave hat, c1960.

$8 - $18   **The Old Lolly Factory, NSW**

Cream feather-trim hat.

$20 - $30   **The Old Lolly Factory, NSW**

SHOES

Men's 'Tom Cat' fur loafers, size 10, England, c1960.

$45 - $65

Clarence Park Bazaar, SA

Charles Jourdan metallic wedge sandal, unworn size 8, France, 6cm high.

$110 - $130

Curve, VIC

Red leather platform shoes, size 7.5, Australia, c1974.

$40 - $50

Clarence Park Bazaar, SA

Hot pink leather plumps with stiletto heels, pointed toes and blue, jade and yellow inserts, size 6 1/2 B, label 'Sacha, London', England, c1980.

NZ$135 - $155

The Modern Miss, New Zealand

Size 6 1/2 stilettos with gold leather uppers, sling back, woven detail and moulded plastic heels, labelled 'Deluxe', New Zealand, c1950.

NZ$165 - $185

The Modern Miss, New Zealand

J. B. Martin all leather knee high boot with stacked heel, size 7 1/2, France, c1975.

$140 - $160

Curve, VIC

Violet knee high lace-up boots with original laces, vinyl lining, plastic block heels and round toes, size 8, labelled 'Dolcis', c1970.

NZ$165 - $185

The Modern Miss, New Zealand

Union made tall blue suede dress cowgirl boots, white, stitched detail, leather upper, size 6B, United States, c1980.

$220 - $260

Shappere, VIC

Via Spiga flat cream leather boots with a real snake skin panel running down front of boot, size 9, Italy, c1980.

$230 - $270

Shappere, VIC

Green leather platforms with faux cork heels (fabric), labelled 'Bruno Manetto', size 6B, New Zealand, c1970.

NZ$115 - $135

The Modern Miss, New Zealand

Green leather sandals by Charles Jourdan, Paris, size 4, France, c1970.

$140 - $160

OK WOW, ACT

Boxed cream mules with moulded honey colour stiletto heels, vinyl and mesh uppers, scallop detailing and a bow, size 7 1/2-8, labelled 'Foxy', New Zealand.

NZ$140 - $160   **The Modern Miss, New Zealand**

Gold glitter shoes with sling backs, brocade heels and heavily glittered vinyl uppers, size 7, labelled 'Deluxe', New Zealand, c1960.

Black platform leather shoes, size 10, Australia, c1970.

$65 - $85   **Clarence Park Bazaar, SA**

Pair of black leather riding boots, size 7.5, c1950.

NZ$645 - $745   **Auburn Antiques, New Zealand**

NZ$115 - $135   **The Modern Miss, New Zealand**

Black suede shoes, size 6, Italy, c1950.

$30 - $40   **Womango, VIC**

Suede maroon and brown pumps, size 7 'Qualtro', United States, c1960.

$85 - $105   **Gorgeous, VIC**

Leopard skin high heel ladies shoes.

$75 - $95   **369 Antiques, VIC**

Wooden platform shoes with woven uppers and studs, size 7.5, Brazil, c1970.

$55 - $75   **Moustache Vintage Clothing, VIC**

Charles Jordan purple suede shoes, France, c1985.

Pair of snake skin and leather cowboy boots, United States, c1980.

$275 - $315   **Goodwood House Antiques, WA**

$275 - $315   **Chapel Street Bazaar, VIC**

Silver and gold Go-Go ankle boots with two inch heel, size 7, United Kingdom, c1960.

$75 - $95   **Moustache Vintage Clothing, VIC**

COSTUME & DRESSING ACCESSORIES

'Essilor' metal sunglasses with case and cloth, France, c1970, 5cm high, 14cm wide.

$115 - $135

Chapel Street Bazaar, VIC

Tortoise 'Sungard' sunglasses with glass lenses and a case, Australia, c1970, 6cm high, 14cm wide.

$55 - $75

Chapel Street Bazaar, VIC

Pair of 'UFO' reflector sunglasses, Australia, c1980, 6cm high, 10cm wide.

$20 - $30

Curve, VIC

Pair of 'New Wave' plastic sunglasses, Australia, c1980, 5cm high, 12cm wide.

$30 - $40

Curve, VIC

White pearlite sunglasses, France, c1960, 13cm wide.

$105 - $125

Chapel Street Bazaar, VIC

Ski glass mirror lens sunglasses, 'Tous Temps', with case and cloth, France, c1970, 6cm high, 14cm wide.

$100 - $120

Chapel Street Bazaar, VIC

Pair of sunglasses, in original case, United States, c1950, 7cm high, 16cm long.

$35 - $45

Marsteen Collectables, VIC

1950's sunglasses, tortoiseshell frames with diamantes, France, 14cm wide.

$135 - $155

Retro Active, VIC

Pair of pink celluloid framed sunglasses, United States, c1950.

$85 - $105

Retro Active, VIC

Original 1950's cats eyes sunglasses with black and silver plastic frames, gold details and diamantes, France.

$255 - $295

Retro Active, VIC

Original fifties sunglasses, with pearly grey frames, carved detailing and diamantes, France, c1950.

$275 - $315

Retro Active, VIC

Belt buckle of playing cards, in chrome plated brass, England, c1950, 8cm high, 8cm wide, 8cm diam.

$70 - $90

Dr Russell's Emporium, WA

Hand made African mask buckle, Australia, c1955, 8cm long.

$30 - $40

Womango, VIC

Pair of large celluloid tight top buttons, c1960, 4cm diam.

$15 - $25

Sew Yesterday, NSW

Child's school uniform, size 28 with a black dress and a Panama hat, New Zealand, c1950.

NZ$70 - $90

Middle Earth Antiques, New Zealand

Very heavy hand woven, shaggy sleeveless jacket in wool, open front style, unisex, one size fits all, Australia, c1965, 90cm long.

$380 - $420

frhapsody, WA

Compact in the form of a basket with a pretty floral Lucite top and a handle that swings independently, England, c1955, 4cm high, 5.5cm diam.

$40 - $50

Chapel Street Bazaar, VIC

Lucite central emblem, 'Le Rage' compact, England, c1958, 8cm diam.

$45 - $55

Chapel Street Bazaar, VIC

Compact in the shape of a handbag and covered in Lurex material, by Pygmalion, England, c1960, 5cm high, 7cm wide.

$35 - $45

Chapel Street Bazaar, VIC

Stratton compact, of black and white enamel painted leaves to the front of compact, England, c1958, 7.5cm diam.

$45 - $55

Chapel Street Bazaar, VIC

Kigu compact with a Lucite centre, depicting daisies, England, c1955, 8cm diam.

$45 - $55

Chapel Street Bazaar, VIC

Boxed set of make up including two New Zealand eye shadows, foundation, skin tone, milk cleanser, lipstick, velva cream, flexi disc and instructions, Australia.

NZ$275 - $315

The Modern Miss, New Zealand

'Le Rage' powder compact with appointment diary on the front, England, c1950, 10cm diam.

NZ$115 - $135

Gales Antiques, New Zealand

COSTUME & DRESSING ACCESSORIES

Matson rose gold gilded vanity mirror, England, c1950, 25cm high, 16cm wide.

$55 - $75

Helen's On The Bay, QLD

Cufflinks with 'White' sewing machine, made by Kinney & Co., United States, c1950.

$55 - $75

Retro Active, VIC

Boxed original three piece petit-pointe dressing table set, England, c1955.

$100 - $120

Womango, VIC

Box of six Eva Gabor design hair wiglets, South Korea, c1976.

$30 - $40

Chapel Street Bazaar, VIC

Boxed dressing table set, hand engraved with birds, England, c1950, 21cm wide, 30cm long, 7cm deep.

NZ$190 - $210

Ascot Collectables, New Zealand

Lambs wool body powder puff pink plastic, c1950, 5cm high, 12cm wide, 27cm.

$75 - $95

Southside Antiques Centre, QLD

Pair of black ladies kid gloves, size 7.5, Italy, c1950.

NZ$20 - $30

Maison Jolie, New Zealand

Original 'Samsonite' leather suitcase from Denver, Colorado, by Shwader Bros, Style 4939, United States, c1950, 74.5cm high, 54cm wide, 23cm deep.

$355 - $395

Etching House, NSW

Travel bag with assorted travel decals, Australia, c1950.

$45 - $65

Wooden Pew Antiques, VIC

Scenic shopping basket, made of stiffened plastic with woven edges and handles, Australia, 45cm high, 22cm deep.

$30 - $40

Cobweb Collectables, NSW

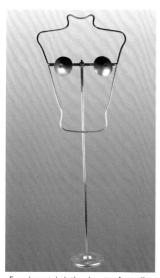

Female metal clothes hanger, Australia, c1950, 116cm high, 42cm wide.

$125 - $145 **Step Back Antiques, VIC**

Wire male mannequin, Australia, c1950, 67cm high, 43cm wide.

$125 - $145 **Step Back Antiques, VIC**

Reproduction Art Deco mannequin, Germany, c1990, 68cm high, 39cm wide, 16cm deep.

$475 - $515 **Wooden Pew Antiques, VIC**

Dressmaker's dummy, in red and black material on a wooden base, c1950, 180cm high, 39cm wide.

$310 - $350 **The Rustic Rose, VIC**

Boxed men's razor made by 'Leresche', France, c1950, 9.5cm long.

$40 - $60 **The Mill Markets, VIC**

'The Dandy Gift Casket' from Priestleys of Melbourne, gentleman's shaving kit containing a shaving stick, styptic pencil and Brilliantine, all in the original packaging, Australia, c1950, 4cm high, 14cm wide, 16cm long.

$40 - $60 **Mt Dandenong Antique Centre, VIC**

Ladies cut glass manicure set, Germany, c1955.

$85 - $105 **Womango, VIC**

Palmolive men's shaving cosmetic kit, Australia, c1950, 14.5cm high.

$25 - $35 **Maryborough Station Antique Emporium, VIC**

Rabaldo 'Dominator' electric razor with original box and documentation, England.

$100 - $120 **The Mill Markets, VIC**

Mitchem lavender 'Imperial' formula perfume bottle, United States, c1960, 6.5cm high, 3.5cm wide.

NZ$15 - $25 **Glenis Parker, New Zealand**

Glass perfume bottle with stopper, original sticker and signed 'Orrefors' to the base, Sweden, c1979, 10.5cm high.

$45 - $55

frhapsody, WA

Signed Mdina perfume bottle with stopper, European, c1960, 15cm high, 9cm diam.

$165 - $185

Obsidian Antiques, NSW

Peach glass perfume bottle, c1960, 14cm high.

$85 - $105

Womango, VIC

Silver cachous (pascall) perfume bottle with a lock of hair inside, c1960, 7.5cm high, 5.5cm wide.

NZ$25 - $35

Glenis Parker, New Zealand

'Tiara' perfume and bottle, c1960, 7cm high, 5cm wide.

NZ$20 - $30

Glenis Parker, New Zealand

Reversible navy and white shape head scarf, c1960.

$5 - $10

The Old Lolly Factory, NSW

Satin acetate scarf with hand rolled edges, Japan, c1969, 65cm wide, 65cm long.

$35 - $45

frhapsody, WA

Satin acetate scarf with hand rolled edges and a Scandinavian style floral pattern, Japan, c1969, 76cm wide, 76cm long.

$35 - $45

frhapsody, WA

St Michael rayon twill scarf with fringed ends, made for Marks and Spencer, Italy, c1967, 31cm wide, 138cm long.

$40 - $50

frhapsody, WA

Acetate scarf with a bold orange and brown flower pattern, Italy, c1969, 67cm wide, 67cm long.

$40 - $50

frhapsody, WA

Marbleised Bakelite expanding bracelet, c1950.

$55 - $75   **Collectors' Cottage Antiques, NSW**

Domino resin bracelet, Germany, c1950, 4cm high, 7cm diam.

$170 - $190   **b bold - 20th Century Furniture & Effects, VIC**

Two bangles, signed 'Givenchy, Paris', France, c1950.

$80 - $100   **L.A. Design, NSW**

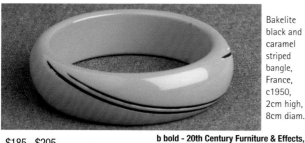

Bakelite black and caramel striped bangle, France, c1950, 2cm high, 8cm diam.

$185 - $205   **b bold - 20th Century Furniture & Effects, VIC**

'United Nations' bracelet of enamelled continents on gold plated bracelet, with a United Nations flag, United States, c1955, 24cm long.

$60 - $80   **Merry's Jewels & Collectables, TAS**

Diamante bracelet, c1950.

NZ$65 - $85   **In Vogue Costumes & Collectables, New Zealand**

Diamante bracelet, England, c1950, 19cm long.

NZ$85 - $105   **Ascot Collectables, New Zealand**

Diamante bracelet, England, c1950, 4cm wide, 19cm long.

NZ$115 - $135   **Ascot Collectables, New Zealand**

Venetian oval mosaic brooch, finely detailed, Italy, c1950, 3cm wide, 4.5cm long.

NZ$85 - $105   **The Wooden Rose, New Zealand**

Brooch featuring an African drummer design, Italy, c1950.

$140 - $160   **Steven Sher Antiques, WA**

COSTUME JEWELLERY

Six white enamel hearts brooch, by Danish silversmith Volmer Bahner, Denmark, c1950, 3cm wide.

$130 - $150
Merry's Jewels & Collectables, TAS

White glass brooch by Coro, United States, c1950, 6cm wide.

$55 - $75
Chapel Street Bazaar, VIC

Enamel flower brooch, United States, c1950, 4.5cm long.

$70 - $90
L.A. Design, NSW

Bakelite brooch of west highland terrier with moveable head, England, c1950, 6cm high, 5cm wide.

$65 - $85
Marsteen Collectables, VIC

Champagne aurora crystal brooch, Australia, c1950, 7cm long.

$40 - $50
Womango, VIC

Flannel flower enamel and rhinestone brooch, by Jewel Crest, United States, c1955, 6cm wide.

$55 - $75
Chapel Street Bazaar, VIC

Costume jewellery spider brooch with diamante legs, c1950, 3cm wide, 4.5cm long.

$55 - $75
Gumleaf Antiques, NSW

Bar brooch with sewing notions on tape measure, England, c1950, 5cm wide.

NZ$40 - $50
Ascot Collectables, New Zealand

Sterling silver and marcasite spray of flowers brooch, England, c1950, 5cm wide.

$60 - $80
Debbie Pech, VIC

Bakelite brooch of bulldog's head, England, c1950, 6cm high, 5.5cm wide.

$65 - $85

Marsteen Collectables, VIC

Costume jewellery brooch with rhinestones, Australia, c1950, 6cm high, 6cm long, 6cm diam.

$50 - $70

Dr Russell's Emporium, WA

Original Simpson signed floral silver and diamante brooch, Australia, c1952, 7cm wide.

$70 - $90

Malvern Antique Market, VIC

Unusual brooch, featuring an Aborigine with tribal weapons, marked EA Australia, c1950, 4cm high, 3cm long, 3cm diam.

$90 - $110

Dr Russell's Emporium, WA

Glass bead necklace of birds and fruit with matching clip-on earrings, Italy, c1950.

$230 - $270

Retro Active, VIC

Crystal and diamante collar necklace, England, c1950, 33cm long.

NZ$330 - $370

Sue Todd Antiques Collectables, New Zealand

European white glass bead choker, c1950.

$65 - $85

Retro Active, VIC

Blue shell costume jewellery necklace, c1950, 30cm long.

$30 - $40

Dr Russell's Emporium, WA

Diamante necklace and clip-on earring set, England, c1950, 43cm long.

NZ$140 - $160

Ascot Collectables, New Zealand

COSTUME JEWELLERY

Souvenir necklace, paua shell set in resin, the centre showing a mountain scene, New Zealand, c1950, 3cm wide, 3.5cm long.

NZ$20 - $30

The Wooden Rose, New Zealand

Cream plastic terrier dog key chain or pendant, c1950.

$20 - $30

Possum's Treasures, QLD

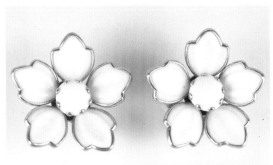

Lucite clip-on ear bobs by Coro, United States, c1950, 3cm wide.

$45 - $65

Chapel Street Bazaar, VIC

Aurora three strand crystal necklace in champagne, Austria, c1950.

$130 - $150

Womango, VIC

Hollywood gold chunky rose necklace, 35cm diameter roses, c1950.

$140 - $160

Gorgeous, VIC

Rhinestone waterfall necklace, c1950, 32cm long.

$110 - $130

L.A. Design, NSW

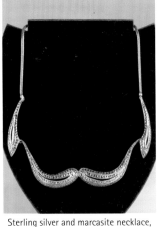

Double strand Aurora Borealis, clear crystal beads, Austria, c1950, 47cm long.

$85 - $105

Out of the Ark, ACT

Sterling silver and marcasite necklace, Germany, c1950.

$135 - $155

Antiques & Collectables On Moorabool, VIC

Aurora Borealis rhinestone necklace with gold tone backing, Austria, c1950, 40cm.

$55 - $75

Out of the Ark, ACT

Black and white graduated glass bead with a gold-toned clasp, c1950, 60cm long.

$40 - $50

**Northside Secondhand Furniture,
QLD**

Bakelite pendant, United States, c1950, 8cm long.

$155 - $175

**Rosebud Antiques,
NSW**

Aurora Borealis black crystal, opera length necklace, single strand with a diamante studded clasp, Austria, c1950, 120cm long.

$135 - $155

**Out of the Ark,
ACT**

Fine quality rhinestone necklace, by Simpson, England, c1959, 41cm long.

$65 - $85

**The Botanic Ark,
VIC**

Castlecliff, New York signed gold plated and plastic sheen three strand choker of white beads, United States, c1955.

$90 - $110

**Malvern Antique Market,
VIC**

NZ$65 - $85

**Gales Antiques,
New Zealand**

Crystal, purple glass and diamante necklace, European, c1950, 24cm long.

$120 - $140

Amethyst glass bead necklace individually set, England, c1950, 38cm long.

NZ$95 - $115

**Ascot Collectables,
New Zealand**

Diamante necklace, the centre having three rows, England, c1950, 40cm long.

NZ$85 - $105

**The Wooden Rose,
New Zealand**

Blue cut glass beads, c1950, 50cm long.

**Northumberland Antiques & Restorations,
NSW**

Oval ribbed paua shell brooch, New Zealand, c1960, 2cm wide, 2.5cm long.

NZ$15 - $25

The Wooden Rose, New Zealand

Powder coated metal daisy flower brooch, the centre button being plastic, United States, c1960, 6cm diam.

NZ$65 - $85

The Wooden Rose, New Zealand

Powder coated metal daisy flower brooch, the centre button of plastic, United States, c1960, 8cm diam.

NZ$55 - $75

The Wooden Rose, New Zealand

Citrine glass brooch, c1960, 6cm high, 4cm wide.

$55 - $75

Codger's Collectables, SA

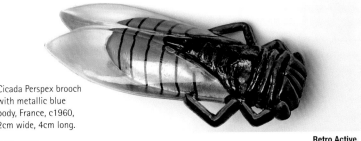

Cicada Perspex brooch with metallic blue body, France, c1960, 2cm wide, 4cm long.

$30 - $60

Retro Active, VIC

Large topaz-like glass round stone brooch with pearl and filigree frame and ornate filigree backing, c1960, 5cm diam.

$60 - $80

Shag, VIC

Galalith plastic bangle with embedded fashion magazine pieces, France, c1960, 4cm wide, 8cm diam.

$205 - $245

Retro Active, VIC

Faux pearls and bullion drop brooch, Czechoslovakia, c1960, 7cm high.

$85 - $105

Chapel Street Bazaar, VIC

Signed designer bracelet in gold metallic, by Les Barnard, New York, United States, c1960.

$75 - $95

Malvern Antique Market, VIC

Lucile white and yellow bangle, France, c1960, 10cm diam.

NZ$245 - $285

Bakelite Belle.com, New Zealand

'Coro' costume bracelet set with blue rhinestones, United States, c1960.

$115 - $135

Southern Antique Centre, NSW

Pair of enamelled violet clip-on earrings, England, c1960, 2cm long.

NZ$15 - $25

The Wooden Rose, New Zealand

Coral style clip-on earrings in various colours, priced per pair.

$4 - $10

The Old Lolly Factory, NSW

Lucite and foil ring, France, c1960.

NZ$225 - $265

Bakelite Belle.com, New Zealand

Diamante necklace and earrings, Czechoslovakia, c1960.

$150 - $170

Pendulum Antiques, SA

Plastic necklace and matching ear clips, United States, c1960.

$25 - $35

Chapel Street Bazaar, VIC

Diamante and marcasite brooch and earring set, the earrings altered for pierced ears, England, c1960, 46cm long.

NZ$120 - $140

Ascot Collectables, New Zealand

Gold coloured metal and imitation pearl, five strand necklace, c1960, 44cm long.

$45 - $65

Classic Vintage, NSW

Plastic amber coloured chain necklace, England, c1960, 92cm long.

NZ$40 - $60

Ascot Collectables, New Zealand

Copper pendant in brown and yellow by Karl Schibensky, Germany, c1960.

$310 - $350

Kaleidoscope Antiques, VIC

Five strand faux pearls and coral with a faux carved coral clasp, United States.

$85 - $105

Chapel Street Bazaar, VIC

Plastic double strand adjustable necklace, c1960, 49cm long.

$45 - $65

Classic Vintage, NSW

Double strand, multi-coloured, beaded necklace, c1960, 55cm long.

$45 - $65

Classic Vintage, NSW

COSTUME JEWELLERY

Stunning orange glass and diamante brooch and clip-on earrings, United States, c1970.

$245 - $285

Chapel Street Bazaar, VIC

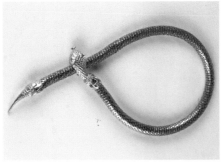

Glow Mesh snake necklace, c1975, 50cm long.

$55 - $75

Fat Helen's, VIC

Multi-coloured plastic necklace with a cube and fern design, Hong Kong, c1970, 118cm long.

$45 - $65

Classic Vintage, NSW

Signed Bakelite piano bangle, France, c1970, 7cm wide, 6cm deep.

NZ$325 - $365

Bakelite Belle.com, New Zealand

Black plastic brooch of a woman's head with hat, England, c1970, 4.5cm high.

$20 - $30

Debbie Pech, VIC

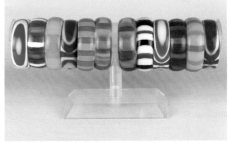

Multiple coloured Lucite bangles. Priced per item, United States, c1980.

$20 - $30

Chapel Street Bazaar, VIC

Clip-on earrings in various colours, priced per pair, c1980.

$4 - $10

The Old Lolly Factory, NSW

Plastic brooches. Priced per item, c1980, 5cm high.

$5 - $15

Fat Helen's, VIC

Lucite carved bangle, Germany, c1980, 4cm high, 8cm diam.

$185 - $205

b bold - 20th Century Furniture & Effects, VIC

Cherry necklace and earrings of Lucite, United States, c1990.

$205 - $245

Chapel Street Bazaar, VIC

Diamante necklace and earring set.

$50 - $70

Pymble Antiques - Linen & Retro, NSW

Banana necklace, of coloured Lucite, United States, c1990.

$205 - $245

Chapel Street Bazaar, VIC

Lea Stein pink plastic bangle, France, c1970, 6.5cm diam.

NZ$185 - $205

Bakelite Belle.com, New Zealand

Lea Stein elasticised bracelet, marked 'Lea Stein, Paris', France, c1960, 7cm wide.

$280 - $320

Kaleidoscope Antiques, VIC

Plastic hedgehog Lea Stein brooch, France, c2002, 6cm high, 4cm wide.

$110 - $130

Chapel Street Bazaar, VIC

Lea Stein Art Deco style brooch of a cat, France, c1970, 8cm high.

$230 - $270

Steven Sher Antiques, WA

Lea Stein Art Deco styled cat brooch, France, c1960, 7.5cm high.

NZ$245 - $285

Bakelite Belle.com, New Zealand

Plastic Lea Stein cat with ball brooch, France, 7cm high, 4.5cm wide.

$120 - $140

Chapel Street Bazaar, VIC

Lea Stein burgundy camel brooch, France, c2000, 4cm high, 4cm wide.

$100 - $120

Chapel Street Bazaar, VIC

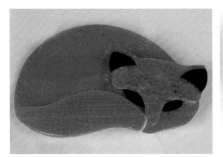

Lea Stein orange cat brooch, France, c1960, 5cm high, 7.5cm wide.

NZ$225 - $265

Bakelite Belle.com, New Zealand

Lea Stein brooch in the form of a butterfly, stamped 'Lea Stein Paris' on the clasp, France, c1970, 5cm long.

$155 - $175

Pendulum Antiques, SA

Lea Stein brooch of a Scotty dog, France, c1980.

$185 - $205

Steven Sher Antiques, WA

Signed Lea Stein brooch, France, c1970.

$150 - $170

L.A. Design, NSW

Blue Lea Stein locust brooch, France, c1960, 9cm long.

NZ$245 - $285

Bakelite Belle.com, New Zealand

Pair of glasses in the style of Lea Stein, made from laminated plastic, France.

$220 - $260

Decorama, VIC

LEA STEIN

Emerald Lea Stein fox brooch, marked 'Lea Stein, Paris', France, c1960, 10cm high.

$170 - $190   **Kaleidoscope Antiques, VIC**

Lea Stein brooch, in the form of a pink fox face, stamped 'Lea Stein Paris' on the clasp, France, c1970, 7cm long.

$155 - $175   **Pendulum Antiques, SA**

Lea Stein of Paris 'Tennis Diver' woman brooch, France, c1960, 13cm high.

$375 - $415   **Esmerelda's Curios, WA**

Lea Stein 'Magenta Girl with Umbrella' brooch, limited edition, France, c2002, 4.5cm high.

$100 - $120   **Chapel Street Bazaar, VIC**

Lea Stein brooch in the form of an Art Deco flapper, stamped 'Lea Stein Paris' on the clasp, France, c1970, 6cm wide.

$175 - $195   **Pendulum Antiques, SA**

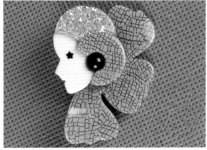

'Deco Lady' carved Lea Stein brooch, France, c1970, 5.5cm high.

$140 - $160   **Circa Vintage Clothing, VIC**

Lea Stein 'Little Girl with Hoop' brooch, limited edition, France, 4.5cm high.

$100 - $120   **Chapel Street Bazaar, VIC**

Lea Stein brooch in the 'Petal Flapper' design, stamped on the clasp 'Lea Stein Paris', France, c1970, 6cm long.

$175 - $195   **Pendulum Antiques, SA**

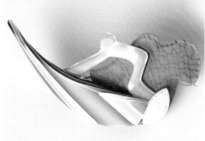

Lea Stein windsurfer brooch, France, 5.5cm high.

$110 - $130   **Chapel Street Bazaar, VIC**

Brooch by Lea Stein, Paris, of a black sax player, France.

$230 - $270   **Steven Sher Antiques, WA**

Lea Stein, plastic brooch of a waistcoat on a coat hanger, France, c2002, 4.5cm high, 3.5cm wide.

$110 - $130   **Chapel Street Bazaar, VIC**

Lea Stein red Christmas tree brooch, France, c1960, 8.5cm high, 5.5cm wide.

NZ$255 - $295   **Bakelite Belle.com, New Zealand**

Lea Stein, handbag brooch, France, c2000, 2.5cm high, 2cm wide.

$90 - $110   **Chapel Street Bazaar, VIC**

Royal Doulton Nesbit collector's dolls in their original boxes including 'Little Model', 'Vera', 'Winter', 'Small Sister' and 'Big Sister', England, c1981.

$935 - $1035

**Collectable Creations,
QLD**

Box of four composition mohair Daisy dolls with their original clothing and labelled box, c1950.

$255 - $295

**Jan James,
NSW**

Celluloid 'Baby Girl' doll in a moulded nappy with beautifully moulded hair and painted features, Japan, c1950, 56cm high.

$500 - $600

**Northside Secondhand Furniture,
QLD**

'Palitoy' celluloid doll with sleepy eyes, original hair, clothes, jewellery and traditional Scottish dress, c1950, 36cm high.

$235 - $275

**Ivanhoe Collectibles Corner,
VIC**

Celluloid baby doll with a moulded face and hair, painted eyes and open/closed mouth with two upper teeth, Japan, c1950, 46cm high.

$330 - $370

**Northside Secondhand Furniture,
QLD**

'Palitoy' celluloid doll with a movable head and limbs, moulded hair and painted intaglio eyes, England, c1950, 56cm high.

$275 - $315

**Northside Secondhand Furniture,
QLD**

'Pedigree' doll with course nylon hair and sleeping eyes, New Zealand, 40cm high.

$255 - $295

**Antiques & Collectables On Moorabool,
VIC**

Pedigree doll with a cryer, blue eyes and blonde hair, England, c1950, 57cm high.

$355 - $395

**Serendipity Antiques - Newcastle,
NSW**

Hard plastic 'Pedigree' black walker doll with a vintage dress, c1950, 55cm high.

$430 - $470

**Jan James,
NSW**

Celluloid and cloth football player doll, Japan, c1950, 20cm high.

$65 - $85

**Decorama,
VIC**

Large, hard-plastic doll in original clothes, Italy, c1962, 77cm high.

$110 - $130

**The Botanic Ark,
VIC**

'Pedigree' doll, c1950, 42cm long.

$90 - $110

**The Mill Markets,
VIC**

Hard plastic African tribal doll, England, c1960, 16cm high.

Hard plastic doll, dressed as a Scottish piper, England, c1960, 15cm high.

Madame Alexander doll with original tagged clothes, United States, c1960, 39cm high.

Brownie Downing Aboriginal doll, of fabric and wood, Australia, c1955, 70cm high,10cm wide.

$205 - $245   **Malvern Antique Market, VIC**

$40 - $50   **Paddington Antique Centre Pty Ltd, QLD**

$40 - $50   **Paddington Antique Centre Pty Ltd, QLD**

$275 - $315   **Lancaster's Toowoomba Antique Centre, QLD**

Plastic Kewpie doll, c1960, 10cm long.

$10 - $20   **Dr Russell's Emporium, WA**

Maori dressed plastic doll, New Zealand, c1960, 12cm high.

$15 - $25   **Dr Russell's Emporium, WA**

Hard plastic black show doll with changing eyes, Australia, c1950, 20cm high,12cm wide.

$65 - $85   **Terrace Collectables, NSW**

Large walking doll, head turns as she walks, Italy, c1950, 71cm high.

$165 - $185   **The Evandale Tinker, TAS**

Plastic walking doll, operated by string pull, United States, c1950, 15cm high.

$65 - $85   **Western District Antique Centre, VIC**

'Ideal' Shirley Temple doll, 40cm high.

$100 - $120   **Coliseum Antiques Centre, NSW**

Miniature Murano glass, doll's tea set, Italy, c1970.

$255 - $295   **Goodwood House Antiques, WA**

Hard plastic, black 'Palitoy' walking doll with astrakhan hair and a vintage dress, c1950, 52.5cm high.

$375 - $415   **Jan James, NSW**

'Holly Hobbie' lunch box, flask and doll, c1980.

$90 - $110   **The Toy Collector, SA**

Child's tin table and chairs, Japan, c1955.

$115 - $135

Chapel Street Bazaar, VIC

Doll's dressing table, United States, c1950, 59cm high, 46cm wide, 25cm deep.

$165 - $185

Dannykay Antiques, NSW

Tin bungalow, made by Mettoy, England, c1955, 50cm long.

$330 - $370

Traffic Developments Pty Ltd, VIC

Tin 'Mettoys' doll house, England, c1960.

$110 - $130

Cat's Cradle Comics, VIC

Child's folding toy pram, Australia, c1970, 70cm high.

$50 - $70

Antiques & Collectables On Moorabool, VIC

Plastic original Cabbage Patch pram, United States, c1984.

$30 - $60

Fat Helen's, VIC

'Singer' sew handy child's sewing machine, model No. 20, United Kingdom, c1950.

$245 - $285

Pedlars Antique Market, SA

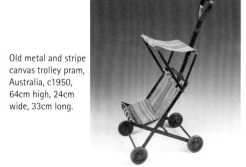

Old metal and stripe canvas trolley pram, Australia, c1950, 64cm high, 24cm wide, 33cm long.

$155 - $175

Serendipity Antiques - Newcastle, NSW

Battery and hand operated 'Zigzag' child's sewing machine, in its original box, Japan, 17cm high, 25cm long.

NZ$45 - $65

Diane Akers, New Zealand

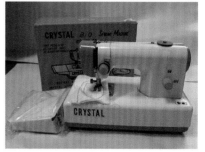

Boxed, toy battery operated sewing machine, Japan, c1960, 11cm high, 17cm wide.

$75 - $95

Collectors' Cottage Antiques, NSW

DOLLS

Steiff 'Hare' hand puppet, Germany, c1950, 30cm high.

$430 - $470   **Esmerelda's Curios, WA**

Steiff elephant with a silver button/label, c1960, 15cm high.

$115 - $135   **Jan James, NSW**

Golly marked 'Dame Wilkinson, Made in England Under Licence James Robertson's', England, c1980, 22.5cm long.

$105 - $125   **Jan James, NSW**

Steiff giraffe, c1950, 27.5cm high.

$155 - $175   **Jan James, NSW**

Steiff fawn with a button/label, c1950, 12.5cm high.

$85 - $105   **Jan James, NSW**

Steiff sparrow, c1960.

$100 - $120   **Jan James, NSW**

Steiff 'Molly Golli and Peg' with leather shoes and the original label, limited edition of 2500 made in 1996, 20cm high.

$265 - $305   **Jan James, NSW**

Steiff mouse, 8.5cm high.

$85 - $105   **Jan James, NSW**

Two golliwog dolls, hand made, Australia, c1960, 45cm high.

$80 - $100   **Mac's Collectables, SA**

Teddy bear with glass eyes, c1950, 38cm high.

$255 - $295　　Ivanhoe Collectibles Corner, VIC

Teddy bear, by Alpha Farnell, England, c1950, 30cm high.

$135 - $155　　Coliseum Antiques Centre, NSW

'Bob's Bear' inscribed on the paw with 'Made in Tasmania' and signed Bob White 1993, dressed with a leather hat and stock whip, Australia, 50cm long.

$375 - $415　　Jan James, NSW

'Gram's', 'Baby Hugs' and 'Baby Tugs', original 1983 'Care Bears,' American Greetings Corp, a Kenner toys product, soft stuffed bears with heart shaped soles of feet, noses and tush button, complete with kiss curl hair, Taiwan, 40cm high, 24cm wide, 13cm deep.

$80 - $100　　The Toy Collector, SA

Brimley Bears 'Charity' No, 10, from a limited edition of 10, and 'Alexia' Limited edition of 1, Australia, c1995, 16cm high.

$140 - $160　　Eagle Antiques, VIC

'Joy Toy' gold mohair bear with glass eyes and tagged on the right paw, c1950, 40cm long.

$375 - $415　　Jan James, NSW

Hand made teddy by Tim Penny Patch, from the series 'The Great Aunts', teddy name, 'Effie McCallum', Australia, c1996, 37cm high.

$215 - $255　　Mentone Beach Antiques Centre, VIC

Panda with glass eyes, by Joy Toys, Australia, c1950, 22cm high, 18cm wide.

$110 - $130　　Shop 77, Centenary Antique Centre, NSW

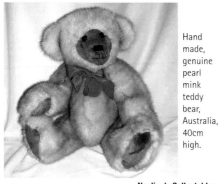

Hand made, genuine pearl mink teddy bear, Australia, 40cm high.

$290 - $330　　Noeline's Collectables, QLD

Steiff original limited edition Teddy Baby Bear, button and tags still attached, genuine mohair, Germany, 16cm high.

$275 - $315　　Chapel Street Bazaar, VIC

Teddy bear a with rubber face, c1950, 33cm high, 21cm wide.

$45 - $65　　Obsidian Antiques, NSW

ENTERTAINMENT EQUIPMENT

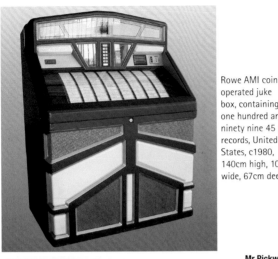

Rowe AMI coin operated juke box, containing one hundred and ninety nine 45 rpm records, United States, c1980, 140cm high, 104cm wide, 67cm deep.

NZ$2500 - $2700

Mr Pickwicks, New Zealand

'Ami Continental 2' juke box with a 200 sound selection, c1962, 158cm high, 87cm wide, 77cm deep.

$10500 - $11500 **Relic, QLD**

5 cent gumball machine, unlocking from the top and set to vend on five cents, with a great stainless steel base and simple yet effective styling, United States, c1950.

$475 - $515 **Retro Antiques, NSW**

'Monarch' battery operated record player by HMV, Australia, c1960.

$175 - $195 **Paddington Antique Centre Pty Ltd, QLD**

MBA velocity microphone, 31cm high, 14cm wide.

$255 - $295 **Chapel Street Bazaar, VIC**

Early Zephyr microphone, 29cm high, 13cm wide.

$325 - $365 **Chapel Street Bazaar, VIC**

GEC '2007' stereo system, with matching '2006' model speakers, Japan, c1970.

$1550 - $1750 **Atomic Pop, SA**

Portable HMV radio record player, plays 45, 78 and LP records, Australia, c1960, 25cm high, 48cm long, 40cm deep.

$255 - $295 **Towers Antiques & Collectables, NSW**

Early Zephyr microphone.

$255 - $295 **Chapel Street Bazaar, VIC**

Astor Mickey 'KM', brown Bakelite radio, Australia, 18cm high, 27cm wide, 17cm.

$325 - $365   **Ace Antiques & Collectables, VIC**

Astor 'Football' brown Bakelite valve mantle radio, Australia, 15cm high, 23cm long, 16cm deep.

$1300 - $1500   **Resurrection Radio, VIC**

Toshiba Radio IC - 310B, in leather case, Japan, c1975.

$65 - $85   **Branxholme Mobile Books, VIC**

'Kriesler' plastic radio, Australia, c1960, 15cm high, 40cm wide, 15cm deep.

$110 - $130   **Towers Antiques & Collectables, NSW**

Hotpoint white Bakelite mantel radio with a perspex dial and original valve chassis, c1950, 18cm high, 28cm wide.

$215 - $255   **Alltime Antiques & Bairnsdale Clocks, VIC**

'AWA Transistor Seven' portable radio, in a black leather case, Australia, c1970, 19cm high, 28cm long, 8cm deep.

$375 - $415   **Ritzy Bits - ACT, ACT**

Cream 'Astor' Bakelite radio, Australia.

$110 - $130   **McKays Mart, SA**

Amalgamated Wireless Australasia (AWA) brown Bakelite radio, Australia, 19cm high, 28cm long, 15cm deep.

$440 - $480   **Resurrection Radio, VIC**

'Ekco' radio, distributed by Australian Electrical Industries, Australia, c1960, 40cm long, 15cm deep.

$475 - $515   **Ritzy Bits - ACT, ACT**

His Masters Voice (HMV), burgundy plastic, valve mantle radio, Australia, c1956, 20cm high, 32cm long, 14cm deep.

$230 - $270   **Resurrection Radio, VIC**

Bakelite valve radio made by G.W. Green & Sons Pty Ltd Melbourne, Australia, c1950, 22cm high, 33cm wide.

$200 - $240

The Mill Markets, VIC

Blue plastic National Panasonic radio, Japan, c1970, 11cm diam.

$40 - $50

506070, NSW

Brown Bakelite cased radio by 'Phillips', England, c1950, 24cm wide, 35cm long, 16cm deep.

NZ$180 - $200

Decollectables, New Zealand

'Healing Moderne' bakelite radio, Australia, c1950, 19cm high, 25cm wide, 19cm high.

$1100 - $1300

Ace Antiques & Collectables, VIC

AWA brown Bakelite valve radio, Australia, c1950, 19cm high, 28cm wide.

$275 - $315

Fyshwick Antique Centre, ACT

Red and white plastic 'Wayfarer' radio, 24cm high, 13cm wide, 32cm long.

$430 - $470

506070, NSW

'Bell' radio with a cream bakelite case, New Zealand, c1950, 17cm high, 14cm wide, 27cm long.

NZ$185 - $225

Decollectables, New Zealand

Philips brown Bakelite radio, c1950, 16cm high, 24cm wide, 15cm deep.

$230 - $270

The Mill Markets, VIC

Astor 'Mickey' brown Bakelite valve mantle radio, Australia, 18cm high, 27cm long, 17cm deep.

$510 - $610

Resurrection Radio, VIC

'Tasmanian' Bakelite radio, made in Sydney by Thomas Smith Radio Co., Australia, 20cm high, 30cm wide, 20cm deep.

$375 - $415

The Bottom Drawer Antique Centre, VIC

Standard telephones and cables (STC) red plastic mantle valve radio, Australia, c1956, 20cm high, 28cm wide, 13cm deep.

$300 - $340

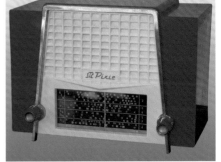

Resurrection Radio, VIC

Beatles 1963 Christmas record, only available to fan club members, the first such record produced, England.

$405 - $445

Relic,
QLD

Beatles 'Hard Days Night', on the Parlophone label, England, c2003.

$25 - $35

Quality Records,
VIC

'The Beatles, More Requests!' E.P. on the EMI label, Australia, c1960.

$35 - $45

Terrace Collectables,
NSW

Three 'Parlophone' Beatles LPs, 'A Hard Days Night', 'Rubber Soul' and 'Help', priced per item, c1960.

$10 - $20

Tyabb Hay Shed,
VIC

Bach Cello Suites Janos Starker, re-issue from Speakers Corner, originally recorded by Mercury Living Presence, a three record set in a box with a booklet on heavy vinyl, Germany, c2003.

$135 - $155

Quality Records,
VIC

'The Beach Boys, Pet Sounds', the classic original stereo pressing, United Kingdom, c1966.

$90 - $110

Licorice Pie Records,
VIC

'The Best of the Beach Boys' Volume 1, 12' LP original soundtrack by EMI Australia, Australia, 31cm wide, 31cm long.

$25 - $35

Towers Antiques & Collectables,
NSW

The Beach Boys, Barbara Ann E.P., by Capital Records in 1965, includes 'Sloop John B', 'The Little Girl I Once Knew', 'There's No Other', 'Barbara Ann'.

$35 - $45

Terrace Collectables,
NSW

Ariel 'Strange Fantastic Dream', a highly creative and coherent package of music and artwork that stands the test of time, Australia, c1973.

$50 - $70

High on Music,
VIC

Ariel 'Strange Fantastic Dream' with a different cover version, than the Australian release, England, c1973.

$50 - $70

High on Music,
VIC

'Spicks & Specks, The Bee Gees' E.P. on the Spin label and featuring Spicks & Specks, Jingle Jangle, Tint of Blue and Where are You, c1960.

$40 - $60

Terrace Collectables,
NSW

RECORDS

Bee Gees 'Massachusetts' EP, original Australian only issue on the 'Spin' label, Australia, c1968.

$95 - $115

High on Music,
VIC

'Pot Luck with Elvis' L.P produced by RCA records SL101311, Australia, c1963.

$60 - $80

The Time Machine,
QLD

'Elvis Presley Sings Flaming Star' 12' LP, original sound track by RCA, Australia, c1960, 31cm wide, 31cm long.

$10 - $20

Towers Antiques & Collectables,
NSW

'The Doors Resurrection' a French fan club release double LP of the Doors music, and Jim Morrison 'Poem's', France, 32cm high, 31cm long.

$255 - $295

The Time Machine,
QLD

Doors 'Best of the Doors', sumptuous three record set on 150g vinyl, with amazing sound brings these classics back to life, from Elektra Records, Germany, c2003.

$40 - $50

Quality Records,
VIC

The Doors 'L. A. Woman' original issue, with a die cut cover, negative photo of the band and a yellow inner sleeve with a nude woman on an electric light pole cross, United States, c1971.

$50 - $70

High on Music,
VIC

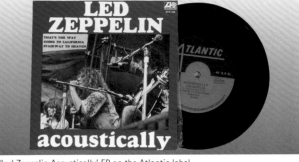

'Led Zeppelin Acoustically' EP on the Atlantic label.

$100 - $120

Relic,
QLD

Led Zeppelin 'Whole Lotta Love' EP, Australian only original issue on the green Atlantic label, Australia, c1969.

$230 - $270

High on Music,
VIC

Led Zeppelin 'Live at the BBC', recorded in studio sound by the BBC between 1969 and 1971, four LP deluxe set on 200g vinyl from Classic Records, United States.

$115 - $135

Quality Records,
VIC

'INXS Decka Dance Promotional Only Vinyl' version of the INXS cassette only release, a white label promotion, Australia, c1985.

$750 - $850

The Time Machine,
QLD

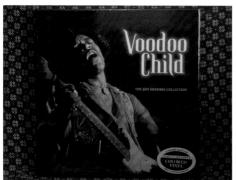

Jimi Hendrix 'Voodoo Child', deluxe four LP box set edition, including four studio sides, four live sides and a colour booklet, compiled from the original analogue masters, United States, c2003.

$85 - $105

Quality Records, VIC

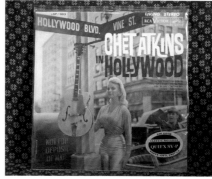

Chet Atkins 'Live in Hollywood', the guitar behind a hundred RCA recordings, including those of Elvis Presley, a virtuoso performance considered to be his best record, from Classic records on 180g vinyl taken from the original master tapes.

$45 - $55

Quality Records, VIC

Original Australian vinyl pressing of 'Hawkwind's Space Ritual', Australia, c1973.

$35 - $45

Rockaway Records, QLD

'Jane Fonda's Workout' record, United States, c1982.

NZ$15 - $25

Hubbers Emporium, New Zealand

Neil Young 'Greatest Hits', two LP sets with a bonus 7 inch record on 200g vinyl, United States, c2003.

$55 - $75

Quality Records, VIC

Thelonious Monk/ John Coltrane 'Live at Carnegie Hall', this record did not receive general release at the time of recording, Audiophile label, Mosaic Records has finally made things right, on 180g vinyl, United States, c2003.

$40 - $60

Quality Records, VIC

John Coltrane 'Blue Train', one of the most famous of jazz albums of all time dating from 1957, on the Blue Note Label, this re issue from Classic Records does the recording full justice, United States, c2003.

$45 - $55

Quality Records, VIC

Tamam Shud, 'Goolutionites and the Real People', Australia progressive rock from 1970 on the Warner Bros. Label, Australia.

$750 - $850

The Time Machine, QLD

Count Basie/Tony Bennett 'Basie/Bennett', re issue from Classic Records, comes as 4x12 inch records playable at 45 rpm, for the ultimate in sound reproduction, United States, c2003.

$70 - $90

Quality Records, VIC

Henri Bource All Stars ' Rock in Roll Party' Australia's first rock and roll LP on the 'Planet' record label 1958, and features great old rock and roll standards, Australia.

$380 - $420

The Time Machine, QLD

RECORDS

'Keith Hudson, Steaming Jungle' LP from the 'Dub Dentist', United Kingdom.

$140 - $160   **Licorice Pie Records, VIC**

Original soundtrack for 'Lupin III', from the cult animated TV series from Guji Ohno, Japan, c1977.

$40 - $60   **Licorice Pie Records, VIC**

'Davy Crockett', 78rpm, two record set, with official Walt Disney cartoons on the inside and back of the cover, c1960, 26cm high, 26cm wide.

$45 - $65   **Chapel Street Bazaar, VIC**

Enid Blyton 'Noddy' record, 78rpm, England, c1950, 26cm long.

$40 - $60   **How Bazaar, VIC**

'Who's Next', considered to be the Who's finest album, this is the latest in Who re- issues from Audiophile Label, Classic Records, superlative sound quality, United States, c2003.

$45 - $55   **Quality Records, VIC**

Miles Davis 'Sketches of Spain', Miles at his most melodic, a follow up to a 'Kind of Blue', this was recorded by Columbia Records and this re issue in on 200g vinyl from Classic Records, United States, c2003.

$45 - $55   **Quality Records, VIC**

Mike Furber and the Bowery Boys, ' Just a Poor Boy' on the 'Kommotion' label 1966 one of Australia's most collectable 60's rock LPs, Australia.

$550 - $650   **The Time Machine, QLD**

Fitzgerald and Gershwin, the clear winner of Audiophile Awards this year, the five LP plus EP, book and prints release on the Verve label is strictly limited and continues Speaker Corner's superlative 'Songbook' series, a re-release of the original, Germany, c2003.

$380 - $420   **Quality Records, VIC**

Kate Bush 'Ariel', a two record set with a twenty four page booklet, on 180g vinyl, England, c2003.

$45 - $65   **Quality Records, VIC**

Eva Cassidy 'Songbird', her only official album release, including the superb 'Fields of Gold' on heavy duty vinyl, England, c2003.

$40 - $50   **Quality Records, VIC**

'Frederick Rzewski, No Place To Go But Around' LP of 'new' piano pieces, United States, c1976.

$40 - $60   **Licorice Pie Records, VIC**

'GTO's Permanent Damage', all girl band on Zappa's Straight Records, United States, c1969, 30cm high, 30cm long.

$90 - $110   **Licorice Pie Records, VIC**

'Marius Popp, Pano Ramic Jazz Rock', eighteen track LP, Romania, c1975, 30cm high, 30cm long.

$70 - $90   **Licorice Pie Records, VIC**

'If I Tony Worsley' mono E.P., on the Sunshine label and featuring 'If I', 'Just a Little Bit', 'I'm so glad', 'If you see my baby', Australia, c1960.

$75 - $95

Terrace Collectables, NSW

'Do the Limbo with the Keil Isles' E. P. on the Viking label and featuring 'Limbo Rock', 'Tequila Limbo', 'Mathilda' and 'Papa loves Limbo', c1960.

$90 - $110

Terrace Collectables, NSW

'The Stone Roses' limited edition package, containing a tee shirt, cassette of ' What the World is Waiting For' and the single picture sleeve record of ' Fools Gold' sealed and never played, Australia, c1989, 32cm high, 32cm long.

$185 - $205

The Time Machine, QLD

Cannonball Adderley 'Somethin Else' original Blue Note jazz LP, United States, c1958, 30cm high, 30cm long.

$90 - $110

Licorice Pie Records, VIC

'Jander Cater ON' 3rd album from Jander, a cult 'coner' four artist, private pressing, United States, c1981.

$140 - $160

Licorice Pie Records, VIC

'The Wind In The Willows', self titled album with Deborah Harry (of Blondie), first record, Australia, c1968, 30cm high, 30cm long.

$35 - $45

Licorice Pie Records, VIC

'Chetarca' progressive rock record, from one of Australia's most underrated bands, Australia, c1975, 32cm high, 32cm long.

$230 - $270

The Time Machine, QLD

'Jimmy Smith, I'm Movin' On', one of the many Smith treasures on Blue Note, United States, c1965.

$35 - $45

Licorice Pie Records, VIC

'Julie Driscol, Jools', classic mod 60's groove's, Australia, c1969.

$25 - $35

Licorice Pie Records, VIC

'The Meters' self titled album, the definitive New Orleans funk LP, United States.

$140 - $160

Licorice Pie Records, VIC

'Tom Waits, Bone Machine' LP, only released in the United Kingdom, c1992.

$140 - $160

Licorice Pie Records, VIC

Twelve inch Duran Duran 'The Reflex' dance mix E.P., England, c1984.

NZ$75 - $95

Banks Peninsula Antiques, New Zealand

ENTERTAINMENT EQUIPMENT

Hank Mobley 'Soul Station', many albums from the Blue Note Label are very collectable, excellent pressing on 180g vinyl, United States, c2003.

$20 - $30

Quality Records, VIC

Twelve inch Queen E.P 'It's a hard Life', picture disc, England, c1984, 30cm diam.

NZ$110 - $130

Banks Peninsula Antiques, New Zealand

Ella Fitzgerald/Joe Pass 'Take Love Easy', from Analogue Productions, on 2 x 45 rpm records for the finest in sound reproduction, United States, c2003.

$75 - $95

Quality Records, VIC

'Smile', by Brian Wilson who considered 'Pet Sounds' to be an unfinished masterpiece, so it was logical he would try and complete the album, United States.

$35 - $45

Quality Records, VIC

'Albatross' a breath of fresh air 1973 record with two members, of the previous band 'Tamam Shud', on the Reprise label, Australia, c1973, 32cm high, 32cm wide.

$255 - $295

The Time Machine, QLD

'Don't Knock the Rock' 33 rpm record featuring Bill Hayley and His Comets from a Columbia Picture, recording in America by Decca Records Inc, United States.

$20 - $30

Towers Antiques & Collectables, NSW

Creedence Clearwater Revival 'Cosmos Factory', one of the entire Creedence Clearwater Revival catalogues released by the audiophile label, Analogue Productions with stunning sound and silent 180g vinyl, United States, c2003.

$35 - $55

Quality Records, VIC

Pattie Smith 'Horses', from the Audiophile, Simply Vinyl Label on 160g vinyl, England, c2003.

$30 - $40

Quality Records, VIC

'Culture Club Colour by Numbers', 12' LP original sound track by Virgin Records 1983, includes a souvenir tour poster.

$40 - $50

Towers Antiques & Collectables, NSW

'Bombora, The Gremlin King, Bluebottles, Turista' E.P. by 'The Atlantics' on the CBS label for Southern Music, Sydney, Australia, c1960.

$60 - $80

Terrace Collectables, NSW

'Pipeline, the Chantey's' mono E.P. by Dot Records and includes 'Pipeline', 'Move It', 'Runaway' and 'Sleepwalk', c1960.

$30 - $40

Terrace Collectables, NSW

Roman Holiday 'Don't Try to Stop It' picture 45. LP, England, c1983, 20cm wide, 22cm long.

NZ$55 - $75

Banks Peninsula Antiques, New Zealand

Australian Gold Award presented to Vince Lovegrove by the executive of Festival Records, for the album 'Desperate' Divinyls, March 1983, Australia, 46cm high, 36cm wide.

$480 - $520

Nicki's Collection, NSW

'Sun 1972' self titled LP, Renee Geyer's first band, all original music written by its six members featuring a blend of guitar, piano and brass instruments playing a hybrid of jazz and rock, Australia.

$140 - $160

High on Music, VIC

'This is Dusty Springfield' L.P. released by Philips.

$10 - $20

Terrace Collectables, NSW

'The Small Faces, Ogden's Nut Gone Flake', first UK (mono) pressing with the fold out sleeve, United Kingdom, c1968, 30cm diam.

$140 - $160

Licorice Pie Records, VIC

Slim Harpo 'Best of', original issue on the 'Excello' label, electric blues played in its purest style, United States, c1969.

$40 - $60

High on Music, VIC

'Stevie Wright, Hard Road' a classic LP from the Easybeats vocalist, featuring the song 'Evie', United States, c1974.

$35 - $45

High on Music, VIC

'Leroy Vinegar, Glass Of Water' LP, United States, c1973.

$140 - $160

Licorice Pie Records, VIC

'Four Shirley Temple Hits for Children', mono E.P. 20th Century Records.

$40 - $60

Terrace Collectables, NSW

The Indo-British Ensemble, 'Curried Jazz', east meets west, sitar tinged melodies combine with mellow laid back jazz, England, c1969.

$15 - $25

High on Music, VIC

La De Das, 'The Happy Prince' classic children's novel written by Oscar Wilde, set to music, in between the finely crafted and played songs, Adrian Rawlins narrates the sad story of the Happy Prince, New Zealand, c1969.

$140 - $160

High on Music, VIC

Jethro Tull 'Stand Up', their second LP released in 1969 on the 'Island' label, the gatefold cover displays a novel 'pop up' cut out of the four band members.

$35 - $45

High on Music, VIC

Dvorak Cello Concerto 'Janis Starker', a classical re issues from Speakers Corner and Classic Records, originally recorded by Mercury Living Presence, Germany.

$45 - $65

Quality Records, VIC

'On your feet, let's dance Aussie Style With the City Slickers' on the W & G label, Australia, c1960.

$5 - $15

Terrace Collectables, NSW

James Brown 'I Got You (I Feel Good)' original release on the legendary 'King' label, eye catching cover, the back cover displays other artist's albums that the King label has to offer, United States, c1966.

$90 - $110

High on Music, VIC

Alice Cooper 'Killer', this original version features a calendar with Alice and a noose around his neck, United States, c1971.

$30 - $40

High on Music, VIC

Think, 'We'll Give You a Buzz', five piece band, playing a mix of hard driving rock with slick funky fills, New Zealand, c1976.

$280 - $320

High on Music, VIC

Original sound track recording LP of ' Lets Make Love' starring Marilyn Monroe, by Philips in Hi-Fi mono, c1958.

$65 - $85

The Time Machine, QLD

'Dig Richards Bad Boy' LP on the Rex label, Australia, c1960.

$205 - $245

Relic, QLD

Scientist - The People's Choice LP. Yet to be re-issued mid period Dub Reggae from King Tubb's No. 1 student, on Kingdom Records KVL-9014, England, c1983.

$70 - $90

Licorice Pie Records, VIC

'Ween, 12 Golden Country Greats', cult band Ween's country pastiche, limited edition vinyl, United Kingdom, c1996.

$190 - $210

Licorice Pie Records, VIC

Bert Newton GTV9 W & G record single 45 rpm, Australia, c1960.

$5 - $10

The Wool Exchange Geelong, VIC

Davy Graham - Folk Blues & Beyond LP. Ground breaking album from Graham of middle eastern flavoured folk, on Decca LK-4649 mono, original pressing, England.

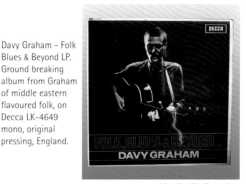

$140 - $160

Licorice Pie Records, VIC

Cream 'Disraeli Gears' original mono pressing on the 'Reaction' label, the album cover by Martin Sharp typifies the music, psychedelic meets electric blues.

$50 - $70

High on Music, VIC

'Tully' self titled album, progressive music with a lot of love, peace and happiness, Australia, c1970.

$90 - $110

High on Music, VIC

Jane 'Lady', progressive rock issued on the original 'Brain' label, music played in the tradition of Pink Floyd meets Uriah Heep but with strong Germanic overtones, Germany, c1974.

$25 - $35

High on Music, VIC

'Les Baxter, Ritual Of The Savage', one of the best from the king, United States.

$15 - $25

Licorice Pie Records, VIC

The Atlantics 'Now Its Stompin' Time', instrumental surf music album, original pressing in mono, Australia, c1963.

$80 - $100

High on Music, VIC

Company Caine 'A Product of a Broken Reality', original issue on the 'Generation' label, Australia, c1971.

$140 - $160

High on Music, VIC

Herbie Hancock 'Head Hunters', Herbie plays a feast of electric keyboards that created a breakthrough album of fusion with jazz, funk and rock, in quadraphonic sound, United States, c1974.

$40 - $60

High on Music, VIC

Ray Brown/Moonstone 'Mad House' 60's pop singing icon Ray Brown's fine attempt at branching out in the 70's with music for the heart and soul, Australia, c1971.

$100 - $120

High on Music, VIC

'Grateful Dead, Aoxomoxoa', Early Dead LP with classic Rick Griffin artwork, United States, c1971, 30cm high, 30cm long.

$25 - $35

Licorice Pie Records, VIC

'Pink Floyd Ummagumma' EP with the banned 'Gigi' cover.

$50 - $70

Relic, QLD

Pink Floyd 'Dark Side of the Moon', this album defined the seventies and this 30th Anniversary edition from EMI, with booklet and on heavy vinyl, United States.

$25 - $35

Quality Records, VIC

The Climax Blues Band 'Plays on', an English blues band that later trimmed their name down to 'Climax' and became fairly popular as a touring band on the American College circuit during the 70's and 80's, Australia, c1969.

$25 - $35

High on Music, VIC

Paul McCartney 'Twin Freaks', released under the name of a mythical DJ, but is McCartney playing about with his own work, old and new, on L.P only, England.

$30 - $40

Quality Records, VIC

Paul McCartney 'Fireman', released under the artist name of Rushes, but in fact Paul McCartney dabbling in ambient music, England, c2003.

$30 - $40

Quality Records, VIC

RECORDS

Paul McCartney 'Chaos and Creation in the Backyard', the latest album from Sir Paul McCartney, in a gatefold cover as a two record set, on heavy vinyl from EMI, England, c2003.

$30 - $40

Quality Records, VIC

'The Rolling Stones, Sticky Fingers', first U.K. pressing with the Andy Warhol designed sleeve with the zipper, United Kingdom, c1971, 30cm high, 30cm long.

$90 - $110

Licorice Pie Records, VIC

Rolling Stones 'abiggabang', a two record set on heavy vinyl from EMI, England.

$35 - $45

Quality Records, VIC

Rolling Stones 'Big Hits (High Tide and Green Grass)', early Stones catalogue from the Decca Label (London in the USA), Germany, c2003.

$30 - $40

Quality Records, VIC

Boxed set of twelve Rolling Stones vinyl records, Germany, c1980.

$230 - $270

Rockaway Records, QLD

Steve Miller Band 'Children of the Future', psychedelic product from the heady days of the San Francisco Haight/Asbury era, United States, c1968.

$35 - $45

High on Music, VIC

'Fidelity' record by Bobby Limb and his band, 'Flying Saucer', Australia, c1954.

$5 - $15

Yarra Valley Antique Centre, VIC

Deep Purple 'Shades of' EP, New Zealand only release on the Parlophone label, New Zealand, c1969.

$165 - $185

High on Music, VIC

Tymepiece 'Sweet Release' LP, progressive rock, features the track 'Shake Off', Australia, c1971.

$330 - $370

High on Music, VIC

Buffalo 'Only Want You for Your Body', issued on the prodigious 'Vertigo' swirl label with a foldout cover and additional lyric sheet, Australia, c1974.

$110 - $130

High on Music, VIC

Stevie Wright 'Hard Road' autographed album, Australian cover version, c1974.

$70 - $90

High on Music, VIC

Piano accordion with a green pearl finish, in its original box, Italy, c1950.

$355 - $395

Colonial Collectables, QLD

'Baile' 12 bass accordion, China, c1950, 50cm high, 40cm wide, 60cm deep.

$330 - $370

Flaxton Barn, QLD

Thirty string Celtic harp, built by George Callaghan, Ireland, c1950, 105cm high, 66cm wide, 36cm deep.

$2400 - $2600

Antique Curiosity Shop, QLD

JVC ball television set, 32cm high.

$365 - $405

The Junk Company, VIC

Novelty music box in the shape of a house and garden, Switzerland, c1950, 10cm high, 14.5cm wide, 9cm deep.

$40 - $60

The Mill Markets, VIC

Super 8 Flintstones film in original box, United States, c1960.

$7 - $17

Marsteen Collectables, VIC

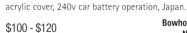

Black and white Thorn television set with a clear acrylic cover, 240v car battery operation, Japan.

$100 - $120

Bowhows, NSW

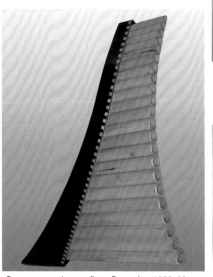

Twenty two tube pan flute, Romania, c1950, 29cm high, 30cm wide.

$200 - $240

Antique Curiosity Shop, QLD

'Bing Crosby' record cleaner by Decca Records, England, 9cm diam.

$125 - $145

The Mill Markets, VIC

FURNITURE

Charles Eames 'Time Life' lobby chair '675' with a chrome plated, cast aluminium frame and black leather upholstery, United States, c1960, 73cm high, 73cm wide.

$2650 - $2850

506070, NSW

American metal office chair, by Shaw and Walker, United States, c1950.

$1150 - $1350

Barry Sherman Galleries, VIC

Art Deco style walnut cocktail cabinet with original fittings such as a lemon squeezer and cocktail sticks, the serving area with original mirrors and the cupboard and a fitted area for bottles and glasses, England, c1950, 114cm high.

NZ$1295 - $1495

Bonham's, New Zealand

Charles and Ray Eames designed 'Segmented base' table, first made in 1964 and produced continually by Herman Miller since then, United States, c1970, 72cm high, 99cm wide, 200cm long.

$940 - $1040

Plasma, VIC

Charles Eames coffee table of walnut veneer on bevelled plywood, manufactured by Herman Miller from a 1960's design, United States, c2000, 42cm high, 89cm diam.

$940 - $1040

506070, NSW

Art Deco style pedestal table, Australia, c1950, 70cm high, 60cm diam.

$455 - $495

Vampt, NSW

Art Deco style cabinet with mahogany marquetry detail and Bakelite handles, New Zealand, c1950, 65cm high, 58cm wide, 30cm deep.

NZ$185 - $205

Mr Pickwicks, New Zealand

Art Deco style telephone table with Bakelite handles to the drawer, Australia, c1950, 86cm wide, 77cm deep.

$550 - $650

Antipodes Antiques, QLD

Fler teak buffet with graduated drawers, Australia, 66cm high, 190cm long, 45cm deep.

$600 - $700

Relic, QLD

Tessa leather and wood two seater couch with two chairs, Australia, c1980.

NZ$2000 - $2200

Maxine's Collectibles, New Zealand

Teak draw leaf extension table and six teak 'Fler' dining chairs with original vinyl upholstery, Australia, c1960.

$1150 - $1350

Retro Active, VIC

Fler three seater couch with original upholstery, Australia, c1970.

$375 - $415

Atomic Pop, SA

DC chair designed for Myer Emporium by Fred Wald, manufactured by Fler, Melbourne, Australia, c1950.

$230 - $270

Tongue & Groove, VIC

'Talking chair' originally made for the World Expo in Montreal, 1967, designed by Grant & Mary Featherston with original fabric and speakers/electronics intact, Australia, 114cm high, 72cm wide.

$4400 - $4600

Plasma, VIC

Contoured organic armchair, in the style of Grant Featherston, reupholstered in period fabric, Australia, c1955.

$1150 - $1350

Design Dilemas, VIC

Featherston number IV modular lounge suite, in original brown wool, Australia, c1970, 85cm high, 76cm wide, 76cm deep.

$1000 - $1200

Relic, QLD

Early R152 contour chair by Grant Featherston in original x-ray leaf fabric with matching footstool, made by Emerson Bros, Melbourne, Australia, c1951.

$2400 - $2600

Tongue & Groove, VIC

FURNITURE

Set of eight Parker dining chairs, Australia, c1960.

$1100 - $1300

The Junk Company, VIC

Teak nest of three tables, by Parker, Australia, c1970.

$200 - $240

506070, NSW

Stylish pair of Parker teak arm chairs with heavy duty vinyl upholstery, Australia, c1970, 90cm high, 66cm long, 60cm deep.

$430 - $470

Towers Antiques & Collectables, NSW

Black vinyl studded bar and four chairs, Australia, c1970, 112cm high, 240cm long.

$1500 - $1700

How Bazaar, VIC

Oversized coffee table by Parker, featuring blackwood struts, solid teak legs and a teak veneer top with a cane magazine rack, Australia, c1965, 52cm high, 60cm wide, 152cm long.

$500 - $600

Design Dilemas, VIC

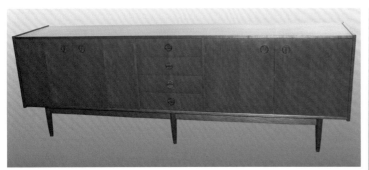

Parker teak sideboard, Australia, c1960, 227cm long.

$1395 - $1595

Paddington Antique Centre Pty Ltd, QLD

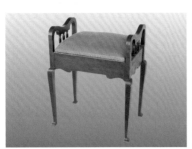

Mahogany piano stool with a lift up seat, Australia, c1950, 61cm high, 49cm long, 34cm deep.

$305 - $345

Edward VIII Antiques, VIC

Small pine stool, Australia, c1950, 14cm high, 32cm long.

$25 - $35

The Mill Markets, VIC

Set of pine pigeon holes on a plinth base with a small bench top, would make an ideal wine rack, Australia, 116cm high, 108cm wide, 34cm deep.

$1150 - $1350

Roger Hose Antiques, QLD

Extension table and six chairs, by Woodlands Furniture, Australia, c1955.

Red vinyl chair with white studs and piping, Australia, c1955.

$600 - $700

Atomic Pop, SA

$45 - $65

Atomic Pop, SA

Butterfly chair with an orange canvas cover, originally designed in 1938 by Jorge Ferrari-Hardoy, Antonio Bonet and Juan, Kurchan, also known as the 'Hardoy Lounge Chair' or '198', with a galvanised and powder coated steel rod frame, Australia, c2005, 87cm high, 75cm wide, 75cm deep.

Pair of kitchen chairs, upholstered in black vinyl with contrasting red piping, Australia, c1955.

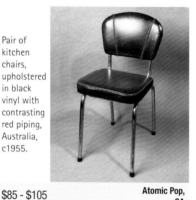

Cord chair by Clement Meadmore, Australia, c1951.

$430 - $470

506070, NSW

$85 - $105

Atomic Pop, SA

$330 - $370

Tongue & Groove, VIC

Webbed Rocker designed by Douglas Shellyns, a close copy of Ralph Rapson's (USA) chair for Knoll, manufactured by Functional Products, Sydney, Australia.

Set of four purple chairs, Australia, c1960.

Early Rondo chair by Gordon Andrews with original cast aluminium base, Australia.

$4400 - $4600

Tongue & Groove, VIC

$1900 - $2100

Tongue & Groove, VIC

$275 - $315

The Junk Company, VIC

Upholstered throne chair, Australia, c1950.

Chair designed by Jens Pison, Australia, c1970, 88cm high, 60cm wide.

Set of three pod chairs, designed by Team Tilburg and produced by Sebel Australia, c1970.

$945 - $1045

Atomic Pop, SA

$365 - $405

The Junk Company, VIC

$330 - $370

Chapel Street Bazaar, VIC

AUSTRALIAN - OTHER

'Cut Away' Kone chair by Roger McLay first made 1947, but associated more with the 1950's. This chair can be dated to the years 1947-51, and was assembled by McLay himself by the registration # 1395 stamped underneath Post 1951, the chair was made by Descon Laminates, and the registration number changed, Australia, c1950, 73cm high, 56cm wide, 60cm deep.

$1350 - $1550

Plasma, VIC

Pair of 'Atelier Designer And Manufacturer' modern design chairs with original upholstery and jarrah timber frames, Australia, 88cm high, 61cm wide, 71cm deep.

$900 - $1000

B'artchi, ACT

Douglas Snelling web chair, a design classic, Australia, c1950, 80cm high, 80cm deep.

$600 - $700

Relic, QLD

Fibreglass 'Gro' chair made in Brisbane, Australia, c1967, 53cm high, 95cm deep.

$500 - $600

Relic, QLD

Pair of chairs with maple frames and full grain leather upholstery, Austria, c1959, 90cm high, 67cm long, 60cm deep.

$600 - $700

Le Contraste, VIC

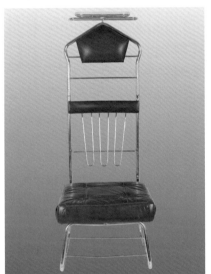

'Relaxa-Leg' gentleman's valet, manufactured in Sydney by K & A Products, Australia, c1950, 126cm high, 45cm wide.

$245 - $285

Out of the Ark, ACT

Pair of bar stools with acrylic velour padded seats on chromed steel, on a swivel cruciform base, Australia, c1970, 105cm high, 47cm wide, 45cm deep.

NZ$430 - $470

Antiques & Decorator Items, New Zealand

Pair of maple arm chairs with green upholstery, Australia, c1950, 90cm high, 64cm long, 60cm deep.

$185 - $205

Towers Antiques & Collectables, NSW

Floral three piece lounge, Australia, c1950.

$465 - $505

**The Junk Company,
VIC**

Teak framed day bed with original wool tweed fabric upholstery, Australia, c1960, 73cm high, 87cm wide, 210cm long.

$800 - $900

**Retro Active,
VIC**

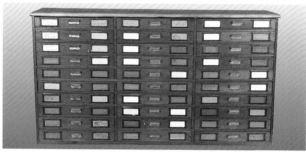

Thirty drawer pharmaceutical drugs storage unit, Australia, c1950, 58cm high, 109cm wide, 22cm deep.

$590 - $690

**Doug Up On Bourke,
NSW**

Pair of modernistic space age bedside cabinets, Australia, c1970, 63cm high, 62cm wide.

$240 - $280

**Paddington Antique Centre Pty Ltd,
QLD**

China display cabinet with a mirror back, Australia, c1960, 100cm high, 120cm long, 30cm deep.

$375 - $415

**Towers Antiques & Collectables,
NSW**

Pair of pink vinyl blow-up pouffes with maple legs, Australia, c1960, 40cm high, 40cm diam.

$110 - $130

**Towers Antiques & Collectables,
NSW**

Designer armchairs in timber and vinyl with a matching coffee table, Melbourne maker, designed by Kral, Australia, c1970, 65cm high, 75cm wide, 70cm deep.

$8300 - $8700

**Capocchi,
VIC**

Australian classic two-seater sofa with arms, designed by architect Douglas Snelling, c1953, 75cm high, 104cm long, 73cm deep.

$4400 - $4600

**506070,
NSW**

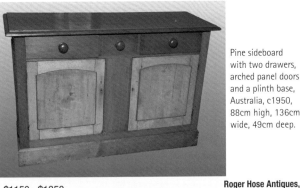

Pine sideboard with two drawers, arched panel doors and a plinth base, Australia, c1950, 88cm high, 136cm wide, 49cm deep.

$1150 - $1350

Roger Hose Antiques, QLD

Buffet by Douglas Snelling, in Victorian ash veneer, four section version made by Functional Products P/L, Australia, c1950, 83cm high, 180cm long, 37.5cm deep.

$1000 - $1200

Plasma, VIC

Chiswell fold out, narrow dining table with a hidden cutlery drawer, Australia, c1970, 73cm high, 45cm wide, 110cm long.

$250 - $290

506070, NSW

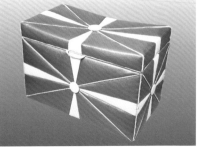

Chest in green and cream vinyl, c1950, 46cm high, 75cm wide, 42cm deep.

$255 - $295

Atomic Pop, SA

Tiled top coffee table with a flat steel base, Australia, c1970, 41cm high, 46cm wide, 107cm long.

$420 - $460

506070, NSW

Stylish credenza/low sideboard by T. H. Brown, Adelaide, teak with roller doors, inspired by 60's 'TV' shape, craftsman built, sliding roller doors are very unusual, Australia, c1964, 80cm high, 46cm wide, 220cm long.

$2400 - $2600

Vintage Living, ACT

Teak four drawer sideboard, Australia, 184cm high, 46cm deep.

$280 - $320

Furniture Revisited, VIC

'Wrightbilt' sideboard in teak, unusual at over two metres in length, finished at the back to allow for use as a room divider, Australia, c1964, 78cm high, 228.5cm wide.

$1150 - $1350

Tiffany Dodd Antique & 20th Century Furniture, QLD

Large silky oak laboratory desk with three drawers, one cupboard and one pullout, Australia, c1950, 75cm high, 182cm long, 105cm deep.

$830 - $930

Doug Up On Bourke, NSW

Three piece coffee table, Australia, c1955, 42cm high, 66cm diam.

$55 - $75

Atomic Pop, SA

Round laminate and chrome side table, Australia, c1955, 69cm high.

$90 - $110

Atomic Pop, SA

Side table, custom made by Rosando in Melbourne with an Afromosia marquetry top and a solid Afromosia frame, Australia, c1962, 55cm high, 41cm wide, 63cm long.

$190 - $230

Plasma, VIC

Laminex table with four matching chairs, Australia, c1950, 77cm high, 123cm long, 76cm deep.

$375 - $415

Chapel Street Bazaar, VIC

Octagonal Tasmanian oak games table and four chairs, converting to a dining table, cards table or chess board, Australia, c1960, 170cm diam.

$945 - $1045

Antique Revivals, VIC

Teak dining suite with six chairs, recently recovered in original 70's fabric, Australia, c1974, 74cm high, 100cm wide, 145cm long.

$545 - $645

Chapel Street Bazaar, VIC

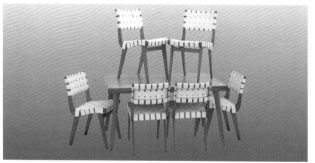

Dining suite, designed by Sydney architect Douglas Snelling, comprising seven pieces, manufactured by Functional Products, Australia, c1955, 74cm high, 84cm wide, 138cm long.

$4300 - $4500

Design Dilemas, VIC

Cuban mahogany Regency style, nine piece dining suite, Australia, c1970, 90cm high, 270cm long, 120cm deep.

$5300 - $5700

Seanic Antiques, VIC

French style, European beech dining table with fruitwood inlay, cabriole legs and ormolu detail, Australia, c1950, 75cm high, 108cm wide, 203cm long.

$2200 - $2400

Roger Hose Antiques, QLD

FURNITURE

Kitchen table and four chairs with a red Formica top and the chairs in their original red, cream and white vinyl upholstery, Australia, c1955, 76cm high, 81cm wide.

$600 - $700

Atomic Pop, SA

Nest of three wrought iron tables, Australia, c1950, 45cm high, 46cm wide, 31cm deep.

$175 - $195   **Step Back Antiques, VIC**

Seven piece laminex table setting with pink and grey vinyl seats, Australia, c1960.

$530 - $630   **Stumpy Gully Antiques, VIC**

Laminex kitchen table with six chairs, Australia.

$430 - $470   **Furniture Revisited, VIC**

Tasmanian oak school desk, on a metal frame, Australia, c1960, 70cm high, 107cm long, 80cm deep.

$115 - $135   **Stumpy Gully Antiques, VIC**

Cane and metal 'Cone' chair, attributed to the English designer Terence Conran, Australia, c1960, 76cm high, 76cm wide, 76cm deep.

$310 - $350   **The Junk Company, VIC**

Rosewood Chiswell sideboard, Australia.

$935 - $1035   **The Junk Company, VIC**

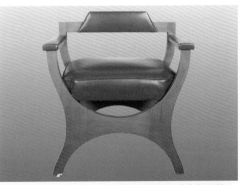

Funky maple chair with a red vinyl seat and back, Australia, c1960.

$225 - $265   **Towers Antiques & Collectables, NSW**

Teak side table and light stand, Australia, c1970, 175cm high, 57cm wide, 43cm deep.

$205 - $245   **Cobweb Collectables, NSW**

Wooden tea trolley, Australia, c1960, 70cm high, 80cm wide, 50cm deep.

$185 - $205   **Chapel Street Bazaar, VIC**

Unusual three wheel tea trolley, in teak and chrome with a hardened plastic top, Australia, c1975, 70cm high, 40cm wide, 73cm long.

$135 - $155   **Burly Babs Collectables/Retro Relics, VIC**

Kartell plastic storage unit, designed by Anna Castelli, Australia, c1960, 66cm high, 42cm diam.

$130 - $150   **Old World Antiques, SA**

Maple telephone stand with lamp, Australia, c1960, 160cm high, 31cm wide, 65cm long.

$180 - $200   **Roger Hose Antiques, QLD**

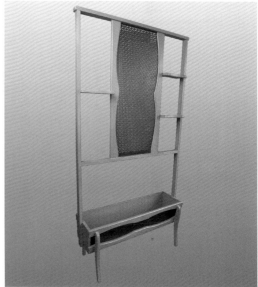

Room divider with a planter box to the base, Australia, c1960, 176cm high, 97cm wide, 35cm deep.

$200 - $240   **Atomic Pop, SA**

Coachwood smoker's stand, Australia, c1950, 64cm high.

$135 - $155   **Rose Cottage Antiques, ACT**

Kartell Designer green plastic, three table set, stamped 'Grotto Stoppino', Australia, c1970, 42cm high, 50cm diam.

$205 - $245   **Towers Antiques & Collectables, NSW**

Coffee table, Australia, c1950, 40cm high, 80cm long, 44cm deep.

$135 - $155   **Rose Cottage Antiques, ACT**

FURNITURE

Deep buttoned leather arm chair with a winged back, England, c1950.

$1550 - $1750

Antiques Restorations of Unley, SA

Matching pair of re-upholstered Robin Day 'Scimitar' chairs, in stainless steel, England, c1962.

$940 - $1040

Design Dilemas, VIC

Pair of mahogany side pedestals, England, c1950, 75cm high, 36cm wide, 32cm deep.

NZ$1495 - $1695

Bonham's, New Zealand

Oak court cupboard, of good colour with bevelled glass to the cupboards, United Kingdom, c1950, 137cm high, 122.5cm long, 50cm deep.

NZ$745 - $845

Antiques in Thames, New Zealand

Walnut veneer cocktail cabinet, made by George Serlin & Sons, London with a light in the top compartment and copper fittings, England, c1958, 110cm high, 107cm wide, 40cm deep.

NZ$475 - $515

Mr Pickwicks, New Zealand

Mahogany adjustable architect's table, England, c1950, 140cm high, 60cm wide, 93cm long.

$1850 - $2050

Shop 12, Armadale Antique Centre, VIC

Pair of reproduction bedside cabinets, parquetry inlaid with carved cabriole legs, France, 86cm high, 39cm wide, 39cm deep.

$1000 - $1200

Malvern Antique Centre, SA

Reproduction marble top bedside cabinet, France, 85cm high, 40cm wide, 40cm deep.

$550 - $650

Malvern Antique Centre, SA

Pair of aqua vinyl and nylon deluxe armchairs with teak bases, Denmark, c1968, 86cm high, 82cm wide, 90cm deep.

$545 - $645

Chapel Street Bazaar, VIC

Painted king size bed in Louis XVI style with flaming torcheres, France.

$13000 - $14000

Capocchi, VIC

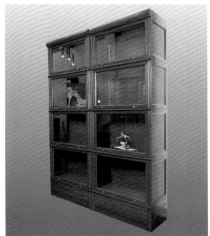

Pair of four sectional mahogany stacking bookcases with bevelled glass, France, c1950, 210cm high, 80cm long, 38cm deep.

$4800 - $5000

**Three Quarters 20th C Furnishings,
VIC**

Set of oak Louis style dining chairs, Belgium, c1960.

$1500 - $1700

**Collector's Corner,
QLD**

McIntosh carver chair, Scotland, c1960.

$275 - $315

**The Junk Company,
VIC**

Set of six chairs by 'Lingna', Czechoslovakia, c1970.

$1550 - $1750

**Cedar Lodge Antiques,
VIC**

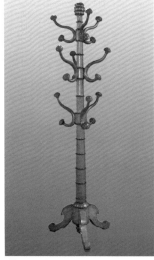

Simulated bamboo coat stand, France, c1950, 200cm high, 50cm wide.

$3150 - $3350

**Capocchi,
VIC**

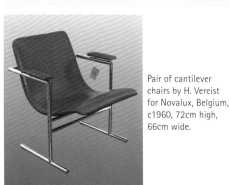

Pair of cantilever chairs by H. Vereist for Novalux, Belgium, c1960, 72cm high, 66cm wide.

$6300 - $6700

**Geoffrey Hatty,
VIC**

Marcel Brever chair with a solid steel frame, elastic webbing and a black leather seat and back rest, c1965.

$70 - $90

**Bowhows,
NSW**

Louis XVI styled, ladies writing desk with an inlaid fall front that depicts a romantic provincial scene of a shepherdess waiting for a letter, France, c1950, 97cm high, 77cm wide, 49cm deep.

$11500 - $12500

**Transference Antiques & Decor,
VIC**

Louis XV style commode, France, c1950, 87cm high, 97cm wide, 46cm deep.

$3850 - $4050

**Antiques On Consignment,
NSW**

FURNITURE

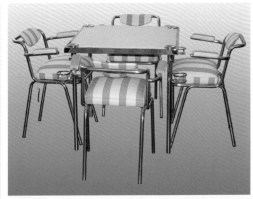

Card table
and chairs,
France, c1950,
72cm high.

$4400 - $4600

**Geoffrey Hatty,
VIC**

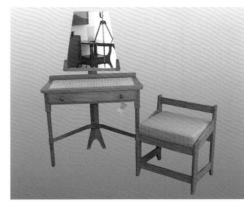

Oak dressing
table and chair
by Guilermeet
Chamber, France,
c1950, 140cm
high, 90cm wide,
41cm deep.

$3400 - $3600

**Geoffrey Hatty,
VIC**

Corner console table with a cherub supporting
a marble top, Italy, c1950, 80cm high, 70cm
wide.

$800 - $900

**Hollywood Antiques,
WA**

Bronzed iron and glass coffee table, with chinoiserie styling, France,
c1960, 40cm high, 54cm wide, 130cm long.

$1850 - $2050

**Capocchi,
VIC**

Unusual cane and glass coffee table,
stacked triangle design, maker's label in
aluminium for 'K de Vries, Amsterdam',
Netherlands, c1950, 44cm high, 64cm
wide.

$115 - $135

**Wendy Morrison Antiques,
VIC**

Wooden and brass palette umbrella stand,
Italy, c1950, 82cm high, 42cm wide.

$1000 - $1200

**Geoffrey Hatty,
VIC**

Lacquered red drinks trolley with brass trim, France, c1950, 60cm high, 75cm wide, 45cm deep.

$4400 - $4600

**Capocchi,
VIC**

Purple plastic surround mirror, by Cartell, Italy, c1973, 60cm diam.

$85 - $105

Chapel Street Bazaar, VIC

White ABS plastic umbrella stand or plan holder, model 'Dedalo' manufactured by Artemide and designed by Emma Gismondi Schweinberger, Italy, c1960, 38cm high, 38cm diam.

$200 - $240

506070, NSW

Chrome occasional table with interesting detail on the central pedestal and an early plastic top, New Zealand, c1952, 47cm high, 43cm diam.

NZ$110 - $130

Mr Pickwicks, New Zealand

Wrought iron hallstand, featuring suits of cards from the Grand Negre Casino, Nice, France, c1950, 285cm high, 100cm wide.

$12250 - $13250

Capocchi, VIC

Set of four painted, steel framed factory chairs with polished timber seats, Australia, c1950, 45cm high, 37cm wide, 35cm deep.

$500 - $600

Doug Up On Bourke, NSW

Chrome and glass Art Deco style tea trolley, Australia, c1950, 70cm high, 50cm wide.

$250 - $290

Chapel Street Bazaar, VIC

Two tier plastic, black and white trolley, European, c1970, 62cm high, 57cm wide.

$1870 - $2070

Victor Harbour Antiques - Mittagong, NSW

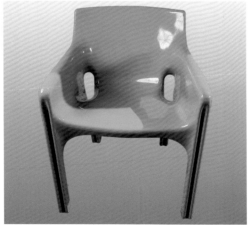

Gaudi chair, designer Vico Magistretti, manufacturer: Artemide, dated 1971 and made of fibreglass reinforced plastic, Italy, 73cm high, 60cm wide, 55cm deep.

$1100 - $1300

506070, NSW

Metal umbrella stand shaped as an umbrella, Italy, c1950, 74cm high, 27cm wide.

$850 - $950

Geoffrey Hatty, VIC

FURNITURE

Hans J. Wegner cabinet and book shelf designed by Hans J. Wegner between 1951-1958 for Ry Møbler, titled 'Model RY15 and RY5', as two separate units. The top and bottom units are part of an extensive modular storage system developed by Wegner, Denmark.

$2400 - $2600

Great Dane Furniture, VIC

Beech armchair designed by Sonna Rosen for Nassjo Stolfback with the original vinyl seat, Sweden, c1950, 73cm high, 62cm wide, 60cm long.

$1000 - $1200

Relic, QLD

Pair of Finn Juhl armchairs '#136', manufactured by France and Sons, in solid teak and retaining original cut velvet upholstery, Denmark, c1954.

$5300 - $5700

Design Dilemas, VIC

Oak easy chair, designed by Hans Wegner with original paper string weaving and manufactured by Carl Hansen, Denmark, c1950.

$2700 - $2900

Danish Vintage Modern, SA

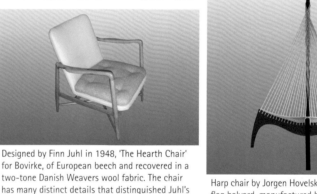

Designed by Finn Juhl in 1948, 'The Hearth Chair' for Bovirke, of European beech and recovered in a two-tone Danish Weavers wool fabric. The chair has many distinct details that distinguished Juhl's designs including the subtle curve of the arm and the seat which is floating free form the chair frame. The X-shaped crossbars under the finely detailed seat are the outstanding features of this chair. Another very similar chair was made by Niels Vodder, Denmark, c1950.

$5300 - $5700

Great Dane Furniture, VIC

Harp chair by Jorgen Hovelskov, of ebonised ash and flag halyard, manufactured by Christensen & Larsen Mobelhandvaerk, design based on the bow section of a Viking ship, Denmark, c1968, 134cm high, 100cm wide, 105cm deep.

$4650 - $4850

Vampt, NSW

Pair of Illum Wikkelsø Easy Chair 'No. 4', designed by Illum Wikkelsø in 1959 for N. Eilersen. During the early 1950's a large surplus of pre-cut teak (1x2x24in) became available. Wikkelsø and Eilersen developed the chair based on the modular chair, e.g. the armrests have a similar construction to a cricket bat, where two modular pieces are glued to the sides of the top of the armrest and rounded. The modular chair was also sold as sofas of varying lengths. Eventually, the chair was manufactured in other timbers, e.g. rosewood and oak.

$1500 - $1700

Great Dane Furniture, VIC

Wingback armchair by Illum Vikkelso, featuring long sweeping rear legs and an egg like chair shell, new upholstery, Denmark, c1950, 100cm high, 80cm wide.

$5300 - $5700

Vampt, NSW

A pair of beech occasional chairs, designed and produced by Fritz Hansen, stamped and dated 'FH 1954', Denmark, 80cm high, 60cm long, 60cm deep.

$750 - $850

Le Contraste, VIC

Spanish chair Model No. 2226 by Borge Mogensen, solid oak and oxhide leather back and seat, classic lines, Denmark, c1959, 68cm high, 82cm wide, 55cm deep.

$3700 - $3900

Vampt, NSW

Open armchair, in palisander and leather, designed by 'Fritz Henning', Denmark, c1950, 89cm high, 55cm wide, 46cm deep.

$1195 - $1395

Virtanen Antiques, VIC

Oak three seat sofa and easy chair, designed by Hans J. Wegner in 1953 and manufactured by Getama, model 'GE 290', Denmark.

$2400 - $2600

Danish Vintage Modern, SA

Hvidt & Mølgaard easy chair designed by Hvidt & Mølgaard for France & Søn in 1953, its distinguishing feature being the curved arms of laminated wood, with dark teak used on the tops of the arms to protect them from stains and lighter beech.

$1650 - $1850

Great Dane Furniture, VIC

Pair of chrome plated, spring steel and leather chairs manufactured by E. Kold Christensen and designed by Poul Kjaerholm, model name 'PK22', Denmark, c1960, 70cm high, 63cm wide, 42cm deep.

$5300 - $5700

506070, NSW

Swan chair in black leather, designed by Arne Jacobsen and manufactured by Fritz Hansen in 1987, Denmark.

$7300 - $7700

Danish Vintage Modern, SA

Teak chair, by Orla Molgaard Nielsen and Peter Hvidt with green wool upholstery, Denmark, c1958, 82cm high, 67cm wide, 67cm deep.

$1700 - $1900

506070, NSW

Hans Wegner designed cane folding chair, Denmark, c1950, 80cm high, 60cm wide, 60cm deep.

$330 - $370

The Junk Company, VIC

FURNITURE

Model CH24, 'The 'Y' Chair' or 'The Wishbone Chair', designed by Hans J. Wegner, the first chair Wegner designed for Carl Hansen & Son, and still in production. This is the most popular of Hans J. Wegner's chairs. Designed in 1949, the Y-Chair is linked to Wegner's Chinese chairs he designed in 1943 and 1949. The name Y-Chair is based on the Y-shaped construction of the back of the chair. Made from oak with paper cord, Denmark, c1950.

$1000 - $1200

Great Dane Furniture, VIC

Chair and ottoman in solid Brazilian rosewood and black leather, designed by Danish Architect Kristian Vedel in 1963, Denmark, 77cm high, 71cm wide.

$1150 - $1350

Plasma, VIC

Wegner coffee table, Denmark, c1960, 49cm high.

$430 - $470

The Junk Company, VIC

Teak coffee table designed by Finn Juhl and made by France & Son, Denmark, c1960, 46cm high, 54cm wide, 145cm long.

$950 - $1050

Danish Vintage Modern, SA

Teak and oak three seat sofa and two single easy chairs, manufactured by Getama 'GE 240' and designed by Hans Wegner in 1955, Denmark, 176cm long.

$2900 - $3100

Danish Vintage Modern, SA

Grete Jalk sofa, designed by Grete Jalk in the late 50's with a Brazilian rosewood frame and recovered in an aniline leather with 100% feather cushions, Denmark.

$3850 - $4050

Great Dane Furniture, VIC

Hans Wegner daybed (#258) with a cane backing, made for Getama, the more common version of this daybed having an upholstered back, Denmark, c1956.

$3150 - $3350

Great Dane Furniture, VIC

Low rosewood sideboard, by Rosengren & Hansen, Denmark, c1960, 80cm high, 47cm wide, 240cm long.

$3300 - $3500

Danish Vintage Modern, SA

Rosewood sideboard, designed by Gunni Omann in 1961, with teak lining (model#13), manufactured by Omann Jun Møbelfabrik, Denmark.

$2400 - $2600

Great Dane Furniture, VIC

Three door fitted cabinet with pull out sections, Denmark, c1960, 143cm high, 158cm long, 48cm deep.

$1850 - $2050   **Three Quarters 20th C Furnishings, VIC**

Two door sliding cabinet, in teak with adjustable internal shelving and storage, Denmark, c1960, 123cm high, 124cm wide, 45cm deep.

$1350 - $1550   **b bold - 20th Century Furniture & Effects, VIC**

Pair of black leather armchairs with rosewood frames, Denmark, c1960.

$1850 - $2050   **Three Quarters 20th C Furnishings, VIC**

Pair of Art Deco style chairs, Denmark, c1950, 80cm high, 43cm wide.

$220 - $260   **Mid Century Modern, SA**

Teak wine back upholstered chair, Scandinavia, c1950, 105cm high, 63cm wide, 80cm deep.

$330 - $370   **Rock N Rustic, SA**

Red leather easy chair with loose cushions, Denmark, c1970.

$650 - $750   **Danish Vintage Modern, SA**

Leather cushioned Tessa style arm chair, Denmark, c1970, 90cm high, 70cm wide, 70cm deep.

$750 - $850   **Mid Century Modern, SA**

Set of six cafe chairs with metal bases and teak ply seats, Denmark, c1950, 75cm high, 50cm wide, 38cm deep.

$300 - $340   **Mid Century Modern, SA**

FURNITURE

Pair of brown leather armchairs, Denmark, c1960.

$2400 - $2600   **Three Quarters 20th C Furnishings, VIC**

Compass chair with black vinyl upholstery, Denmark, c1950, 74cm high, 50cm wide, 45cm deep.

$190 - $210   **Mid Century Modern, SA**

Leather swivel armchair, Denmark, c1960, 95cm high, 75cm wide, 73cm deep.

$945 - $1045   **b bold - 20th Century Furniture & Effects, VIC**

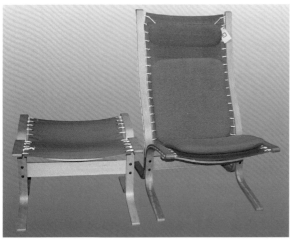

Early model 'Siesta' chair and footstool, Norway, c1960, 98cm high, 63cm wide.

$1400 - $1600   **Geoffrey Hatty, VIC**

Three seater red leather sofa with rosewood legs, Denmark, c1960, 67cm high, 190cm wide, 73cm deep.

$2650 - $2850   **b bold - 20th Century Furniture & Effects, VIC**

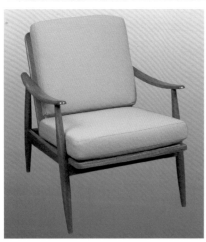

Arm chair with loose cushions, Denmark, c1950, 75cm high, 63cm wide, 70cm deep.

$230 - $270   **Mid Century Modern, SA**

Pair of leather cushioned reclining arm chairs with oak frames, Denmark, c1950, 90cm high, 75cm wide, 85cm deep.

$1500 - $1700   **Mid Century Modern, SA**

Red 'Little Tulip Chair' with upholstery and a painted steel base, Holland, c1970, 77cm high, 70cm wide, 50cm deep.

$1100 - $1300   **506070, NSW**

Teak and Aframosia chest of drawers, Denmark, c1960, 119cm high, 85cm wide, 42cm deep.

$700 - $800

Danish Vintage Modern, SA

Teak bureau raised on legs, Denmark, c1950, 110cm high, 90cm wide, 46cm deep.

$360 - $400

Mid Century Modern, SA

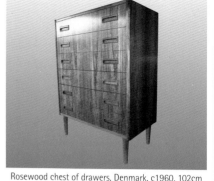

Rosewood chest of drawers, Denmark, c1960, 102cm high, 77cm wide, 42cm deep.

$850 - $950

Danish Vintage Modern, SA

Teak desk with six drawers, Denmark, c1960, 73cm high, 123cm long, 61cm deep.

$900 - $1000

Three Quarters 20th C Furnishings, VIC

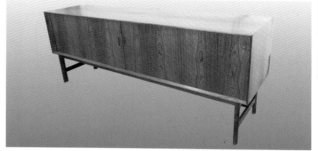

Free standing rosewood tambour fronted sideboard with an interior of oak drawers, Denmark, c1960, 74cm high, 51cm wide, 204cm long.

$3100 - $3300

Danish Vintage Modern, SA

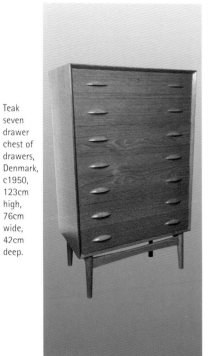

Teak seven drawer chest of drawers, Denmark, c1950, 123cm high, 76cm wide, 42cm deep.

$630 - $730

Mid Century Modern, SA

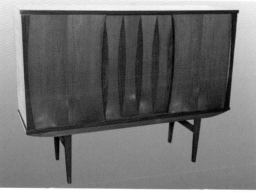

Sliding door teak side board, Denmark, c1950, 114cm high, 155cm wide, 43cm deep.

$950 - $1050 **Mid Century Modern, SA**

Teak four drawer chest of drawers, Denmark, c1950, 80cm high, 100cm wide, 45cm deep.

$360 - $400 **Mid Century Modern, SA**

FURNITURE

Two seat and three seat white leather sofas, Denmark.

$3400 - $3600

Danish Vintage Modern, SA

Three seat leather sofa, Denmark, c1970, 198cm long.

$3100 - $3300

Danish Vintage Modern, SA

Oak six to eight seater classic style, Scandinavian refectory table manufactured in the Netherlands with a stretcher base, classic shaped legs, detailed carvings and the top more than 8cm thick, c1960, 76cm high, 80cm wide, 170cm long.

$2100 - $2300

Whimsical Notions, NSW

A dining suite with two extension leaves, made in veneered and solid Brazilian rosewood, with original black vinyl upholstered seats, Norway, c1965, 74cm high, 120cm wide, 160cm long.

$2300 - $2500

Plasma, VIC

Rosewood coffee table with a solid top, Denmark, c1960, 40cm high, 45cm wide, 122cm long.

$280 - $320

Relic, QLD

Solid and veneered rosewood coffee table with a black laminate slide-out end, Denmark, c1960, 50cm high, 60cm wide, 160cm long.

$475 - $515

Plasma, VIC

Rosewood circular dining table, Denmark, c1950, 120cm high, 73cm diam.

$550 - $650

Mid Century Modern, SA

Oak hallstand with fabric pockets, Denmark, 113cm high, 107cm wide.

$1000 - $1200

Vampt, NSW

Three piece leather lounge suite with deep buttoning, Denmark, c1960, 80cm high, 187cm wide, 75cm deep.

$2700 - $2900

Mid Century Modern, SA

Nest of three teak tables, Denmark, c1950, 46cm high, 62cm wide, 39cm deep.

$260 - $300

Mid Century Modern, SA

Two section telephone table, Denmark, c1950, 61cm high, 55cm wide, 48cm deep.

$170 - $190

Mid Century Modern, SA

Teak single drawer suspended side table, Denmark, c1950, 48cm high, 62cm wide, 40cm deep.

$260 - $300

Mid Century Modern, SA

Coffee table in poplar with a chrome base, Sweden, c1960, 42cm high, 90cm wide, 90cm diam.

$1150 - $1350

Capocchi, VIC

Two tiered rosewood sofa table, Denmark, c1950, 54cm high, 170cm long, 63cm deep.

$380 - $420

Mid Century Modern, SA

Teak coffee table, Scandinavian design, with a magazine rack, Denmark, c1960, 46cm high, 44cm wide, 120cm long.

$230 - $270

Vintage Living, ACT

Teak extending auto trolley, Denmark, c1960, 63cm high, 75cm long, 48cm deep.

$695 - $795

Three Quarters 20th C Furnishings, VIC

Rosewood coffee table, Norway, c1960, 52cm high, 80cm wide, 145cm long.

$850 - $950

Danish Vintage Modern, SA

FURNITURE

Double cabinet in solid mahogany with Formica drawers and door fronts, New Zealand, c1955, 123cm high, 122cm long, 41cm deep.

NZ$475 - $515

Maxine's Collectibles, New Zealand

Two-tiered coffee table with a teak base and glass top layer, New Zealand, c1968, 48cm high, 70cm wide, 132cm long.

$475 - $515

Chapel Street Bazaar, VIC

Beech coffee table with a grey Formica shelf, New Zealand, c1950, 46cm high, 42cm wide, 117cm long.

NZ$140 - $160

Strangely Familiar, New Zealand

Pair of solid kauri pine church pews. Priced per item, New Zealand, c1950, 96cm high, 164cm long, 46cm deep.

NZ$545 - $645

Mr Pickwicks, New Zealand

Formica and chrome extension dining table and four upholstered chairs, New Zealand, c1951, 78cm high, 79cm wide, 165cm long.

NZ$775 - $875

Glenis Parker, New Zealand

Split cane chair, c1950.

$110 - $130

Paddington Antique Centre Pty Ltd, QLD

Blue and white saucer chair, c1960, 70cm high, 70cm wide.

$60 - $80

Relic, QLD

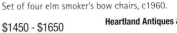

Set of four elm smoker's bow chairs, c1960.

$1450 - $1650

Heartland Antiques & Art, NSW

'Jetson' chair in metal with a blackbean base and a moulded foam top, c1960, 77cm high, 67cm wide, 70cm deep.

$355 - $395

Relic, QLD

Orange slice chair of moulded ply and stainless steel, designed and made by Relic, 72cm high, 72cm wide, 70cm deep.

$405 - $445

Relic, QLD

Pair of black and white woven plastic and cane chairs, c1950, 75cm high, 60cm wide, 65cm deep.

$155 - $175

Relic, QLD

Leather and steam pressed plywood reclining and swivel armchair with footstool, in the style of Charles and Ray Eames, Canada, c1960.

$3200 - $3400

Design Dilemas, VIC

Classic shaped cane suite of four single chairs, c1950, 90cm high, 65cm wide, 90cm deep.

$430 - $470

Relic, QLD

Butterfly chair with a steel frame and canvas seat, c1950, 85cm high, 85cm wide, 95cm deep.

$205 - $245

Relic, QLD

Red and blue chair by Gerrit Rietveld 1918 for Cassina, fully signed with Cassina tags, c1970, 90cm high, 62cm wide, 88cm deep.

$2200 - $2400

Relic, QLD

Belmont barber's chair with manually operated height and reclining adjustments, Japan, c1960, 115cm high, 72cm wide, 115cm deep.

$800 - $900

Doug Up On Bourke, NSW

Set of six green vinyl and fabric, tub dining chairs, c1970, 87cm high, 52cm wide, 49cm deep.

$255 - $295

Relic, QLD

Teak and vinyl lounge suite with an ottoman, of unusual design, c1960.

$500 - $600

Relic, QLD

FURNITURE

Classic lounge in original three toned vinyl, c1950, 88cm high, 205cm long.

$330 - $370

Relic,
QLD

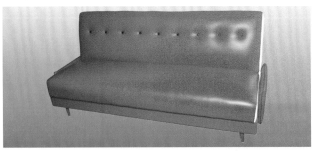

'Click-Clack' lounge, folding down to a bed with storage under, c1960, 85cm high, 196cm long, 80cm deep.

$675 - $775

Relic,
QLD

'Genda' three seater lounge with wonderful arms, c1950, 75cm high, 187cm wide, 98cm deep.

$950 - $1050

Relic,
QLD

Round glass topped coffee table with a carved timber base in the form of four bull dogs, Indonesia, 41cm high, 90cm diam.

$2100 - $2300

Architectural Décor Australia,
NSW

Red laminex dining suite with chrome chairs and base, circa 1950, length 153cm, height 80cm.

$500 - $600

Relic,
QLD

Van Treight extension dining table, and ten chairs, c1950.

$1400 - $1600

Heartland Antiques & Art,
NSW

Chrome, glass and perspex dining suite by Ultra Furniture with original red velvet seats, c1970, 83cm high, 159cm wide, 190cm long.

$500 - $600

Relic,
QLD

Laminated six seater table with a central pedestal and six framed chairs with black vinyl seats, c1950, 76cm high, 91cm wide, 154cm long.

NZ$1800 - $2000

Decollectables,
New Zealand

Fenton milk glass, lidded compote, United States, c1970, 20cm high.

$45 - $65   **Antique General Store, NSW**

Fenton milk glass vase, United States, 19cm high, 12cm wide.

$115 - $135   **Half Moon Antiques & Interiors, SA**

Footed amber glass divided server, United States, c1970, 6cm high, 19cm wide, 31cm long.

$65 - $85   **Antipodes Antiques, QLD**

Whitehill sterling silver and crystal claret jug, United States, c1955, 29cm high.

$1265 - $1465   **Victor Harbour Antiques - Mittagong, NSW**

Iridescent water jug by Jeannette Glass Company, pattern 'Floragold', United States, c1950, 24cm high.

$40 - $50   **Olsens Antiques, QLD**

Multi-coloured glass sugar bowl, Australia, c1970, 17cm high.

$55 - $75   **Paddington Antique Centre Pty Ltd, QLD**

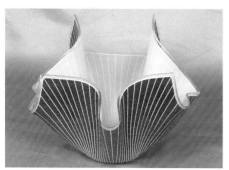

Red and white striped glass bowl, Australia, c1950.

$25 - $35   **Baxter's Antiques, QLD**

Large blue hand blown glass epergne, by Peter Crisp, Australia, c1960, 23cm high, 28cm wide.

$1195 - $1395   **Victor Harbour Antiques - Mittagong, NSW**

Ted Secombe crystaline vase, Australia, c1990, 29cm high, 29cm wide.

$530 - $630   **Tarlo & Graham, VIC**

Large blue glass urn, Australia, c1970, 38cm high.

$85 - $105   **The Junk Company, VIC**

Crackle lustre finish vase by Colin Heaney, Australia, c1988, 28cm high, 15cm wide, 8cm deep.

$115 - $135   **Forever Amber @ The Tyabb Grainstore, VIC**

Flashed ruby art glass footed bowl with an engraved signature, 'Came Weston', Australia, c1990, 24.5cm diam.

$135 - $155   **Graham & Nancy Miller, VIC**

Depression glass bowl with a pink glass foot, c1950.

$55 - $75

Helen's On The Bay, QLD

Fenton amethyst carnival glass mermaid planter with original sticker, United States, c1960, 17cm high, 19cm wide.

$375 - $415

The Bottom Drawer Antique Centre, VIC

Carnival glass cherry bowl, United States, c1948, 14cm high, 16cm diam.

$75 - $95

Dr Russell's Emporium, WA

'Lemon and Poeroa Sparkling Mineral Water' 750ml. brown glass bottle, New Zealand, c1967, 27.5cm high, 8cm diam.

NZ$5 - $15

Peachgrove Antiques, New Zealand

Transfer printed 'Fanta' bottle dated 1970, New Zealand, 30cm high, 8.5cm diam.

NZ$5 - $15

Peachgrove Antiques, New Zealand

Green glass 'Lead' bottle, New Zealand, c1967, 30cm high, 8cm diam.

NZ$5 - $15

Peachgrove Antiques, New Zealand

'Buckham's' flavoured beverage, transfer printed bottle, New Zealand, c1967, 29.5cm high, 7cm diam.

NZ$5 - $15

Peachgrove Antiques, New Zealand

Carnival glass vase in the 'beehive' shape, England, c1950, 23.5cm high.

$85 - $105

Woodside Bazaar, SA

Green glass penguin float bowl, Czechoslovakia, c1950, 25cm high, 22cm diam.

$200 - $240

Malvern Antique Market, VIC

'Highland Queen Scotch Whisky' bottle with a plastic stopper, c1970, 23cm high, 10cm wide.

$20 - $30

Chapel Street Bazaar, VIC

Whitefriars green and blue glass bowl, England, c1950, 28cm high, 30cm diam.

$345 - $385

The Junk Company, VIC

Pair of aubergine and tangerine 'random strapping' vases by Geoffrey Baxter, for Whitefriars, England, c1965, 20cm high.

$200 - $240

Design Dilemas, VIC

Large Whitefriars blue glass Kingfisher slab vase, England, c1970, 26.5cm high, 13cm wide.

$675 - $775

Chapel Street Bazaar, VIC

Whitefriars vase, England, c1960, 28cm high.

$205 - $245

The Junk Company, VIC

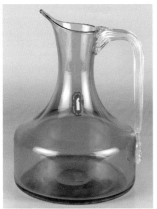

Blue Whitefriars jug with original sticker, England, 16cm high.

NZ$150 - $170

Gales Antiques, New Zealand

Whitefriars jug in the glacier pattern, designed by Geoffrey Baxter, England.

$55 - $75

frhapsody, WA

Whitefriars bamboo patterned, blue glass vase, England, c1960.

NZ$115 - $135

Peachgrove Antiques, New Zealand

Whitefriars bud vase, England, c1968, 22cm high, 40cm wide.

NZ$215 - $255

Oxford Court Antiques Centre, New Zealand

Glass paperweight, made by Langham, England, c1950, 8cm diam.

$185 - $205

Kings Park Antiques & Collectables, SA

Large Geoffrey Baxter designed aubergine 'Drunken Bricklayer' vase, England, c1970, 34cm high.

$4300 - $4500

Design Dilemas, VIC

Yellow coloured glass vase with a red interior and frilled rim, England, 21cm high, 12cm wide.

$45 - $65

Half Moon Antiques & Interiors, SA

Wedgwood black glass vase, England, 20cm high, 7cm wide.

$110 - $130

Galeria del Centro, NSW

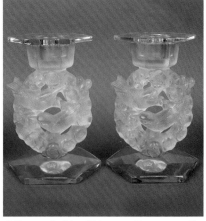

Lalique candlesticks with hexagonal bases, removable sconces and frosted stems of birds within a wreath of flowers and fruit, engraved signatures, 'Lalique France', c1950, 17.5cm high.

NZ$3400 - $3600

Tinakori Antiques, New Zealand

Pair of milk glass decanters with stoppers, Portugal, c1970, 24.5cm high.

$50 - $70

Atomic Pop, SA

Orrefors vase, in blue cased, over clear glass, signed, c1950, 13.5cm high, 11cm Wide.

$280 - $320

Isadora's Antiques, NSW

Leadglass vase by Val St. Lambert, Belgium, c1950, 34cm high, 10cm wide.

$255 - $295

Collector's Cottage, NSW

Tall cameo-cut baluster shape lipped vase with acorn pattern decoration of three colours, post Emile Galle period, asterisk star signature, France, c1966, 30cm high.

$7300 - $7700

Showcase Antiques, NSW

Cased glass sculptured vase, signed Pavel Hlava, Czechoslovakia, c1950, 17cm high, 6cm wide.

$305 - $345

Chapel Street Bazaar, VIC

Vintage crystal figure of two dancers, designed by Marc Lalique in 1960, 'Lalique France', 27cm high, 13cm wide.

$2400 - $2600

Kaleidoscope Antiques, VIC

Tall 'Flash-cut' crystal vase, marked 'Eybor Czechoslovakia' to the base, c1950, 30cm high.

$125 - $145

Born Frugal, VIC

Crystal vase by Baccarat, France.

$750 - $850

Casey Antiques, VIC

Set of six mid size green and amber glasses with clear stems, France, c1970, 10cm high.

$35 - $45

frhapsody, WA

Set of eight green stem wine goblets, by Luminarc, France, c1970, 10.5cm high.

$45 - $55

frhapsody, WA

Signed Daum Nancy crystal vase, France, c1950, 18cm high.

$430 - $470

Hollywood Antiques, WA

Orange Pyrex cup and saucer, France.

$55 - $75

Victor Harbour Antiques - Mittagong, NSW

Blue glass mortar and pestle, by Daum, France, c1950, 13cm high, 20cm wide.

$800 - $900

Capocchi, VIC

Seven piece glass drink set, consisting of a glass decanter with white enamel and gold rings applied to turquoise coloured glass and six matching drinking glasses, Czechoslovakia, c1950, 22cm high, 9cm diam.

$20 - $30

Woodside Bazaar, SA

Bohemian ruby glass decanter and six matching wine goblets, etched and embossed in gold with twisted clear stems, Czechoslovakia, c1960.

$185 - $205

Helen's On The Bay, QLD

Crystal champagne bucket, Poland, c1995, 19.5cm high, 20cm diam.

NZ$135 - $155

Gregory's of Greerton, New Zealand

Bohemian ruby glass bell, etched and embossed in gold with a twisted handle, Czechoslovakia, c1960, 16cm high, 8cm wide.

$45 - $65

Helen's On The Bay, QLD

Beautiful crystal vase with original stickers, 'Lead crystal 26% Pho ® hand crafted Yugoslavia', c1950, 16cm high, 15.5cm diam.

$40 - $50

Maryborough Station Antique Emporium, VIC

GLASS

Red cased glass bottle, designed by Micheal Bang of the Holmgaard Factory, Denmark, c1970, 55cm high.

$345 - $385   **How Bazaar, TAS**

Holmgaard 'brandy' decanter in blue glass with the original label intact, Denmark, c1960, 30cm high, 13cm wide, 12cm deep.

$170 - $190   **Lesley's Treasures, NSW**

'Gulvase' by Otto Brauer for Holmgaard, Denmark, c1970, 50cm high.

$1000 - $1200   **Vampt, NSW**

Signed Holmgaard asymmetrical blue glass bowl, by Per Lutkin, c1965, 5cm high, 14cm diam.

$130 - $150   **Relic, QLD**

Glass goblet commemorating 150 years of 'Holmgaard 1825-1975', limited edition of 3500, Denmark, 19cm high.

$305 - $345   **Collectable Creations, QLD**

Unusual Holmgaard vase with a black highlighted rim and signed by Michael Bang, Sweden, c1980, 15cm high, 14cm wide.

$260 - $300

Three Holmgaard blue bottle vases, Denmark, c1950, 44cm high.

$750 - $850   **Mid Century Modern, SA**

Holmgaard glass bowl, Denmark, c1960, 18cm wide, 5cm deep, 18cm diam.

$75 - $95   **Pedlars Antique Market, SA**

Holmgaard paper weight with original label, Denmark, c1960, 7cm diam.

$85 - $105   **Marge's Antiques & Collectables, NSW**

$260 - $300   **Chapel Street Bazaar, VIC**

Amber glass Holmgaard 'bottle' vase, Denmark, c1950, 58cm high.

$360 - $400   **Mid Century Modern, SA**

Kastrup/ Holmgaard Viking bottle designed by Ole Winther in smoke grey glass, Denmark, c1970, 23cm high.

$40 - $50   **frhapsody, WA**

Heavy glass ashtray or dish, Scandinavia, c1969, 14cm wide.

$45 - $55

frhapsody, WA

Sea Glasbruk/Glassworks (Kosta) goblet with a moustache decoration, Sweden, c1969, 13.5cm high.

$30 - $40

frhapsody, WA

Kosta 'Snowball' tea light holder designed by Ann Warff, Sweden, c1979, 8cm high.

$25 - $35

frhapsody, WA

Lind Strad Kosta vase, Sweden, 20cm high.

$245 - $285

The Junk Company, VIC

Pair of lead crystal Granna glass birds, hand made in Sweden, paper label, c1970, 6.5cm high, 6cm wide, 9cm long.

$65 - $85

Kilbarron Antiques and Collectables, VIC

'Hadelands' glass charger, by Willy Johannson, Norway, c1964, 30cm diam.

$165 - $185

Forever Amber @ The Tyabb Grainstore, VIC

Lattichino bowl, Scandinavia, c1950, 7cm high, 19cm diam.

NZ$260 - $300

Peachgrove Antiques, New Zealand

Ekness art glass vase, signed, Sweden, c1950, 19cm high, 20cm diam.

NZ$185 - $205

Peachgrove Antiques, New Zealand

Aseda glass bowl 'Svenska' from Bo Borgstrom, Sweden, 85cm high, 135cm diam.

$115 - $135

Shop 26, Antiques & Collectables - Hamilton, NSW

Glass bowl in the Kraka technique, manufactured by Orrefors and designed by Sven Palmquist, Sweden, c1960, 10cm high, 20cm diam.

$500 - $600

506070, NSW

GLASS

Pair of Scandinavian art glass vases, Scandinavia, c1950.

$200 - $240

Obsidian Antiques, NSW

Signed Orrefors, sommerso art glass vase, Sweden, c1950, 16cm high, 12cm wide.

$330 - $370

Obsidian Antiques, NSW

Hoglund vaseline vase, c1960, 7cm high, 17cm wide.

NZ$175 - $195

Oxford Court Antiques Centre, New Zealand

The apple vase, designed by Ingeborg Lundin (1919-1992) for Orrefors for the 1957 exposition, signed and dated to the base, the idea from Andromeda and Greek antiquity, Sweden, c1957, 39cm high, 29cm diam.

$3200 - $3400

Warwick Oakman Antiques, TAS

Moulded glass vase with original sticker, by Sea Glassworks (Kosta Sweden), Sweden, c1970, 16.5cm high.

$30 - $40

frhapsody, WA

Steel blue vase by Riihimaen Lasi Oy designed by Helena Tynell, translated means 'fence lock' or 'large padlock', Finland, c1970, 21cm high, 14cm wide.

$495 - $595

Capocchi, VIC

Signed Kraka vase by Sven Palmqvist for Orrefors, featuring controlled bubbles within netting and the original label, Sweden, c1960, 22cm high, 14cm wide.

$1600 - $1800

Relic, QLD

Ekenas glass orange vase, signed John Orwar Lake, Sweden, 16.5cm high, 14cm wide.

NZ$255 - $295

Maxine's Collectibles, New Zealand

Blue Orrefors vase, signed to base 'Palmquist Kraka' from the series created in 1944, Sweden, c1950, 23cm high, 12cm wide.

$1150 - $1350

Capocchi, VIC

Red art glass bowl, Italy, c1970, 10cm high, 22cm long, 22cm diam.

$135 - $155

Dr Russell's Emporium, WA

Yellow uranium glass bowl 'Murano', 9cm high, 10cm wide, 15cm long.

$110 - $130

The Junk Company, VIC

Murano gold foil Seguso fish with original sticker, Italy, c1950, 18cm high, 19cm wide.

$455 - $495

Archers Antiques, TAS

Archimede Seguso vase of ovoid shape with controlled bubbles on a black ground and gold accents, signed plus paper label, Italy, c1970, 11cm high, 16cm diam.

$845 - $945

Kilbarron Antiques and Collectables, VIC

Murano latticino glass bowl, Italy, c1960, 5.5cm high, 11.5cm long.

$75 - $95

Pedlars Antique Market, SA

Luxardo Murano glass fish liquor bottle with a green base, Italy, c1969, 30cm high, 27cm wide.

$330 - $370

Victor Harbour Antiques - Mittagong, NSW

Sommerso Murano glass bowl by Archimedes Seguso, Italy, c1950, 7.5cm high, 22cm diam.

NZ$185 - $205

Peachgrove Antiques, New Zealand

Seguso Viro (Murano) signed oval platter, featuring the 'Fireworks' pattern with an engraved signature, paper label and an amethyst background, Italy, c1992, 38cm wide, 47cm long.

$1500 - $1700

Pastimes Antiques, NSW

Murano art glass basket with a fluted handle and orange flower, Italy, c1970, 27cm high.

$255 - $295

Victor Harbour Antiques - Mittagong, NSW

Murano blue and peach glass vase, Italy, c1960, 17cm high, 16.5cm wide, 42cm long.

$85 - $105

Newport Temple Antiques, VIC

Murano glass, turtle shell replica bag with a gold threaded handle, Italy, c1950, 21cm high.

$140 - $160

Nicki's Collection, NSW

GLASS

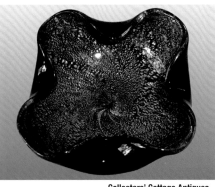

Murano art glass dish with copper and gold inclusions, Italy, c1960, 12cm wide, 12cm long.

$75 - $95

Collectors' Cottage Antiques, NSW

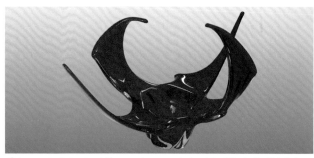

Scissor-cut, abstractural Murano glass console bowl, by Alfredo Barbini, Italy, c1955, 82cm wide.

$610 - $710

Design Dilemas, VIC

Murano glass bowl with silver foil inclusions and the original sticker to the base, Italy, c1960, 6cm high, 14cm diam.

$80 - $100

Born Frugal, VIC

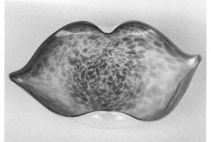

Murano pink overlay glass bowl with gold inclusions, Italy, c1950, 8cm high, 17cm wide, 28cm long.

$265 - $305

Patrick Colwell, NSW

Murano Art Glass ash tray, clear to ruby with aventurine trapped flakes, Italy, c1960, 5cm high, 17cm diam.

$55 - $75

Yande Meannjin Antiques, QLD

Murano pink glass ashtray, Italy, c1950, 5.5cm high, 16cm wide, 15.5cm long.

NZ$115 - $135

Peachgrove Antiques, New Zealand

Large centrepiece Venetian dish in blue, green and clear glass, Sommerso style, Italy, c1950, 10cm high, 34cm wide, 24cm deep.

$135 - $155

Born Frugal, VIC

Murano cased glass sculpture in blue, Italy, c1950, 15cm wide, 19cm long.

$205 - $245

Obsidian Antiques, NSW

Red art glass fruit bowl with a heavy clear glass base, Italy, c1960, 16cm high, 32cm wide, 16.5cm deep.

$65 - $85

Sweet Slumber Antiques & Collectables, NSW

Murano Barbini, four sided, folded glass bowl, in the biomorphic shape decorated with gold flakes and tiny air bubbles, Italy, c1950, 8cm high, 20cm wide, 20cm wide.

$155 - $175

Towers Antiques & Collectables, NSW

Red and green, scissor-cut Murano glass bowl, by Alfredo Barbini, Italy, c1960, 23cm high.

$225 - $265

Design Dilemas, VIC

Pair of glass figures for Barovier & Toso, Adventurine inclusions, Italy, c1950.

$2700 - $2900

Gallery Narcisse, NSW

Murano glass clown bowl, Italy, 18cm wide, 25cm long.

$345 - $385

Sherwood Bazaar, QLD

Hand blown pair of red and clear glass vases, shaped as fish with open mouths, Italy, c1950, 15.5cm high, 7cm wide, 9cm deep.

$430 - $470

Claringbold's Fine Jewellery, Antiques & Gifts, NSW

Murano glass Dolphin on a ball, Italy, c1985, 31cm high, 23cm wide.

NZ$330 - $370

Hubbers Emporium, New Zealand

Sommerso glass 'Rooster' vase of flowing lines, clear glass and inner layers of red and orange, Italy, c1960, 21cm high, 32cm long.

$165 - $185

Born Frugal, VIC

Multi-coloured Murano glass clown decanter, Italy, c1950, 35cm high.

$245 - $285

How Bazaar, TAS

Murano glass figure of a Chinese woman with the original Murano label to the base, Italy, c1950, 19cm high.

$155 - $175

Malvern Antique Market, VIC

Pair of Murano glass figurines of a gentleman and a lady, in opalescent glass with gold inclusions, Italy, 22cm high.

$745 - $845

Jack Maas, VIC

Stylized glass bird, Italy, c1970, 38cm high.

$135 - $155

The Junk Company, VIC

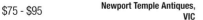

Art glass, red fish vase, Italy, c1960, 15cm high, 23cm long.

$75 - $95

Newport Temple Antiques, VIC

Hand blown art glass multi-coloured fish, Italy, c1950, 12cm high, 30cm long, 7cm deep.

$85 - $105

Towers Antiques & Collectables, NSW

GLASS

Venetian glass figure with a crown, Italy, c1950, 16cm high.

$100 - $120   **Malvern Antique Market, VIC**

Twelve Bohemian ruby red wine glasses with gilt etched decorations, Italy, c1970, 19cm high.

$275 - $315   **Northumberland Antiques & Restorations, NSW**

Solid glass dog, Italy, c1960, 22cm high.

$190 - $210   **frhapsody, WA**

Fine Venetian opalescent compote with blue detail, Italy, c1980, 17.5cm high, 15cm wide.

$135 - $155   **Chapel Street Bazaar, VIC**

Set of six hand blown Venetian wine glasses, Italy, 17cm high.

$305 - $345   **Capocchi, VIC**

Murano gold foil dolphin in ruby glass, with the original sticker, Italy, c1950, 18cm high.

$215 - $255   **Archers Antiques, TAS**

Pair of signed Murano glass goblets, Italy, c1970, 22.5cm high.

$430 - $470   **Newlyn Antiques & Cottage Garden Nursery, VIC**

Murano clear art glass centrepiece, Italy, c1950, 20cm high.

$155 - $175   **Gumnut Antiques & Old Wares, NSW**

Large blue brandy balloon, Italy, c1960, 34cm high, 21cm wide.

$40 - $50   **Helen's On The Bay, QLD**

Large orange satin glass brandy balloon, Italy, c1960, 20cm high, 19cm wide.

$55 - $75   **Helen's On The Bay, QLD**

Murano glass duck ornament, Italy, c1960.

$205 - $245   **Antiques & Heirlooms, WA**

Hand painted glass comport with a 22ct gold, twisted stem, Italy, c1950, 24cm high, 17cm wide, 17cm diam.

$165 - $185   **Dr Russell's Emporium, WA**

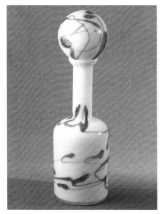

Art glass decanter and stopper, of white glass with swirling colour, Italy, c1965, 40cm high.

$75 - $95

Atomic Pop, SA

Art glass decanter and stopper in blue glass with original label, Opalina Fiorentina manufacturer, Italy, c1965, 44cm high.

$75 - $95

Atomic Pop, SA

Cased glass bottle with a ball stopper, Italy, c1950, 40cm high, 19cm wide.

$175 - $195

Chapel Street Bazaar, VIC

Murano glazed red and black opaque jug with a translucent handle, c1960, 17cm high.

$260 - $300

Shenton Park Antiques, WA

Murano blue and white clear cased sauce jug, Italy, c1950, 18cm high, 8cm wide.

$210 - $250

Isadora's Antiques, NSW

Green art glass jug with a marker's label, 'Opalina Florentina', Italy, c1970, 30cm high, 19cm diam.

$25 - $35

Atomic Pop, SA

Venetian glass jug in red cased glass with a black trailing swag design and an applied clear twist glass handle, Italy, c1960, 23cm high, 18cm wide.

$130 - $150

Bowerbird Antiques & Collectables, SA

Green art glass jug with 'Opalina Fiorentina' written on the label and a clear glass handle, Italy, c1950.

$200 - $240

Dr Russell's Emporium, WA

Red glass vessel with a clear glass bubble stopper, the body in ruby red sitting on a clear glass decorated stem and foot, the stopper of hollow hand blown glass, Italy, c1960, 42cm high.

$45 - $65

Born Frugal, VIC

Blue cased Venetian glass claret jug with a clear glass base, handle and stopper, Italy, c1960, 42cm high, 10cm wide.

$105 - $125

Bowerbird Antiques & Collectables, SA

Blue art glass jug with a clear handle, Italy, c1965, 36cm high.

$30 - $40

Atomic Pop, SA

GLASS

VENETIAN

Murano glass figure of birds, Italy, c1950, 20cm high.

$100 - $120

Malvern Antique Market, VIC

Signed Murano glass fish, Italy, c1950, 26cm high, 23cm wide.

$430 - $470

Coliseum Antiques Centre, NSW

Green Murano glass duck, Italy, c1950, 20cm high.

$85 - $105

Accent on Gifts, NSW

Magnificent Murano glass bird, Italy, c1950, 35cm high.

$260 - $300

Hollywood Antiques, WA

Murano red and blue coloured glass swan with sticker, Italy, c1950.

$330 - $370

Lucilles Interesting Collectables, NSW

Pair of Murano ruby coloured fish, Italy, c1960, 30cm high, 6cm wide.

$130 - $150

Antiques As Well, VIC

Signed art glass figurine of an oriental themed person, in cased amber and clear glass, Italy, c1955, 27cm high, 12cm wide.

$500 - $600

ShopAtNortham, WA

Murano glass rooster with original label, Italy, c1950, 22cm high.

$185 - $205

Antipodes Antiques, QLD

Murano glass bird, featuring gold decoration and bubbles in the body, Italy, c1950, 12cm high, 31cm wide.

$305 - $345

Bathurst Street Antique Centre, TAS

Red Murano glass dog, Italy, c1960, 9cm high, 6cm wide, 19cm long.

$175 - $195

Pedlars Antique Market, SA

Murano glass figure of 'The Cymbal Man', attributed to Barovier, Italy, c1950, 20cm high.

$115 - $135

Steven Sher Antiques, WA

Large and colourful art glass vase, Italy, c1970, 35cm high.

$100 - $120

Atomic Pop, SA

Murano art glass vase, in orange on a clear foot, Italy, c1960, 38cm high, 12cm diam.

$85 - $105

Obsidian Antiques, NSW

Tall Incalmo vessel by Venini, Italy, c1960, 42cm high.

$1400 - $1600

Geoffrey Hatty, VIC

Purple art glass vase, Italy, 22cm high, 16cm deep, 16cm diam.

$110 - $130

Dr Russell's Emporium, WA

Ruby glass Murano vase, Italy, c1970, 15cm high.

$55 - $75

Graham & Nancy Miller, VIC

Incalmo small vessel with collar by Venini, Italy, c1960, 13cm high.

$900 - $1000

Geoffrey Hatty, VIC

Blue and gold fleck Murano vase, Italy, c1970, 17cm high.

$110 - $130

The Junk Company, VIC

Pair of amethyst vases with sterling silver overlay, original sticker shows a Venetian gondola, Italy, c1960, 10cm high, 8cm wide.

$100 - $120

Helen's On The Bay, QLD

Pair of Venetian glass vases with raised floral designs, Italy, c1960, 25cm high, 8cm wide.

$110 - $130

Helen's On The Bay, QLD

Orange and black striped glass vase, Italy, c1970, 26cm high, 19cm diam.

NZ$185 - $205

Maxine's Collectibles, New Zealand

Contemporary green glass vase, Italy, 47cm high, 19cm diam.

$40 - $50

Furniture Revisited, VIC

Brown and yellow Murano glass vase, Italy, c1960, 20cm high, 14cm diam.

$85 - $105

The Junk Company, VIC

Pair of art glass fish, from the Crown Crystal, Christchurch factory, New Zealand, c1960, 33cm long.

NZ$130 - $150   **Middle Earth Antiques, New Zealand**

Hand blown glass flagon by Ray Hooper, Auckland, New Zealand, c1970, 16cm high, 13cm diam.

NZ$85 - $105   **Maxine's Collectibles, New Zealand**

Set of six dessert bowls with star decorations, c1955, 8cm high.

$40 - $50   **Atomic Pop, SA**

Orange, black and white glass basket, China, c2000, 23cm high, 14cm wide.

$35 - $45   **Maryborough Station Antique Emporium, VIC**

Blue glass, Deco styled, fish float bowl, Bohemia, c1970, 22cm high.

$245 - $285   **Paddington Antique Centre Pty Ltd, QLD**

Pink glass lidded punch bowl with ten cups and a pink glass ladle, c1950, 28cm high, 23cm diam.

$120 - $140   **Antiques at Redbank, QLD**

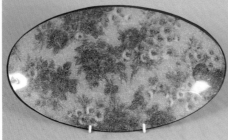

Oval shaped dish with rose fabric encased between the glass, Japan, c1950, 17cm wide, 30cm long.

$45 - $65   **Helen's On The Bay, QLD**

Clear art glass bowl with a spiky design, 13cm high.

$20 - $30   **Atomic Pop, SA**

Blue glass epergne, c1960.

$2395 - $2595   **Casey Antiques, VIC**

Large, heavy crystal punch bowl with a lid and ladle, c1960, 34cm high, 27cm diam.

$375 - $415   **Fyshwick Antique Centre, ACT**

Blue glass 'Genie' bottle decanter with stopper, c1965, 41cm high.

$25 - $35   **Atomic Pop, SA**

Amber glass 'Genie' bottle decanter with stopper, c1965, 43cm high.

$25 - $35   **Atomic Pop, SA**

Bohemian decanter with six gl...

Blu...
32c...

$65 -

Crystal decanter set with six whisky glasses, signed 'Edinburgh. Made In Scotland', c1960, 25cm high, 9cm wide.

$275 - $315

Helen's On The Bay, QLD

Carafe and set of six matching glasses, all in different colours, Australia, c1950.

Helen's On The Bay, QLD

Green glass 'Genie' bottle decanter with an inlaid grape pattern and complete with stopper, c1970, 54cm high.

$25 - $35

Atomic Pop, SA

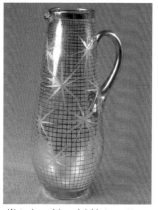

Water jug with an inlaid star pattern design, c1965, 30cm high.

$15 - $25

Atomic Pop, SA

THYME SEEDS

SOW IN MOIST COMPOST IN A POT OR TRAY. DO NOT COVER WITH COMPOST AS THEY NEED LIGHT TO GERMINATE. COVER WITH PLASTIC OR GLASS UNTIL LARGE ENOUGH TO HANDLE AND RE-POT

WWW.WAYSTOSAYTHANKYOU.CO.UK.

Colourful cased glass water jug and glasses with multi coloured swirls on aqua backgrounds, Japan, c1950, 18cm high, 17cm wide.

$175 - $195

Chapel Street Bazaar, VIC

Four harlequin glass brandy balloons, in blue, green, pink and aqua, Japan, c1970, 11cm high.

$20 - $30

frhapsody, WA

Water set with a jug and six glasses, in colourful frosted glass, c1965, 18cm high.

$25 - $35

Atomic Pop, SA

Set of six drinking glasses with different coloured patterns and a wire carrier, c1970, 32cm diam.

$40 - $50

Relic, QLD

Green glass water jug and set with six glasses, c1970, 26cm high.

$20 - $30

Atomic Pop, SA

Bohemia lustre, Czechoslovakia, c1960, 32cm high, 9cm wide.

$230 - $270 **Green Gables Collectables, NSW**

Heavy glass body shaped vase, China, c2000, 45cm high, 19cm wide.

$75 - $95 **Maryborough Station Antique Emporium, VIC**

Pressed glass vase, c1950, 35cm high.

$40 - $50 **Flaxton Barn, QLD**

Seven piece glass water set with textured rings of red and gold, c1960, 19cm high.

$60 - $80 **Sweet Slumber Antiques & Collectables, NSW**

Selkirk glass paperweight in the 'Primrose' design from the Hedgerow series, No. 113 of 500, designed by Peter Holmes, Scotland, c1996, 8cm diam.

$110 - $130

Selkirk Antiques & Restorations, ACT

Paperweight in the 'Mardi Gras' design, by Selkirk Glass, Scotland, c2000.

$70 - $90 **Selkirk Antiques & Restorations, ACT**

Glass paperweight with a blue trail pattern, c1980, 11cm high.

$85 - $105 **Goodwood House Antiques, WA**

Pink opalescent glass vase, c1960, 23cm high, 26cm wide, 19.5cm deep.

NZ$185 - $205

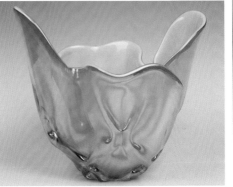

Amour Antiques & Collectables, New Zealand

Unusual art glass vase, c1975, 30cm high.

$25 - $35 **Atomic Pop, SA**

Amber glass vase with gold decoration, c1950, 23cm high, 16cm diam.

$55 - $75 **Mockingbird Lane Antiques, NSW**

Whisky crystal decanter and measure, c1950, 32cm high, 12cm wide.

$430 - $470 **Maryborough Station Antique Emporium, VIC**

Louis XV style bracket clock by Franz Hermle and Sons, the case, made in Italy, fully inlayed with scrolls of flowers and brass inlay, Germany, c1965, 57cm high, 28cm wide, 12cm deep.

$1850 - $2050   **Willi - The Clockman, WA**

Pagoda style enamelled carriage clock, c1950, 12cm high.

$105 - $125   **Goodwood House Antiques, WA**

Ceramic Kaiser horses figural clock, Germany, c1950, 30cm high, 40cm long.

$155 - $175   **Antique Revivals, VIC**

Racing pigeon mantle clock with an eight day movement, Germany, c1950, 23cm high, 9cm wide, 52cm long.

$230 - $270   **Antique Curiosity Shop, QLD**

Swallow clock, 'Jema' glazed ceramic, Holland, c1960, 17cm high, 26.5cm wide.

$195 - $235   **Cobweb Collectables, NSW**

Mercedes clock set in lustre glazed ceramic in the form of budgerigars on a branch, inscribed 'Jema Holland' on the base, Germany, c1950, 21cm high, 32cm wide.

$120 - $140   **Dorn Frugal, VIC**

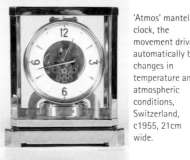

'Atmos' mantel clock, the movement driven automatically by changes in temperature and atmospheric conditions, Switzerland, c1955, 21cm wide.

$2100 - $2300   **Master Clockmakers, NSW**

Arts & Crafts eight day Westminster chime with allumion Lauris movement, allumion dial with chrome weights and pendulum in a case of ebonised wood plastic and two glass doors, features two glass windows in the sides, Switzerland, c1955, 182cm high, 36cm wide, 25cm deep.

Ceramic clock by 'Peter', Australia, c1950, 19cm high, 28cm wide.

$115 - $135   **Antique Revivals, VIC**

'Unicorn' mantle clock, Germany, c1950, 23cm high, 45cm wide.

$245 - $285   **Newport Temple Antiques, VIC**

$1750 - $1950   **Neville Beechey Antiques, VIC**

Lunar thirty day torsion clock with original Arabic dial, solid brass, Germany, 30cm high, 16cm wide.

$900 - $1000 **Alltime Antiques & Bairnsdale Clocks, VIC**

'Cyma' brand Art Deco style travelling clock, in an engine turned brass and crocodile case, with its original box, Switzerland, c1950, 8cm diam.

$375 - $415 **Pastimes Antiques, NSW**

Wind up 'Elypso' desk clock, manufactured by Emes, Germany, c1970, 14cm high, 10cm wide, 6cm deep.

$60 - $80 **506070, NSW**

Flamingo clock made from tin, Australia, c1950, 40cm high, 22cm wide.

$155 - $175 **Antique Revivals, VIC**

'Hordovar' flying pendulum mantel clock with original box and books, c1950, 16cm high, 16cm wide, 6cm deep.

$740 - $840 **Master Clockmakers, NSW**

Lime green battery operated wall clock, Hong Kong, c1970, 30cm high, 30cm wide.

$115 - $135 **Chapel Street Bazaar, VIC**

Teak veneer battery operated 'Starburst' clock by Junghams, Germany, c1960, 40cm diam.

$120 - $140 **Chapel Street Bazaar, VIC**

Anodised star clock with astrological motifs, battery operated, made by Sunbeam, England, c1950, 54cm diam.

$205 - $245 **Retro Active, VIC**

'Junghans' sunburst clock, in orange, c1970, 65cm high, 65cm wide.

$205 - $245 **Relic, QLD**

Colourful 'Viva' kitchen clock with seven rubies, battery operated, Germany, c1950, 20cm high, 23cm long.

$85 - $105 **Towers Antiques & Collectables, NSW**

Double dial 'Imhof' partner's clock, Switzerland, c1960, 10cm high, 10cm wide, 5cm deep.

$800 - $900 **Master Clockmakers, NSW**

Smiths lantern clock with timepiece movement, England, c1950, 18cm high, 7cm wide, 7cm deep.

$340 - $380   **Master Clockmakers, NSW**

'Blessing', chromed plastic alarm clock, Germany, c1958, 22cm high, 12cm diam.

NZ$45 - $55   **Amour Antiques & Collectables, New Zealand**

Swiss eight day Imhof night clock with a battery button on the top and a gilt finish, Switzerland, c1970, 19cm high, 8cm diam.

$430 - $470   **Camberwell Antique Centre, VIC**

'Tokyo Tokei' two jewel plastic alarm clock, Japan, c1960, 13cm high, 31cm wide, 60cm deep.

NZ$25 - $35   **Right Up My Alley, New Zealand**

Chrome alarm clock, Germany, c1970, 12.5cm diam.

NZ$120 - $140   **Decollectables, New Zealand**

'Westclox' alarm clock, Scotland, c1950, 9.5cm diam.

NZ$40 - $50   **Decollectables, New Zealand**

Tokei ball clock, c1960.

$85 - $105   **The Junk Company, VIC**

Battery operated ceramic clock, marked 'Lohmann Quartz', c1972, 22cm wide, 22cm long.

$45 - $65   **frhapsody, WA**

Wall regulator by David Walters, Perth (WA.) with a duration of thirty one days, this clock was made for the 'Great Western Gold exchange' in 1979, has a silvered dial, Arabic numerals, sweep centre seconds, walnut top case and a birds eye maple back, Australia, c1979, 162cm high, 38cm wide.

$9300 - $9700   **Willi - The Clockman, WA**

Junghans wall clock with a timber veneered face and twin weight chiming movement, Germany, c1960, 28cm high, 28cm wide, 11cm deep.

$255 - $295   **Antique Effects, VIC**

Triangular shaped clock, back stamped 'The Brian Wood Collection', England, c2000, 12cm high, 22cm long.

$175 - $195   **Decodence Collectables, VIC**

Pair of space age, ABS plastic, bedside alarm clocks, c1970.

$80 - $100   **Design Dilemas, VIC**

Cyma, Deco style pocket watch in a stainless steel case with fifteen jewels, Switzerland, c1950, 4.4cm diam.

$430 - $470

Ferntree Gully Watch & Clock Company, VIC

'Cyma' delux with a rolled gold case, fifteen jewels and a silver dial, Switzerland, c1950, 4.4cm diam.

$430 - $470

Ferntree Gully Watch & Clock Company, VIC

Omega gold plated fob watch, Switzerland, c1950, 3.5cm diam.

$205 - $245

Fyshwick Antique Centre, ACT

'Solvil et Titus Geneve' ball pendant watch, Switzerland, c1950.

$275 - $315

George Magasic Antiques & Collectables, QLD

Sterling silver and marcasite, 'Cinderella' coach, lapel watch, c1950.

$375 - $415

Reflections Antiques, NSW

Red banded Le Coultre ladies wrist watch with a stainless steel case and manual movement, one of the smallest movements made by Le Coultre, France, c1950.

$800 - $900

Vintage Times, NSW

18ct yellow gold, Vacheron Constantin ladies watch with a round face bordered by round brilliant diamonds and an elegant gold mesh bracelet, Switzerland, c1970.

$19000 - $20000

Sue Ellen Gallery, QLD

'The Clocke' 18ct solid gold, inverted horseshoe gold cased Cartier ladies watch with a brown crocodile band, c1960.

$4400 - $4600

Vintage Times, NSW

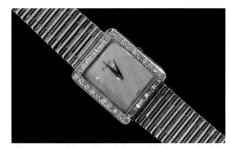

Piaget 18ct white gold and diamond ladies watch with a square face, bordered by round brilliant and baguette cut diamonds, Switzerland, c1970.

$18000 - $19000

Sue Ellen Gallery, QLD

Small square 18ct gold Rolex lady's wristwatch, Switzerland, c1960.

NZ$1100 - $1300

Lord Ponsonby Antiques, New Zealand

Lady's automatic Cartier 'Santos' in steel and gold, Switzerland, c1994.

NZ$1800 - $2000

Lord Ponsonby Antiques, New Zealand

Lady Rolex in steel and gold 'date just' automatic date chronometer, Switzerland, c1998.

NZ$4400 - $4600

Lord Ponsonby Antiques, New Zealand

Ladies 18ct white gold Omega with integrated bracelet and a diamond bezel, Switzerland.

NZ$1800 - $2000 **Lord Ponsonby Antiques, New Zealand**

18ct Ladies Longines watch with a solid gold band, 43.1 gm., Switzerland, c1955.

$1750 - $1950 **Alexa's Treasures, VIC**

'Piccadilly', shock protected, anti magnetic, wind-up watch with a suede band, Switzerland, c1960, 40cm wide, 50cm long.

$165 - $185 **Retro Active, VIC**

Cartier manual wind tank watch with an 18ct case and taupe band, Switzerland.

$4400 - $4600 **Vintage Times, NSW**

Stainless steel Lucerne gents 'Jump Hour' watch with large rectangular case, blue band and 'Rolling' register for the dial, Switzerland, c1970.

$680 - $780 **Vintage Times, NSW**

Large sized 18ct rose gold cased chronograph with a tachometer ring, sweep and minute recorders, silvered dial signed 'Formida', good quality 'Landeron 48' manual wound seventeen jewel lever, double button movement. Many watches of this period carried the names of retailers or wholesalers, Switzerland, c1950.

$1400 - $1600 **Colman Antique Clocks, VIC**

Art Deco style 14ct gold Wittnauer, manual wind gent's wristwatch, United States.

$475 - $515 **George Magasic Antiques & Collectables, QLD**

Rolex 'Explorer II', Switzerland, c2006, 4cm diam.

NZ$5500 - $5900 **Lord Ponsonby Antiques, New Zealand**

Rolex Oyster 18ct gold case, super Oyster crown automatic (ref. 6084), Switzerland, c1950, 3.5cm wide, 4cm long.

$6800 - $7200 **Armadale Antique Centre, VIC**

International Watch Company 'Schafhausen' 18ct gold watch, c1950.

$2200 - $2400 **Armadale Antique Centre, VIC**

International Watch Co. manual wind in 18ct gold with original box and certificate, signed for 'Beyer', c1950, 3.3cm diam.

NZ$2500 - $2700 **Lord Ponsonby Antiques, New Zealand**

Omega 18ct gold gent's Seamaster Automatic movement cal 505 with date, beefy lugs, snap on case back, and the Seamaster logo on the back, Switzerland, c1961.

$2200 - $2400

Brisbane Vintage Watches, QLD

Breitling gold filled 806 Navitimer with a black gilt dial, manual wind chronograph and a turning tachymeter bezel, Switzerland, c1960, 4cm diam.

$3100 - $3300

Brisbane Vintage Watches, QLD

'Omega Seamaster', in a stainless steel case, CAL 500 automatic movement, textured two tone dial, nineteen jewels, Switzerland, c1956.

$470 - $510

Camberwell Antique Centre, VIC

Omega, 9ct rose gold case, fifteen jewels and manual wind, Switzerland, c1950, 2.9cm diam.

$500 - $600

Ferntree Gully Watch & Clock Company, VIC

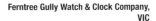

'Hamilton Military' with a stainless steel case and seventeen jewels, United States, c1980, 3.3cm diam.

$280 - $320

Ferntree Gully Watch & Clock Company, VIC

'Omega Seamaster Cosmic', stainless steel case, CAL 601 manual wind, adjusted two positions seventeen jewels, Switzerland, c1968.

$470 - $570

Camberwell Antique Centre, VIC

C.W.C military with a stainless steel case and seventeen jewels, made for the English military, Switzerland, c1970, 3.5cm diam.

$480 - $520

Ferntree Gully Watch & Clock Company, VIC

Omega I.W.C Stainless steel wristwatch with centre seconds and a silvered/pearl dial, Switzerland, 3.4cm diam.

$900 - $1000

Willi - The Clockman, WA

Tudor oyster with a stainless steel case, twenty one jewels and manual wind, Switzerland, c1962, 3.4cm diam.

$600 - $700

Ferntree Gully Watch Clock Company, VIC

Tudor by Rolex, steel oyster, manual wind with a unusual applied gold dial and hands, Switzerland, c1950.

$700 - $800

Brisbane Vintage Watches, QLD

Stainless steel Seiko chronograph, automatic with day and date, Japan, c1968, 4cm diam.

NZ$430 - $470

Lord Ponsonby Antiques, New Zealand

'Omega Constellation' chronometer #504 in an 18ct gold capped stainless steel shaped lug case with a champagne dial, gold batons and date at 3, early full rotor automatic and a twenty four jewel movement, serial number #16725600.

$1600 - $1800 **Colman Antique Clocks, VIC**

Seiko bulls head chronograph with pushers at 11:00 and 1:00, Japan.

NZ$950 - $1050 **Lord Ponsonby Antiques, New Zealand**

Duke gold filled cased, Art Deco style wrist watch, Switzerland.

$75 - $95 **Bob Butler's Sentimental Journey, QLD**

Large Seiko automatic diving watch, Japan, c1970, 4.4cm diam.

NZ$380 - $420 **Lord Ponsonby Antiques, New Zealand**

Omega stainless, automatic, day and date 'Seamaster Cosmic' with a one piece case, Switzerland, c1970.

NZ$500 - $600 **Lord Ponsonby Antiques, New Zealand**

Cyma navy star, gold capped with manual wind and eighteen jewels, Switzerland, c1960, 3.4cm diam.

$380 - $420 **Ferntree Gully Watch & Clock Company, VIC**

Rolex boys size 'Oyster Date' manual winding and stainless steel, Switzerland, 3cm diam.

NZ$1800 - $2000 **Lord Ponsonby Antiques, New Zealand**

Omega rose gold automatic 'Seamaster', Switzerland, c1960.

NZ$600 - $700 **Lord Ponsonby Antiques, New Zealand**

Swiss Omega military style watch with a stainless steel case, luminous hands, cal 26.5 manual wind movement and fifteen jewels, Switzerland.

$300 - $340 **Camberwell Antique Centre, VIC**

Tissot Seastar with an auto date stainless case and twenty one jewels, Switzerland, c1970, 3.4cm diam.

$280 - $320 **Ferntree Gully Watch & Clock Company, VIC**

Jaeger LeCoultre automatic wrist watch in a stainless steel case, water and shock resistant, original clasp bracelet, screw case back and a pearl white dial with silver batons and date, JLC Cal: K881, case #832406, Mvt: #1492882 (fully automatic), Switzerland, c1965.

$2200 - $2400 **Colman Antique Clocks, VIC**

Omega stainless 'Dynamic' with an automatic day date movement and a one piece bracelet, Switzerland, c1972, 4cm diam.

NZ$900 - $1000

Lord Ponsonby Antiques, New Zealand

Classic rose gilt manual 'Omega Seamaster' in a stainless steel, solid lugged water resistant case with a linen silvered dial, gilt batons and hands. Omega Cal: 264, seventeen jewel, shock protected manual movement, serial #16599578, Switzerland, c1959.

$850 - $950

Colman Antique Clocks, VIC

Top quality, Pulsar (Seiko) spoon alarm chrono with a mineral glass face, Japan.

$115 - $135

Chapel Street Bazaar, VIC

Omega Seamaster Chronostop with a stainless steel case, manual wind and seventeen jewels, Switzerland, c1970, 4.1cm diam.

$1050 - $1250

Ferntree Gully Watch & Clock Company, VIC

Stainless steel Rolex 'Oyster Date' on an Oyster bracelet, Switzerland, c1970, 3.5cm diam.

NZ$1800 - $2000

Lord Ponsonby Antiques, New Zealand

Rolex stainless steel, 'Oyster Perpetual' on an Oyster bracelet, Switzerland, c1960, 3.5cm diam.

NZ$2300 - $2500

Lord Ponsonby Antiques, New Zealand

Omega steel gent's 'Seamaster Automatic' with a cream dial, rose gold hour markers and hands with the original 'grain of rice' Omega bracelet, Switzerland c1953.

$950 - $1050

Brisbane Vintage Watches, QLD

Boxed Rontex seventeen jewel, self winding wrist watch, Switzerland.

$70 - $90

Whimsical Notions, NSW

Omega ladies watch with a 9ct gold case and a cord band, Switzerland, c1950, 1.9cm diam.

$330 - $370

Ferntree Gully Watch & Clock Company, VIC

Blue and white wall, mounted coffee grinder, Holland, c1950, 30cm high.

$185 - $205

Victor Harbour Antiques - Mittagong, NSW

Stainless steel and red enamel espresso maker, by Casalinghi, Italy, c1960, 22cm wide.

$200 - $240

Design Dilemas, VIC

Red plastic and stainless steel coffee machine, Italy, c1970, 30cm high, 35cm long, 20cm deep.

$275 - $315

Towers Antiques & Collectables, NSW

Brown enamelled 'Atomic' expresso machine, Italy, c1970, 23cm high, 16cm wide.

$500 - $600

506070, NSW

'Nacional' brand metal and timber coffee mill, c1950, 25cm high, 14cm wide, 19cm deep.

$155 - $175

Southside Antiques Centre, QLD

'Atomic' espresso machine with original instructions, Italy, 25cm high.

$630 - $730

Hunters & Collectors Antiques, NSW

UFO fan heater, c1950, 20cm high, 39cm diam.

$55 - $75

Obsidian Antiques, NSW

Electric heater of Art Deco style with an artificial log fire which lights up, Australia, c1950, 50cm high, 65cm wide.

$115 - $135

Collectable Creations, QLD

Red and cream enamelware Speedee electric jug, 21cm high.

NZ$20 - $30

Glenis Parker, New Zealand

Ceramic 'Lightening Bolt' electric jug, Australia, c1950.

$30 - $40

Colonial Collectables, QLD

Chrome electric tea pot, Australia, c1960, 26cm high.

$65 - $85

Coliseum Antiques Centre, NSW

HOUSEHOLD OBJECTS

HOME APPLIANCES

'Leonard' refrigerator in working condition, Australia, c1950.

$1400 - $1600

**Antique Revivals,
VIC**

Goblin 'Teasmade' automatic tea-making outfit, model D.28 complete with instructions, England, c1952, 25cm high, 27cm long, 22cm deep.

$390 - $430

**Gaslight Collectables And Old Books,
SA**

Art Deco styled, Xylonite 'Teasmade' with clock and alarm, England, c1950.

$280 - $320

**Half Moon Antiques & Interiors,
SA**

Red Bakelite blender, Australia, c1950, 37cm high, 17cm wide, 17cm deep.

$185 - $205

**Ace Antiques & Collectables,
VIC**

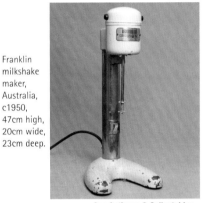

Franklin milkshake maker, Australia, c1950, 47cm high, 20cm wide, 23cm deep.

$255 - $295

**Ace Antiques & Collectables,
VIC**

'Rotafrig' made by James Kirby Camperdown, Sydney, produced in limited numbers only, Australia, c1953, 153cm high, 67cm diam.

$3850 - $4050

**Flaxton Barn,
QLD**

'Chanty' electric hair dryer, Japan, c1950, 15cm long.

NZ$40 - $50

**Decollectables,
New Zealand**

'Can-O-Matic' wall mount can opener with a magnetic lid lifter, made by C.C. Engineering Industries Pty. Ltd., South Granville NSW, Australia, c1975.

$55 - $75

**Dejanvou Antiques & Bric a Brac,
VIC**

Tilley kerosene iron, England, c1950, 23cm long.

$25 - $35

**The Mill Markets,
VIC**

Boxed 'Smoothie Portable Electric Iron', England, 6cm high, 11.5cm long.

NZ$25 - $35

**Moa Extinct Stuff,
New Zealand**

'Birko' travelling iron with cord and case, Australia, c1960, 10cm high, 20cm long.

$40 - $50

**Forever Amber @ The Tyabb
Grainstore, VIC**

Pair of footed, anodised aluminium wine beakers, Japan, c1960, 14cm high.

$20 - $30

Antipodes Antiques, QLD

Large anodised bread tin, Australia, c1960, 30cm high, 26cm wide.

$60 - $80

Newport Temple Antiques, VIC

Soda siphon by BOC, in anodised bronze, England, c1965, 30cm high, 11cm diam.

$70 - $90

J. R. & S.G. Isaac-Cole, NSW

Set of five anodised aluminium canisters, by 'Raco Quality Kitchenware'.

$55 - $75

Treats & Treasures, NSW

Set of three Gayware cannisters, c1960, 8.5cm high.

$45 - $65

Olsens Antiques, QLD

Blue anodised, apple shaped ice bucket, Australia, c1960, 22cm high.

$40 - $50

Paddington Antique Centre Pty Ltd, QLD

Plastic stacking snack containers, the set separating into individual snack bowls, 12cm high, 15cm diam.

$25 - $35

Jan Johannesen, VIC

Round anodised red soda siphon, by BOC, England, c1963, 28cm high, 17cm diam.

$200 - $240

J. R. & S.G. Isaac-Cole, NSW

Anodised aluminium, clover 'Mixi-Mini', whipped cream siphon, by Lehel, Hungary, c1980, 22cm high.

$30 - $40

Dejanvou Antiques & Bric a Brac, VIC

HOUSEHOLD OBJECTS

Plastic pancake maker, by Majestic, Australia, c1950, 17cm high.

$5 - $10   **Paddington Antique Centre Pty Ltd, QLD**

Art Deco chrome and Bakelite four tier cake stand, Australia, c1950, 80cm high.

$420 - $460   **Design Dilemas, VIC**

Orange, stackable plastic character mugs, c1970, 34cm high.

$65 - $85   **Classic Vintage, NSW**

'Nally Ware', Art Deco style sandwich server, in Bakelite and chrome with four removable plates, Australia, c1950, 80cm high, 25cm diam.

$305 - $345   **The New Farm Antique Centre, QLD**

Set of five plastic pink and grey kitchen canisters, by Gayware, Australia, c1955.

$100 - $120   **Atomic Pop, SA**

'Clementine' conservateur a glace ice pail in its original box, France, c1960, 14cm high, 20cm diam.

$85 - $105   **Retro Active, VIC**

Five piece plastic canister set, in yellow and grey by Nally, Australia, c1960.

$45 - $65   **Atomic Pop, SA**

Set of five Bristolite pink and cream spice jars, England, c1950, 10cm high, 7cm diam.

$65 - $85   **Alltime Antiques & Bairnsdale Clocks, VIC**

Multicoloured set of five plastic canisters, in graduated sizes, Australia, c1960.

$125 - $145   **Shop 5, The Centenary Centre, NSW**

Set of six plastic party tumblers in a carrier, c1965, 14cm high, 15cm wide, 22cm long.

$20 - $30   **P. & N. Johnson, NSW**

Set of five plastic kitchen containers with white tops, for 'Flour', 'Sugar', 'Rice', 'Tea' and 'Coffee', Australia, c1960, 25cm high.

NZ$65 - $85   **The Curiosity Shoppe, New Zealand**

Orange plastic revolving party set with original box, assembles in a variety of configurations and consists of five bowls with a revolving stand, Hong Kong, c1974, 35cm high, 70cm wide.

$35 - $45

frhapsody, WA

Cream and red Bakelite electric juicer manufactured by Ellis, has separate chutes for juice and residues, Switzerland, c1950, 34cm high, 28cm wide, 18cm deep.

$85 - $105

Burly Babs Collectables/Retro Relics, VIC

Hand painted 'Parrot' brand hor d'ourves set, in plastic with one large plate and six small plates, Australia, 26cm diam.

$35 - $45

Cobweb Collectables, NSW

'Tiny Plastic TV' salt and pepper set in original box, United States, c1950, 8cm high, 9cm wide.

$85 - $105

Chapel Street Bazaar, VIC

Set of plastic cake and biscuit canisters, by Nally, Australia, c1955, 23cm high, 25cm diam.

$30 - $40

Atomic Pop, SA

Tilley plastics revolving cruet set, on a blue base and decorated with raised flowers, Australia, c1950, 11cm high, 10cm diam.

$75 - $95

Nana's Pearls, ACT

Metal and plastic bookends by Carl, No. B-330, titled 'White Book Ends', Japan, c1970, 19cm high, 23cm wide.

NZ$75 - $95

Maxine's Collectibles, New Zealand

Set of three plastic boxes, marked 'Honey', 'Cheese' and 'Sugar' made by 'Gay Ware', Australia, c1950, 7.5cm high, 8cm wide, 8cm deep.

$40 - $50

Fat Helen's, VIC

Sandwich cover by Krista ware, Melbourne, made to fit six thick sandwiches, Australia, c1970, 32cm long, 16cm deep.

$20 - $30

Cobweb Collectables, NSW

Set of five plastic spice containers made by Iplex Industrial Plastics, Adelaide, Australia, c1950, 8cm high.

$35 - $45

The Mill Markets, VIC

HOUSEHOLD OBJECTS

Le Creuset 'Volcanique' cast iron and enamel fondue set, in original box, with fondue forks, France, c1970.

$185 - $205

Retro Active, VIC

Enamel bread tin, with a red lid and a cream base, c1950, 32cm high, 34cm wide.

$50 - $70

Tyabb Hay Shed, VIC

Original cream and red 'Coronation Ware' enamel bread bin with a Bakelite knob, the label still attached, Australia, c1950, 31cm high, 31cm diam.

$275 - $315

Step Back Antiques, VIC

Red enamelled steel bowl, manufactured by Torben Orskov, designed by Herbert Krenchel 1953, Denmark, 7cm high, 12cm diam.

$70 - $90

506070, NSW

Orange enamelled bowl with leaf decorations, by Catherine Holm, Norway, c1960, 12cm wide, 29cm diam.

$90 - $110

506070, NSW

Set of five green and white enamel bowls, Denmark.

NZ$100 - $120

Moa Extinct Stuff, New Zealand

Green enamel milk jug, Denmark, 19.5cm high, 17cm diam.

NZ$85 - $105

Moa Extinct Stuff, New Zealand

Pair of enamel bowls, one red, one white, with 'mushroom' designs in black, Finland, c1960, 14cm high, 21cm diam.

$90 - $110

506070, NSW

Assorted Kaj Franck designed enamel bowls, by Finel, Finland, c1965, 14cm high.

$110 - $130

Design Dilemas, VIC

Bernard Hesling enamel cat plate, Australia, 22.5cm diam.

$600 - $700

Ancanthe Antiques, TAS

Boxed cream enamel 'Harper No. 1500 Clampless Food Mincer' with a detachable handle, England, c1960, 33cm high, 32cm long.

$65 - $85

Trinkets & Treasures, VIC

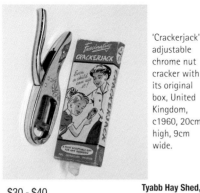

'Crackerjack' adjustable chrome nut cracker with its original box, United Kingdom, c1960, 20cm high, 9cm wide.

$30 - $40

Tyabb Hay Shed, VIC

Pyrex glass rolling pin, Australia, c1950, 38cm long.

$55 - $75

Paddington Antique Centre Pty Ltd, QLD

Rolling pin made by Portmeirion pottery, 'Magic City', designed by Susan Williams-Ellis, England, c1963, 35cm long.

NZ$205 - $245

Banks Peninsula Antiques, New Zealand

Brass hood with a lion crest, c1975.

$1100 - $1300

InPlace Antiques & Homewares, NSW

Home made six bottle milk carrier with a bird proof lid and six, one pint milk bottles, Australia, c1950, 25cm high, 18cm wide, 25cm long.

$110 - $130

Bob & Dot's Antiques & Old Wares, NSW

Chromed metal juicer, England, c1980, 20cm high.

$45 - $65

Steven Sher Antiques, WA

Complete seventy two piece canteen of 'Paramount' cutlery, Australia, c1950, 46cm wide, 30cm deep.

$275 - $315

Newport Temple Antiques, VIC

Set of ten Wiltshire bone handled knives, England.

$85 - $105

Archers Antiques, TAS

Fruit knife set in an anodised aluminium stand, England, c1955, 17cm high.

$55 - $75

Antipodes Antiques, QLD

Aluminium 'Tala Cook's Measure', England, c1952, 14.5cm high, 11cm diam.

NZ$20 - $30

Glenis Parker, New Zealand

Willow tin measuring cup with a plastic base, c1955, 14cm high, 11cm diam.

NZ$15 - $25

Glenis Parker, New Zealand

Wire whisk with a red wooden handle, Australia, c1954, 20cm high.

$20 - $30 **Step Back Antiques, VIC**

Boxed 'Tala Icing Set', England, c1950, 12cm wide, 15.5cm long.

NZ$5 - $15 **Moa Extinct Stuff, New Zealand**

'Tala Queen Icing Set' in original box, England, c1960, 5cm high, 12cm wide.

$40 - $50 **J. R. & S.G. Isaac-Cole, NSW**

Bonco flour sifter, c1960, 16cm high, 14cm diam.

NZ$20 - $30 **Glenis Parker, New Zealand**

Bonco flour sifter, c1950, 170cm high, 160cm wide, 140cm deep.

NZ$20 - $30 **Glenis Parker, New Zealand**

Soda siphon by Sparklets Ltd., in silver with red bands and a platform base, England, c1965.

$110 - $130 **J. R. & S.G. Isaac-Cole, NSW**

'Kande' one hand flour sifter, Australia, c1950, 13.5cm high, 11cm diam.

$30 - $40 **The Restorers Barn, VIC**

Willow, all over floral sifter, Australia, 16cm high, 18cm wide.

$25 - $35 **Archers Antiques, TAS**

Ceylon tea dispenser, for attachment to a wall and with a perspex lid, c1950, 19cm high, 14cm wide.

$30 - $40 **Baxter's Antiques, QLD**

Pro Hart set of five canisters, tray, miniature print, four place mats and bread container, Australia, c1970.

$245 - $285 **Lydiard Furniture & Antiques, VIC**

Plastic 'Home Pride Fred', the body dissembles to become kitchen utensils, England, c1970, 33cm high, 15cm wide.

$125 - $145 **Chapel Street Bazaar, VIC**

Pale green tin bread bin, Australia, c1954, 27cm high, 30cm wide, 27cm deep.

$45 - $65

Step Back Antiques, VIC

'Pro Hart' cake tin with an orange plastic lid, dated 1975 and depicting the Pro Hart painting titled 'Mining Landscape', Australia, 12cm high, 23cm wide, 29cm long.

$45 - $65

Treats & Treasures, NSW

Aluminium double boiler saucepan with lid, Bakelite handles and knob, Waratah brand, Australia, c1950, 13cm high, 18cm diam.

$45 - $65

Step Back Antiques, VIC

Large patterned bread bin by Willow, Australia, c1970, 30cm high, 26cm wide

$20 - $30

Newport Temple Antiques, VIC

Storage jar by Ganiopta, Sweden, 15cm high, 12cm diam.

NZ$20 - $30

Antiques & Curiosities, New Zealand

Pressed tin, hanging green meat safe, Australia, c1950, 38cm high, 38cm wide, 38cm deep.

$75 - $95

Step Back Antiques, VIC

Storage jar by Ganiopta, Sweden, 12cm high, 11cm diam.

NZ$35 - $45

Antiques & Curiosities, New Zealand

Three tiered aluminium cake, biscuit and scone containers, c1950.

$35 - $45

Flaxton Barn, QLD

Aluminium three piece storage marked for 'Cakes', 'Scones' and 'Biscuits', with a Bakelite handle, Australia, c1950, 38cm high, 27cm diam.

$55 - $75

Northside Secondhand Furniture, QLD

Stacking aluminium canisters for 'Biscuits', 'Cakes' and 'Pastry', Australia, c1960, 27cm high, 21cm diam.

NZ$115 - $135

Glenis Parker, New Zealand

'Picquot' ware tea and coffee service on a tray with a timber base and handles, England, c1950, 28cm wide, 42cm long.

$255 - $295

Obsidian Antiques, NSW

Picquot Ware tea and coffee service with tray, England.

$455 - $495

Vampt, NSW

Modernist five piece Dutch pewter tea/coffee service by Royal Holland Pewter.

$310 - $350

Design Dilemas, VIC

Green salt and pepper shakers by Inno, made of rubber with plastic, 8cm high.

$10 - $20

Cobweb Collectables, NSW

Fondue set with six forks, burner and stand, c1970, 26cm high.

$20 - $30

Atomic Pop, SA

Pair of bright coloured kitchen themed tins, Australia, c1970, 18cm high, 13cm diam.

$5 - $13

Woodside Bazaar, SA

'Thermos' vacuum jar, by appointment to her Majesty the Queen, England, c1950, 27cm high.

$55 - $75

The Mill Markets, VIC

Set of four coasters for drinks and nuts and with a tray for savouries, c1970, 23cm wide, 38cm long.

$7 - $17

Jan Johannesen, VIC

Metal ice bucket, Australia, c1960, 20cm high.

$40 - $50

The Junk Company, VIC

Aluminium gravy shaker, New Zealand, c1960, 16cm high, 8.5cm diam.

NZ$5 - $15

The Curiosity Shoppe, New Zealand

Teak salt and pepper grinders, Denmark, c1950, 13cm high, 5cm diam.

$40 - $50

Obsidian Antiques, NSW

Plastic napkin holders, Australia, c1970, 13cm high, 10cm wide.

$10 - $20

Fat Helen's, VIC

Tin 'Cook's' measure, Australia, c1954, 14cm high, 10.5cm diam.

$15 - $25

Step Back Antiques, VIC

'Donald Duck' plastic money box, for Walt Disney Productions, c1950, 20cm high, 10cm diam.

$75 - $95   **Southside Antiques Centre, QLD**

Mickey Mouse plastic money box, c1960, 14cm high.

$20 - $30   **Dr Russell's Emporium, WA**

Gold metal, mechanical rocket money box with key, United States, c1960.

$275 - $315   **Chapel Street Bazaar, VIC**

Commonwealth Savings Bank elephant money box, Australia, c1970, 8cm high, 13cm wide.

$20 - $30   **Lucilles Interesting Collectables, NSW**

Clockwork novelty money box, in tinplate and plastic, 'Applebank' with a worm that collects the coins, Japan, c1960, 12cm high, 12cm diam.

$175 - $195   **Beehive Old Wares & Collectables, TAS**

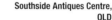

Comical ceramic piggy bank, c1950, 12cm high, 7cm wide, 6cm deep.

$120 - $140   **Southside Antiques Centre, QLD**

Plastic money box in the shape of an 'Esso' tanker truck, 6cm high, 17cm long.

$185 - $205   **Decorama, VIC**

Carlton Ware money box, England, c1960, 15cm high, 17cm long, 5cm deep.

$275 - $315   **True Blue Antiques, NSW**

Novelty money box, in the form of a black child with a nodding head, and seated on bananas, 16cm high, 18cm wide.

$80 - $100   **Nana's Pearls, ACT**

Ceramic money box with a mouse playing a violin, Japan, c1950, 12.5cm high, 9cm long, 6cm deep.

$115 - $135   **Now & Then Antiques & Collectables, QLD**

Metal 'Popeye Daily Dime Bank', $5 capacity with a counter for daily and total amounts, copyright King Features Syndicate, United States, c1956, 12cm long.

$245 - $285   **Decorama, VIC**

HOUSEHOLD OBJECTS

Australian PMG, black Bakelite phone, Australia, c1950, 14cm high.

$165 - $185   **Northside Secondhand Furniture, QLD**

'Roxanne' style, clear acrylic telephone with neon tube lighting, Japan, c1980, 9cm high, 18cm wide, 18cm long.

$125 - $145   **Chapel Street Bazaar, VIC**

ACF ivory, 802 rotary dial telephone, from Telecom Australia, the standard phone in Australia in the 1960's and 70's, Australia, c1965, 15cm high, 24cm wide, 20cm deep.

$45 - $55   **The House of Oojah, SA**

Red 'Ericofon' rotary dial telephone, dial is in the base, Sweden, c1960, 22cm high, 9cm wide, 12cm long.

$370 - $410   **The House of Oojah, SA**

Pink boudoir telephone, Hong Kong, c1980, 20cm high, 20cm wide.

$115 - $135   **Chapel Street Bazaar, VIC**

Novelty cucumber shaped telephone, by Tasca International, England, c1985, 25cm long.

$45 - $65   **The Mill Markets, VIC**

Reproduction brass telephone, Japan, c1970, 23cm high, 26cm long, 26cm deep.

$185 - $205   **Towers Antiques & Collectables, NSW**

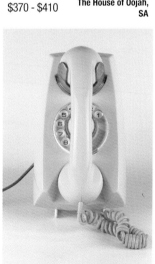

Crystal mint 'Ericofon' rotary dial telephone, this colour was not available in Australia, Sweden, c1960, 22cm high, 9cm wide, 12cm long.

$370 - $410   **The House of Oojah, SA**

Yellow Telecom issued wall phone, Australia, c1978, 20cm high.

$85 - $105   **Chapel Street Bazaar, VIC**

Telephone shaped like a red handbag, China, c1970, 35cm high, 39cm wide.

$800 - $900

Victor Harbour Antiques - Mittagong, NSW

GEC black Bakelite phone with a number keypad, England, c1950.

$220 - $260

Flaxton Barn, QLD

Gold 'Ericofon' rotary dial telephone, this colour was not available in Australia, Sweden, c1960, 22cm high, 9cm wide, 12cm long.

$270 - $310

The House of Oojah, SA

Gold ball phone, United States, c1970, 18cm high, 15cm wide.

$135 - $155

The Junk Company, VIC

Cream 'Ericofon' cobra phone, by Ericsson, Sweden, c1960, 21cm high, 8cm wide, 8cm long.

$145 - $165

Dr Russell's Emporium, WA

First edition Mickey Mouse telephone on wooden base, United States, c1978, 38cm high.

$255 - $295

Max Rout, NSW

Blue 'Multicoin' pay phone, accepting 10c, 20c, 50c, $1 and $2 coins, Australia, c1990, 33cm high, 24cm wide, 17cm deep.

$55 - $75

McKays Mart, SA

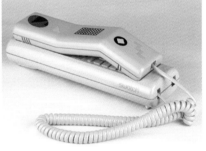

Original 'Swatch' telephone, Switzerland, c1980.

$400 - $440

Malvern Antique Market, VIC

Volvo 740, novelty car shaped telephone, by Tasca International, England, c1985, 24cm long.

$40 - $50

The Mill Markets, VIC

Boulle inlaid telephone, made by Telcer with twin bells on the back, Italy, c1970, 30cm high, 25cm wide, 22cm deep.

$800 - $900

Camberwell Antique Centre, VIC

Cream Bakelite telephone, Australia, c1950, 25cm high, 16cm wide.

$275 - $315

Towers Antiques & Collectables, NSW

HOUSEHOLD OBJECTS

'Stork' baby's pram, England, c1950, 92cm high, 50cm wide, 105cm long.

$375 - $415

Fyshwick Antique Centre, ACT

Cyclops dolls pram, c1950, 86cm high, 34cm wide, 82cm long.

$225 - $265

Twice Around, NSW

Childs pram, c1950, 118cm high, 120cm wide, 60cm long.

$375 - $415

Twice Around, NSW

Small beaded basket, edged with shells, c1950, 16cm high, 7cm diam.

$20 - $30

Southside Antiques Centre, QLD

Large scales with tray and a set of weights, 15kg capacity by Avery Birmingham, sole agent W. T. Avery Australia, England, 50cm wide.

$320 - $360

Sweet Slumber Antiques & Collectables, NSW

Aldo Tura parchment thermos flask, Italy, c1950, 40cm high, 12cm diam.

$420 - $460

506070, NSW

Drink set with six cups and a bottle, Australia, c1955, 60cm high.

$55 - $75

Atomic Pop, SA

Avery counter scales with an original painted finish, a stainless steel weighing basket and two weights, Australia, c1950, 43cm high, 42cm wide, 23cm deep.

$215 - $255

Whimsical Notions, NSW

Poodle made from a sand filled bottle used as a door stop, Australia, c1970, 32cm high.

$20 - $30

Cobweb Collectables, NSW

Brexton picnic set, England, c1955, 15cm high, 52cm wide, 33.5cm deep.

NZ$245 - $285

Bonham's, New Zealand

'Ariki', paua shell dish with its original label, New Zealand, c1970, 10cm wide, 25cm long.

$10 - $20

Cobweb Collectables, NSW

Tortoiseshell rimmed glasses with original cleaning cloth and box, Australia, c1950.

$40 - $50

The Mill Markets, VIC

Leather and plastic frames with case, France, c1960, 5cm high, 15cm wide.

$85 - $105

Chapel Street Bazaar, VIC

'Vaxomatic' vaccination kit by Monsanto Australia Ltd, Australia, 9cm wide, 17cm long.

$40 - $50

The Restorers Barn, VIC

Silver and marcasite folding lorgnette, c1950.

$345 - $385

Reflections Antiques, NSW

Optometrists torch in original box, maker Welch Allyn, United States, c1970, 23cm long.

$85 - $105

Kingston Antiques, VIC

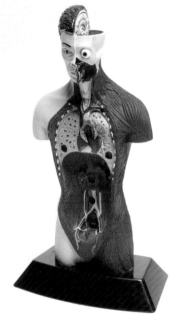

Anatomical plastic figure of a man, showing the muscular system, China, c1960, 12cm high, 8cm wide, 12cm long, 8cm deep.

$65 - $85

Dr Russell's Emporium, WA

Dentist's model of teeth, in painted plaster construction of two parts, made by Columbia Dentalform, United States, c1950, 10cm high, 13cm wide, 12cm deep.

$190 - $210

Dr Russell's Emporium, WA

Reflex hammer, England, c1950, 20cm long.

$15 - $25

Chapel Street Bazaar, VIC

Original fifties 'look-over' eye glass frames, black with gold details and diamantes, France.

$205 - $245

Retro Active, VIC

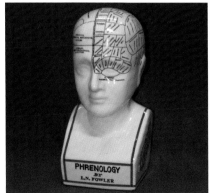

Ceramic Phrenology head by L. N. Fowler, Ludgate Circus, London, England, c1960, 30cm high.

$200 - $240

Granny's Market Pty Ltd, VIC

Original 1950's eye glass frames cats eyes with diamantes, France, c1950.

$205 - $245

Retro Active, VIC

Monte Carlo opera glasses, 10cm wide, 5cm deep.

$55 - $75

Archers Antiques, TAS

Red plastic binoculars, Italy, 13cm high, 15.5cm wide.

NZ$30 - $40

Antiques & Curiosities, New Zealand

Four porcelain chemist mixing bowls with a hand blown and etched fluid ounce measure glass, United Kingdom.

$55 - $75

Robyn's Nest, VIC

Electric globe with an internal light, Australia, c1970, 55cm high, 40cm diam.

$85 - $105

Towers Antiques & Collectbles, NSW

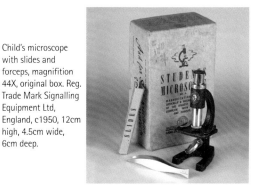

Child's microscope with slides and forceps, magnifition 44X, original box. Reg. Trade Mark Signalling Equipment Ltd, England, c1950, 12cm high, 4.5cm wide, 6cm deep.

NZ$85 - $105

Fendalton Antiques, New Zealand

'Culmak' advertising shaving brush, England, c1950, 20cm high.

$305 - $345

The Glass Stopper, NSW

Chemist scales, by Avery, Australia, 128cm high, 34cm wide, 64cm deep.

$500 - $600

Doug Up On Bourke, NSW

Ceramic mortar and pestle, size 1, England, c1950, 10cm wide.

$80 - $100

The Glass Stopper, NSW

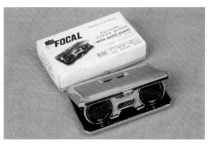

Boxed 'Focal Folding Opera Glass', made for S.S. Kresge Company, Troy, Michigan, Japan, c1960, 10cm wide.

$15 - $25

Dr Russell's Emporium, WA

Windmill model made of metal and wood, Australia, c1950, 185cm high.

$600 - $700

Tarlo & Graham, VIC

Taxidermy specimen puppy, Australia, c1960.

$275 - $315

Parramatta Antique Centre, NSW

Professionally mounted kangaroo head on a board, Australia, c1960, 25cm high.

$275 - $315

Rose Cottage Antiques, ACT

Handsomely preserved and mounted game fish, Australia, 105cm long.

$200 - $240

Furniture Revisited, VIC

Glass laboratory scales in an oak case, made by 'Griffin & George Limited, London, G. Britain', England, c1950, 40cm high, 40cm long, 17cm deep.

$220 - $260

Towers Antiques & Collectables, NSW

Mounted Scottish highland cow, Australia, c1990, 100cm high, 130cm wide, 125cm deep.

$2750 - $2950

Tarlo & Graham, VIC

Zebra skin, South Africa, c1950.

$2150 - $2350

Grafton Galleries, NSW

Sea turtle shell, c1950, 42cm wide, 48cm long.

$360 - $400

Tarlo & Graham, VIC

Genuine five leaf clover, a freak of nature, Australia, c2005.

$90 - $110

Island & Continent Coins & Stamps, NSW

White ceramic electricity insulator marked ' Dulmas (Aust) 48 Made in Occupied Japan', Japan, c1950, 9cm high.

$20 - $30

Cobweb Collectables, NSW

BRACELETS/BANGLES

18ct yellow and white gold bracelet, with a central white gold inlay set with S4 x 0.01 carat single cut diamonds, box clasped and two figures of eight safety clips, Italy, c1960, 19cm long.

$4350 - $4550   **Toowoomba Antiques Gallery, QLD**

Silver, pearl and moonstone bracelet, by designer Antonio Pineda, Mexico.

$1700 - $1900   **Armadale Antique Centre, VIC**

Sterling silver hand engraved hinged bangle, New Zealand, c1950, 1.5cm wide.

NZ$275 - $315   **Pleasant Place Antiques, New Zealand**

Oriental 18ct gold multi-coloured precious stone bracelet set with a centre line of carved sapphires, emeralds and rubies supported by carved emeralds, cabochon cut rubies, emeralds and sapphires and two hundred and seventy brilliant cut diamonds (6.45ct total) valued at $71,900, c1960, 2.5cm wide, 20cm long.

$38750 - $40750   **Bygone Beautys, NSW**

18 carat yellow gold bracelet, with links that display a man with hay, a llama and a man feeding a llama (50.66 grms), 1.3cm wide, 18cm long.

$4400 - $4600   **Adornments, QLD**

Kenneth J. Lane pearl and turquoise bracelet, England, c1960.

$180 - $200   **L.A. Design, NSW**

Japanese damascene (gold and silver inlay in steel) bracelet, Japan, c1955.

$85 - $105   **Merry's Jewels & Collectables, TAS**

Sterling silver hand engraved hinged bangle, New Zealand, c1950, 5.5cm high, 2cm wide, 6.5cm long.

NZ$230 - $270   **Pleasant Place Antiques, New Zealand**

9ct charm bracelet set with eight jade charms, c1950.

$475 - $515   **Lancaster's Toowoomba Antique Centre, QLD**

Pair of silver and enamel bluebird brooches on a chain, Australia, c1950, 2cm high, 4cm wide, 4cm diam.

$165 - $185

Dr Russell's Emporium, WA

14ct gold brooch with round brilliant cut diamonds and cabochon jadeites, c1950, 5cm wide.

$8300 - $8700

Trinity Antiques, WA

Large vintage brooch by JOMAZ (Joseph J. Mazer, NY), carved white rose with rhinestone leaves and gold finish metal stem, United States, c1955, 9.5cm long.

$475 - $515

Pastimes Antiques, NSW

18ct yellow gold mother of pearl plaque brooch, with underwater scene in gold, diamonds and Keshi pearl, Australia, c2000, 4.5cm wide.

$2200 - $2400

Catanach's Jewellers Pty. Ltd., VIC

18ct yellow gold plique a jour and diamond dragonfly brooch, designed and made by Tony Wilson, New Zealand, c2000, 7cm wide.

$6800 - $7200

Catanach's Jewellers Pty. Ltd., VIC

Sterling silver and gold plate brooch, stamped 'Flora Danica Denmark', Denmark.

$115 - $135

Malvern Antique Market, VIC

Sterling silver and jade brooch, Mexico, c1980.

$115 - $135

Antipodes Antiques, QLD

Simpson brooch in its original box in the style of 'The Wattle Brooch' presented to Queen Elizabeth II during her 1954 Royal visit, Australia.

$430 - $470

Sherrill Grainger, NSW

Sterling silver turquoise brooch with inlay, designed and manufactured in Taxco, a Mexican artist community, Mexico, c1960.

$75 - $95

Vintage Times, NSW

Sterling silver brooch, featuring two birds sitting in a nest with a pearl egg, marked 925, European, c1950, 3cm long.

NZ$120 - $140

Sue Todd Antiques Collectables, New Zealand

Pair of silver 'Destino' cufflinks, Italy, c1950.

$140 - $160

Vintage Times, NSW

Hand blown eye ball cufflinks, Italy, c1950.

$140 - $160

Vintage Times, NSW

18ct white gold, ruby and diamond tassel earrings in Art Deco style, England, c2005, 5cm long.

$9800 - $10200

Catanach's Jewellers Pty. Ltd., VIC

Kiwi shaped paua shell and silver cufflinks, New Zealand, c1960.

NZ$55 - $75

Queens Gardens Antique Centre, New Zealand

Silver cufflinks by Kitch Currie of Western Australia, Australia, c1950.

$1300 - $1500

Mary Titchener Antique Jewels, VIC

14ct white gold and diamond pave earrings, Italy, c1970.

$4100 - $4300

Martin of Melbourne - Fine Jewels, VIC

Port and starboard lantern earrings, in 9ct gold and hallmarked for Birmingham, 1976, England.

$370 - $410

Imogene Antique & Contemporary Jewellery, VIC

Shield shape sterling silver and enamel screw-on earrings, stamped 'Siam Sterling', Thailand, c1950, 2.5cm wide, 2.5cm long.

$30 - $40

Possum's Treasures, QLD

Art Deco style, 18ct white gold diamond earrings (1.25ct diamond weight), England, c2000.

$4900 - $5100

Steven Sher Antiques, WA

18ct filigree design, hand made drop ear pendants, Australia, c1970.

$945 - $1045

Carillon Antiques, WA

Sterling silver tie-clip, by Georg Jensen, Denmark, c1970, 0.7cm high, 3.5cm long, 0.7cm deep.

$190 - $210

Dr Russell's Emporium, WA

Georg Jensen silver bracelet, by Jarum, c1970.

$1400 - $1600

Steven Sher Antiques, WA

Georg Jensen silver bangle, weight 67.6g, Denmark, c1952.

$1150 - $1350

Glenelg Antique Centre, SA

Pierre Cardin necklace and pendant, Italy, c1970.

$115 - $135

Classic Vintage, NSW

18ct hand made chain and patterned heavy collar, Italy, c1950.

$3400 - $3600

Carillon Antiques, WA

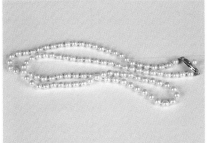

9ct yellow gold snake necklace with ruby eyes, Birmingham, England, c1965.

$2400 - $2600

Sue Ellen Gallery, QLD

Malachite necklace, South Africa, c1950, 68cm long.

NZ$330 - $370

Sue Todd Antiques Collectables, New Zealand

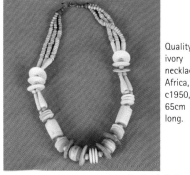

Quality ivory necklace, Africa, c1950, 65cm long.

$475 - $515

Isadora's Antiques, NSW

Top quality cultured pearls with a silver push clasp and set with a cultured pearl, c1960, 62cm long.

NZ$945 - $1045

Kelmscott House Antiques, New Zealand

Hand made emerald cut diamond clasp with brilliant cut diamond details, on two rows of creamy cultured Akoya pearls, Australia, c1970, 45cm long, 9.5cm diam.

$56000 - $61000

Catanach's Jewellers Pty. Ltd., VIC

9ct (250g) men's gold chain, made in Melbourne by Colonial Gold Sales, Australia, c1970.

$4900 - $5100

Castlemaine, VIC

PENDANTS/LOCKETS & RINGS

Large Baltic amber, lobed pendant with a mount in .835 silver, Germany, c1955, 4.5cm high, 2.5cm wide, 1cm deep.

NZ$155 - $175 **Anticus Antiques, New Zealand**

Platinum gold and diamond pendant on 18ct gold chain, the pendant is a medallion-style with diamond and platinum filigree edge and an embossed image of a woman with a small diamond set in her necklace (33 small diamonds in total).

NZ$575 - $675 **Anticus Antiques, New Zealand**

18ct gold, enamel and diamond jester pendant with original 18ct gold and enamel chain, c1970, 38cm long.

NZ$7300 - $7700 **Queens Gardens Antique Centre, New Zealand**

Large hand made 18ct gold, sterling silver, amethyst and garnet cross, commissioned from The Brisbane Silversmith by the late Frank Thring, Australian actor and film star, Australia, c1975, 9.5cm wide, 16.5cm long.

$1150 - $1350 **Scheherazade Antiques, VIC**

18ct white gold pendant and chain, set with a 1.3ct pear-shaped emerald and a small diamond, chain length 42cm, Germany, c1980, 2cm high, 1cm wide.

NZ$1100 - $1300 **Anticus Antiques, New Zealand**

Artisan made ring, of sterling silver and garnets with etched panels of silver between the stones, New Zealand, c1960, 1.5cm high, 2cm diam.

NZ$155 - $175 **Anticus Antiques, New Zealand**

18ct yellow white gold ring set and one natural Columbian emerald approx 1.30ct, surrounded by twelve brilliant cut diamonds, c1980, 1.7cm wide, 2cm long.

$5500 - $5900 **Pendulum Antiques, SA**

18ct blur sapphire solitaire ring, England, c1950.

$525 - $625 **Antiques & Collectables Centre - Ballarat, VIC**

Large cabochon ruby with natural inclusions, set in 14ct, leaf shape patterns surround this bezel set ring, Australia, c1950.

$845 - $945 **Lancaster's Toowoomba Antique Centre, QLD**

Large chrysoprase ring, cabochon cut set in sterling silver, Australia, c1960.

$700 - $800 **Lancaster's Toowoomba Antique Centre, QLD**

Square bright citrine ring, surrounded with claw set diamonds on an 18ct white gold shank, Australia, c1990.

$1750 - $1950

Carillon Antiques, WA

14ct gold and diamond tremblant ring, c1970.

$185 - $205

Antipodes Antiques, QLD

18ct gold ring with diamonds and blue and green enamel, United States, c1980.

$640 - $740

Imogene Antique & Contemporary Jewellery, VIC

9ct rose and yellow gold ring, with a solid white opal (12x10x2.3mm) and a maker's mark of 'P7K', of approximately 1.5 carats, Australia, c1950.

$840 - $940

Imogene Antique & Contemporary Jewellery, VIC

Silver ring with natural sunstone, Afghanistan, c1960.

$220 - $260

Vintage Times, NSW

9ct gold ring, with a single claw set amethyst, Australia, c1970, 1.3cm wide, 1.9cm long, 1cm deep.

$750 - $850

Isadora's Antiques, NSW

Diamond dress ring, featuring twelve baguette diamonds in each of the two slanted ribbons of gold in the shape of a bow across a setting of fourteen tiny diamonds in a sparkly low setting, either side of the tapered 18ct yellow gold shank, Australia, c1970.

$800 - $900

I.S. Wright, VIC

14ct yellow gold, three across pearls retro ring, c1950.

$645 - $745

Chilton's Antiques & Jewellery, NSW

Ruby and diamond cluster ring, featuring one round bright red ruby, twelve diamonds around 18ct yellow gold set, Australia, c1970, 0.5cm wide.

$970 - $1170

Accent on Gifts, NSW

Signed heavy 18ct ring, set with a side-on cross of diamonds by Chaumet, France, c1950.

$3850 - $4050

Carillon Antiques, WA

Set of old cut diamonds from a Brazilian mine circa 1880, re-set in a hand made coronet mount, centre diamond of 2.38ct and two shoulder diamonds of 2.10ct total, Australia, c2000.

$58000 - $63000

Catanach's Jewellers Pty. Ltd., VIC

Art Deco style onyx and diamond ring, Australia, c1988.

$1450 - $1650

Malvern Antique Market, VIC

Hand made 18ct garnet and ten diamond ring, New Zealand, c1950.

NZ$600 - $700

Pleasant Place Antiques, New Zealand

9ct gold men's ring with red glass stone, c1970, 1.5cm high.

$275 - $315

Maryborough Station Antique Emporium, VIC

9ct white gold and platinum setting daisy ring, England, c1960.

$2850 - $3050

Trinity Antiques, WA

18ct yellow gold and citrine ring, England, c1970.

$900 - $1000

Martin of Melbourne - Fine Jewels, VIC

Rectangular aquamarine of approximately 10.5cts (13.1mm x 11mm x 9.6mm depth), mounted in a 14ct white gold ring with engraved shoulders.

$3850 - $4050

Rutherford Fine Jewellery & Antique Silver, VIC

18ct gold, seven stone diamond ring, Australia, c1990.

$4895 - $5095

Malvern Antique Market, VIC

14ct and quartz dress ring, New Zealand, c1960.

NZ$330 - $370

Pleasant Place Antiques, New Zealand

Pair of hand blown glass, signed and dated candlesticks, c1992, 28cm high, 9cm diam.

$475 - $515   **Coliseum Antiques Centre, NSW**

Pair of Zanfirico candle sticks with latticino canes, signed Venini, Murano, Italy, c1950, 26cm high.

$2800 - $3000   **Sue Ellen Gallery, QLD**

Pair of carved wooden blackamoors, holding a five branch metal candelabrum, Italy, c1960, 208cm high.

$6800 - $7200   **Hollywood Antiques, WA**

Teak candlestick, Denmark, c1960, 22cm high.

$20 - $30   **506070, NSW**

Boxed pair of wax candlesticks by Timo Sarpaneva, Finland, c1970, 35cm high.

$60 - $80   **Chapel Street Bazaar, VIC**

Pair of Ronson four hour burning candlesticks with stands, Australia, c1960, 40cm high, 85cm wide.

$230 - $270   **Calmar Trading, VIC**

Pair of Murano candlesticks in latticino with dolphin supports, Italy, 17cm high.

$545 - $645   **Brae-mar Antiques, NSW**

Nagel Variante modular candle supports made up of eight units, Germany, 6cm high, 10cm long.

$200 - $240   **B'artchi, ACT**

Silver plated three branch candelabra, England, c1970, 20cm high, 27cm wide.

$155 - $175   **Yande Meannjin Antiques, QLD**

Signed Lalique candlestick with a rope edge design, France, c1970, 12cm high, 7.5cm wide, 7.5cm deep.

$700 - $800   **Pendulum Antiques, SA**

CEILING LIGHTS

Six light chrome and smoke glass light fitting, Italy, c1970, 29cm high.

$155 - $175

frhapsody, WA

Pair of chrome cubist style ceiling lights with white glass globe shades, Italy, c1972, 50cm high, 50cm diam.

$355 - $395

Chapel Street Bazaar, VIC

Heavy metal and chunky broken glass light fitting, made in Eltham, Victoria, Australia, c1970.

$230 - $270

Retro Active, VIC

Hanging six branch light, in chrome and copper with original shades, France, c1950, 60cm high, 90cm diam.

$4400 - $4600

Capocchi, VIC

Metal tole light with original painted foliage, re-wired, Italy, c1955, 40cm high, 50cm wide.

$375 - $415

Prism Original Lighting, VIC

Scandinavian white and amber glass ceiling light, c1960, 32cm diam.

NZ$115 - $135

Maxine's Collectibles, New Zealand

Ceiling light with a yellow coloured glass bowl and white fillings, Australia, c1950.

$130 - $150

Towers Antiques & Collectables, NSW

Jute and teak light shades with a teak hanging rod, Denmark, c1962, 21cm high, 19cm wide.

$200 - $240

frhapsody, WA

Tobia Scarpa 'Nuvola' hanging light 1962, Italy, 50cm high, 65cm wide.

$1750 - $1950

Geoffrey Hatty, VIC

White glass with gold trim hanging light, Sweden, c1950, 26cm diam.

NZ$140 - $160

Maxine's Collectibles, New Zealand

'Spaghetti' plastic sphere light fitting, Hong Kong, c1974, 40cm diam.

$60 - $80

Chapel Street Bazaar, VIC

Jo Hammerborg cone lamp, designed in the late 60's and manufactured from anodised aluminium with black and pink detail, by Fog & Mørup, Denmark, c1970.

$475 - $515

Great Dane Furniture, VIC

Large Venetian milk glass chandelier of eight lights, Italy, c1950, 92cm high, 60cm wide.

$3700 - $3900   **Miguel Meirelles Antiques, VIC**

Murano glass, eight branch chandelier in champagne tones with ornate hand blown floral decorations, Italy, c1950, 80cm high, 65cm wide.

$3400 - $3600   **Whimsical Notions, NSW**

Crystal electric chandelier, France, c1980.

$545 - $645   **Ardeco Antiques & Collectables, WA**

Blue Venetian light, Italy, c1950, 80cm high, 55cm wide.

$8300 - $8700   **Capocchi, VIC**

Chrome timber ceiling light with five moulded, blue cube shape shades, Italy, c1970, 40cm high, 50cm diam.

$115 - $135   **Chapel Street Bazaar, VIC**

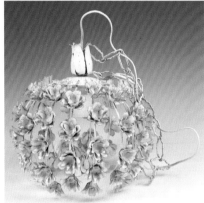

Enamel toleware chandelier, in a 'bird cage design' of pink and white flowers, France, 102cm long, 30cm deep, 81cm diam.

$230 - $270   **Auld & Grey 20th Century Antiques, NSW**

Solid brass and crystal chandelier with five arms, Australia, 35cm high, 45cm long, 45cm deep.

$230 - $270   **Towers Antiques & Collectables, NSW**

'Sputnik' chrome light fitting, Italy, c1960, 64cm high, 62cm wide.

$1300 - $1500   **Tarlo & Graham, VIC**

Brass frame chandelier with individual glass prism drops, Italy, c1980, 39cm high, 40cm wide.

$275 - $315   **Chapel Street Bazaar, VIC**

LAMPS - TABLE & DESK

Large white Bakelite table lamp, Australia, c1950, 69cm high.

$80 - $100   **Chapel Street Bazaar, VIC**

Black, red and white Bakelite hanging/table lamp, battery operated, Hong Kong, c1960, 33cm high, 14cm diam.

$55 - $75   **Burly Babs Collectables/ Retro Relics, VIC**

Studio pottery lamp, by Ellis, Australia, c1960, 42cm high, 23cm wide.

$185 - $205   **Armadale Antique Centre, VIC**

Original pink black and white ceramic lamp with two tier original shade, United States, c1955, 72cm high, 42cm wide.

$410 - $450   **Chapel Street Bazaar, VIC**

Barsony black lady lamp with its original shade, Australia, c1950, 61cm high.

$280 - $320   **Relic, QLD**

Barsony black lady lamp with original shade, c1950, 45cm high.

$280 - $320   **Relic, QLD**

Barsony black lady lamp with its original pink shade, hand painted, stamped underneath, 'Barsony FL-27', Australia, c1950, 50cm high, 11cm long, 15cm deep.

$325 - $365   **Towers Antiques & Collectables, NSW**

Barsony black lady lamp with original shade, Australia, c1950, 56cm high.

$305 - $345   **Relic, QLD**

Barsony black lady lamp with original shade, 'Silver Cloud' sticker on base and incised 'Mark FL 32', Australia, c1950, 42.5cm high, 30cm wide.

$290 - $330   **Bowerbird Antiques & Collectables, SA**

Pottery lamp, signed 'MF l411', Australia, 80cm high, 28cm wide.

$130 - $150   **Lesley's Treasures, NSW**

Pair of ceramic lamps, France, c1950, 55cm high, 27cm wide.

$2850 - $3050   **Capocchi, VIC**

Ceramic black lady lamp of a young girl with a pony tail, c1955, 38cm high.

$100 - $120   **The Botanic Ark, VIC**

Moorcroft pottery lamp, in the 'Oberon' pattern, England, c1993.

$1225 - $1425 **The New Farm Antique Centre, QLD**

Barsony ceramic lamp, Australia, c1960, 36cm high.

$340 - $380 **The Junk Company, VIC**

Presley purple pottery lamp, Japan, c1970, 54cm high.

$45 - $65 **Fat Helen's, VIC**

Ceramic Soholm lamp base, Denmark, c1960, 22.5cm high, 7cm wide, 5cm deep.

NZ$185 - $205 **Maxine's Collectibles, New Zealand**

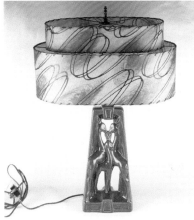

Ceramic lamp base with a vellum, two tiered shade, United States, c1950, 65cm high.

$275 - $315 **Chapel Street Bazaar, VIC**

Pair of blue ceramic oriental style lamps, Italy, 50cm high.

$225 - $265 **Newport Temple Antiques, VIC**

Large pottery lamp, Italy, c1970, 85cm high, 36cm diam.

NZ$185 - $205 **Maxine's Collectibles, New Zealand**

Ceramic lamp with a two-tiered, fibreglass printed shade, United States, c1950, 69cm high.

$345 - $385 **Chapel Street Bazaar, VIC**

Ceramic lamp with a pale green and speckled white metal base and fitting and a two-tiered fibreglass original shade, United States, c1955, 71cm high.

$375 - $415 **Chapel Street Bazaar, VIC**

Archimede Seguso Murano glass ribbed lamp base, in Alexandrite lilac with three applied flowers and the original silk base, Italy, c1955, 75cm high.

$1150 - $1350 **Design Dilemas, VIC**

Murano glass lamp with the original shade, Italy, 32cm high, 15cm wide.

NZ$255 - $295 **Antiques & Curiosities, New Zealand**

LAMPS - TABLE & DESK

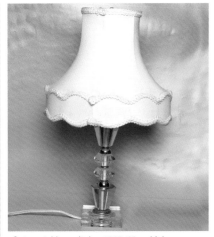

Cut crystal lamp, Italy, c1960, 60cm high.

$115 - $135

Womango, VIC

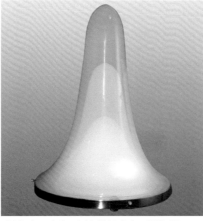

Triple domed glass table light, Italy, c1960, 60cm high, 45cm diam.

$4400 - $4600

Geoffrey Hatty, VIC

Murano glass lamp, in the form of a fish with a shade, Italy, c1950, 37cm high, 24cm wide.

$330 - $370

Thompsons Country Colectables, NSW

Barovier and Toso Murano glass lamp in citrine yellow with gold foil inclusions, Italy, c1955, 75cm high.

$1150 - $1350

Design Dilemas, VIC

Heavy black wrinkle finish, tension arm 'Planet' desk lamp. Planet originated in Brighton, Victoria and moved to Bellingen NSW in the late 60's. This design had mostly industrial, commercial and medical applications (chrome standard in the floor mount model is very desirable), Australia, c1955, 20cm wide.

$275 - $315

Industria, VIC

Red metal, accordion neck lamp, Italy, c1970, 56cm high.

$48 - $68

Chapel Street Bazaar, VIC

Bino light by Fontana Arte, 1967, Italy, 26cm high, 35cm wide.

$2650 - $2850

Geoffrey Hatty, VIC

Pair of contemporary wrought iron painted lamps and shades, France, 70cm high, 30cm wide.

$1550 - $1750

Capocchi, VIC

Desk lamp, the yellow enamel shade raised on a brass stem from the base, Australia, 51cm high.

$135 - $155

B'artchi, ACT

Aluminium table lamp, Australia, c1955, 50cm high, 48cm diam.

$100 - $120

Atomic Pop, SA

Orange ribbon shade lamp, 37cm high.

$25 - $35
**Atomic Pop,
SA**

Crown Lynn lamp, made for the Gaylight Studios as illustrated on page 203 of Gail Henry's book 'New Zealand Pottery - Commercial and Collectable', New Zealand, c1950, 49cm high, 11cm wide, 18cm deep.

NZ$600 - $700
**Maxine's Collectibles,
New Zealand**

Table lamp with original shade, Italy, c1970, 79cm high.

$375 - $415
**Victor Harbour Antiques
- Mittagong, NSW**

Metal and cherub lamp with a pull chain switch, United States, c1995, 70cm high.

NZ$230 - $270
**Middle Earth Antiques,
New Zealand**

Ceramic and metal lamp base with a vellum, two tiered shade, United States, c1958, 60cm high.

$255 - $295
**Chapel Street Bazaar,
VIC**

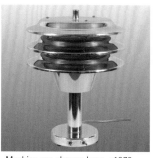

Machine age chrome lamp, c1970, 45cm high, 36cm diam.

$355 - $395
**Relic,
QLD**

Adjustable desk lamp on a swivel metal base, wooden stem and metal and glass shade, made in Paris, France, c1955, 45cm high, 30cm wide, 60cm long.

$545 - $645
**Le Contraste,
VIC**

Pair of solid brass table lamps with gold foil and brown velvet shades, Australia, c1960, 90cm high, 45cm diam.

$345 - $385
**The New Farm Antique Centre,
QLD**

Hand painted Carlton Ware lamp, England, 23cm high.

$145 - $165
**Cobweb Collectables,
NSW**

Anodised desk lamp, Australia, c1950, 30cm high.

$40 - $50
**Fat Helen's,
VIC**

Blue anodised electric lamp with brass legs, Australia, c1950, 30cm high, 32cm long, 32cm deep.

$155 - $175
**Towers Antiques &
Collectables, NSW**

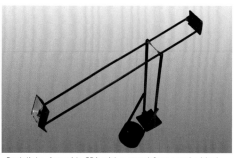

Desk light, Artewide SPA with a metal frame and a black plastic base, Tizio, Milano, R. Sadder, Italy, c1970.

$260 - $300
**Bowhows,
NSW**

Red planet studio or desk lamp by Planet Products with an extendable arm, made in Brighton, Melbourne, catalogue No. 'K', Australia, c1975, 80cm high, 37cm wide.

$75 - $95
**Image Objex,
VIC**

LAMPS - TABLE & DESK

Woven plastic pink lamp, Australia, c1950, 48cm high.

$45 - $65   **Fat Helen's, VIC**

'Mushroom' shaped orange plastic lamp, Australia, 43cm high, 34cm wide.

$75 - $95   **Victor Harbour Antiques - Mittagong, NSW**

Plastic toffee lamp, Hong Kong, c1970, 47cm high.

$85 - $105   **Chapel Street Bazaar, VIC**

Large capodimonte table lamp with shade, decorated with hand painted moulded relief of classical figures, Italy, c1960, 86cm high, 38cm wide.

$545 - $645   **Bowerbird Antiques & Collectables, SA**

Ceramic and wooden table lamp with the original cloth shade, Italy, c1970, 67cm high.

$65 - $85   **Chapel Street Bazaar, VIC**

Barsony lady lamp, mounted on a teak base with the original textured shade, model FL55, Australia, c1960.

$545 - $645   **Vampt, NSW**

Teak tripod table lamp with the original shade, c1960, 47cm high, 20cm diam.

$145 - $165   **Vampt, NSW**

Table lamp, composed of multiple Australian native woods with a waisted cream shade and tan velour edging, Australia, c1970, 80cm high.

$55 - $75   **Born Frugal, VIC**

Black lady lamp with an Hawaiian girl design and a pink shade, Australia, c1960, 60cm high, 30cm wide.

$230 - $270   **Shop 5, The Centenary Centre, NSW**

Black lady Art Deco style table lamp, Australia, c1950, 60cm high, 12cm wide.

$275 - $315   **Newport Temple Antiques, VIC**

Black lady lamp, Australia, 48cm high.

$275 - $315   **Coliseum Antiques Centre, NSW**

Nina Ricci 'Factice' container, for Deci Delia launched in 1994, converted to lamp, France, 45cm high.

$275 - $315   **Armadale Antique Centre, VIC**

Fabulous fifties lamp and shade, made in Chicago, United States.

$330 - $370   **Retro Active, VIC**

Barsony yellow ceramic lustre fish lamp with the original yellow plastic ribbon shade, marked to the base 'FL 52', Australia, c1950, 46cm high, 30cm wide.

$205 - $245   **Bowerbird Antiques & Collectables, SA**

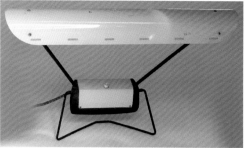

Bill Igulsden desk lamp designed for Planet Lighting, Australia, c1952, 55cm high.

$225 - $265   **Design Dilemas, VIC**

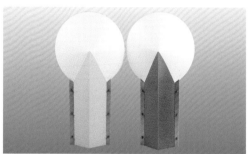

Pair of lamp shades, in the 'Moon' design by Samuel Parker, Italy, c1994, 56cm high, 30cm wide, 14cm deep.

$310 - $350   **Vampt, NSW**

Lamp shade and base, Australia, c1970, 67cm high.

$115 - $135   **Victor Harbour Antiques - Mittagong, NSW**

Black and orange perspex lamp, 46cm high, 30cm wide, 30cm long.

$160 - $180   **Relic, QLD**

Crown Devon, leaping deer lamp, England, 26cm high.

$115 - $135   **Archers Antiques, TAS**

Large lamp base with relief patterns, attributed to Bitossi, Italy, c1970, 45cm high.

$155 - $175   **frhapsody, WA**

Wembley Ware fish lamp, Australia, c1950, 27cm high.

$405 - $445   **Antiques & Collectables Centre - Ballarat, VIC**

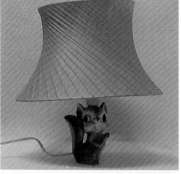

Novelty lamp base with pink shade, c1960, 33cm high.

$125 - $145   **Olsens Antiques, QLD**

Floor lamp with bendable heads, c1980, 160cm high.

$175 - $195

Image Objex, VIC

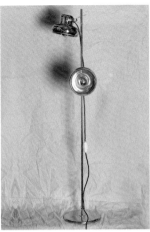

Chrome twin standard lamp with adjustable twin spot lights, c1965.

$190 - $230

Bowhows, NSW

Funky metal standard lamp with its original shades and a cast iron base, Australia, c1950, 170cm high, 30cm long, 30cm deep.

$275 - $315

Towers Antiques & Collectables, NSW

Chrome ball downlight, adjustable 360 degrees.

$130 - $150

Bowhows, NSW

Floor lamp with a four legged base and table, Australia, c1955.

$185 - $205

Atomic Pop, SA

Two arm adjustable standard light, Italy, c1970, 195cm high.

$2400 - $2600

Geoffrey Hatty, VIC

Lamp with table on wheels with original celluloid shade, Australia, c1955, 155cm high.

$220 - $260

Atomic Pop, SA

Black metal standard lamp, c1950, 140cm high.

NZ$185 - $205   **Maxine's Collectibles, New Zealand**

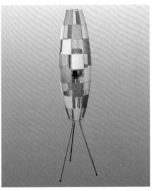

Rocket shaped lamp with plastic ribbon panels and three splayed legs, Denmark, c1960, 138cm high, 26cm diam.

NZ$240 - $280   **Decollectables, New Zealand**

Jean Royere 1950's metal standard light, France, 180cm high.

$8300 - $8700   **Geoffrey Hatty, VIC**

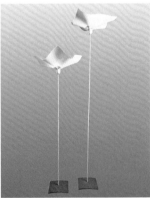

Pair of Mario Bellini floor lamps by Aero, Italy, c1974, 220cm high.

$1600 - $1800   **b bold - 20th Century Furniture & Effects, VIC**

Green and brown woven wool standard lamp, c1970, 160cm high, 55cm diam.

$940 - $1040

506070, NSW

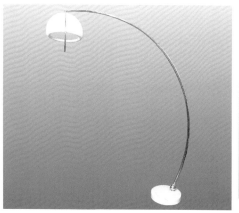

Adjustable arc lamp in brass with a carrera round marble base and a Perspex ringed shade, France, c1960, 240cm high, 220cm wide.

$1495 - $1695

Le Contraste, VIC

Paired Louis Poulsen panthella lamps, designed by Verner Panton, in the standard version, Denmark, c1979, 130cm high, 50cm diam.

$1490 - $1690

Le Contraste, VIC

Flower power floor lamp, European, c1960, 115cm high, 21cm diam.

$545 - $645

Vampt, NSW

Art Deco style smoker's table lamp in chrome and Bakelite, Australia, c1950, 169cm high.

$140 - $160

Chapel Street Bazaar, VIC

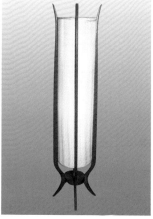

'Rocket' standard lamp, c1960, 149cm high, 32cm diam.

$115 - $135

Relic, QLD

Teak and fabric floor lamp, c1960, 150cm high, 30cm wide, 30cm deep.

$105 - $125

Willunga Antiques, SA

Art Deco style chrome and Bakelite standard lamp with a large red cloth shade, smokers table and ashtray, c1950, 167.5cm high, 70cm diam.

$330 - $370

River Emporium, NSW

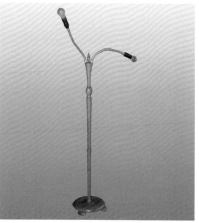

Art Deco style timber lamp stand, c1950, 1.2cm high.

$185 - $205

Home Again, NSW

Floor lamp with a table and the original celluloid shade, Australia, c1955.

$115 - $135

Atomic Pop, SA

Raspberry coloured spaghetti light shade, c1970, 40cm diam.

$60 - $80

Relic,
QLD

Fibre optic lamp with an unusual chrome base, Taiwan, 35cm high.

$45 - $65

Atomic Pop,
SA

Metal lighthouse lamp, Australia, c1950, 37cm high.

$265 - $305

The Junk Company,
VIC

Wall mounted light fitting, c1960, 31cm high.

$185 - $205

Victor Harbour Antiques - Mittagong,
NSW

Crystal drop five branch wall bracket, Italy, c1950, 55cm high.

$1150 - $1350

Antique Décor,
VIC

Cobra light by Angelo Lelli, Italy, c1964, 55cm high.

$4400 - $4600

Geoffrey Hatty,
VIC

Unused double bedside or wall lamp with orange fibreglass shades and a white plastic base, stamped 'Duperite', Australia, c1960, 20cm high, 25cm long.

$50 - $70

Trinkets & Treasures,
VIC

Jro Globus glass light up world globe, by Jro-Verlag Munchen, Germany, c1958, 35cm high, 25cm diam.

$490 - $590

Vampt,
NSW

Signed photograph of Winnifred Attwell from 1956, 20cm high, 25cm wide.

$15 - $25

The Nostalgia Factory, NSW

John Astin, otherwise known as Gomez Addams, from the TV series 'The Addams Family', signed and framed colour photo, United States, c1997, 35cm high, 30cm wide.

$190 - $210

Rockaway Records, QLD

Autographed black and white photo of famed actress Lauren Bacall, whose real name was Betty Joan Peiske, United States, c1990, 35cm high, 30cm wide.

$230 - $270

Rockaway Records, QLD

Autographed by the late great Johnny Cash and Waylon Jennings, two of country music's greatest acts, obtained at the Hilton Hotel in Brisbane in the 1980's, Australia, 93cm wide, 110cm long.

$1695 - $1895

Rockaway Records, QLD

Autographed black and white photo of Barbara Eden, of 'I Dream of Jeannie' TV series fame, United States, c1997, 35cm high, 30cm wide.

$280 - $320

Rockaway Records, QLD

Elvis Presley autograph inset with a photo of his 1968 comeback special, United States, c1960, 43cm high, 32cm wide.

$2400 - $2600

Rockaway Records, QLD

Alice Cooper autographed 'Time Off' newspaper, issue 681 of August 3-9, 1994 featuring Alice Cooper on the cover, clearly signed in black marker pen on the front cover, Australia, c1994, 29cm wide, 40cm long.

$90 - $110

Rockaway Records, QLD

Kylie Minogue autographed 'Cowboy Style' mini poster, large photo, framed with unique photo plaque, Australia, c1999, 55cm high, 40cm wide.

$640 - $740

Rare Memorabilia Gallery, VIC

Guitar signed by members of the heavy metal band Pantera, at an in store signing at HMV Brisbane, including the autograph of the late Daniel Abbott (AKA Dimebag) who met a tragic end when shot by a fan during a performance in 2004, Australia.

$550 - $650

Rockaway Records, QLD

Coloured autographed photo of country and western singer Johnny Lee, United States, c1980, 20cm wide, 25.5cm long.

$20 - $30

Abra Card Abra Roycroft, VIC

Home made 'Beatles' polished cotton shift dress, fully lined, size 8-10, c1965.

$475 - $515

OK WOW, ACT

Beatles 'Remco' dolls complete with instruments, c1964, 12cm high.

$800 - $900

Relic, QLD

Plastic figurines of the Beatles, with moving heads, Japan, c1960, 10cm high.

$550 - $650

Marsteen Collectables, VIC

Unique Beatles era dress, made and worn by the owner to Brisbane's Festival Hall Concert June 1964, Australia, 42cm wide, 90cm long.

$1000 - $1200

Relic, QLD

John Lennon 'Imagine' gold record, the first piece of memorabilia allowed to be licensed by Yoko Ono following John's death. Numbered 1042 of 2500 and licensed by Bag One Arts Inc, United States, c1992, 51cm high, 41cm wide.

$1800 - $2000

Rockaway Records, QLD

Beatles cup and saucer/snack set, by Washington Pottery, England, c1964, 7cm high, 20cm wide, 18cm long.

$230 - $270

Relic, QLD

Beatles sun hat, England, c1964.

$255 - $295

The Time Machine, QLD

Beatles stockings with their heads and guitars in the weave and the original packaging, c1964.

$205 - $245

Relic, QLD

Mounted 1960's Beatles poster, England, 90cm high, 60cm wide.

$85 - $105

Retro Active, VIC

'Beatlemania in Australia', this Beatles automata was used as a shop display to promote and sell Beatles records during their visit to Australia in the 1960's, Australia, 83cm high, 83cm wide.

$6300 - $6700

Hunters & Collectors Antiques, NSW

Perthshire limited edition Christmas paperweight, No. 45 of 400, the centre cane contains the letter 'P' and '1987', England, 9cm diam.

$455 - $495
Glenelg Antique Centre, SA

Plastic 'Merry Christmas' wall decoration, Japan, c1960, 20cm high, 30cm long.

NZ$20 - $30
Bakelite Belle.com, New Zealand

Plastic Santa Clause lamp, Japan, c1950, 43cm high, 18cm wide.

NZ$165 - $185
Bakelite Belle.com, New Zealand

Melrose pottery figure of Father Christmas, Australia, 18cm high, 10cm wide.

$745 - $845
Armadale Antique Centre, VIC

Pair of plastic choir singers, Japan, c1960, 47.5cm high, 16cm wide.

NZ$155 - $175
Bakelite Belle.com, New Zealand

'Wee Winking Christmas Tree', battery operated and boxed, Japan, c1960, 17cm high, 6cm diam.

NZ$40 - $50
Bakelite Belle.com, New Zealand

Battery operating moving toy Santa with flashing eyes and ringing bell, with original box, Japan, c1970, 33cm high.

$135 - $155
How Bazaar, VIC

Plastic nativity scene, dated 1974, Hong Kong, 17.5cm high, 36cm long.

NZ$40 - $50
Bakelite Belle.com, New Zealand

Tim Burton's 'Nightmare Before Christmas' Santa Claus soft toy, China, c1994, 22cm high, 25cm wide.

$115 - $135
Chapel Street Bazaar, VIC

Tinsel Christmas centrepiece, Japan, c1965, 14cm wide.

NZ$20 - $30
Bakelite Belle.com, New Zealand

Commemorative plate for the bi-centenary of the discovery of Australia, 1770-1970, Australia, c1970, 25cm diam.

$55 - $75

Antique Revivals, VIC

Glass plate, made to commemorate the opening of the Sydney Opera House in 1973, Australia, 30.5cm diam.

$55 - $75

Newport Temple Antiques, VIC

Wedgwood plate, commemorating the centenary of The Exhibition Building, Melbourne, 1880-1980, limited edition of 2000, made exclusively for Buckley & Nunn, England, 15cm wide.

$95 - $115

Karlia Rose Garden Antiques & Collectables, VIC

Royal Winton pin tray. Picture depicting Buckley & Nunn shop front. Commemorative 1851-1951, stamped 'Made in Australia', Australia, c1951, 11cm wide.

$65 - $85

Pearl Rose, VIC

Boxed set of silver coins commemorating the Korean War, 1950-1953, issued in 2003 by the Perth Mint, set no. 0121, Australia.

$125 - $145

Island & Continent Coins & Stamps, NSW

Boxed set of seven silver coins commemorating the 75th Anniversary of Australian Federation, 1901-1970, Australia.

$230 - $270

Island & Continent Coins & Stamps, NSW

Pewter tankard, commemorating the 150th Anniversary of the State of Victoria, the front surmounted with the Coat of Arms of Victoria, the back engraved with details of milestones of the state's history, dated 1984-5, Australia, 14cm high.

$40 - $60

Trinkets & Treasures, VIC

Royal Doulton loving cup commemorating Captain Cook's Bicentenary, No. 78 of 250, England, c1970, 21cm high, 28cm wide.

$1650 - $1850

Collectable Creations, QLD

Commemorative bust of Queen Elizabeth II, made in 1953, England, 16.5cm high.

$55 - $75 · **Antiques & Collectables Centre - Ballarat, VIC**

Guinness stout green glass bottle, commemorating the 'Royal Visit 1953-4' of 'The Queen, God Bless Her', Ireland, 20.5cm high, 6cm diam.

NZ$20 - $30 · **Peachgrove Antiques, New Zealand**

Gilt and enamel 'ER' pin, commemorating the commemoration of Elizabeth II in 1953, England, 1cm high, 3cm wide, 4cm diam.

$70 - $90 · **Dr Russell's Emporium, WA**

Coronation Queen Elizabeth II paperweight, printed tin over lead weight, England, c1950, 5cm diam.

$55 - $75 · **Chapel Street Bazaar, VIC**

Set of six glasses commemorating the Queens 1954 visit to Australia.

$15 - $25 · **Goodwood House Antiques, WA**

Boxed set of matches, commemorating the Queens 1954 visit to Australia.

$35 - $45 · **Goodwood House Antiques, WA**

1oz silver coin commemorating Prince Harry's 21st birthday, 15/9/05, issued by the Perth Mint, Australia.

$100 - $120 · **Island & Continent Coins & Stamps, NSW**

Royal Perth Mint issued 1oz silver coin, commemorating 'HRH Prince William's 21st Birthday' 21/6/03, Australia.

$100 - $120 · **Island & Continent Coins & Stamps, NSW**

'The Queen Mother 1900-2002' one ounce pure silver $5 proof commemorative coin. Complete with all packaging and booklet, issued by the Royal Mint, Australian.

$45 - $65 · **Island & Continent Coins & Stamps, NSW**

Coronation perfume bottle in red, white and blue stripes with a crown stopper, England, c1953, 1cm wide, 7cm long.

NZ$40 - $50 · **Memory Lane, New Zealand**

Catherine Ferguson tin commemorating the coronation of Queen Elizabeth II, 2nd of June 1953, 12cm long.

$30 - $40 · **Dr Russell's Emporium, WA**

Aynsley china mug, commemorating the coronation of Queen Elizabeth II in 1953, England.

NZ$40 - $50

Colonial Antiques, New Zealand

Royal Doulton loving cup, commemorating the silver jubilee of Queen Elizabeth II, number 37 of a limited run of only 250 produced in 1977, England, 27cm high, 30cm wide.

$1750 - $1950

Collectable Creations, QLD

Aynsley china cup and saucer, to commemorate Queen Elizabeth II coronation in 1953, England, 6cm high.

NZ$40 - $50

Colonial Antiques, New Zealand

Aynsley China cup, commemorating the coronation of Queen Elizabeth II in 1953, England.

NZ$40 - $50

Colonial Antiques, New Zealand

Royal Doulton Charles and Diana wedding cup, England, c1981, 9.5cm high, 8cm diam.

$35 - $45

Woodside Bazaar, SA

Beaker commemorating the Queens Coronation, 1953.

$20 - $30

The Nostalgia Factory, NSW

Norville ceramic beaker, commemorating the 1937 Coronation of King George VI, England, 4cm high.

$30 - $40

Paddington Antique Centre Pty Ltd, QLD

Set of six glasses commemorating the Queens 1954 visit to Australia.

$15 - $25

Goodwood House Antiques, WA

Queen Elizabeth II and Duke of Edinburgh commemorative tin plates, 'Portland Ware' made by The Metal Box Company Limited, England, c1950, 35cm diam.

$80 - $100

Lucilles Interesting Collectables, NSW

Aynsley bone china plate, commemorating the coronation of Queen Elizabeth II in 1953, England, 26.5cm diam.

NZ$190 - $210

Colonial Antiques, New Zealand

Spode 'The Westminster Abbey Plate', 1965 celebrating the Nine-Hundredth Anniversary, England, 26cm diam.

$135 - $155

The Restorers Barn, VIC

'Buckingham Palace, London' souvenir compact, England, c1965, 6.5cm wide.

$45 - $65

Journey to the Past Antiques & Collectables, QLD

45 rpm record of the 'Star Wars Title Theme', made by RCA Limited, Sydney Australia in 1977, 'Funk' on side two, Australia.

$10 - $20

Vintage Replacement Parts, NSW

Set of videos of the original Star Trek series, seventy three episodes, United States, c1990.

$380 - $420

Vintage Replacement Parts, NSW

A boxed double deck of Marilyn Monroe playing cards, manufactured under special exclusive franchise with Tom Kelly Studios, Hollywood California. E. H. Walker Supply Co, Washington, Richmond, United States, 8.5cm wide, 22cm long.

$275 - $315

Decorama, VIC

'Sunnyside Up' early television studio HSV7 publicity photos, autographed by Syd Heylen and Honest John in pen, cards both black and white, Australia, c1960.

$35 - $45

Savers, VIC

'Phantom', print, signed and numbered by the artist Glenn Ford, Australia, c1990, 62.5cm high, 92cm long.

$85 - $105

Cat's Cradle Comics, VIC

'Fight for the Ashes', an 8mm film, with four hundred feet of film, England, c1953.

$175 - $195

How Bazaar, VIC

'Noddy' lunch tin by Playworks International, China, 15cm high, 19cm wide, 8.5cm deep.

$25 - $35

Treats & Treasures, NSW

Sticker sheet of 'Mr. Magoo and Friends' featuring characters from the cartoon series, made by UPA Pictures, Taiwan, c1979, 45cm high, 30cm wide.

$15 - $25

Chapel Street Bazaar, VIC

Unused book of paper dolls from the TV show 'Laugh-in', United States, c1960, 26cm high, 20cm wide.

$40 - $50

Chapel Street Bazaar, VIC

'The Racers' photograph outside of the Regent picture show in 1953, Australia.

$20 - $30

The Nostalgia Factory, NSW

Tin 'Tuck Tape' dispenser depicting Jerry Lewis and Dean Martin, 3/4 inch width. 'American Tuck Corp. New Rochelle, NY, Made in USA', United States, c1950.

$40 - $50

Decorama, VIC

Davy Crocket mug and bowl duo, United States, c1950, 7cm high.

$85 - $105

Decorama, VIC

Porcelain figurine of the 'Centaurette' character, from the Disney film 'Fantasia', Thailand, c1995, 16cm high, 20cm long.

$205 - $245

Chapel Street Bazaar, VIC

Set of four 'Nightmare Before Christmas', watches in their original boxes, China.

$170 - $190

Chapel Street Bazaar, VIC

Snoopy watch with manual movement, c1975, 3cm diam.

NZ$60 - $80

Lord Ponsonby Antiques, New Zealand

Porcelain wall plate featuring the character 'Jock' from the Walt Disney film 'Lady and the Tramp', manufactured by the same company that made Brownie Downing plates, Japan, c1955, 10cm diam.

$40 - $50

Chapel Street Bazaar, VIC

Donald Duck egg cup stamped 'Walt Disney Productions', Japan, c1950, 7cm high.

$185 - $205

Pearl Rose, VIC

Miniature 'Marge Simpson' in a plastic bubble, China, c1980, 3.5cm high.

$5 - $10

Chapel Street Bazaar, VIC

Porcelain plate, featuring 'Felix the Cat', manufactured by Monkeys of Melbourne, Australia, c1994, 24cm diam.

$85 - $105

Chapel Street Bazaar, VIC

'Masters of the Universe' cold cast hand painted mini 'Evil-Lyn' bust, limited edition of 2500 pieces, designed and sculptured by the Four Horsemen, made by 'Neca', China, c2004, 20cm high.

$75 - $95

Go Figure Collectables, VIC

Solid resin figurine of the Japanese cartoon character, 'Astro Boy', China, c2004, 25cm high.

$85 - $105

Chapel Street Bazaar, VIC

Elvis Presley licensed commemorative plaque numbered 30 of 2500, inset with original concert tickets and two concert photos, United States, c1994, 30cm high, 40cm wide.

$700 - $800   Rockaway Records, QLD

Original 1978 packet of Elvis trading cards with original price tag, United States.

$15 - $25   Rockaway Records, QLD

Licensed 'Kiss' badges, sought after by collectors. Priced per item, Australia, c1980.

$15 - $25   Rockaway Records, QLD

Original Kiss badges, c1980, 6cm wide.

$25 - $35   Fat Helen's, VIC

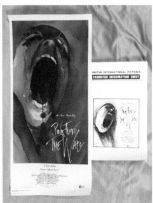

'Pink Floyd The Wall' daybill poster and exhibitor's information sheet, for the 1982 Alan Parker directed film starring Sir Bob Geldof, United States, 33cm wide, 71cm long.

$230 - $270   Rockaway Records, QLD

'Bill Haley and his Comets The Big Show', 1957 Australian tour programme, Australia.

$75 - $95   369 Antiques, VIC

Jimi Hendrix original Fillmore, San Francisco concert ticket depicting 'Flying Eyeball' artwork framed with official photo from 1969 concert and a unique Hendrix photo plaque, United States, 90cm high, 60cm wide.

$700 - $800   Rare Memorabilia Gallery, VIC

'We Love the Beatles' plastic mug, Australia, c1960, 14cm high.

$65 - $85   Antiques & Collectables On Moorabool, VIC

Gumbi as 'Elvis', a hard plastic figure with removable hair and sunglasses, China, c1995, 27cm high, 11cm wide.

$55 - $75   Chapel Street Bazaar, VIC

Kiss Creatures – 'The Demon' limited edition exclusive figure by McFarlane, United States, c2002, 41cm high, 28cm wide, 15cm deep.

$65 - $85   Cardtastic Collectables, VIC

SOUVENIR WARE

View Ware souvenir ashtray of 'Sydney Harbour Bridge', Australia, c1955, 2.5cm high, 12cm diam.

$5 - $15

Woodside Bazaar, SA

Sydney Harbour Bridge souvenir matchbox holder, made of anodised aluminium, Australia, 6cm wide, 3.5cm deep.

$5 - $15

Furniture Revisited, VIC

Souvenir brooch with blue enamel bow and resin pendant, attached with a picture of Big Ben in London, England, c1950, 3cm wide, 4.5cm long.

NZ$55 - $75

The Wooden Rose, New Zealand

Hand crafted shell collage featuring the Sydney Opera House, Australia, c1970, 63cm high, 75cm long.

$45 - $65

Chapel Street Bazaar, VIC

Shell and coral TV lamp with a 'Seaworld Gold Coast' sticker, Australia, c1960, 25cm high, 30cm wide, 18cm deep.

$165 - $185

Vampt, NSW

Goss Ware souvenir featuring the 'City of Sydney' coat of arms, England, c1950, 8cm high.

$20 - $30

Dr Russell's Emporium, WA

Child's souvenir enamelled bracelet depicting Perth, Adelaide, Melbourne, Parliament House and City Hall, Brisbane, Australia, c1955.

$25 - $35

Patti K Temporary Interiors, VIC

Pair of Queenstown souvenir egg cups, made by 'Royal Grafton Bone China', New Zealand, c1960, 4cm high, 4.5cm diam.

NZ$15 - $25

Moa Extinct Stuff, New Zealand

Circular mirror with a scene from a mud pool in Rotorua, New Zealand, c1960, 39cm diam.

NZ$190 - $210

Colonial Heritage Antiques Ltd, New Zealand

Cushion cover as a souvenir of Las Vegas, on glittery felt, Japan, c1970, 50cm high, 50cm wide, 10cm deep.

$55 - $75

Dr Russell's Emporium, WA

View Ware souvenir ashtray of Sydney Harbour Bridge, Australia, c1955, 3cm high, 8cm wide, 14cm long.

$20 - $30

Woodside Bazaar, SA

Goss Ware, 'Queensland' souvenir vase, England, c1950, 5cm high.

$20 - $30

Dr Russell's Emporium, WA

Kornies footy card of R. Featherby, Australia, c1950.

$7 - $17   **Chapel Street Bazaar, VIC**

Geelong Football Club 1980 album, complete with cards for each player and each player's autograph, Australia.

$380 - $420   **Marsteen Collectables, VIC**

Kornies footy card of N. Trezise from Geelong, Australia, c1950.

$7 - $17   **Chapel Street Bazaar, VIC**

Coles Footy Card of Don Williams from Melbourne, Australia, c1950.

$15 - $25   **Chapel Street Bazaar, VIC**

Complete set of forty 'Mobil' VFL football trading cards, Australia, c1965, 22cm high, 28.5cm wide.

$225 - $265   **The Bottom Drawer Antique Centre, VIC**

Kornies footy card of K. Shears, Australia, c1950.

$7 - $17   **Chapel Street Bazaar, VIC**

Coles Footy Card of Bill Stephen from Fitzroy, Australia, c1950.

$15 - $25   **Chapel Street Bazaar, VIC**

Coles footy card of Hawthorn's Clayton Thompson, Australia, c1950.

$20 - $30   **Chapel Street Bazaar, VIC**

'Scanlens' football card for Graham Farmer, Australia, c1964.

$280 - $320   **Camberwell Antique Centre, VIC**

'Kornies' football card for John Reeves, North Melbourne, Australia, c1953.

$7 - $17   **Camberwell Antique Centre, VIC**

AFL Melbourne Football Club, signed Russell Robertson Collectors card (#116 of 300), Australia, c2006, 8cm high.

$90 - $110   **Carnegie Collectables, VIC**

'Easi Oats' football card, Lionel Blackmore, Australia, c1951.

$550 - $650   **Camberwell Antique Centre, VIC**

Set of twelve packs of cards, one pack for each VFL team, issued by Ardmona, Australia, c1981, 33cm high.

$950 - $1050

Carnegie Collectables, VIC

'Ampol VFL Champions' vinyl record, 1st series, one player from each of the twelve VFL clubs, Bob Skilton (Sth Melbourne), Len Thompson (Collingwood), Barry Davis (Essendon), Alex Ruscuklic (Fitzroy), Ted Whitten (Footscray), Peter Hudson (Hawthorn), Ron Barassi (Carlton), Hassa Mann (Melbourne), Laurie Dwyer (North Melbourne), Royce Hart (Richmond), Carl Ditterich (St Kilda) and Doug Wade (Geelong). Priced per item, Australia, c1960, 24cm high, 20cm wide.

$65 - $85

Memorabilia on Parade, VIC

Set of Victorian State women's, 2004 football team cards, Australia, 8.5cm high.

$25 - $35

Carnegie Collectables, VIC

'Easi-Oats' trade card. After five years, 'Easi-Oats' breakfast cereal issued a fifth series consisting of twenty four South Australian league footballers. Each card featured a coloured photograph of a player superimposed onto a blue background depicting a football ground, Australia, c1960, 4.8cm high, 7.8cm wide.

$35 - $45

At The Toss of A Coin, SA

A series footy card of Laurie Sandiland from Footscray, Australia, c1968.

$5 - $10

Chapel Street Bazaar, VIC

'The Footy Show' promotional card, signed by Jim Stynes, Australia, c1990, 14cm wide.

$15 - $25

Carnegie Collectables, VIC

'Carlton Premiers, 1981 Commemorative Souvenir' badge, Australia, 6cm diam.

$10 - $20

Chapel Street Bazaar, VIC

Football badge, 'Dick Reynolds Testimonial', Australia.

$200 - $240

Gardenvale Collectables, VIC

St Kilda Football Club official team photograph for 2006, Australia, 74cm wide.

$40 - $50

Carnegie Collectables, VIC

'Milo' VFL team tokens. Priced per item, Australia, c1950, 3.5cm long.

$55 - $75

Memorabilia on Parade, VIC

Geelong Football Club '1951 Grand Final Living Legends' photograph, signed by members of the team, Australia, c1951, 39cm high, 27cm wide.

$500 - $600

Marsteen Collectables, VIC

Melbourne Football Club figurine issued by Ansett Australia, in its original packaging, China, c1990, 11cm high.

$15 - $25   **Carnegie Collectables, VIC**

Carlton doll made by Hunter toys, Australia, c1960, 30cm high.

$110 - $130   **Around The Grounds Football Memorabilia, VIC**

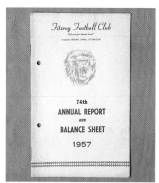

'Fitzroy Football Club, 74th Annual Report and Balance Sheet 1957', Australia, 21cm high.

$35 - $45   **Carnegie Collectables, VIC**

Collingwood Football Club ring cushion, Australia, c1950, 27cm high, 35cm long.

$165 - $185   **Carnegie Collectables, VIC**

Richmond Tigers (AFL/VFL) grand final team flag for the 1982 premiership, Australia, 43cm long.

$40 - $50   **Carnegie Collectables, VIC**

Collingwood badge on a black ribbon, Australia, c1960, 30cm long, 3.5cm diam.

$15 - $25   **Chapel Street Bazaar, VIC**

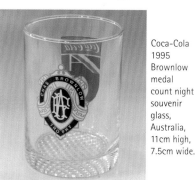

Coca-Cola 1995 Brownlow medal count night souvenir glass, Australia, 11cm high, 7.5cm wide.

$15 - $25   **Wooden Pew Antiques, VIC**

'Greig's Honey' football glass, Australia, c1950, 12cm high.

$115 - $135   **Around The Grounds Football Memorabilia, VIC**

VFL yo-yo for the Essendon Football Club with the name on one side and the mascot on the other, Australia, c1970, 5.5cm diam.

$25 - $35   **Carnegie Collectables, VIC**

VFL yo-yo for the Geelong Football Club, the name on the side, the mascot on the other, c1970, 5.5cm diam.

$25 - $35   **Carnegie Collectables, VIC**

Fitzroy badge on tri-coloured ribbons, Australia, 14cm long, 4.5cm diam.

$30 - $40   **Chapel Street Bazaar, VIC**

Scanlen emblems, The Swans from the 1968 series, Australia.

$110 - $130

Ian's Cards, VIC

Scanlen emblems, 'The Cats' from the 1968C series, Australia.

$50 - $70

Ian's Cards, VIC

Grand Final 'Record', 1956. Melbourne defeated Collingwood 17.19 (121) to 6.12 (48), the second of Melbourne's Premierships in the 1950s when they won 55, 56, 57 and 59, Australia, 21cm high, 11cm wide.

$310 - $350

Carnegie Collectables, VIC

Australian Football League team, 'Sydney Swans' plaque, Australia, c1980, 10.5cm wide, 20cm long.

$35 - $45

Decorama, VIC

'Twisties' VFL team logos. Priced per item, Australia, c1950, 4cm diam.

$80 - $100

Memorabilia on Parade, VIC

VFL 'Courage' beer tray for the Melbourne Football Club, Australia, c1970, 30cm diam.

$140 - $160

Memorabilia on Parade, VIC

Geelong Football Club pennant. Geelong was previously known as the Black Cats, Australia, c1950, 41cm long.

$50 - $70

Carnegie Collectables, VIC

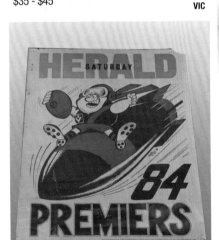

Original 'Weg' art featuring Essendon as the premiers. ('Weg' is a Melbourne based cartoonist.), Australia, c1984, 67cm high, 50cm wide.

$210 - $250

Wooden Pew Antiques, VIC

Richmond Football Club member's ticket for 1971, Australia, 8cm high.

$30 - $40

Carnegie Collectables, VIC

Collingwood Football Club member's ticket for 1976, Australia, 8cm high.

$25 - $35

Carnegie Collectables, VIC

'The Herald', September 29th 1980 Grand Final souvenir edition with the Tigers (Richmond AFL/VFL) as champions, Australia, c1980, 60cm high.

$30 - $40   Carnegie Collectables, VIC

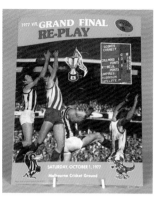

'Grand Final Replay' football record, between North Melbourne and Collingwood when North Melbourne won their second Premiership, Australia, c1977, 28cm high.

$40 - $60   Carnegie Collectables, VIC

Grand final 'Football Record', when Richmond defeated Collingwood. This was Richmond's last Premiership, Australia, c1980, 28cm high, 21cm wide.

$40 - $50   Carnegie Collectables, VIC

Grand final 'Football Record', for the famous drawn grand final between North Melbourne and Collingwood, Australia, c1977, 28cm high, 21cm wide.

$35 - $45   Carnegie Collectables, VIC

Collingwood Football Club 'Team of the Century' print by Jamie Cooper, signed by six Collingwood team of the century players, limited edition of 1000 with full certificate of authenticity, Australia, c2002, 95cm high, 113cm wide.

$1100 - $1300   Memorabilia on Parade, VIC

Victoria Park, Collingwood in 1903, reprint by Paul Crampton, Australia, c1990, 72cm wide.

$100 - $120   Carnegie Collectables, VIC

Herald Sun 1980's premiers, Tigers (Richmond Football Club) poster, Australia, c1980, 66cm high.

$280 - $320   Carnegie Collectables, VIC

Hawthorn Football Club member's tickets from 1958, Australia, 8cm high.

$65 - $85   Carnegie Collectables, VIC

Pre-season interstate trial game programme for Port Adelaide vs. Melbourne, played at Alberton oval on Sunday March 14th 1971, 8 pages, Australia, 21.7cm high, 14.4cm wide.

$40 - $50   At The Toss of A Coin, SA

Dick Reynolds 'Old Style' woollen jumper signed by Dick Reynolds on his famous number 3, framed and matted with photos, Australia, c1990, 140cm high, 90cm wide.

$1100 - $1300   Memorabilia on Parade, VIC

A cricket bat from the Centenary Test Match at Lords, August 1980, signed by the full squad of Australian and English teams, Australia, 41cm high, 6cm wide.

$475 - $515

Miniature Gunn & Moore cricket bat from the 1950/51 Ashes Series in Australia, signed by all of the players, England, 19cm long.

$230 - $270

Grey Nicholls bat, 1983-84 Australian team original signatures, on the reverse side the Pakistani team original signatures and West Indies team with the original signatures plus Wes Hall as manager, Australia.

$2400 - $2600

Bat from Kerry Packer's 1979 World Series Cricket with eighteen Australian signatures, twelve West Indies signatures plus Tony Greig, Clive Rice, Alan Nott and Imran Khan, England.

$4400 - $4600

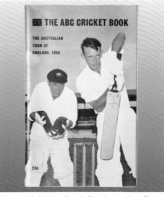

'The ABC Cricket Book, The Australian Tour of England, 1968', Australia, 21cm high.

$15 - $25

Dennis Lillee souvenir spoon, for world record test wickets 27.12.1981, Australia, 13.5cm long.

$15 - $25

Signed 'Victorian cricket Association Cricketer of the Year Dinner and presentation of The Jack Ryder Medal for 1975-76, MCC dining room 10th March 1976' menu and procedure book, Australia, 20cm high.

$115 - $135

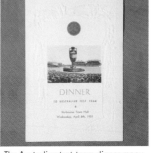

The Australian test team dinner menu and order of service for Wednesday April 8th 1959, signed by guests of honour and the Australian test team, Australia, 20cm high.

$945 - $1045

Richie Benaud badge from the Australian 1950-1951 cricket series, Australia, 3cm diam.

$35 - $45

Etched wine glass, commemorating the 'First Test Victory by New Zealand over England on British soil, Headingley Leeds August 1st 1983', with etched team signatures, New Zealand, 16cm high, 7.5cm diam.

NZ$185 - $205

Novelty ash tray, cigarette dispenser and matchbox holder, 'Keep the Ashes Here'. 'Reg. Design No. 11675. Olympia Smoker's Compendium', Australia, c1960, 10.5cm long, 9.5cm deep.

$75 - $95

Melbourne Cricket Club carpet cutting from the 'Bullring Bar' and 'Dining Room', Australia, c1950, 37cm high, 35cm wide.

$140 - $160

Cheeky 'Misha', the Moscow Olympics bear mascot, c1980, 11cm high, 6.5cm wide.

$75 - $95 **Maryborough Station Antique Emporium, VIC**

The Australian Women's Weekly, October 28, 1964 featuring Dawn Fraser on the cover for the 1964 Olympics, Australia, 38cm high, 30cm wide.

$25 - $35 **Towers Antiques & Collectables, NSW**

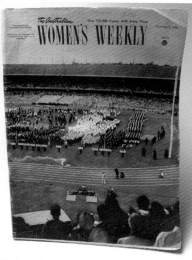

'The Australian Women's Weekly' Melbourne Olympics issue, for December 1956, Australia.

$15 - $25 **The Nostalgia Factory, NSW**

1956 Olympic games badges, on their original display card, Australia.

$40 - $50 **Yarra Valley Antique Centre, VIC**

Two Holden car badges as used on the official cars during the Sydney 2000 Olympic Games, featuring the Sydney 2000 logo, Australia, 3cm wide, 7.5cm long.

$5 - $15 **Lucilles Interesting Collectables, NSW**

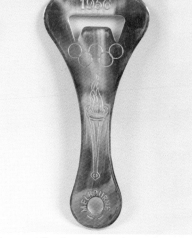

Large metal bottle opener, featuring the Olympic rings from the Melbourne 1956 games, and the Melbourne 1956 Olympic torch, Australia, 25.5cm long.

$230 - $270 **Lucilles Interesting Collectables, NSW**

Two packs of cards in plastic containers commemorating the 1956 Melbourne Olympic Games, one pack representing the Olympic Swimming Pool and the other, the MCG, Australia.

$70 - $90 **Robyn's Nest, VIC**

Royal Australian Mint $5 silver proof coin, commemorating the Olympic Journey from Sydney to Athens, 2001-2004, Australia.

$80 - $100 **Island & Continent Coins & Stamps, NSW**

Brooch in the form of a 1949 Winter Olympics, St Moritz stamp, Switzerland, c1950.

$55 - $75 **Steven Sher Antiques, WA**

SPORTING - OLYMPICS

1956 Melbourne Olympic Games cup and saucer, made by Rostyn Fine Bone China, England.

$215 - $255

Memorabilia on Parade, VIC

Royal Albert 1956 Melbourne Olympic Games trio, Australia, c1956.

$140 - $160

Antiques & Collectables Centre - Ballarat, VIC

Sydney 2000 Olympic Games 'Thank You' pin, as given to the staff and volunteers of the Games, still sealed in the original packet, Australia, 3cm high.

$20 - $30

Lucilles Interesting Collectables, NSW

Original lithographed poster for the Melbourne Olympics 1956, designed by Richard Beck, Australia, 100cm high, 70cm wide.

$4300 - $4500

Vintage Posters Only, VIC

1956 Melbourne Olympics face washer, Australia, 27cm wide, 26cm long.

$55 - $75

Antipodes Antiques, QLD

Cadbury's chocolate tin made in Claremont, Tasmania, for the 1956 Olympic Games in Melbourne, Australia, c1956, 14.5cm high, 17cm wide.

$120 - $140

The Rustic Rose, VIC

XVIth Melbourne 1956 Olympic Games Phoenix biscuit tin made by Willow, Australia, 24cm diam.

$75 - $95

Memorabilia on Parade, VIC

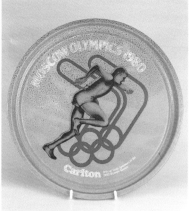

Moscow Olympics 1980 beer tray, advertising Carlton United Beer, Official State, Olympic sponsors, 31cm diam.

$35 - $45

Burly Babs Collectables/Retro Relics, VIC

'The Rugby League News', July 1968, Australia.

$4 - $10

The Nostalgia Factory, NSW

'Big League 1986 Annual', rugby league magazine featuring the 1986 premiers, the Parramatta Eels, Australia, 27.5cm high, 20.5cm wide.

$15 - $25

Mark's Book Barn, NSW

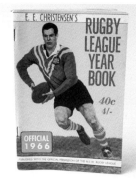

Official 'Rugby League Year Book', Australia, c1966, 18cm high, 12.5cm wide.

$20 - $30

Mark's Book Barn, NSW

Hand knitted Parramatta Eels Rugby league mascot doll, Australia, c1970, 20cm high.

$20 - $30

Terrace Collectables, NSW

'The Official 2003 Rugby League Album' of football cards, complete set, Australia.

$40 - $60

Modelcraft Miniatures, NSW

Three fridge magnets featuring Illawarra Steelers, North Sydney Bears, Eastern Suburbs Roosters, all NSW Rugby League teams, Australia, c1990, 6.5cm diam.

$25 - $35

Lucilles Interesting Collectables, NSW

Western Suburbs Magpies vinyl and fabric lined carry bag, Australia, c1960, 50cm high.

$55 - $75

Barry McKay, NSW

Parramatta Eels 'Canterbury' brand jersey, New Zealand, c1970.

$40 - $50

Barry McKay, NSW

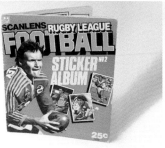

'State Bank Big Games, Western Suburbs Magpies' money box, in a cardboard container, Australia, c1980, 14cm high.

$15 - $25

Terrace Collectables, NSW

'Scanlen's Rugby League Football Sticker Album No. 2', complete with all full colour stickers, 1984, Australia, 27cm high, 24cm wide.

$60 - $80

Mark's Book Barn, NSW

'The Ring' boxing magazine, for June 1962, United States.

$15 - $25

The Nostalgia Factory, NSW

Jim Beam bourbon decanter commemorating fifth 'Kaiser International Golf Open' October 1971 at Silverado, Napa Valley, California, United States, 28cm high, 18cm wide.

$65 - $85

Lucilles Interesting Collectables, NSW

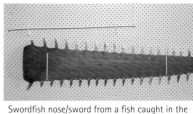

Swordfish nose/sword from a fish caught in the Gulf of Carpentaria, Australia, c1950, 20cm wide, 150cm long.

$330 - $370

Collectable Creations, QLD

102 silver proof coin issued by the Perth Mint to commemorate the 100th anniversary of the Australian Open, 1905-2005, Australia.

$70 - $90

Island & Continent Coins & Stamps, NSW

Aulsebrooks 4lb cake tin featuring 'Cardigan Bay', the highest stakes winner in the world, New Zealand, c1957, 10cm high, 24cm wide, 24cm long.

NZ$190 - $210

Hubbers Emporium, New Zealand

Waterford crystal decanter, commemorating the '1991 World Rugby Classic' tournament in Bermuda, England, 27cm high, 10cm diam.

NZ$200 - $240

Gregory's of Greerton, New Zealand

'The Argus' Melbourne to Warnambool bike ride, October 9th 1954 fixture, Australia, 23cm wide.

$25 - $35

Carnegie Collectables, VIC

Twentieth century sterling silver pill box with an enamelled picture on the lid of Victorian ladies and gentleman playing golf, titled 'The Game of Golf', England, 2.5cm wide, 5cm long, 1cm deep.

$170 - $190

Mac's Collectables, SA

Framed racing pigeon photograph, 'National Racing Pigeon federation, Mr. T. Knight, blue bar hen, 'Kempsey Girl' first prize Kempsey Combine', Australia, c1964, 45cm high, 43cm wide.

$35 - $45

Mark's Book Barn, NSW

'Sports Novels' March 1961, Australia.

$5 - $15

The Nostalgia Factory, NSW

'Charles Buchan's Football Monthly', January 1962, England, 37.5cm high, 25cm wide.

$5 - $15

The Nostalgia Factory, NSW

ANA (Australian National Airways) ceramic, double lipped milk jug made by Globe Pottery Co.Ltd., Shelton, England, supplied by John Dynon & Sons, Melbourne, England, c1950, 7cm high, 7cm diam.

$45 - $65 **Lucilles Interesting Collectables, NSW**

Small silver plated desk blotter, stamped 'Made for British Airways', also stamped 'Concorde' on the top and 'England' on the side, England, c1985, 5cm high, 9cm long, 5cm deep.

$40 - $50 **Trinkets & Treasures, VIC**

Fine bone Wedgwood Qantas coffee cup and saucer with Qantas cresting, England, c1980.

$70 - $90 **Global Transport Collectables Pty/Ltd, NSW**

Qantas travel bag, Australia, c1960, 25cm high, 45cm long.

$35 - $45 **Chapel Street Bazaar, VIC**

'Ansett Airlines of Australia' flight shoulder bag, featuring a Boeing jet, Australia, c1960, 35cm high, 30cm wide, 14cm long.

$55 - $75 **The Evandale Tinker, TAS**

BOAC World Timetable 1952, containing, fares and schedules, world offices and a diagram of world routes, England, 10cm wide, 22cm long.

$165 - $185 **Global Transport Collectables Pty/Ltd, NSW**

'Air India' advertising, papier mache, plaster covered figure of a genie on a flying carpet, India, c1990, 31cm high, 12cm wide, 18cm deep.

$140 - $160 **The Evandale Tinker, TAS**

Set of TAA brochures. Priced per item, Australia, c1950, 22cm high, 10cm wide.

$23 - $33 **Chapel Street Bazaar, VIC**

TAA (Trans Australia Airways) pair of metal cuff links, made by Stokes, Australia, 2.3cm wide.

$45 - $65 **Lucilles Interesting Collectables, NSW**

Three TAA uniform buttons, Australia, c1960, 1cm high, 1.5cm wide.

$25 - $35 **Yarra Valley Antique Centre, VIC**

Pair of Ansett Airlines metal cufflinks, Australia, 2.3cm wide.

$45 - $65 **Lucilles Interesting Collectables, NSW**

Australian Airlines 'Kanga Crew' badge, Australia.

$10 - $20   **Military Antiques Warehouse, WA**

'MMA' (Macrobertson Miller Airlines) pilot's hat, c1950.

$230 - $270   **Military Antiques Warehouse, WA**

TAA Junior Flyers Club wings, Australia.

$20 - $30   **Military Antiques Warehouse, WA**

Model aluminium aeroplane on a chrome stand, with 'Air New South Wales'. Livery, Australia, c1970, 130cm high, 85cm wide, 100cm deep.

$2700 - $2900   **Tarlo & Graham, VIC**

Sepia picture postcard of a 'Sunderland' flying boat, England, c1950, 9cm wide, 14cm long.

$20 - $30   **Abra Card Abra Roycroft, VIC**

Large Art Deco style chrome aeroplane on a stand, Australia, c1960, 23cm high.

$275 - $315   **Chapel Street Bazaar, VIC**

Model of a MacRobertson Miller Airlines DC3, made from mahogany with company livery, England, 36cm long.

$430 - $470   **Global Transport Collectables Pty/Ltd, NSW**

'Martinair Holland' plastic Boeing 747 model, on a stand, c1980, 30cm high, 50cm long.

$20 - $30   **The Nostalgia Factory, NSW**

Model of a BOAC 747–Classic, made from mahogany and with company livery, England, 50cm long.

$430 - $470   **Global Transport Collectables Pty/Ltd, NSW**

Model of a BOAC Super-VC10, made from mahogany and with company livery, England, 50cm long.

$430 - $470   **Global Transport Collectables Pty/Ltd, NSW**

Michelin man paperweight, in high gloss ceramics, England, c1970.

$75 - $95 **Rare Old Times Antiques & Collectables, SA**

Genuine original hard plastic Michelin Man, France, c1951, 36cm high, 15cm wide.

$900 - $1000 **Chapel Street Bazaar, VIC**

Sample bottle of 'Crude Oil' from 'Shell B.P & Todd Oil Services Ltd', oil strike 20.3.69, New Zealand, 8.5cm high, 3.5cm wide.

NZ$30 - $40 **Memory Lane, New Zealand**

AA car badge (Automobile Association) for Auckland, with an enamelled centre shield, New Zealand.

NZ$135 - $155 **Bulls Antiques & Collectables, New Zealand**

EJ Holden steering wheel, Australia, c1965.

$250 - $290 **Patrick Colwell, NSW**

$15 - $25

Scrapbook style booklet, 'Mobil Album/Top Performance Car', includes actual colour photographs affixed into the pages, Australia, c1970, 28cm high, 21.5cm wide.

Mark's Book Barn, NSW

Mobil petrol station attendant's hat, Australia, c1950, 30cm long.

$190 - $210 **How Bazaar, VIC**

'Vesta Ignition Condensers' wall cabinet, c1950, 40cm high, 40cm wide.

$100 - $120 **Flaxton Barn, QLD**

'Ford Custom' sales brochure, for the Ford Motor Company of Australia Pty. Ltd, Australia, c1950, 18.5cm high, 23.5cm wide.

$70 - $90 **Mark's Book Barn, NSW**

'Holden' utility and panel van brochure, distributed by Sundell Motors Pty. Ltd., Chatswood, Australia, c1958, 24cm high, 29cm wide.

$90 - $110 **Mark's Book Barn, NSW**

Model of a 'Golden Fleece' petrol pump, Australia, 50cm high, 15cm wide.

$85 - $105 **Newport Temple Antiques, VIC**

Small Gilbarco, industrial 'Golden Fleece' petrol pump, Australia, 164cm high.

$1400 - $1600

The Mill Markets, VIC

A silvered bronze robot car mascot, mounted on a marble base for use as a paperweight, 17.5cm high.

$845 - $945

Barry Sherman Galleries, VIC

Pair of BSA Motorcycle decals, in chromed and enamelled metal, c1960, 10cm high, 16cm long, 1cm deep.

$135 - $155

Patinations, NSW

'AA New Coventry London', auto badge, England, c1960, 11cm high, 10cm wide.

$85 - $105

How Bazaar, VIC

NSW enamelled car badge 'No 16110', Australia, 10cm high.

$85 - $105

Journey to the Past Antiques & Collectables, QLD

'Golden Fleece' bowser, with a refrigerator fitted behind the bottom hinged panel and a storage compartment behind the top door, Australia, c1960.

$2050 - $2250

Yarra Valley Antique Centre, VIC

RACV car badge, Australia, c1960, 9cm high, 9cm wide.

$35 - $45

How Bazaar, VIC

R.A.A. South Australian auto badge, Australia, c1960, 11cm high, 10cm wide.

$65 - $85

How Bazaar, VIC

Collection of four handy oil tins for Shell and Mobil. Priced per item, Australia, c1965, 9cm high.

$35 - $45

How Bazaar, VIC

One pint 'Castrol' oil bottle with a 'Red XL' top, Australia, c1960, 33cm high.

$125 - $145

Chapel Street Bazaar, VIC

'Golden Fleece' illuminated ram petrol bowser sign in fibre glass, Australia, c1950, 33cm high, 20cm wide, 53cm long.

$500 - $600

The Evandale Tinker, TAS

Original heavy plastic 'Taxi' sign with a meter system and six different signs including 'Vacant', Australia, c1950, 18cm high, 55cm long, 20cm deep.

$220 - $260

Towers Antiques & Collectables, NSW

Service station attendant's cap badge, 'Vacuum Quality Product' (now Mobil oil) made by 'Stokes', Australia, c1950.

$430 - $470 **Marsteen Collectables, VIC**

'General Motors Holdens' factory employees badge, Australia, c1955.

$280 - $320 **Marsteen Collectables, VIC**

'General Motors Holdens' (GMH) factory inspector's badge, Australia, c1950.

$600 - $700 **Marsteen Collectables, VIC**

'Kayesel' car polish, Australia, c1950, 4cm high, 10cm diam.

$5 - $15 **Castlemaine, VIC**

Chrome 'Holden' ashtray, Australia, c1960, 9cm high, 18cm wide.

$15 - $25 **Wooden Pew Antiques, VIC**

'Shell Road Map' of 'Western Australia', Australia, c1960.

$55 - $75 **Colonial Antiques & Tea House, WA**

Brass and plastic service indicator card for motor vehicles, supplied by 'Mortlock & Co', Hawera, New Zealand, c1950, 3cm high, 8cm long.

NZ$25 - $35 **Maison Jolie, New Zealand**

'Third James Flood Book of Early Motoring', #968 of 2000, Australia, c1970, 33cm high, 28cm wide.

$155 - $175 **How Bazaar, VIC**

'Second James Flood Book of Early Motoring', #576 of 2000, Australia, c1970, 33cm high, 28cm wide.

$355 - $395 **How Bazaar, VIC**

Original sales brochure for the Holden special, 'The New Holden', 1957, Australia, 22.5cm high, 28.5cm wide.

$70 - $90 **Mark's Book Barn, NSW**

Limited edition wooden model of an Australian Navy Bathurst class corvette, hand carved and painted, with a brass engraved story board, housed in a solid mahogany and flexiglass display case, Australia, c2004, 45cm long.

$700 - $800

Global Transport Collectables Pty/Ltd, NSW

Model of the P & O 'Himalaya', with extended funnel, a handcarved wooden hull and superstructure engraved brass storyboard and a solid polished mahogany and flexiglass display case, Philippines, c2005, 45cm long.

$670 - $770

Global Transport Collectables Pty/Ltd, NSW

Model of the 'Endeavour' sailing ship, China, c2000, 91cm high, 10.5cm wide.

NZ$140 - $160

Pleasant Place Antiques, New Zealand

Art Deco chrome yacht atop a mirror, c1940, 37cm high.

$345 - $385

Design Dilemas, VIC

Barque type model sailing ship in a glass case, depicting a ship from the Loch Shipping Line with false gun portals to give the impression of being a naval vessel, New Zealand, c1950.

NZ$1850 - $2050

Mr Pickwicks, New Zealand

Model cabin cruiser, made from king billy pine, Australia, c1960, 23cm high, 24cm wide, 60cm long.

$465 - $505

The Evandale Tinker, TAS

All timber model of the HMS Victory, famous for Lord Nelson at the Battle of Trafalgar with fine detail and metal guns, Australia, c1960, 76cm high, 110cm wide, 36cm deep.

$1400 - $1600

Peter French Antiques, VIC

Later plastic cruise liner doll with sleeping doll eyes, from the 'Oriana', England, c1980, 16cm high.

$15 - $25

Max Rout, NSW

Cruise ship dinner menu, printed on a flag from V. M. 'Oranje' cruise liner, Norway, c1951, 33cm high.

$20 - $30

Marsteen Collectables, VIC

Scratch made huon pine sailing boat with oiled cotton masts, Australia, c1955, 40cm high, 11cm wide, 58cm long.

$185 - $205

Woodside Bazaar, SA

Model of a schooner, scratch built from a photograph, Australia, c1975, 48cm high, 10cm wide, 62cm long.

$645 - $745

Rare Old Times Antiques & Collectables, SA

'Halcyon Days' 'Britannia' enamel box, England, c1970, 5cm high, 6cm wide.

$275 - $315

Trinity Antiques, WA

Unused 'Orient Line' cardboard baggage tag, England, 14cm wide.

$5 - $10

Chapel Street Bazaar, VIC

Unused 'Orient Line' cardboard baggage tag, England, 16cm long.

$5 - $13

Chapel Street Bazaar, VIC

'The Blue Funnel Line' shipping company shop counter display sign, England, c1950, 23cm high, 30cm long.

$60 - $80

Wooden Pew Antiques, VIC

Replica diver's helmet made of chromed copper, India, c2004, 45cm high, 35cm wide, 40cm deep.

$305 - $345

Wooden Pew Antiques, VIC

Cruise line souvenir doll from the 'Fairstar', England, c1950, 21cm high.

$40 - $50

Max Rout, NSW

Unused 'Orient Line' first class baggage tag for Melbourne, England, c1950, 14cm long.

$5 - $13

Chapel Street Bazaar, VIC

Scale size ornamental copper and brass diving helmet, c1980, 23cm high, 19cm wide.

$230 - $270

Bob & Dot's Antiques & Old Wares, NSW

TRANSPORT - NAUTICAL & OTHER

Royal Winton three piece set, consisting of one trio, a candy box and an ash tray with transfer prints of 'Princess of Tasmania' a passenger ferry running between Melbourne and Devenport, England, c1950.

$185 - $205

Whimsical Notions, NSW

New Zealand railways 'tablet', collected by the train driver at end of the station before proceeding, New Zealand, c1955, 50cm long.

NZ$75 - $95

Camelot Antiques, New Zealand

Brass bell souvenir from 'P & O Iberia', England, c1960, 10cm high, 5cm wide.

$30 - $40

Wooden Pew Antiques, VIC

Reproduction target railway station sign for 'Essendon' made to the specifications of the original station signs, but on sheet metal, Australia, c2004, 51cm high, 81cm wide.

$140 - $160

Memorabilia on Parade, VIC

Melbourne Tram Destination Roll used between 1950-1980, with forty one destinations, wound with a mechanism on the side of the box, destinations include: St Kilda Beach, City, Olympic Park, University, Football, Special, Racecourse, East Brighton and Coburg, Australia, 32cm high, 108cm wide, 30cm deep.

$750 - $850

Memorabilia on Parade, VIC

Railway signal lights, Australia, c1950, 120cm high, 20cm wide, 20cm deep.

$350 - $390

Cobweb Collectables, NSW

Certificate of recognition by the Union of Locomotive Engineman to Mr. Warnock for services as Chairman 1951, 1952 and 1953, Australia, 60cm high, 46cm wide.

$255 - $295

Alltime Antiques & Bairnsdale Clocks, VIC

Royal Australian Mint, $5 silver proof coin commemorating '150 years of Steam Railways in Australia', 1850-2004, issue number 11066, Australia.

$65 - $85

Island & Continent Coins & Stamps, NSW

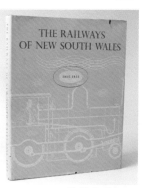

Book of 'The Railway of New South Wales 1855-1955', published by The Department of Railways, NSW, Australia, c1955, 29.5cm high, 24cm wide.

$65 - $85

Mark's Book Barn, NSW

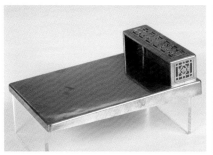

Art Nouveau styled brass note pad holder, by 'Tiffany & Co.'.

$770 - $870

Centuries Past, NSW

Brass school bell with a wooden handle, Australia, c1950, 30cm high.

$75 - $95

Chapel Street Bazaar, VIC

Georg Jensen brass tray, designed by Piet Hein Denmark, design no. 7002, Denmark, c1980, 32cm wide, 24.5cm deep.

$225 - $265

Bathurst Street Antique Centre, TAS

Georg Jensen brass hot water jug, designed by Henning Koppel, design no. 7011, features a black plastic handle and lid, and lined in stainless steel, Denmark, c1980, 12cm high, 10cm diam.

$455 - $495

Bathurst Street Antique Centre, TAS

Brass monkey shaped bottle opener, c1980.

$20 - $30

Wooden Pew Antiques, VIC

Pewter, brass and copper bust of an African woman, signed, European, c1960, 7.5cm high.

NZ$745 - $845

Shand's Emposium, New Zealand

Figure of a kangaroo, stamped 'Pewter WA', Australia, c1980, 10cm high, 20cm long.

$55 - $75

Ritzy Bits - ACT, ACT

Stainless steel drink set with a jug and six tumblers, in a Greek key type pattern, manufacturer's mark to the base 'Aloe', c1970, 18.5cm high.

$60 - $80

frhapsody, WA

Set of four teak and stainless serving trays, made in Denmark, Denmark, c1970, 40cm wide.

$70 - $90

frhapsody, WA

Unusual dog door stop.

$80 - $100

Memorabilia on Parade, VIC

Copper, green and blue enamel wall plate, signed, c1970, 49.5cm diam.

NZ$230 - $270

Maxine's Collectibles, New Zealand

Hand painted metal, 'rose' candlestick centrepiece, Australia, c1960.

$20 - $30

Cobweb Collectables, NSW

Souvenir Ghurka fighting knife, England, c1970.

$55 - $75

Whimsical Notions, NSW

Prototype combat knife and scabbard, Australia, c1980.

$115 - $135

Military Antiques Warehouse, WA

Complete set of thirty six 'Golden Fleece' swap cards, including Ballarat and Victorian militia uniforms, Australia, c1960.

$55 - $75   **Forever Amber @ The Tyabb Grainstore, VIC**

Anti-Vietnam war booklet published in 1966, New Zealand, 27cm high, 22cm wide.

NZ$5 - $13

Memory Lane, New Zealand

Paratroopers beret, Israel, c1980.

$50 - $70   **Military Antiques Warehouse, WA**

RAAF/RNZAF flight helmet and mask, Australia, c1968.

$255 - $295   **Military Antiques Warehouse, WA**

US Army Vietnam era steel helmet, United States.

$205 - $245   **Rare Old Times Antiques & Collectables, SA**

Australian Army slouch hat, Australia, c1953, 38cm long.

$55 - $75   **The Junk Company, VIC**

Chinese army officer's cap, China, c1960.

$75 - $95   **Malvern Antique Market, VIC**

MEDALS, BADGES & INSIGNIA

'City of Stirling Senior Ranger' badge.

$35 - $45   **Military Antiques Warehouse, WA**

Greek Special Forces shoulder flash, patch and wing badge.

$90 - $110   **Military Antiques Warehouse, WA**

Africa General Service Medal, awarded in 1955 with the clasp 'Kenya' to troops who participated in operations against the Mau Mau in Kenya, England.

$150 - $170   **John Burridge Military Antiques, WA**

Western Australian Ministry of Justice cloth badge, Australia.

$5 - $15   **Military Antiques Warehouse, WA**

Two Korean War medals, awarded to leading stoker mechanic A. W. Tyler for service aboard the HMAS Anzac, Australia, c1950.

$700 - $800   **Marsteen Collectables, VIC**

Victorian Police sleeve patch, Australia.

$5 - $15   **Military Antiques Warehouse, WA**

NSW Police cloth badge, Australia.

$5 - $15   **Military Antiques Warehouse, WA**

Queensland Police cloth badge, Australia.

$5 - $15   **Military Antiques Warehouse, WA**

Russian badge, for 400 parachute jumps.

$35 - $45   **Military Antiques Warehouse, WA**

'British Ex-services Association' car badge, England, c1970, 8cm diam.

$45 - $65   **Dr Russell's Emporium, WA**

Western Australian Department of Corrective Services cloth badge, Australia.

$5 - $15   **Military Antiques Warehouse, WA**

307

Bullion Coldstream guard's badge, for a colour sergeant, England, c1955.

$140 - $160 — **Fyshwick Antique Centre, ACT**

Manila Police badge, number 168, Philippines.

$115 - $135 — **Military Antiques Warehouse, WA**

Western Australian Police breast pocket badge, Australia.

$25 - $35 — **Military Antiques Warehouse, WA**

Malay Police badge, number 1957, Malaysia.

$115 - $135 — **Military Antiques Warehouse, WA**

Victorian Prison Services badge, Australia, c1970, 6.5cm high, 5.5cm wide.

$60 - $80 — **Wooden Pew Antiques, VIC**

Victorian Federation Army belt buckle, Australia.

$255 - $295 — **Military Antiques Warehouse, WA**

Fisheries & Wildlife badge and slide-on epaulettes, Australia.

$65 - $85 — **Military Antiques Warehouse, WA**

Royal Flying Doctor Service half wing badge, Australia.

$65 - $85 — **Military Antiques Warehouse, WA**

The St John Ambulance Association Police badge, Australia.

$65 - $85 — **Military Antiques Warehouse, WA**

Australian Protective Service badge, Australia.

$90 - $110 — **Military Antiques Warehouse, WA**

Aviation Rescue, Fire Fighting, Australia badge, Australia.

$50 - $70 — **Military Antiques Warehouse, WA**

'Royal Army Service Corps' car badge, England, c1970, 8cm diam.

$45 - $65 — **Dr Russell's Emporium, WA**

High quality replica of a medieval suit of shining armour.

$3400 - $3600   **Casey Antiques, VIC**

Trench art model of a Boeing 'Globe Master', of large proportions on a cast iron base, Australia, c1960, 39cm high, 50cm wide, 37cm long.

$430 - $470   **The Evandale Tinker, TAS**

Department of Defence morse code tapper, Australia, c1950, 4cm wide, 12cm long.

$25 - $35

Curtis's and Harvey's gunpowder tin, England, c1950, 16cm high, 10cm wide, 4cm deep.

$35 - $45   **Parramatta Antique Centre, NSW**

Marsteen Collectables, VIC

$65 - $85   **M J Durand, VIC**

Trench art, probably executed in Afghanistan on a Russian aircraft cannon shell, Russia, c1990.

Irish guard's tunic with Corporal ranks on the sleeves, Ireland, c1950.

$355 - $395   **All In Good Time Antiques, SA**

Brass Indonesian police belt buckle, Indonesia.

$35 - $45   **Military Antiques Warehouse, WA**

Osama Bin Laden 'Wanted' poster on a match book.

$20 - $30   **Military Antiques Warehouse, WA**

Limited edition (number 118) plaque, from 1992 commemorating the 50th anniversary of the Battle of the Coral Sea, Australia.

$40 - $60   **Military Antiques Warehouse, WA**

Water bottle captured in Mozambique, Russia.

$40 - $60   **Military Antiques Warehouse, WA**

Boxed set of silver coins issued in 2003 by the Perth Mint to commemorate the Boer War, 1899-1902, set no. 0410, Australia.

$125 - $145

Island & Continent Coins & Stamps, NSW

Uncirculated 1952 George VI Sixpence, Australia.

$1900 - $2100

The Rare Coin Company, WA

NSW Fire Brigades volunteer hat badge, Australia, c1950, 4cm wide.

$110 - $130

Canberra Cards & Colectables, ACT

1964 New Zealand shilling, New Zealand, c1964.

$2 - $6

Alan McRae, NSW

New Zealand, 1964 one penny, New Zealand.

$185 - $205

Island & Continent Coins Stamps, NSW

Protest button, 'Stop the 81 Tour', New Zealand, c1981.

NZ$40 - $50

Banks Peninsula Antiques, New Zealand

1951 New Zealand florin, New Zealand, c1951.

$4 - $10

Alan McRae, NSW

New Zealand, 1963 halfpenny, New Zealand.

$2 - $6

Island & Continent Coins & Stamps, NSW

Greenpeace protest button, 'You can't sink a rainbow', New Zealand, c1980.

NZ$30 - $40

Banks Peninsula Atiques, New Zealand

1970 New Zealand, Mount Cook one dollar coin, New Zealand, c1970.

$5 - $10

Alan McRae, NSW

NSW Bicentenary 1988 commemorative coin/medallion, in original presentation case, Australia.

$5 - $15

Lucilles Interesting Collectables, NSW

1954 ten pound note, Renniks Code R62, Australia.

$500 - $600

**The Time Machine,
QLD**

Four twenty dollar, first series, consecutive notes, XAA 933236- to 9,
Coombs/Wilson, some of the first $20 notes issued in 1966, Renniks
Code R401a.

$1300 - $1500

**Collectable Creations,
QLD**

Brazilian over printed bank note, one centavo on ten cruzeiros, Brazil.

$3 - $7

**Alan McRae,
NSW**

1967 Malta P30, Five Pounds, uncirculated with Queen Elizabeth II at
the right and Grand Harbour on the back, 8cm high, 14.5cm wide.

$480 - $520

**Trevor Wilkin Banknotes,
NSW**

100 Cambodian riels, Cambodia.

$50 - $70

**Alan McRae,
NSW**

Two Dollar Coombs Wilson, Star replacement note, serial number 2FB 60043*,
Renniks Code R81s, Australia, c1966.

$1850 - $2050

**Collectable Creations,
QLD**

Type 3 specimen banknote set, produced for distribution to senior banking staff and
dignitaries at the changeover from 'Commonwealth of Australia' to 'Australia'
(1974-1983), Australia.

$140000 - $150000

**Monetarium,
NSW**

National Australia Bank specimen cheques, from 1984, Australia, 8cm high, 16cm wide.

$30 - $40   **The Bottom Drawer Antique Centre, VIC**

1986 Gibraltar, P24, Fifty Pounds, uncirculated with Queen Elizabeth II at the centre and The Rock on the back, 9.5cm high, 16.5cm wide.

$355 - $395   **Trevor Wilkin Banknotes, NSW**

Brunei 1967 P5, One Hundred Ringgit, uncirculated with the Sultan Omar Ali Saifuddin II at the right and a mosque on the back, Brunei, 9.5cm high, 16cm wide.

$1150 - $1350   **Trevor Wilkin Banknotes, NSW**

Bahamas 1953 P14b, Ten Shillings, uncirculated with Queen Elizabeth II at right, ships at left and the Coat of Arms on the back, 8.5cm high, 15cm wide.

$455 - $495   **Trevor Wilkin Banknotes, NSW**

1968 Australia $5 note, Randal signature, Serial No. NCS 669968, Australia, 8cm high, 15.5cm wide.

$45 - $65   **Wooden Pew Antiques, VIC**

The National Bank of Scotland one pound note, issued on the 4th of January, 1951, Scotland.

$30 - $40   **Dr Russell's Emporium, WA**

Professional Philatelists

...n you afford to risk ...teral anywhere else?

$9,200

$55,000

$60,375

$86,800

$10,350

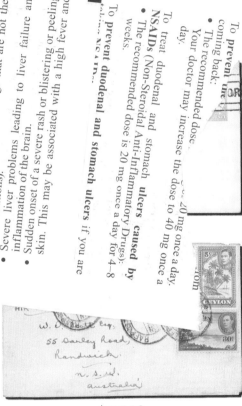
$4,140

$2,300

$20,700

$1,725

$1,200

$3,220

$2,645

$10,925

NUMISMATICS, STAMPS & SCRIP

'Marine Stores Collector' armband, bottle collector's licence, number 345 and dated 1969.

$35 - $45   **Military Antiques Warehouse, WA**

Set of solar system stamps, souvenirs only, issued by Broadway Approvals, United States, c1980, 6cm high, 8cm wide.

$5 - $15   **Chapel Street Bazaar, VIC**

Australia Post issued envelope commemorating 'National Stamp Week 1982', featuring images of postage stamps, and one 27 cent commemorative stamp, Australia, c1982, 9.4cm wide, 16.5cm long.

$4 - $10   **Alan McRae, NSW**

1971 RAAF Anniversary, 6c with black printing ('Australia' and value etc), omitted BW#558c, unmounted, Cat $4000, Australia.

$3350 - $3550   **Prestige Philately, VIC**

1956 Olympic Games, 3 1/2d carmine-lake, BW #332E(1), well centred, unmounted, ex Australia Post Archives, because of an increase in the postage rate to 4d, this stamp was never issued and all but a few were officially destroyed.

$11575 - $12575   **Prestige Philately, VIC**

First day cover with commemorative medallion, for the golden jubilee of the coronation of Queen Elizabeth II, 1953-2003, Australia.

$25 - $35   **Island & Continent Coins & Stamps, NSW**

First day cover with a commemorative medallion for the 150th anniversary of the Eureka stockade, issued in 2004, Australia.

$20 - $30   **Island & Continent Coins & Stamps, NSW**

Australian Open 2005 first day cover with commemorative medallion postmarked Melbourne, Victoria, Australia.

$15 - $25   **Island & Continent Coins & Stamps, NSW**

1975 45C bottlebrush stamps in a vertical strip of five, one stamp showing green leaves completely missing with another showing green partially omitted, SG 609b. ACSC 727ce, Australia, 12.5cm high, 2.5cm wide.

$610 - $710   **Pittwater Philatelic Service, NSW**

1973 1c 'Banded Coral Shrimp' with black completely omitted, inscription and face value missing, spectacular error (shown with normal version for comparison) SG 545a. ACSC 635c, Australia, 2.1cm high, 2.5cm wide.

$480 - $520   **Pittwater Philatelic Service, NSW**

Acorn No. 4 wood plane (Sheffield), England, 14cm high, 6cm wide, 23cm long.

$65 - $85   **Old Bank Corner Collectables, NSW**

Stanley box plane, United States, c1950, 33cm long.

NZ$265 - $305   **Ikon Antiques, New Zealand**

Handmade infill plane with a dovetailed metal base, England, c1960, 13cm high, 24cm long.

NZ$400 - $440   **Pleasant Place Antiques, New Zealand**

Rapier 500 jack plane, England, c1950, 12cm high, 35cm long.

NZ$100 - $120   **Pleasant Place Antiques, New Zealand**

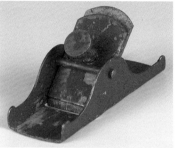

Metal plane stamped 'Ellar, Made in England', England, c1950, 2.5cm wide, 8.5cm long.

NZ$25 - $35   **Deans Antiques, New Zealand**

Mathieson badger plane, England, c1950, 18cm high, 43cm long.

NZ$50 - $70   **Pleasant Place Antiques, New Zealand**

Matheson timber grooving plane, England, c1960.

NZ$25 - $35   **Pleasant Place Antiques, New Zealand**

Boxed Stanley No. 71 router plane, with original tag and instruction, England, c1967, 19cm wide, 10cm deep.

NZ$65 - $85   **Pleasant Place Antiques, New Zealand**

'Record 077A' adjustable bull nose plane, England, c1950, 7cm high, 3cm wide, 10cm long.

$115 - $135   **The Gizmo, SA**

Record No. 020 wheel plane, England, c1960, 15cm high, 25cm long.

NZ$290 - $330   **Pleasant Place Antiques, New Zealand**

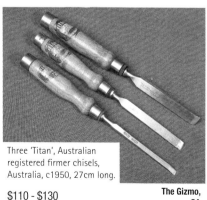

Three 'Titan', Australian registered firmer chisels, Australia, c1950, 27cm long.

$110 - $130   **The Gizmo, SA**

Boxed Stanley 'Dowel Jig' with original instructions, England, c1970, 12cm long.

NZ$45 - $65   **Pleasant Place Antiques, New Zealand**

Darlton soldering blow torch, Australia, c1950, 15cm high, 47cm long.

NZ$120 - $140

Pleasant Place Antiques, New Zealand

Large Primus 607 blow lamp, Sweden, c1954, 36cm high, 33cm wide.

NZ$190 - $230

Pleasant Place Antiques, New Zealand

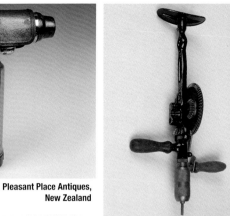

Millers Falls two speed breast drill, United States, c1950, 44.5cm long.

NZ$45 - $65

Pleasant Place Antiques, New Zealand

Brass well depth measure, made by Chesterman, measures to 40ft, England, c1954, 10cm wide, 38cm long.

$65 - $85

The Bottom Drawer Antique Centre, VIC

'Crain' vinyl and ceramic tile carrying tool in its box, United States, c1965, 15cm high, 11cm diam.

NZ$15 - $25

Ikon Antiques, New Zealand

Wallpaper trimmer by Ridgely, England, c1970, 7.5cm high, 11cm long.

NZ$25 - $35

Ikon Antiques, New Zealand

Two speed breast drill, France, c1950, 39cm long.

NZ$30 - $40

Pleasant Place Antiques, New Zealand

Workman's tape measure, Flag Brand, c1950, 8cm diam.

$40 - $50

Pearl Rose, VIC

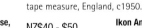

Imperial leather, brass and canvas tape measure, England, c1950.

NZ$40 - $50

Ikon Antiques, New Zealand

'Leidreiter's' tanner's tool for scraping animal hides, c1970, 16.5cm long.

NZ$10 - $20

Ikon Antiques, New Zealand

Telex technicians tool kit, the tools stamped 'Gedore' and 'Wilo', in canvas carrying case, England, c1970.

$330 - $370

Branxholme Mobile Books, VIC

Adjustable bevel, England, c1960, 26cm long.

NZ$5 - $15

Ikon Antiques, New Zealand

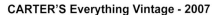

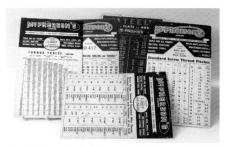

Set of five mechanical charts for McPherson's Limited, 51 Bathurst Street, Sydney, Australia, c1950, 34cm high, 21.5cm wide.

$70 - $90

Mark's Book Barn, NSW

Darlton brass blow lamp, Sweden, c1960, 21.5cm high, 24cm wide.

NZ$40 - $60

Pleasant Place Antiques, New Zealand

'Abbey & Hockley' leather and brass encased tape measure, measures in inches and links, England, c1950.

$25 - $35

Chapel Street Bazaar, VIC

Hardwood apple boxes, many with individual stamps, grower's names and places of origin. Priced per item, Australia, c1956, 38cm high, 23cm wide, 50cm long.

$5 - $10

Tyabb Hay Shed, VIC

Boxed, Stanley tools, 'The Fuller Calculator' with scales of sines and logs, England, c1955, 12cm wide, 36cm long.

$640 - $740

Wooden Pew Antiques, VIC

'Cut-All' swivel saw, England, c1950, 9cm high, 30cm long.

$40 - $50

The Restorers Barn, VIC

Butcher's price tags for meat, Australia, c1955, 45cm long.

$115 - $135

How Bazaar, VIC

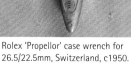

Rolex 'Propellor' case wrench for 26.5/22.5mm, Switzerland, c1950.

$230 - $270

Paddington Antique Centre Pty Ltd, QLD

'Victa 18in. lawn mower with original white wall tyres and an all-wheel height adjuster, Australia, c1953, 40cm high, 43cm wide, 65cm long.

$330 - $370

The Evandale Tinker, TAS

'BP' fuel mixture chart, c1950, 40cm high, 50cm wide.

$65 - $85

Flaxton Barn, QLD

'Anchor' open face pulley, rated for 1000 Kg, Australia, c1970, 45cm long, 15cm diam.

$65 - $85

Bob & Dot's Antiques & Old Wares, NSW

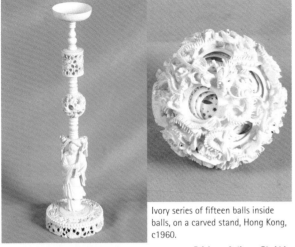

Carved ivory figure, China, c1950, 36cm high, 8cm wide.

Ivory series of fifteen balls inside balls, on a carved stand, Hong Kong, c1960.

$2550 - $2750

Brisbane Antiques Pty Ltd, QLD

Pair of early figures of ladies, China, c1950, 14cm high, 7cm wide, 5cm deep.

$1495 - $1695

Patrick Colwell, NSW

$1300 - $1500

Patrick Colwell, NSW

Brocade caftan with blue and silver details, China, c1970.

$25 - $35

The Old Lolly Factory, NSW

Lacquered Guanyin on stand from late 20th century, China, 56cm high.

$600 - $700

Eagle Antiques, VIC

'Ando' cloisonne vase with a chrome rim and base, beautiful dark jade enamel and a floral design to the top, Japan, c1960, 25cm high, 14cm wide.

$475 - $515

Isadora's Antiques, NSW

White jade incense burner with a wooden stand, China, c1950, 30cm high, 20cm wide.

$1900 - $2100

Qian Long Antiques, NSW

Chinese hand-made, signed ink block, China, 24cm high, 13cm wide.

$500 - $600

Kollectik Pty Ltd, NSW

Internally hand painted glass snuff bottle, China, 8.5cm high, 4.5cm wide.

NZ$30 - $40

Diane Akers, New Zealand

'Anxious Love' wood block print by Utamaro (1733-1806), Showa period reissue with a mica background, Japan, c1970, 38cm high, 26cm wide.

$280 - $320

Cabinet of Discoveries, ACT

John Deacons magnum paperweight, of a large red/white millefiori overlay enclosing a lace cushion under pink lampwork flowers and leaves, paper label, signature and date cane in base, Scotland, c2005, 9cm wide.

$1100 - $1300

Pastimes Antiques, NSW

Peter McDougall lampwork paperweight with five flowers each with a central cane on a blue ground, signature cane in base, Scotland, c2005, 6.5cm wide.

$375 - $415

Pastimes Antiques, NSW

Perthshire PP81 large limited edition paperweight with a central golfer figure surrounded by rings of twists and blue/pink/lemon millefiori canes on lace ground, dated 'P' cane in base, Scotland, c1985, 8cm wide.

$575 - $675

Pastimes Antiques, NSW

Perthshire Annual Collection paperweight, 1981B Limited Edition with a pink lampwork flower surrounded by green and pink millefiori panels, divided by millefiori twists on translucent ruby ground, date cane in base, Scotland, c1981, 7cm wide.

$725 - $825

Pastimes Antiques, NSW

Grant Randolph paperweight, with three applied fish set over an internal design of weed and barnacles on a green ground, signed and dated on the base, United States, c1992, 9cm wide.

$575 - $675

Pastimes Antiques, NSW

Perthshire PP178, medium sized weight with close-packed simple millefiori canes on blue ground, 'P' cane in setup, Scotland, c1997, 6cm wide.

$245 - $285

Pastimes Antiques, NSW

Perthshire (Scotland) crown weight, from the Annual Collection 1996 with red and blue twists, white Latticino over ruby layer, the top facet showing a floating flower and buds, and date in base, Scotland, c1996, 7cm diam.

$775 - $875

Pastimes Antiques, NSW

Lampworked paperweight, by Grant Randolph with two deep hibiscus blooms set over two leaves, on a deep mauve translucent background, United States, c2003.

$475 - $575

Pastimes Antiques, NSW

Strathearn magnum crown paperweight, brick red ground with polychrome flecks, 'quilted' controlled bubble effect, Scotland, c1970, 10cm high.

$475 - $515

Pastimes Antiques, NSW

PAPERWEIGHTS

Ken Rosenfeld small lampwork paperweight with a central pink dahlia and a bud on a stalk over a translucent blue ground, 'R' cane, signed and dated on side, United States, c2005, 6cm wide.

$745 - $845   **Pastimes Antiques, NSW**

Perthshire millefiori glass paperweight, Italy, 5cm high, 7cm wide.

$345 - $385   **Sherwood Bazaar, QLD**

Cenedese magnum paperweight with a high dome and close-packed cog canes on a polychrome/aventurine ground, paper label, Italy, c1950, 9.5cm wide.

$405 - $445   **Pastimes Antiques, NSW**

Perthshire millefiori paperweight, the central cane contains the letter 'P' for Perthshire, England, c1980, 9cm diam.

$330 - $370   **Glenelg Antique Centre, SA**

Molina glass paperweight in the shape of a seahorse, European, c1970, 16cm high, 6cm diam.

NZ$55 - $75   **Maxine's Collectibles, New Zealand**

A.V.E.M scrambled paperweight with polychrome bits, twists and latticino, Italy, c1980, 7cm wide.

$330 - $370   **Pastimes Antiques, NSW**

Ken Rosenfeld small lampwork paperweight with a bee hovering over flowers and berries on a clear ground, signed and dated on the side, United States, c2005, 6cm diam.

$745 - $845   **Pastimes Antiques, NSW**

Glass paperweight by Liskeard Glass, Cornwall, impressed mark 'L' to the base, United Kingdom, c1980, 10cm diam.

$165 - $185   **Glenelg Antique Centre, SA**

John Deacons medium crown paperweight, white latticinio and ribbon twists in various colours, top complex cane, signature and date cane in the base, Scotland, c2005, 6.5cm wide.

$645 - $745   **Pastimes Antiques, NSW**

'Love is...being swept off your feet', ceramic trinket box in a love heart shape, Brazil, c1970, 8cm long.

$20 - $30

Shop 8 Mittagong Antiques Centre, NSW

Plastic musical trinket box, in the form of a record player, plays 'Stranger in the Night', Japan, c1960, 11cm high, 24cm wide, 9cm deep.

NZ$40 - $50

Diane Akers, New Zealand

Designer's collection 'Holly Hobbie' by Sands Trinket Box, Japan, c1974, 4.5cm high, 7cm long.

$10 - $20

Jan Johannesen, VIC

Faux tortoise shell musical trinket box, in the shape of a radiogram, the end doors opening to reveal dancing ballerinas, Japan, c1950, 13cm high, 19cm long.

$275 - $315

Brae-mar Antiques, NSW

Wedgwood green heart shaped lidded trinket box, England, c1970, 5cm high, 13cm wide.

$55 - $75

Lucilles Interesting Collectables, NSW

9ct Holy Bible charm, opening to reveal a folded paper with a list of the books in the Old and the New Testament, c1960.

$310 - $350

H.O.W Gifts & Collectables, QLD

Australian mass 'Bridal Missal' with a Lucite cover, gilt edge pages and a mother-of-pearl and gold plate crucifix on the inside cover, Belgium, c1968, 10cm wide, 16cm long, 2cm deep.

$25 - $35

Possum's Treasures, QLD

Wooden tea caddy, China, c1965, 13cm high, 10cm wide, 9cm deep.

NZ$30 - $40

Moa Extinct Stuff, New Zealand

Tortoise shell and mother-of-pearl miniature mandolin, 3.5cm high, 4.5cm wide, 17cm long.

$25 - $35

Maryborough Station Antique Emporium, VIC

'Nursery Rhymes, Illustrated by Peg Maltby' children's booklet.

$35 - $45

The Nostalgia Factory, NSW

'A Big Book of Animals' by Syd Nicholls.

$30 - $40

The Nostalgia Factory, NSW

'Biggles Works it Out' by W. E. Johns, England, c1952, 20cm high, 12.5cm wide.

$50 - $70

The Nostalgia Factory, NSW

TV book 'Circus Boy' starring Mickey Dolenz, who later gained fame in 'The Monkees' TV rock group, England, c1960, 28cm high, 21cm wide.

$35 - $45

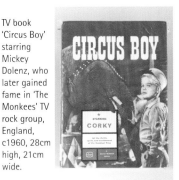

P. & N. Johnson, NSW

'Tinka and the Bunyip' book by Brownie Downing, Australia, c1966.

$60 - $80

Decorama, VIC

'Five Fall Into Adventure' By Enid Blyton, 1962, Australia, 19cm high, 12cm wide.

$30 - $40

Terrace Collectables, NSW

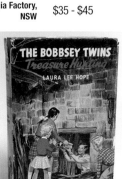

'The Bobbsey Twins Treasure Hunting' by Laura Lee Hope, published in 1955, 19cm high, 13cm wide.

$10 - $20

Terrace Collectables, NSW

Children's book, 'Teddy Edwards Visitor' by Patrick and Mollie Matthews, beautifully photographed in real scenery, published by Golden Pleasure Books, England, c1962, 28cm high, 21cm wide.

$30 - $40

Patinations, NSW

'The Girl' annual, Australia, c1950, 28cm high.

$5 - $15

Chapel Street Bazaar, VIC

'The Girl' annual, Australia, c1950, 28cm high.

$5 - $15

Chapel Street Bazaar, VIC

'The So Long Book of Golliwog Tales', c1950.

$40 - $60

The Nostalgia Factory,
NSW

Children's book ' The Golliwogs Polar Adventures'
1967 edition by Florence K. Upton, published by
Longmans Green & Co, England, 13cm high,
20cm wide.

$45 - $65

Patinations,
NSW

'Biggles Cuts
it Fine' by
W. E. Johns,
England,
c1954, 20cm
high, 12.5cm
wide.

$40 - $50

The Nostalgia Factory,
NSW

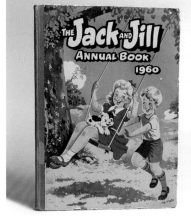

'The Jack and Jill Annual Book 1960', 27cm high,
20cm wide.

$40 - $60

Terrace Collectables,
NSW

$40 - $60

Three books from the Magic
Boomerang series, each with
Hoadley's Violet Crumble
advertisements on the back
pages. Priced per item,
Australia, c1950, 28cm high,
22cm wide.

Lydiard Furniture & Antiques,
VIC

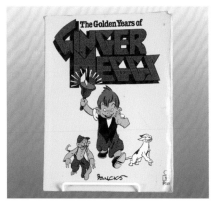

Soft cover 192 page book, 'The Golden Years of
Ginger Meggs' edited by John Horgan, Pan Books,
Sydney 1982, contains some of the best Ginger
Meggs cartoons by J. C. Bancks, Australia.

$55 - $75

Titles & Treasures,
QLD

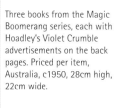

'A Little Golden Book, The Life and Legend of
Wyatt Earp', Australia, c1960.

$5 - $15

The Nostalgia Factory,
NSW

'Noddy and His
Car', book No. 3
by Enid Blyton,
England, c1958,
17.5cm high,
12.5cm wide.

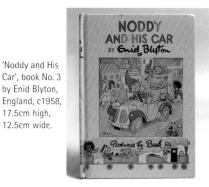

$15 - $25

The Nostalgia Factory,
NSW

'Rawhide Annual
Starring Clint
Eastwood and
Eric Fleming', a
children's book,
1961, United
States.

$20 - $30

The Nostalgia Factory,
NSW

'Gun Smoke Annual Starring James Aznes', 1963.

$20 - $30

The Nostalgia Factory,
NSW

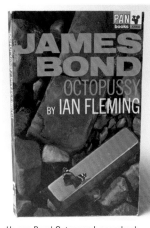

'James Bond Octopussy', paperback by Ian Fleming, England, c1966.

$15 - $25   **The Nostalgia Factory, NSW**

'James Bond 007, Licence Renewed' by John Gardner.

$20 - $30   **The Nostalgia Factory, NSW**

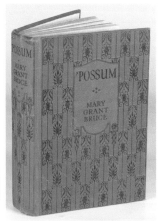

Book 'Possum' by Mary Grant Bruce, 1st edition, England, c1950.

$40 - $50   **The Restorers Barn, VIC**

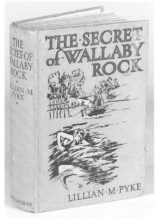

Book 'The Secret of Wallaby Rock' by Mary Grant Bruce, 1st edition, England.

$40 - $60   **The Restorers Barn, VIC**

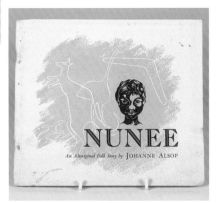

'Nenee, An Aboriginal Folk Story by Johanne Alsop' with illustrations, released by the Vacuum Oil Company and printed by G. W. Green Pty. Ltd., Melbourne, Australia, c1952, 22cm long, 18cm deep.

$25 - $35   **Mt Dandenong Antique Centre, VIC**

Norman Lindsay 'Tales from the Heptameron' of Marguerite of Navarre Melbourne 1976, 1st edition, original posting box, limited edition of 1000 copies, Australia.

$200 - $240   **Australian Antiquarian Book Centre, NSW**

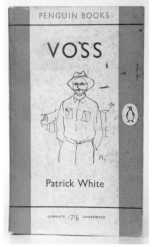

Patrick White's 'Voss', Penguin Books 1960, autographed by 'Patrick White', Australia, 18cm high, 11cm wide.

$180 - $200   **Australian Antiquarian Book Centre, NSW**

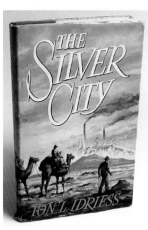

Book 'The Tower Rooms' by Mary Grant Bruce, 1st edition, England, c1950.

$40 - $60   **The Restorers Barn, VIC**

'The Silver City' by Ion Idress, 1956 first edition, 22cm high, 14cm wide.

$25 - $35   **Terrace Collectables, NSW**

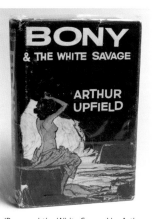

'Bony and the White Savage' by Arthur Upfield, 1961 first edition, Australia, 19cm high, 13cm wide.

$190 - $210   **Terrace Collectables, NSW**

'Serpents in Paradise' by Nancy Phelan, 1967 edition, England.

$5 - $15   **Terrace Collectables, NSW**

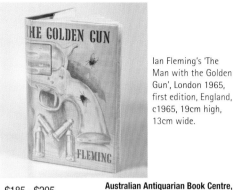

Ian Fleming's 'The Man with the Golden Gun', London 1965, first edition, England, c1965, 19cm high, 13cm wide.

'Bound for the Goldfields' by Charles Dickens, first published in 1855, this edition published by the Wayzgoose Private Press in Katoomba, linocuts and wood engravings, number 7 of only 55 copies, Australia, c1990.

$480 - $520

Antiquariat Fine Books, NSW

$185 - $205

Australian Antiquarian Book Centre, NSW

Pulp fiction novel, 'The Shrinking Man', printed 1956 by 'Gold Medal' publishers, England, 18cm high, 12cm wide.

$30 - $60

Born Frugal, VIC

'The End of the Harbour' By Elise Locke, 1968 first edition, New Zealand, 20cm high, 13cm wide.

$5 - $10

Terrace Collectables, NSW

'The Captain's Death Bed and Other Essays' by Virginia Woolf, with dust jacket, England, c1981.

$65 - $85

Antiquariat Fine Books, NSW

'The Remains of the Day' by Kazuo Ishiguro, hardcover first edition, England.

$190 - $210

Antiquariat Fine Books, NSW

Collins Street Directory, Melbourne and Suburbs, 1954, Australia, 12.5cm wide, 15.3cm long.

$15 - $25

Retro Relics, VIC

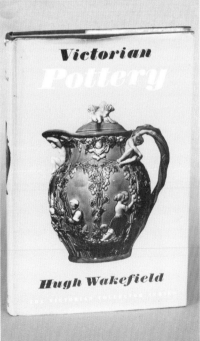

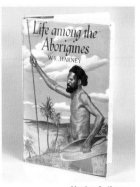

Life Among the Aborigines by W. E. Harney, a unique study of the Aborigines of the Northern Territory by an authority on the subject, published by Robert Hale Limited 1957, first edition, Australia.

$35 - $45

Ainsley Antiques, VIC

'Ladies Handbook', leather bound by Gulalia S. Richard.

$90 - $110

Home Again, NSW

'Victorian pottery by Hugh Wakefield, 1962 London, with dust jacket, England.

$20 - $30

Baxter's Antiques, QLD

'The Facsimile Kelmscott Chaucer' and companion volume, published by the Basilisk Press December 31, 1974, No.145 of 500, England, 44cm high, 30cm wide.

$2650 - $2850

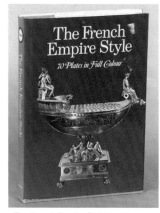

'The French Empire Style' by Alwar Gonzalez-Palacios, 1966, with dust jacket.

The Botanic Ark, VIC

$15 - $25

Houdini paperback By William Lindsay Gresham, c1970.

Baxter's Antiques, QLD

$10 - $20

The Nostalgia Factory, NSW

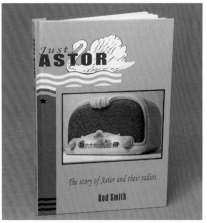

'Just Astor' radio book by Rod Smith, Australia, c2005, 30cm high, 22cm wide.

$45 - $65

Ace Antiques & Collectables, VIC

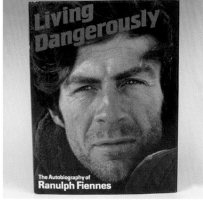

'Living Dangerously, The Autobiography of Ranulph Fiennes' hard cover book, published by MacMillan, London in 1987, England, 25.5cm high, 20cm wide.

NZ$5 - $13

Maison Jolie, New Zealand

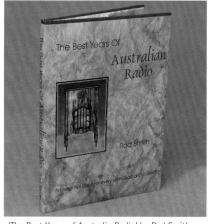

'The Best Years of Australia Radio' by Rod Smith, Australia, c1988, 30cm high, 22cm wide.

$40 - $50

Ace Antiques & Collectables, VIC

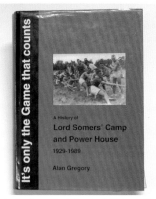

'Its only the Game That Counts, A History of Lord Somers Camp and Power House 1929 - 1989' by Alan Gregory, published by the camp in 1994 with the foreword by the Queen Mother, Australia.

$40 - $60

Yarra Valley Antique Centre, VIC

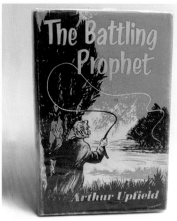

'The Battling Prophet' by Arthur Upfield, 1956 first edition, Australia, 19cm high, 13cm wide.

$190 - $210

Terrace Collectables, NSW

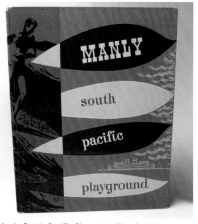

'Manly South Pacific Playground' book, 1956, Australia.

$40 - $60

The Nostalgia Factory, NSW

'The Panther Comic #45', an original Australian character, art by Paul Wheelahan, colour cover; black and white interior, Australia, c1960, 17.5cm high, 25cm deep.

$30 - $40

Comics R Us, VIC

First issue 'Futurama' comic book, published under licence by Other Press Pty. Ltd., Thornleigh NSW in 2002, Australia, 26.5cm high, 17cm wide.

$5 - $15

Vintage Replacement Parts, NSW

'The Potts Annual ' by Jim Russell, a 'Courier Mail' feature, 28 pages, Australia, c1957.

$30 - $40

369 Antiques, VIC

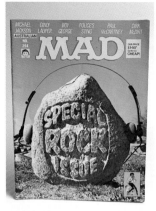

'MAD' Magazine, 'Special Rock Issue' no. 254, 1985, Australia.

$15 - $25

Terrace Collectables, NSW

'Commando war stories in pictures' comic books. Priced per item, Australia, c1960, 17cm high, 14cm wide.

$3 - $9

Terrace Collectables, NSW

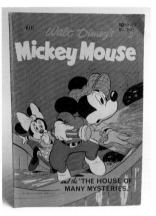

'Walt Disney's Mickey Mouse, and the House of Many Mysteries', comic, no. 111 released in 1966, Australia.

$20 - $30

Terrace Collectables, NSW

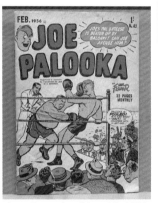

Australian reprint of the original USA comic 'Joe Palooka' by Ham Fisher, Australia, c1956, 18.5cm high, 26.5cm deep.

$10 - $20

Comics R Us, VIC

Australian reprint of the USA Lone Ranger Comic #42 published in 1957, with a colour cover; black and white interior, Australia, 18.5cm high, 26cm deep.

$15 - $25

Comics R Us, VIC

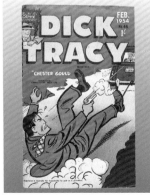

Australian reprint of the USA comic, Dick Tracy Comic #46 by Chester Gould, Australia, c1954, 18cm high, 28cm deep.

$25 - $35

Comics R Us, VIC

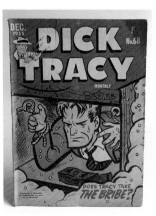

'Comic Dick Tracy Monthly' by Chester Gould, no. 68. Dec, 1955, Australia.

$20 - $30

Terrace Collectables, NSW

'Vic Flynt Private Eye Comic #3', Australian reprint of the original American comic strips in the style of Dick Tracy, with a colour cover and a black and white interior, Australia, c1955, 18cm high, 25cm deep.

$25 - $35

Comics R Us, VIC

Phantom comic No. 217, Australia, c1959, 30cm high, 20cm wide.

$35 - $45   **The Nostalgia Factory, NSW**

Phantom comic, No. 186 by Frew, Australia, c1950.

$85 - $105   **Paddington Antique Centre Pty Ltd, QLD**

'The Phantom, No. 270' comic, by Frew, Australia, c1964.

$20 - $30   **The Time Machine, QLD**

'The Phantom, No. 265' comic, by Frew, Australia, c1964.

$20 - $30   **The Time Machine, QLD**

'Phantom' comic #298, Australian black and white, pre-decimal, Australia, c1960, 26cm high, 17cm wide.

$35 - $45   **Cat's Cradle Comics, VIC**

Third American issue, Gold Key's 'Phantom' comic, series #3, colour, United States, c1963, 26cm high, 17cm wide.

$55 - $75   **Cat's Cradle Comics, VIC**

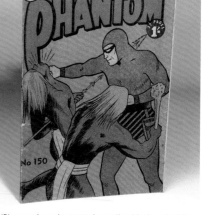

'Phantom' comic #150, Australian black and white shilling issue, Australia, c1950, 17cm high, 26cm deep.

$60 - $80   **Cat's Cradle Comics, VIC**

'Phantom' comic, No. 334.

$20 - $30   **Terrace Collectables, NSW**

Comics 'Phantom', No. 131, Australia, c1956.

$65 - $85   **The Nostalgia Factory, NSW**

Phantom Comic, No. 553.

$15 - $25   **Terrace Collectables, NSW**

Phantom comic, No. 214, Australia, c1959, 30cm high, 20cm wide.

$35 - $45   **The Nostalgia Factory, NSW**

Peter Parker, 'Spectacular Spiderman' comic #2, United States, c1976, 26cm high, 17cm wide.

$30 - $40

Cat's Cradle Comics, VIC

'Spiderman' comic #1, United States, c1990.

$40 - $60

Cat's Cradle Comics, VIC

'Amazing Spiderman' comic #26, fourth Green Goblin appearance, United States, c1965, 26cm high, 17cm wide.

$135 - $155

Cat's Cradle Comics, VIC

Marvel comic 'The Amazing Spiderman' No. 31, December 1965. 'Pop Art' issue, United States, c1965.

$105 - $125

George Magasic Antiques & Collectables, QLD

'Superman Vs. Spiderman' comic, double sized treasury edition, very early DC/Marvel crossover, United States, c1976, 26cm wide, 34cm long.

$65 - $85

Cat's Cradle Comics, VIC

Marvel comics 'The Amazing Spiderman' No. 28, September 1965. 'Pop Art' issue, United States, c1965.

$130 - $150

George Magasic Antiques & Collectables, QLD

'Amazing Spiderman' comic #17, 2nd Green Goblin, United States, c1964, 26cm high, 17cm wide.

$65 - $85

Cat's Cradle Comics, VIC

'X-Men' comic #35, Spiderman crossover, United States, c1967, 26cm high, 17cm wide.

$50 - $70

Cat's Cradle Comics, VIC

'Amazing Spiderman' comic book with record, United States, c1975, 26cm high, 17cm wide.

$20 - $30

Cat's Cradle Comics, VIC

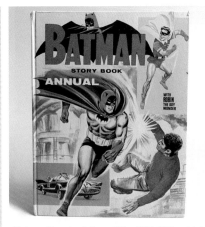

'Batman Story book Annual' for 1967, 26.5cm high, 20.5cm wide.

$35 - $45

Terrace Collectables, NSW

'Fantastic Four' comic #48, first Silver Surfer, and the first Galactus, United States, c1966, 26cm high, 17cm wide.

$140 - $160

Cat's Cradle Comics, VIC

'X-Men' comic 94, new 'X-Men' comic, United States, c1975, 26cm high, 17cm wide.

$185 - $205

Cat's Cradle Comics, VIC

Marvel comics 'The X-Men' No. 12, July 1965, featuring 'The Juggernaut', the origin of Professor X, United States.

$120 - $140

George Magasic Antiques & Collectables, QLD

'Master of the World' movie comic from 1961, from the Jules Verne's story of a media mogul, United States, 26cm high, 17cm wide.

$15 - $25

Cat's Cradle Comics, VIC

'Dr. Who and the Daleks' movie comic, Peter Cushing photo cover, United States, c1966, 26cm high, 17cm wide.

$70 - $90

Cat's Cradle Comics, VIC

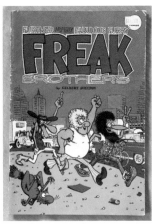

'Freak Brothers' comic, a 1980 reprint by Rip-Off Press, United States.

$15 - $25

The Time Machine, QLD

'The Man from U.N.C.L.E' comic, 1968, United States, 35cm high, 20cm wide.

$15 - $25

The Nostalgia Factory, NSW

'Classic Illustrated, Treasure Island' comic, no. 64, 24cm high, 18cm wide.

$25 - $35

Terrace Collectables, NSW

Dell 'Flying Saucers Comics' no. 4, November 1967, 18cm high, 26cm long.

$15 - $25

Terrace Collectables, NSW

'Zerinza 8 and 9, The Australian Doctor Who Fanzine, January 1979, Ice Warriors', Australia, 26cm high, 22cm wide.

$40 - $60   **Terrace Collectables, NSW**

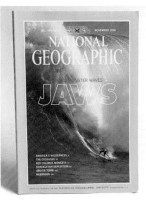

'National Geographic: Vol. 194 No.5. November 1998, Maui's Monster Waves Jaws', United States, 25cm high, 17cm wide.

$5 - $15   **Terrace Collectables, NSW**

'The Australian Women's Weekly' April 1945 with Winston Churchill on the cover, Australia.

$15 - $25   **The Nostalgia Factory, NSW**

'Oz Magazine, 'no. 11 July 1964, featuring a satirical Mona Lisa on the cover, Australia, 28cm high, 22cm wide.

$20 - $30   **Terrace Collectables, NSW**

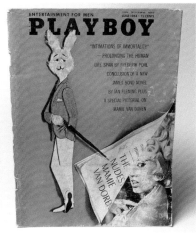

'Playboy' June 1964, United States.

$30 - $40   **The Nostalgia Factory, NSW**

'Picture Goer with Disc Parade' magazine for April 1959 and featuring Frank Sinatra on the cover, Australia.

$7 - $17   **The Nostalgia Factory, NSW**

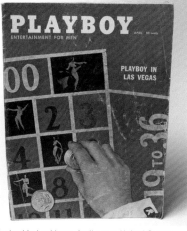

'Playboy' in Las Vegas, April 1958, United States.

$30 - $40   **The Nostalgia Factory, NSW**

'Sports' Novel's' magazine for July 1950, Australia.

$5 - $10   **Dr Russell's Emporium, WA**

'Pix' for October 29, 1955, Melbourne Cup issue, Australia.

$5 - $13   **The Nostalgia Factory, NSW**

'MacLean's', June 23 1956, Canada's National Magazine, Canada.

$10 - $20   **Antipodes Antiques, QLD**

'Sports Novels' magazine for December 1950, Australia.

$4 - $10   **Dr Russell's Emporium, WA**

MAGAZINES

'Pix' magazine for March 7, 1959 with Jayne Mansfield on the cover, Australia.

$10 - $20

The Nostalgia Factory, NSW

'TV Week', November 12th 1966, featuring Roger Moore on the cover, Australia.

$15 - $25

The Nostalgia Factory, NSW

'Woman's Day' March 1962 featuring Marilyn Monroe on the cover, Australia.

$25 - $35

The Nostalgia Factory, NSW

'Pix' December 1963, features 8 pages of photo's of the Kennedy assassination, Australia.

$30 - $40

The Time Machine, QLD

Highly collectable 'Women's Weekly' with a Wep cover, November 2nd 1955 and includes a full page Holden advertisement inside, Australia.

$40 - $50

The Time Machine, QLD

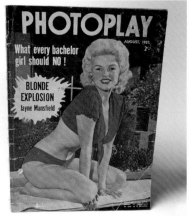

'Photo Play' Magazine for August 1957 featuring Jayne Mansfield on the cover.

$10 - $20

The Nostalgia Factory, NSW

'New Screen News', March 1950, Australia.

$15 - $25

The Nostalgia Factory, NSW

' Australian Disc & Tape Review', May 1972, Australia.

$10 - $20

The Nostalgia Factory, NSW

March 1969 'Women's Weekly', Australia.

$10 - $20

The Time Machine, QLD

Last edition of the large format 'Women's Weekly', July 30th 1975, Australia.

$10 - $20

The Time Machine, QLD

Movie poster for 'Twist Around The Clock', Australian daybill, classic movie about 'The Twist' dance craze in the 1960s starring twist king, Chubby Checker, Australia, c1961, 76cm high, 33cm wide.

$75 - $95 **Malvern Antique Market, VIC**

'New York, New York' daybill, Australia, 76cm high, 33cm wide.

$25 - $35 **Chapel Street Bazaar, VIC**

'G.I. Blues' Elvis Presley daybill, Australia, c1959, 76cm high, 33cm wide.

$100 - $120 **Chapel Street Bazaar, VIC**

'U2 Rattle and Hum The Movie' 1988 daybill, Australia, 76cm high, 33cm wide.

$5 - $15 **Chapel Street Bazaar, VIC**

'World of Abbot and Costello', Australian daybill, starring the famed comedy duo, Australia, c1965, 76cm high, 33cm wide.

$65 - $85 **Malvern Antique Market, VIC**

'The Graduate', Australian daybill, starring Dustin Hoffman and Anne Bancroft, Australia, c1967, 76cm high, 33cm wide.

$65 - $85 **Malvern Antique Market, VIC**

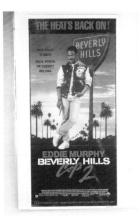

Daybill for 'Beverly Hills Cop 2', Australia, c1988, 76cm high, 33cm wide.

$5 - $15 **Chapel Street Bazaar, VIC**

'Revenge of the Pink Panther' daybill, Australia, c1978, 76cm high, 33cm wide.

$5 - $15 **Chapel Street Bazaar, VIC**

Daybill for 'The Empire Strikes Back', Australia, c1980, 76cm high, 33cm wide.

$90 - $110 **Chapel Street Bazaar, VIC**

Daybill for 'Robinson Crusoe on Mars', Australia, c1964, 76cm high, 33cm wide.

$80 - $100 **Chapel Street Bazaar, VIC**

'Spiderman 2' 2004 daybill, Australia, 76cm high, 33cm wide.

$15 - $25   **Chapel Street Bazaar, VIC**

Foyer card, John Wayne, 'North to Alaska', United States, c1960, 28cm high, 36cm wide.

$65 - $85   **Parramatta Antique Centre, NSW**

Original Australian daybill, for the US movie 'Duel', the cult road movie directed by Steven Spielberg (his first major hit), Australia, c1971.

$45 - $65   **Malvern Antique Market, VIC**

'Cocktail' daybill, Australia, c1988, 76cm high, 33cm wide.

$15 - $25   **Chapel Street Bazaar, VIC**

Foyer card for 'The Undefeated' starring 'The Duke', United States, c1969, 28cm high, 36cm wide.

$50 - $70   **Parramatta Antique Centre, NSW**

Original Australian daybill, for the English cult horror movie 'Mark of the Devil' starring Herbert Lom, Australia, c1973.

$30 - $40   **Malvern Antique Market, VIC**

Original Australian daybill, for the US anti-war film 'Catch 22', Australia, c1970.

$35 - $45   **Malvern Antique Market, VIC**

Original Australian daybill, for the US western 'Frenchie' starring Joel McCrea and Shelley Winters, Australia, c1950.

$20 - $30   **Malvern Antique Market, VIC**

Original Australian daybill, for the US movie 'Arabesque' starring Gregory Peck and Sophia Loren, Australia, c1966.

$75 - $95   **Malvern Antique Market, VIC**

Framed movie poster for 'The Day Mars Invaded Earth', Australia, c1950, 120cm high, 80cm wide.

$500 - $600   **Parramatta Antique Centre, NSW**

'Holly Hobbie' playing cards, United States, c1972.

$7 - $17 **Jan Johannesen, VIC**

Two full sets of 'Fournier' playing cards, boxed, Spain, c1970.

$10 - $20 **Bill Millar, VIC**

Selection of Humerpus greeting cards, typifying styles of the era, Canada, c1966, 24cm high, 10cm wide.

$25 - $35 **P. & N. Johnson, NSW**

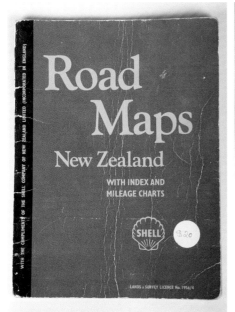

Shell Road Maps of New Zealand, 24 pages, New Zealand, c1960, 24cm high, 18cm wide.

$15 - $25 **Barry McKay, NSW**

Photo of 'Eastern Beach Geelong, Victoria', taken in 1960, and framed in a mirrored box, Australia, 10cm high, 15cm wide.

$40 - $50 **Karlia Rose Garden Antiques & Collectables, VIC**

Manly Marineland postcard, Australia, c1955.

$10 - $20 **The Nostalgia Factory, NSW**

'Cousin of Mine, by Sam Cooke', sheet music, Australia.

$40 - $60 **The Nostalgia Factory, NSW**

Sheet Music ' When the Girl in Your Arms is the Girl in your Heart' By Cliff Richard and Connie Francis, Australia.

$7 - $17 **The Nostalgia Factory, NSW**

Johnny O'Keefe sheet music, ' She Wears My Ring', Australia, c1960.

$5 - $13 **The Nostalgia Factory, NSW**

'Hound Dog' by Sherbet, released by Edwin H. Morris & Co, Ltd., 68-70 Clarence Street, Sydney, Australia, c1970.

$5 - $15   **Terrace Collectables, NSW**

'Beg, steal or borrow', 'Britain's Eurovision Song 72' by Leeds Music Pty. Ltd. Australia.

$4 - $10   **Terrace Collectables, NSW**

Englebert Humperdinck sheet music for 'The Last Waltz', Australia, c1967.

$5 - $10   **The Nostalgia Factory, NSW**

Col Joye sheet music, 'Oh Yeah Uh Huh', Australia, c1959.

$5 - $10   **The Nostalgia Factory, NSW**

'I honestly love you', by Olivia Newton-John, words and music by Peter Allen, 1973, Australia.

$5 - $15   **Terrace Collectables, NSW**

'The Maori Action song' by Jennifer Shennan, No. 36 1984, New Zealand, 17cm high, 23cm long.

$5 - $13   **Terrace Collectables, NSW**

'Gosford District School - Commonwealth, Jubilee Celebration' program April 6th 1951, Australia.

$4 - $10   **The Nostalgia Factory, NSW**

Louis Armstrong and Trini Lopez concert programme, presented by Harry M. Miller in 1964, Australia.

$15 - $25   **The Nostalgia Factory, NSW**

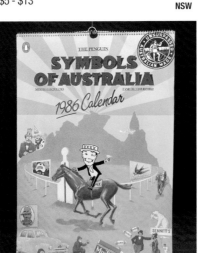

'Symbols of Australia 1986' calendar featuring swallows Ariell Sennitts, etc Australia.

$10 - $20   **369 Antiques, VIC**

Record card for 'A Golden Treasury of Mother Goose and Nursery Songs, under the direction of Mitch Miller'.

$25 - $35   **Terrace Collectables, NSW**

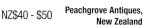

Musical spirit pourer, England, c1950, 13.5cm long.

NZ$40 - $50   **Peachgrove Antiques, New Zealand**

Cut crystal decanter, Poland, c1970, 27cm high, 9cm diam.

$55 - $75   **Obsidian Antiques, NSW**

Yellow opaque glass decanter, Italy, c1960, 11cm high, 10cm diam.

$100 - $120   **Obsidian Antiques, NSW**

'Johnnie Walker' novelty whisky decanter with a glass body and Bakelite hat, c1960, 28cm high.

$50 - $70   **Newport Temple Antiques, VIC**

Boxed metal and vinyl 'Ice Bucket' with horse adornments, Australia, c1970, 26cm high, 14cm diam.

$20 - $30   **Cobweb Collectables, NSW**

Six plastic sword shaped cocktail spikes, Australia, c1960, 6cm long.

$4 - $10   **Cobweb Collectables, NSW**

Funky orange collapsible bar on castors, Australia, c1970, 93cm high, 75cm long, 100cm deep.

$255 - $295   **Towers Antiques & Collectables, NSW**

Ceramic bar accessory, complete with bar tools, corkscrew, etc, c1965, 33cm high.

$40 - $50   **Atomic Pop, SA**

Set of four silver plate and wooden bottle stoppers, c1990, 14cm long.

$20 - $30   **Trinkets & Treasures, VIC**

Bob Hawke cork stopper, Australia, c1985.

$35 - $45   **Robyn's Nest, VIC**

ALCOHOL RELATED

EPNS cylindrical spirit flask, by E & Co., c1950, 17cm high, 3.5cm diam.

$150 - $170 **Claringbold's Fine Jewellery, Antiques & Gifts, NSW**

Boxed and unused 'Spring Irish Coffee Set' complete with the directions booklet, Sweden, c1960.

$45 - $55 **Cobweb Collectables, NSW**

EPNS cocktail shaker, England, c1950, 30cm high.

$55 - $75 **Paddington Antique Centre Pty Ltd, QLD**

Sparkless soda syphon, in stainless steel, England, c1970, 29cm high.

$40 - $50 **Victor Harbour Antiques - Mittagong, NSW**

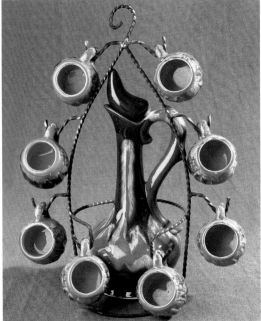

Ceramic decanter with eight mugs on a wire stand, France, c1970, 33 cm high.

$25 - $35 **Atomic Pop, SA**

Silver cocktail shaker with six drinking beakers, China, 24cm high.

$800 - $900 **Barry Sherman Galleries, VIC**

Brass and chrome beer tap with a 'Carlton Draught' handle, Australia, c1965, 53cm high, 19cm wide.

$115 - $135 **Tyabb Hay Shed, VIC**

Brass novelty poodle corkscrew and bottle opener, France, c1950, 7cm long.

$175 - $195 **Womango, VIC**

Wallpaper depicting leading alcohol labels, fully washable, United States, c1970.

$85 - $105 **Chapel Street Bazaar, VIC**

'Hopalong Cassidy' board game, United States, c1950.

$10 - $20 — **Collectable Creations, QLD**

'Careers' board game, Australia, c1959.

$15 - $25 — **Antiques & Collectables Centre - Ballarat, VIC**

'Magic Robot' board game, England, c1955.

$35 - $45 — **Antiques & Collectables Centre - Ballarat, VIC**

Duperlite carpet bias bowls in their original box with original rules, manufactured by Moulded Products (Australasia) Ltd, 5cm high, 23cm long, 11cm deep.

$35 - $45 — **Antique General Store, NSW**

Rubik's cube puzzles, Taiwan, c1980, 5.5cm high, 5.5cm wide.

$10 - $20 — **Fat Helen's, VIC**

'Spy Ring' board game, complete, Australia, c1960.

$5 - $15 — **Cat's Cradle Comics, VIC**

Chess set with a double sided inlaid board and carved wooden pieces, Australia, c1950, 12cm high, 45cm wide, 45cm deep.

$245 - $285 — **The New Farm Antique Centre, QLD**

Hinged box with a carrying handle that opens into a chess board, with enclosed wooden chess pieces, England, c1960, 25cm wide, 50cm long, 6cm deep.

$115 - $135 — **J. R. & S.G. Isaac-Cole, NSW**

Boxed spirograph set, England, c1960.

$30 - $40 — **Antiques & Collectables Centre - Ballarat, VIC**

GAMES & PUZZLES

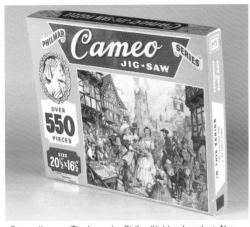

Cameo jig-saw, 'The Lavender Girl', a 'Holdson' product, New Zealand, c1950, 42cm wide, 52cm long.

NZ$10 - $20   **Old & Past Antiques & Collectables, New Zealand**

'Tops and Tails' card game by Ferd, Piatnik & Sons, Vienna, Austria, c1955, 11.5cm high, 14.5cm wide.

NZ$7 - $17   **Maison Jolie, New Zealand**

Boxed set of 'Modernik Indoor Bowls', New Zealand.

NZ$230 - $270   **Auburn Antiques, New Zealand**

Toy motorcycle puzzle with a tin rider under glass, Japan, c1950, 1cm high, 5cm diam.

$40 - $50   **Mt Dandenong Antique Centre, VIC**

Mammoth jig-saw puzzle of a Belgian street, England, c1959, 38cm wide, 48cm long.

NZ$10 - $20   **Old & Past Antiques & Collectables, New Zealand**

'Apollo Series 7440, 1500 Piece' jigsaw puzzle of Sydney Skyline and Cahill Expressway by Whitman Publishing UK Limited, Australia, c1985.

$40 - $50   **Antique Toy World, VIC**

Philmar Ensign jig-saw, 'To the Rescue' scene, England, c1950, 37cm wide, 50cm long.

NZ$10 - $20   **Old & Past Antiques & Collectables, New Zealand**

'Pirates of the Spanish Main' game pack, contains two constructable ships, treasure, crew, an island, game rules and a die, China, c2004, 1cm wide, 12cm long.

$5 - $10   **Cardtastic Collectables, VIC**

Large Masonic medallion, made from brass, and engraved, Australia, c1979, 8cm high, 8cm wide, 8cm diam.

$115 - $135

Dr Russell's Emporium, WA

Full freemason's case with apron, smock, diary, threshold and book of craft masonry, England, c1955, 21cm wide, 46cm long.

NZ$185 - $205

Memory Lane, New Zealand

Masonic jewel, England, c1955, 3cm wide, 9.5cm long.

NZ$65 - $85

Memory Lane, New Zealand

Boxed Masonic jewel, engraved on the back, England, c1955, 3.5cm wide, 11cm long.

NZ$115 - $135

Memory Lane, New Zealand

'Prince Edward Lodge No, 2109' mason's jewel, in 14ct gold with enamel work, Australia, c1962, 6cm wide, 11.5cm long.

$550 - $650

Isadora's Antiques, NSW

'Waterworth' projector, made in Hobart, Australia, c1959.

$55 - $75

Antiques & Collectables Centre - Ballarat, VIC

Kodachrome II colour movie film, 8mm in its original box, Australia, c1970, 2cm high, 8cm wide, 8cm long.

$25 - $35

Vintage Replacement Parts, NSW

Nikon 05 under water flash, Japan.

$70 - $90

Jack Ross Antiques, VIC

'Cineman Editor Special' 8mm electric film viewer, used for editing, c1965, 18cm high, 20cm wide, 15cm deep.

$15 - $25

Manfred Schoen, NSW

Nikon 'Nikonos II' underwater 35mm camera, Japan, c1970, 10cm high, 14cm wide.

$100 - $120

Manfred Schoen, NSW

Kodak Retinette IA Pronto 35mm camera, Germany, c1960, 9.5cm high, 13cm wide, 7cm deep.

$15 - $25

Manfred Schoen, NSW

PHOTOGRAPHY

Flexaret twin lens 120 roll film camera with a 35 mm film adapter.

$75 - $95   **Jack Ross Antiques, VIC**

Kodak 'Sterling II' folding camera, England, 16cm high, 9cm wide.

$65 - $85   **George Magasic Antiques & Collectables, QLD**

Rolleicord camera, c1950.

$170 - $190   **The Junk Company, VIC**

Rollei camera, Germany, c1950.

$200 - $240   **The Junk Company, VIC**

German 'Praktika IV' camera lens with a detachable E Ludwig 1341835, Germany, c1950, 11cm high, 6cm wide.

$225 - $265   **Towers Antiques & Collectables, NSW**

Mini camera in original leather case, marked on upper side 'Hit Camera', Japan, c1960, 6cm long.

$125 - $145   **Decorama, VIC**

Rolex Paillard cinema camera, Switzerland, c1950.

$155 - $175   **Pedlars Antique Market, SA**

Black cased 'Box Brownie' camera, c1950, 12cm wide.

$30 - $40   **Dr Russell's Emporium, WA**

'Diana-F' camera complete in its original box, Hong Kong, c1960.

$45 - $65   **Goodwood House Antiques, WA**

Wirgin stereo camera.

$280 - $320   **Jack Ross Antiques, VIC**

Kodak Polaroid 80 'Land camera', c1970, 12cm high.

$20 - $30   **Dr Russell's Emporium, WA**

'Six- 20 Brownie B' camera, Australia, c1950, 12cm high.

$20 - $30   **Dr Russell's Emporium, WA**

Kiev 4 35mm camera, c1957.

$85 - $105   **Jack Ross Antiques,**
VIC

Duca miniature camera.

$45 - $65   **Jack Ross Antiques,**
VIC

Olympus 35 mm camera with two Uiko f.2.8 lenses, c1959.

$30 - $40   **Jack Ross Antiques,**
VIC

Canon 110Ed camera with an external flash.

$40 - $50   **Jack Ross Antiques,**
VIC

Voigtlander prominent camera.

$230 - $270   **Jack Ross Antiques,**
VIC

'Agfa Silette' 35 mm camera with lens hood and flashgun, Japan.

$20 - $30   **Jack Ross Antiques,**
VIC

Exacta Varex camera, Mod II A with three lenses and a leather case, Germany.

$405 - $445   **Paddington Antique Centre Pty Ltd,**
QLD

Diax L1 camera.

$90 - $110   **Jack Ross Antiques,**
VIC

Minolta A 35mm camera, Japan, c1957.

$55 - $75   **Jack Ross Antiques,**
VIC

Kodak six-20 'Brownie Model D' box camera, United States, c1950.

$15 - $25   **Antiques & Collectables**
On Moorabool, VIC

Nikkormat SLR camera, Japan, c1980.

$185 - $205   **Steven Sher Antiques,**
WA

'Peter Pan' sewing machine, Australia, c1955, 18cm high, 8cm wide, 20cm long.

$20 - $30

Yarra Valley Antique Centre, VIC

'The Favourite Needle Case', a cardboard needle holder complete with all thirty five original, nickel plated needles, Japan, c1950, 17cm wide.

$25 - $35

Needlewitch, ACT

Brass Art Nouveau style needle case, by Copestake & Moore Crampton.

$310 - $350

Esmerelda's Curios, WA

Three booklets of needles, England, c1950.

$20 - $30

Yarra Valley Antique Centre, VIC

Turned wooden cotton reel stand with a six peg gallery and topped with a velvet 'tomato' pin cushion and waxer, United States, 20cm high, 10cm diam.

$115 - $135

Pymble Antiques - Linen & Retro, NSW

Six assorted paper patterns, New Zealand, c1980.

$5 - $15

Bill Millar, VIC

Set of seven boxed ceramic thimbles, in the form of Henry VIII and his six wives, England, c1960.

$205 - $245

Goodwood House Antiques, WA

Large red plastic tatting shuttle, 'Tatsy', England, c1960, 8.5cm wide, 11cm long.

NZ$15 - $25

Maison Jolie, New Zealand

Red and white plastic darning mushroom, New Zealand, c1950, 9cm long, 6.5cm diam.

NZ$15 - $25

Maison Jolie, New Zealand

Sewing bag with a metal stand, Australia, c1950, 49cm wide, 53cm long, 24cm deep.

$115 - $135

Step Back Antiques, VIC

Large plastic woven yellow sewing work basket with cotton reels, Australia, c1950, 19cm high, 35cm wide, 25cm deep.

$65 - $85

Obsidian Antiques, NSW

Art glass yellow ashtray, c1960, 8cm high, 18cm wide.

$35 - $45   **Old Bank Corner Collectables, NSW**

Glass Holmgarrd ashtray by Per Lutkin, signed on the base, Denmark, c1960, 6cm high, 13cm wide, 15cm long.

$125 - $145   **Forever Amber @ The Tyabb Grainstore, VIC**

Art glass, bright blue ashtray, c1960, 8cm high, 16cm wide.

$45 - $55   **Old Bank Corner Collectables, NSW**

'Marlboro' mini ashtray in the form of a cigarette packet, Hong Kong, c1950, 2cm high, 4cm wide, 8cm deep.

$50 - $70   **Stumpy Gully Antiques, VIC**

Bendigo pottery ashtray, in the form of a frog on the edge of a shell, Australia, c1960, 14cm wide.

$230 - $270   **Marsteen Collectables, VIC**

Scandinavian heavy glass ashtray with a textured base, c1970, 12.5cm wide.

$45 - $55   **frhapsody, WA**

Rosenthal ashtray with printed scene, Mouson Lavender with the mailcoach, stamped 'Rosenthal Germany', 17cm long, 15cm deep.

$55 - $75   **Pearl Rose, VIC**

Stacking ashtray in orange melamine, designed by Walter Zeischegg in 1966 and originally produced by Helit, Germany, Hong Kong, c1970, 13cm wide.

$20 - $30   **frhapsody, WA**

Silvered alloy 'Chesterfield Filter' ashtray, United States, c1960, 16cm diam.

$35 - $45   **Decorama, VIC**

Souvenir ceramic ashtray from Las Vegas, United States, c1970, 12cm diam.

$25 - $35   **Decorama, VIC**

Pressed glass souvenir ashtray from the 'Silver Slipper Gambling Casino, Las Vegas', United States, c1960, 9cm wide, 9cm long.

$25 - $35   **Decorama, VIC**

Burslem ashtray, stamped 'M.T. Co. Ltd. Burslem', England, c1960, 13cm long, 13cm deep.

$30 - $40   **Pearl Rose, VIC**

Musical lighter plays the Danube Waltz, in original box, by Crown Musical, England, c1960, 6.7cm high, 3.5cm wide, 1.3cm deep.

$115 - $135

Calmar Trading, VIC

Small pistol cigarette lighter, 'Aurora 45', patent No. 519285, Japan, c1960, 10cm long.

$40 - $60

Sweet Slumber Antiques & Collectables, NSW

New Zealand design cigarette case, New Zealand, c1960, 8.5cm wide, 13cm long.

NZ$20 - $30

Gales Antiques, New Zealand

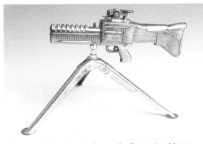

Chrome lighter, in the form of a Browning M-60 machine gun, Japan, c1970, 12cm high, 20cm wide, 20cm diam.

$85 - $105

Dr Russell's Emporium, WA

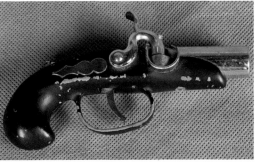

Gun cigarette lighter, Patent 204961, Japan, c1960, 15cm long.

$45 - $65

Sweet Slumber Antiques & Collectables, NSW

Novelty lighter of a cowboy on a barrel, c1950, 10cm high, 8cm wide.

$105 - $125

Goodwood House Antiques, WA

Sea lion and ball, table cigarette lighter with a copper finish, metal, Hong Kong, c1960, 17cm high, 8cm wide, 13cm long.

$40 - $50

Burly Babs Collectables/Retro Relics, VIC

Brass plated kiwi table lighter on a carved wooden base, New Zealand, c1950, 9cm high, 8cm long.

NZ$115 - $135

Collectamania, New Zealand

Chrome lighter in the form of a hand-grenade, marked 'Combat, Windsor', with patent numbers, England, c1960, 12cm high, 6cm deep, 6cm diam.

$85 - $105

Dr Russell's Emporium, WA

'Maruman T36' table lighter, made of black and clear plastic, Japan.

$155 - $175

Adornments, QLD

Ronson lighter in its original box, England, c1960.

$25 - $35

Journey to the Past Antiques & Collectables, QLD

'Maruman T26, Sharon Piezo-Electric Table Lighter', Japan, 11.5cm high, 8.5cm wide.

$155 - $175

Adornments, QLD

Boxed Penn Delmor fishing reel (#285), United States, c1950, 10cm wide.

$75 - $95

Victor Harbour Antiques - Mittagong, NSW

'Pacific Trolling Reel for Fresh & Saltwater' fishing, made of Bakelite and steel, with its original box, Japan, c1960, 15cm long.

$75 - $95

The Mill Markets, VIC

Automatic aluminium fly reel, by Southbend (#1130), United States, c1960, 8cm wide.

$45 - $65

Victor Harbour Antiques - Mittagong, NSW

Zebco spinning reel, model 33, United States, c1960, 9cm long.

$40 - $50

Victor Harbour Antiques - Mittagong, NSW

Murray Cod fishing lure, Australia, c1980, 55cm long.

$155 - $175

How Bazaar, VIC

1950's Brass cannon yabbie pump, Australia.

$45 - $65

Antipodes Antiques, QLD

Charles William Labertauche plastic fishing reel, c1970, 4cm deep, 10cm diam.

$50 - $70

How Bazaar, VIC

ABU 5500 metal fishing reel, 11cm wide, 6cm diam.

$110 - $130

How Bazaar, VIC

Bakelite Alvey fishing reel, c1956, 10cm diam.

$30 - $40

Flaxton Barn, QLD

Seamartin fishing reel with original timber spool and body, patented No-242,286, serial 4-2-60, Australia, c1960, 16cm high, 14cm wide.

$1550 - $1750 **Alltime Antiques & Bairnsdale Clocks, VIC**

Hot Shot fishing lure M307, United States, c1960.

NZ$30 - $40 **Antiques On Victoria, New Zealand**

Flat fish lure size F7 by United States tackle, United States, c1960.

NZ$40 - $50 **Antiques On Victoria, New Zealand**

Alvey Bakelite and chrome 'Surf Champion' fishing reel, c1960, 15cm diam.

$40 - $50

Flaxton Barn, QLD

RECREATIONS & PURSUITS

Fencing mask made by 'Paul', c1960, 34cm long.

$65 - $85

Tarlo & Graham, VIC

Roller skates, Taiwan, c1980.

$45 - $65

Fat Helen's, VIC

Dunlop wooden tennis racquet clamp, c1960, 23cm high, 25cm wide.

$10 - $20

Castlemaine, VIC

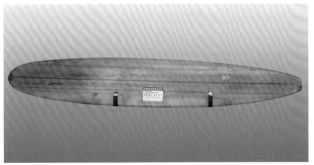

Maraha surf board, Australia, c1960, 320cm long.

$480 - $520

How Bazaar, VIC

Woolami surf rescue board, Australia, c1970, 55cm wide, 350cm long.

$950 - $1050

How Bazaar, VIC

Gray Nicholls cricket bat with 'Keith Stackpole' branding, Australia, c1958.

$65 - $85

Tyabb Hay Shed, VIC

Table size croquet set with five mallets, hoops and balls, England, c1955.

$40 - $50

Max Rout, NSW

'Wilson' Maureen Connolly, picture decal tennis racket, United States, c1960, 69cm high, 23cm wide.

$40 - $50

The Bottom Drawer Antique Centre, VIC

Slazenger 'Colin Cowdrey' model cricket bat and ash stamps, England, c1965.

NZ$205 - $245

Country Antiques, New Zealand

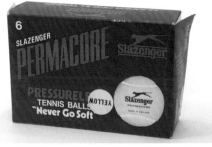

Boxed Slazenger tennis balls, England, c1970, 7cm high, 14cm wide, 21cm long.

$30 - $40

Wooden Pew Antiques, VIC

Flexi-deck skateboard with pop art decoration, c1970, 16cm wide, 62.5cm long.

$70 - $90

506070, NSW

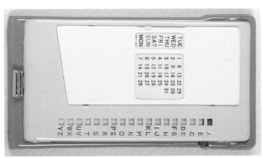

Metal blue and yellow address index and calendar with its original box, Japan c1960.

$30 - $40

Nana's Pearls, ACT

Red ABS plastic 'Valentine' portable typewriter, designed in 1969 by Ettore Sottsass and Perry King, Spain, c1969, 11.5cm high, 34.5cm long, 35cm deep.

$120 - $140

506070, NSW

Plastic elephant pencil sharpener, Germany, c1950, 4.5cm high.

NZ$5 - $15

Sue Todd Antiques Collectables, New Zealand

'Camel Pompadour Pen' with original box, England, c1950, 7cm long.

NZ$70 - $90

Bonham's, New Zealand

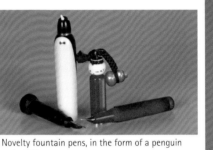

Novelty fountain pens, in the form of a penguin and a Chinese man.

$120 - $140

Ruth Howlett Collectables, VIC

Conway Stewart, 14 carat gold nib and features a model No. 2 lever filler and a green 'marble' case, England, c1950, 125cm long.

$85 - $105

Antique General Store, NSW

Celluloid alligator holding a black boy pencil, design reg. no. 93652, Japan, c1950, 13cm long.

$85 - $105

Decorama, VIC

Sheaffer Nostalgia pen, in sterling silver, with a cartridge/converter filler and a 14ct gold nib, unused, United States, c1970, 13.3cm long.

$650 - $750

Melbourne Vintage Pens, VIC

Parker 65 'Flighter' pen in stainless steel, a cartridge/converter filler with a 14ct gold nib, England, c1975, 13.5cm long.

$190 - $210

Melbourne Vintage Pens, VIC

Parker Slimford pen in black, aerometric filler with a 14ct gold nib, c1952, 12.5cm long.

$70 - $90

Melbourne Vintage Pens, VIC

Onoto fountain pen, c1950, 12cm long.

$40 - $50

Dr Russell's Emporium, WA

NZ$330 - $370

Sheaffer PFM III pen, black with gold fitted trim, in original box, 14 ct gold nib, Australia, c1959.

Collectamania, New Zealand

ANIMALS & BUSTS

Hand carved and highly detailed bird group featuring a male eagle, female eagle and two eagles in a nest on a gnarled tree, Indonesia, 81cm high, 30cm wide, 53cm deep.

$2850 - $3050　**Architectural Décor Australia, NSW**

Marble group of three dolphins, Italy, c1950, 100cm high, 50cm wide.

$1150 - $1350　**Hollywood Antiques, WA**

Ceramic wall hanging of an African princess, Germany, c1959, 28cm high.

$88 - $108　**Chapel Street Bazaar, VIC**

Set of five plaster flying ducks, Australia, c1950, 18cm high, 18cm wide, 3cm deep.

$255 - $295　**Dr Russell's Emporium, WA**

Hand painted figure of a marlin, Italy, c1960, 40cm high, 102cm long.

$1350 - $1550　**Alltime Antiques & Bairnsdale Clocks, VIC**

Three wise monkey's plaster statue, Italy, c1950, 20cm high, 26cm wide.

$55 - $75　**Fat Helen's, VIC**

Plaster hand painted Indian bust, Italy, c1960, 43cm high, 30cm wide.

$185 - $205　**Chapel Street Bazaar, VIC**

Sculpted bust in terracotta of R. J. Hawke, P.M., signed 'Slater' on the back, Australia, c1983, 22cm high, 15cm wide, 13cm deep.

$110 - $130　**Cherished Memories, VIC**

Wonderful and detailed, hand carved bird group, featuring two eagles on a gnarled tree, Indonesia, 81cm high, 47cm wide, 34cm deep.

$2350 - $2550　**Architectural Décor Australia, NSW**

Cement seagull, from a seaside café at Le Grand Motte, France, c1950, 50cm high, 35cm wide.

$355 - $395　**Capocchi, VIC**

Papier mache wall head by W. Goebel, Germany, c1957, 31cm high, 18cm wide, 11cm deep.

NZ$275 - $315　**Maxine's Collectibles, New Zealand**

Bronze cast and brass sleeve Hagemeyer style figure of an African woman, c1970, 47cm high, 25cm wide.

$500 - $600   **ShopAtNortham, WA**

Large figure of an Australian stockman in ceramic and metal, signed/dated and numbered, Australia, c1983, 45cm high, 33cm wide.

$200 - $240   **Antiques As Well, VIC**

Plaster figurine of a gentleman resting and listening to records with his pet dog, by Naturecraft Ltd. England, c1950, 16cm high, 17cm long, 24cm deep.

$55 - $75   **Nicki's Collection, NSW**

Venetian carved wooden blackamoor, on a pedestal holding a two handle basket and a cornucopia, Italy, c1950, 150cm high.

$2750 - $2950   **Hollywood Antiques, WA**

Plaster figure of a seated woman on a skin rug with a drum, Australia, c1950, 20cm high, 20cm long.

$120 - $140   **Chapel Street Bazaar, VIC**

Plaster figure of a seated woman with a basket, Australia, c1950.

$110 - $130   **Chapel Street Bazaar, VIC**

Studio ceramic sculptural work, by Hilary Bartok, Australia, c1980, 13cm high, 22cm wide.

$520 - $620   **Malvern Antique Market, VIC**

Pair of hand made figurines signed 'Berani Italy', c1960.

$180 - $200   **Helen's On The Bay, QLD**

Signed ceramic sculpture by Alaxander Danial, in fine porcelain, of Cinderella and her carriage, England, c1790, 16cm high, 16cm wide, 29cm long.

$165 - $185   **The Evandale Tinker, TAS**

Boxed sterling silver cruet set consisting of a salt, pepper and mustard with spoons and Bristol blue liners, hallmarked Birmingham 1950, England, 7cm high, 22cm long, 11cm deep.

NZ$500 - $600   **Fendalton Antiques, New Zealand**

Superb sterling silver four piece tea and coffee service, of heavy weight with floral decorations, England, c1950.

$5800 - $6200   **Hollywood Antiques, WA**

Enamel tea spoons, on silver gilt, Denmark, c1950.

$125 - $145   **Antiques & Collectables On Moorabool, VIC**

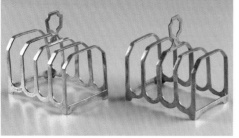

Pair of sterling silver toast racks, Birmingham 1954, England, 7cm high, 7cm long.

$165 - $185   **Eagle Antiques, VIC**

Pair of sterling silver and paua shell open salt dishes, New Zealand.

$125 - $145   **Reflections Antiques, NSW**

Pair of boxed spoons labeled 'Sterling Silver by Harris & Son' Perth WA, Australia, c1960, 11cm long.

$205 - $245   **Ritzy Bits - ACT, ACT**

A pair of Middle Eastern silver fighting birds, with gold wash finishes, c1955.

$2650 - $2850   **Adornments, QLD**

Sterling silver mounted horn, hallmarked for London 1963, England, 25cm long.

$600 - $700   **Discovery Corner, QLD**

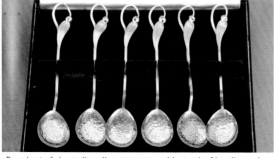

Boxed set of six sterling silver teaspoons with gum leaf handles and hand beaten bowls, weight 53 gm, Australia, c1950, 12cm long.

$275 - $315   **Toowoomba Antiques Gallery, QLD**

Sterling silver olive spoon, Continental, c1970.

$55 - $75   **Camberwell Antique Centre, VIC**

Set of six Georg Jensen Acorn teaspoons, gilded on sterling silver, weight 84 gm, Denmark, 11cm long.

$900 - $1000   **Roy's Antiques Pty Ltd, VIC**

Walker and Hall silver plated rose bowl with lion head handles, England, c1970, 13.5cm high, 25.5cm diam.

NZ$130 - $150

Gregory's of Greerton, New Zealand

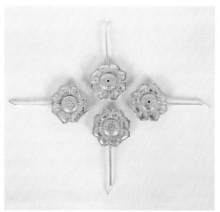

Two sets of silver plated novelty salt and pepper shakers in flower designs, made by Perfection Plate and with the original box, Australia, c1950.

$50 - $70

Nana's Pearls, ACT

Silver plated and milk glass cake stand or centerpiece, England, c1950, 11cm high, 36cm diam.

$600 - $700

Southside Antiques Centre, QLD

Four piece silver plated cruet set with blue glass inserts, Australia, c1960, 7.5cm high, 8cm wide, 20cm long.

$75 - $95

Newport Temple Antiques, VIC

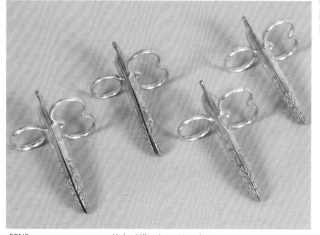

EPNS asparagus server set, United Kingdom, 11cm long.

$75 - $95

Helen's On The Bay, QLD

Art Deco style cruet set, c1950, 8cm high.

$55 - $75

Olsens Antiques, QLD

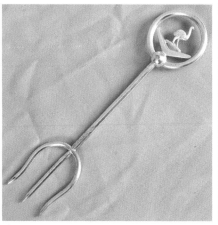

Silver plate bread fork with an emu and boomerang handle, Australia, 21cm long.

$85 - $105

Titles & Treasures, QLD

Silver plated napkin rings, by Paramount Australia, in the Ophelia pattern, Australia, 3cm high, 5cm wide.

$50 - $70

Rathdowne Antiques, VIC

SMALL WOODEN ITEMS

Mahogany box with the Australian coat of arms, c1960, 10cm high, 18cm wide, 39cm long.

$85 - $105

Green Gables Collectables, NSW

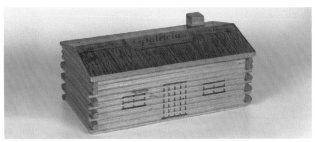

Novelty wooden log cabin shaped chocolate box for 'Patricia's, Sydney, Chocolates and Candies', Australia, c1950, 7cm high, 11cm wide, 18.5cm long.

$65 - $85

Decorama, VIC

Teak instrument box with dovetail joints, England, 15cm high, 20cm wide, 33cm long.

$165 - $185

Bob & Dot's Antiques & Old Wares, NSW

Inlaid timber box, made by an inmate of Boggo Road prison, Brisbane, Australia, c1950, 8cm high, 25cm wide, 16cm deep.

$85 - $105

Antipodes Antiques, QLD

Mulga wood stud bowl, on a flat base with the original decal, 'Australian Mulga, Southern Series', Australia, c1955, 5.5cm high, 9.5cm diam.

$5 - $15

Dejanvou Antiques & Bric a Brac, VIC

Mulga wood lidded container, in the form of a galvanised water tank with taps, Australia, c1955, 11cm high, 7cm diam.

$5 - $15

Dejanvou Antiques & Bric a Brac, VIC

Pair of mulga wood serviette rings with the original sticker inside, Australia, c1950, 4cm high, 5cm diam.

$10 - $20

Mockingbird Lane Antiques, NSW

Mulga wood cigarette holder with a decorative silver plated kangaroo and a decal, 'Greetings from Melbourne', Australia, c1960, 8cm high, 8cm wide, 20cm long.

$30 - $40

Ritzy Bits - ACT, ACT

Mulga wood specimen vase, Australia, c1955, 11cm high.

$10 - $20

Dejanvou Antiques & Bric a Brac, VIC

Mulga wood souvenir desk calendar with the metal kangaroo, Australia, c1950, 9cm high, 15cm wide, 6.5cm deep.

$35 - $45

Galeria del Centro, NSW

Circular mulga wood pin box with the Australian Commonwealth Military Forces badge, Australia, c1950, 8cm diam.

$25 - $35

Marsteen Collectables, VIC

Pokerwork cigarette box, Australia, c1950.

$10 - $20   **Dr Russell's Emporium, WA**

Chip carved kauri pine tray, New Zealand, 55cm wide.

NZ$125 - $145   **Albany Hill Cottage, New Zealand**

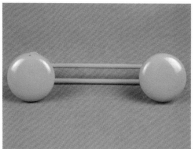

Coat hooks, painted blue, France, c1950, 20cm long.

$40 - $50   **Step Back Antiques, VIC**

EPNS and timber tray in the Art Deco style, by 'APW', c1960, 30cm wide, 45cm long.

NZ$80 - $100   **Gregory's of Greerton, New Zealand**

Four piece lacquered timber cruet set, in orange, Japan, c1970, 12.5cm high.

$30 - $40   **frhapsody, WA**

Hand painted wooden wall plaque, New Zealand, c1950, 25cm diam.

NZ$40 - $50   **Collectamania, New Zealand**

Chip carved kauri tray, New Zealand, 50cm wide.

NZ$125 - $145   **Albany Hill Cottage, New Zealand**

Three teak bowls, Thailand, c1969.

$45 - $55   **frhapsody, WA**

Hand painted wooden wall plaque, New Zealand, c1950, 25cm diam.

NZ$40 - $50   **Collectamania, New Zealand**

Inlaid Australiana timber tray, Australia, 35cm wide, 50cm long.

$40 - $50   **Newport Temple Antiques, VIC**

Home made construction model, of timber, with removable walls, Australia, c1960, 40cm high, 90cm wide, 70cm deep.

$180 - $200   **The Bottom Drawer Antique Centre, VIC**

Hand carved wooden flying fish made by Lancy Christian, c1950, 19cm high.

NZ$185 - $205   **Antiques & Curiosities, New Zealand**

EMBROIDERY, LINEN & RUGS

Embroidered tray cloth, Australia, c1950.

$25 - $35

**Antipodes Antiques,
QLD**

Embroidered table or supper cloth, Australia, c1950, 132cm wide, 132cm long.

$90 - $110

**Antipodes Antiques,
QLD**

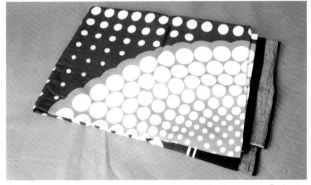

Brown and white poly cotton tablecloth with pop art circular patterns, England, c1970, 120cm wide, 180cm long.

$30 - $40

**frhapsody,
WA**

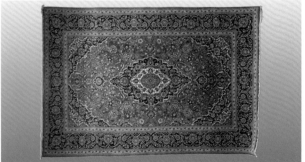

'Kashan' hand knotted Persian rug with a central medallion on a red field, covered with floral motifs, c1950.

$3150 - $3350

**Phoenix Persian Gallery,
NSW**

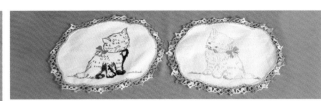

Pair of doilies with needlework cats, Australia, c1950.

$15 - $25

**Paddington Antique Centre Pty Ltd,
QLD**

Large white tablecloth with an applied pattern and twelve matching serviettes, Australia, c1960, 340cm wide, 178cm long.

$230 - $270

**Shaws Antiques,
NSW**

Poly cotton tablecloth in orange, brown and purple with psychedelic patterns, England, c1968, 124cm wide, 160cm long.

$75 - $95

**frhapsody,
WA**

'Rosely' patterned four napkin and tablecloth set with the original label, Ireland.

NZ$25 - $35

**Maison Jolie,
New Zealand**

Woollen pictorial rug of the Melbourne skyline, Australia, c1965, 69cm wide, 140cm long.

$185 - $205

**Gorgeous,
VIC**

Screen printed drapery fabric by Rowe fabrics, 'Rainforest'. 1969. Priced per metre, Australia, 120cm wide.

$55 - $75   **Atomic Boom, QLD**

Screenprinted cotton fabric. Priced per metre, Scandinavia, c1970, 120cm wide.

$55 - $75   **Atomic Boom, QLD**

Large scale numbers print attributed to Alexander Girard for Herman Miller 1965, 100% cotton. Priced per metre, United States, c1965, 120cm wide.

$115 - $135   **Atomic Boom, QLD**

Medium weight hand printed soft furnishing fabric, 'Bolda' by Robyn Versluys, Australia, c1969, 122cm wide.

$110 - $130   **frhapsody, WA**

Soft furnishing fabric, screenprint on cotton bark cloth paint palettes. Priced per metre, Australia, 120cm wide.

$60 - $80   **Flashback, VIC**

Huge scale print, screen printed wallpaper. Priced per metre, Scandinavia, c1968, 52cm wide.

$70 - $90   **Atomic Boom, QLD**

Screen printed drapery fabric, 'Cherry Blossom'. Priced per metre, 100% cotton, Denmark, c1975, 120cm wide.

$55 - $75   **Atomic Boom, QLD**

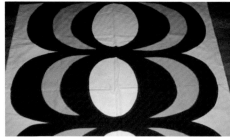

Marimekko of Finland 'Kaivo', designed by Maija Isola in 1965, 100% cotton screen printed, Marimekko's most sought after design, priced per metre, Finland, 138cm wide.

$130 - $150   **Atomic Boom, QLD**

Soft furnishing screen printed fabric, by Boras Wafueiri of Sweden. Priced per metre, Sweden, c1968, 125cm wide.

$85 - $105   **Atomic Boom, QLD**

Soft furnishing paisley cotton fabric with fibreglass backing. Priced per metre, England, c1968, 125cm wide.

$55 - $75   **Atomic Boom, QLD**

Medium weight furnishing fabric design 'Flowers' by Pamela Walker for Austfield Fabrics. Priced per metre, Australia, c1969, 120cm wide.

$70 - $90   **frhapsody, WA**

Barkaloth large scale print on 100% cotton drapery fabric. Priced per metre, England, c1965, 125cm wide.

$75 - $95

Atomic Boom, QLD

Screen printed drapery fabric, 'Contessa' by Rowe in 1971, cotton sateen. Priced per metre, Australia, c1971, 120cm wide.

$75 - $95

Atomic Boom, QLD

Textured screen printed wallpaper, full roll, Netherlands, c1967, 52cm wide, 1000cm long.

$115 - $135

Atomic Boom, QLD

Soft furnishing cotton fabric by International Printworks, sold by the panel, Finland, c1979, 65cm wide, 45cm long.

$40 - $50

Atomic Boom, QLD

Full roll of wallpaper, Netherlands, c1972, 52cm wide, 1000cm long.

$115 - $135

Atomic Boom, QLD

Full unused roll of geometric wallpaper, Netherlands, c1972, 52cm wide, 1000cm long.

$115 - $135

Atomic Boom, QLD

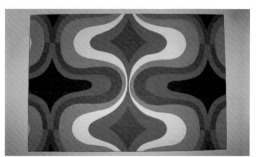

Wall hanging, drapery cotton fabric, Denmark, c1968, 60cm high, 90cm wide.

$115 - $135

Atomic Boom, QLD

Geometric soft furnishing fabric, 100% cotton screen printed. Priced per metre, England, c1972, 120cm wide.

$75 - $95

Atomic Boom, QLD

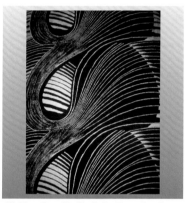

Highly collectable 'Hyoky' by Tampella of Finland, 100% cotton screen printed, sold by the panel, Finland, c1972, 160cm wide, 218cm long.

$230 - $270

Atomic Boom, QLD

Vinyl wallpaper of black and white paisley girls, France, c1960, 52cm wide, 100cm long.

$165 - $185

Flashback, VIC

Tapestry by Ben Shearer, signed on the back, titled 'Courage', Australia, c1970, 114cm high, 190cm wide.

$5800 - $6200 **Mondo Trasho, VIC**

Macrame wall hanging of an owl, Australia, c1970.

$10 - $20 **Atomic Pop, SA**

Dress fabric, screenprint on cotton, featuring abstract flowers, Japan, c1965, 90cm wide, 250cm long.

$65 - $85 **Flashback, VIC**

Dress fabric, featuring cigarette packets, screenprint on cotton, c1955, 90cm wide, 300cm long.

$90 - $110 **Flashback, VIC**

Yellow check gingham fabric, decorated with girls in orange dresses, England, c1960, 120cm wide, 400cm long.

NZ$25 - $35 **The Wooden Rose, New Zealand**

Cotton quilt, Australia, c1950, 120cm wide, 170cm long.

$85 - $105 **Step Back Antiques, VIC**

Heavy velvet quilt with acrylic trim, England, c1972, 230cm wide, 250cm long.

$260 - $300 **frhapsody, WA**

Pink lace. Priced per metre, c1950, 17cm wide.

$4 - $10 **Pitt Trading, NSW**

Pink lace depicting a bunch of flowers in a bow. Priced per metre, c1950, 4cm wide.

$4 - $10 **Pitt Trading, NSW**

Heavily decorated pink lace fabric. Priced per metre, c1960, 144cm wide.

$50 - $70 **Pitt Trading, NSW**

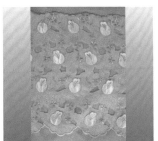

Mauve lace with tulip decorations. Priced per metre, c1955, 39.5cm wide.

$50 - $70 **Pitt Trading, NSW**

Bolt of blue cotton material, Australia, c1950, 120cm wide, 1200cm long.

$200 - $240 **Step Back Antiques, VIC**

Frame photo-print of 1950's fabric, Australia, c2003, 56cm high, 72cm wide.

$430 - $470 **Cool & Collected, SA**

Hand knitted dolly tea cosy, New Zealand.

NZ$45 - $65 **Shand's Emposium, New Zealand**

'Action Man' action figure, 'Underwater Photographer' model, China, c1998, 30cm high.

$20 - $30

Woodside Bazaar, SA

Pond yacht with original sails, Australia, c1950, 61cm high, 48cm long.

$150 - $170

Eclectica, TAS

Die cast figure of 'Queen Elizabeth', Hong Kong, c1970, 8cm high, 25cm long.

$15 - $25

Canberra Cards & Collectables, ACT

Submarine, 'Nautilus', Japan, c1960, 42cm long.

$175 - $195

The Junk Company, VIC

Timber model of the 'Titanic', c1970, 25cm high, 53cm long.

$330 - $370

Terrace Collectables, NSW

Alloy spirit fired speed boat, by Victory Industries, Guildford, England.

$700 - $800

Adornments, QLD

Tri-ang Minic toy speed boat by 'Sutcliffe Models', 'Racer I', England, c1960, 6cm high, 9cm wide, 24cm long.

$230 - $270

Adornments, QLD

'All metal Valiant clockwork battleship', Sutcliffe model with its original box and key, England, c1950, 32cm long.

NZ$545 - $645

Queens Gardens Antique Centre, New Zealand

Motorised model of the 'White Rose', 38cm long.

NZ$845 - $945

Auburn Antiques, New Zealand

Scale model boat CYC 15 'Solo', c1965, 102cm high, 18cm wide, 79cm long.

$1000 - $1200

Heartland Antiques & Art, NSW

Corgi classics Thornycraft van with roof rack die cast model, featuring 'Arnotts Milk Arrowroot Biscuits' livery, code C859/3, England, c1986, 6.5cm high, 13cm long.

$45 - $65

Lucilles Interesting Collectables, NSW

Die cast 'Corgi' car with 'Noddy', 'Big Ears' and 'Golly', c1960.

$330 - $370

Jan James, NSW

Corgi 'Tour de France' cameraman's car, England, c1950.

$65 - $85

Steven Sher Antiques, WA

Boxed Corgi farm set (No. 5), England, c1960, 30cm wide, 30cm long.

$600 - $700

Dr Russell's Emporium, WA

Corgi police car with original box (#419), England, c1950.

$140 - $160

Steven Sher Antiques, WA

Corgi Toys die cast Citroen DS19 model car, England, c1950, 10cm long.

$5 - $15

The Restorers Barn, VIC

Boxed 'Lotus Elan S2', # 318 by Corgi Toys, England, c1964, 8cm long.

$230 - $270

Traffic Developments Pty Ltd, VIC

Corgi toys die cast Hillman Husky model car, England, c1950, 8.5cm long.

$35 - $45

The Restorers Barn, VIC

Boxed 'Massey-Ferguson Tractor' by Corgi, England, c1965, 12cm long.

$135 - $155

Traffic Developments Pty Ltd, VIC

Boxed '1927 Bentley', from the Corgi Classics series, England, c1964, 11cm long.

$135 - $155

Traffic Developments Pty Ltd, VIC

Boxed '1910 Daimler', from the Corgi Classics series, England, c1964, 11cm long.

$125 - $145

Traffic Developments Pty Ltd, VIC

Dinky 'Robertson's Golden Shred' toy truck featuring Guy Golly, 15cm long.

$115 - $135

Jan James,
NSW

Dinky Toys Road Sign Set, No. 47 in original box, England, c1980.

$170 - $190

Antique Toy World,
VIC

Die cast Dinky toy no. 162, 'Ford Zephyr' model car, England, c1950, 9.5cm long.

$55 - $75

The Restorers Barn,
VIC

Dinky brand die cast farm trailer, England, c1950, 13cm long.

$15 - $25

Chapel Street Bazaar,
VIC

Hand made reproduction of a French 'Dinky' fire truck, England, c2002.

$140 - $160

Modelcraft Miniatures,
NSW

Boxed 'Foden Flat Truck' by Dinky Super Toys, # 902, England, c1957, 18cm long.

$745 - $845

Traffic Developments Pty Ltd,
VIC

Dinky Supertoys No. 661 'Army Recovery Tractor' by Meccano, England, c1960, 14cm long.

$205 - $245

Antique Toy World,
VIC

Boxed Dinky toy 'Triumph Spitfire Sports', die cast car No. 114, England, c1960, 4cm high, 10cm long, 3cm deep.

$375 - $415

Philicia Antiques & Collectables,
SA

Hand made copy of a pre-war Dinky delivery van, with its original box, England, c2005, 3.5cm high, 3.5cm wide, 8.5cm long.

$110 - $130

Modelcraft Miniatures,
NSW

Boxed 'R.A.C' patrol minivan, by Dinky, England, c1964, 8cm long.

$330 - $370   **Traffic Developments Pty Ltd, VIC**

Boxed 'ABC Transmitter Van' by Dinky, England, c1962, 11cm long.

$545 - $645   **Traffic Developments Pty Ltd, VIC**

Boxed 'Packard Convertible' by Dinky Toys, England, c1956, 11cm long.

$275 - $315   **Traffic Developments Pty Ltd, VIC**

Boxed 'Aveling-Brarford Diesel Roller' by Dinky, #279, England, c1965, 11cm long.

$185 - $205   **Traffic Developments Pty Ltd, VIC**

Boxed 'Turntable Fire Escape Truck' by Dinky, # 956, England, c1963, 20cm long.

$355 - $395   **Traffic Developments Pty Ltd, VIC**

Boxed Dinky Toys '448', 'Chevrolet Pick-Up & Trailers', England, c1964, 22cm long.

$465 - $505   **Traffic Developments Pty Ltd, VIC**

Boxed 'Medium Artillery Tractor' by Dinky, # 689, England, c1957, 13cm long.

$265 - $305   **Traffic Developments Pty Ltd, VIC**

Boxed 'Plymouth Canadian Taxi', Dinky Toys #266, England, c1958, 11cm long.

$430 - $470   **Traffic Developments Pty Ltd, VIC**

Boxed 'Vauxhall Ambulance' by Dinky, England, c1962, 9cm long.

$165 - $185   **Traffic Developments Pty Ltd, VIC**

Dinky Supertoys Fire engine with extending ladder, by Meccano, England, c1960, 14cm long.

$205 - $245   **Antique Toy World, VIC**

Boxed 'Austin Healy 100 Sport', Dinky Toys (109), England, c1956, 8cm long.

$325 - $365   **Traffic Developments Pty Ltd, VIC**

Matchbox 'Models of Yesteryear', boxed 1955 Holden FJ panel van, commissioned by Automodels in Sydney and featuring the Australian business logo and their German business logo on the other side, China, c1997, 9.5cm long.

$45 - $65

model-cars.com.au, NSW

Boxed 'Matchbox Models of Yesteryear' limited edition die cast model of a 1920 Leyland three tone subsidy lorry, No. B0003, England, c1985.

$25 - $35

Modelcraft Miniatures, NSW

Hornby cattle wagon, O size, England, c1950, 15cm long.

$115 - $135

How Bazaar, VIC

Hornby wind-up train engine, O size, England, c1950, 20cm long.

$245 - $285

How Bazaar, VIC

Hornby Tipping Wagon, O size, McAlpine & Sons, with box, England, c1950, 18cm long.

$190 - $210

How Bazaar, VIC

Wyn-Toy grader with transfers, Australia, c1950, 19cm high, 16cm wide, 40cm long.

$110 - $130

The Evandale Tinker, TAS

Matchbox Collectables series, die cast model of a 1920 Texaco Mack truck, China, c1990, 12cm long.

$15 - $25

Modelcraft Miniatures, NSW

Boxed 'Sky-Busters' by Matchbox, 'SB-25 Helicopter Rescue' with original 'Myer' price tag an a 'SB-5 Starfighter F104', c1978.

$80 - $100

The Toy Collector, SA

Matchbox die cast FJ Holden panel van features 'Gowings, 130 Years of Trading, Pioneer Distributors of Australian Goods' livery, China, c1997, 3cm high, 7cm long.

$7 - $17

Lucilles Interesting Collectables, NSW

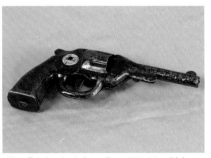

Wyn-Toy tin pistol, Australia, c1950, 10cm high, 20cm long.

$65 - $85

Southside Antiques Centre, QLD

'Philips Mechanical Engineer' children's building set, Holland, c1966, 56cm wide.

$140 - $160

The Mill Markets, VIC

'The New Buz Builder No. 6' set in original box, Australia, c1950, 27cm wide, 43cm long, 4cm deep.

$115 - $135

Mockingbird Lane Antiques, NSW

'Kelloggs' football 'Rou-a-goals'. Priced per item, Australia, c1950, 4cm long.

$55 - $75

Memorabilia on Parade, VIC

'Weet-Bix' and -Weet-a-Flakes', football cereal figures, priced per item, Australia, c1950, 4.5cm high.

$35 - $45

Memorabilia on Parade, VIC

Tin toy monkey swinging on bars, England, c1957, 30cm high, 17cm wide, 6cm deep.

$190 - $210

Dr Russell's Emporium, WA

Tinplate clockwork of a coalmine head, the coal wagon runs back and forth turning around at each end, made by Arnold, Germany, c1950, 35cm long.

NZ$330 - $370

Tinakori Antiques, New Zealand

Tin bodied clockwork toy monkey with cymbals, Australia, c1950, 27cm high.

$115 - $135

Graham & Nancy Miller, VIC

Wind-up tin duck with legs moving in a shuffle motion and glass eyes, Japan, c1950, 14cm high, 10cm deep.

$135 - $155

Towers Antiques & Collectables, NSW

Clockwork tin toy of a clown riding a donkey which walks, Germany, c1950, 16cm high, 13cm long.

$140 - $160

Collectable Creations, QLD

Plastic key wind, tin toy girl with moving head and hands that play the xylophone, China, c1988, 23cm high.

$375 - $415

Chapel Street Bazaar, VIC

Clockwork tin plate 'Funny Tiger' by Marx Toys, Japan, c1950, 16.5cm high.

NZ$85 - $105

Maison Jolie, New Zealand

Wind-up monkey with symbols trade mark 'ALPS', Japan, c1950, 17cm high.

$115 - $135

Forever Amber @ The Tyabb Grainstore, VIC

Plastic wind-up dog, Japan, 10cm high.

$35 - $45

Fat Helen's, VIC

'Austin J40' pedal car with an electric light and horn, England, c1954, 150cm long.

$6750 - $7150

Traffic Developments Pty Ltd, VIC

Pedal driven child's red fire truck, 'Jet Flow Drive' No. 281 with bell and hose, United States, c1960, 97cm long.

$405 - $445

Max Rout, NSW

Britains boxed set of six Gordon Highlanders, England.

$330 - $370

Southside Antiques Centre, QLD

The Bahamas Police Band, a boxed set of eleven lead figures by W. Britain, United Kingdom, c1987.

$165 - $185

Antique Toy World, VIC

Lilliput lead farm figures in original box, by Wittartans, England.

$115 - $135

Antiques & Collectables On Moorabool, VIC

Metal pedal car in fire engine red, c1960, 100cm long.

$375 - $415

Chapel Street Bazaar, VIC

Red metal child's wheelbarrow, Australia, c1950, 31cm wide, 74cm long.

$55 - $75

Step Back Antiques, VIC

'Happynak' tin plate pull cart toy, England, c1950, 8cm high, 13cm wide, 24cm long.

$55 - $75

Antipodes Antiques, QLD

Child's 'Cyclops' trotting horse tricycle, c1950.

$1100 - $1300

Shenton Park Antiques, WA

Single seat, vintage junkyard style pedal car, c1960, 45cm wide, 300cm long.

$945 - $1045

Chapel Street Bazaar, VIC

'Skateboarding Snoopy', a promotional toy from McDonalds, China, c1995, 19cm high.

$5 - $13   **Chapel Street Bazaar, VIC**

'Snoopy with Suitcase', a give-away toy from McDonalds, China, c1995, 15cm high.

$5 - $13   **Chapel Street Bazaar, VIC**

Candle holding Snoopy, promotional toy from McDonalds, China, c1995, 15cm high.

$5 - $13   **Chapel Street Bazaar, VIC**

Woodstock on Snoopy's hat, McDonald's promotional toy, China, c1995, 19cm high.

$5 - $13   **Chapel Street Bazaar, VIC**

'X-7 Space Explorer Ship' in tin, by Modern Toys, Japan, c1963, 20cm diam.

$375 - $415   **Traffic Developments Pty Ltd, VIC**

Tin 'Machine Robot' by S.H Toys, with its original box, Japan, c1961, 28cm high.

$645 - $745   **Traffic Developments Pty Ltd, VIC**

Tin 'Martian Robot', Japan, c1962, 30cm high.

$275 - $315   **Traffic Developments Pty Ltd, VIC**

Toy monkey, battery operated, with moving eyes and clapping hands, Japan, c1960, 24cm high.

$175 - $195   **How Bazaar, VIC**

Toy Clown with box, battery powered with lighting nose and playing the drums, Japan, c1960, 23cm high.

$155 - $175   **How Bazaar, VIC**

Battery operated plastic robot which moves in circles, with flashing eyes, Hong Kong, c1984, 28cm high.

$40 - $50   **The Mill Markets, VIC**

Wailing toy lion with battery power in external control, Japan, c1960, 15cm high, 40cm long.

$110 - $130   **How Bazaar, VIC**

Lindemar, battery operated 'Spanking Bear', c1950, 22.5cm high.

$165 - $185   **Jan James, NSW**

Tinplate battery operated Fire Chief car, by Taiyo, Japan, c1969, 26cm long.

$75 - $95

Antique Toy World, VIC

Unmarked, superb moulded plastic, flat head hot rod with a friction mechanism, c1955, 7cm high, 16cm long.

$185 - $205

Chapel Street Bazaar, VIC

'Trax' Holden special die cast Sydney taxi for 'De-Lux Red Cabs', China, c1994, 10cm long.

$110 - $130

model-cars.com.au, NSW

Mamod live steam power fire engine, England, c1980, 22cm high, 16cm wide, 45cm long.

$595 - $695

Beehive Old Wares & Collectables, VIC

Pair of tin toy yellow taxi cabs with friction drive, Japan, c1955, 5.5cm high, 7.5cm wide, 18cm long.

$75 - $95

Palliaer Antiques, QLD

Haji lady motor cyclist toy, friction driven, Japan, c1960, 14cm high, 20cm long.

NZ$130 - $150

The Wooden Rose, New Zealand

Haji Lady friction motorcycle toy, Japan, c1960, 10cm high, 14cm long.

NZ$80 - $100

The Wooden Rose, New Zealand

Boxed Budge motorcycle toy, No. 262, England, c1950, 7cm high, 4cm wide, 10.5cm long.

NZ$190 - $210

The Wooden Rose, New Zealand

Boxed friction Codec toy motor cyclist, Hong Kong, c1970, 6.5cm high, 13cm long.

NZ$75 - $95

The Wooden Rose, New Zealand

Boxed Sanchis plastic friction motorcycle toy, No. 3, Spain, c1970, 14cm high, 25cm long.

NZ$140 - $160

The Wooden Rose, New Zealand

Sanchis Harley Davidson friction powered plastic motorcycle toy, Spain, c1970, 20cm high, 26cm long.

NZ$175 - $195

The Wooden Rose, New Zealand

Classic Model Cars limited edition die cast model of Paul Morris' 2002 'Sirromet' V8 super car VX Commodore, No. 1269 of 2500, China, c2003.

$25 - $35

Modelcraft Miniatures,
NSW

Classic Model Cars die cast model, limited edition of David Besnard's 2002 V8 super car AU Falcon, No. 2111 of 3000, China, c2003.

$25 - $35

Modelcraft Miniatures,
NSW

Large die cast Ferrari Ascari by Toschi, a promotional model, Italy, c1953, 55cm long.

$4400 - $4600

Antique Toy World,
VIC

Tin plate, battery operated VM race car, Japan, c1980, 25cm long.

$100 - $120

Paddington Antique Centre Pty Ltd,
QLD

Schuco tin wind-up car, sport racing model 1050, Germany, c1958, 6cm high, 8cm wide, 14cm long.

$220 - $260

Dr Russell's Emporium,
WA

Clockwork tin, 1917 Ford Coupe T, made by Schuco, Germany, c1960, 20cm long.

$375 - $415

Traffic Developments Pty Ltd,
VIC

Danbury Mint die cast model car, 1958 Chevrolet Impala convertible, China, c1992, 8cm wide, 23cm long.

$175 - $195

The Restorers Barn,
VIC

Replica vintage toy car made of tin, with a mechanical lever the makes car move, Japan, c1980, 11cm high, 13cm long.

$65 - $85

Jan Johannesen,
VIC

'Wayne Gardiner's WGR Racing Commodore', die-cast model of the Coca-Cola sponsored Holden by Classic Collectables, in its original box, and autographed by Wayne Gardiner, China, c1990, 11cm high, 18cm long.

$205 - $245

Terrace Collectables,
NSW

'Trax' Ford Falcon GTHO die cast, highly detailed model in Ford True Blue, China, c1998, 20cm long.

$190 - $210

model-cars.com.au,
NSW

Model of the Crocodile Audi, winner of the 24 hour race in Adelaide, January 1st 2000, China, c2000, 10cm long.

$50 - $70

Modelcraft Miniatures,
NSW

MOTOR VEHICLES

Die cast 'Promotional Models' Ford delivery truck by Lledo (London) Ltd, England, c1980, 4.5cm high, 7cm long.

NZ$20 - $30

John Varney, New Zealand

Boxed 'Days Gone', die cast 1930 model A Ford Stake truck, Nestles Milk by Lledo PLC, England, c1980, 3cm high, 9cm long.

NZ$15 - $25

John Varney, New Zealand

Boxed die cast 'Days Gone' Ford delivery truck by Lledo (London) Ltd, England, c1983, 4.5cm high, 7cm long.

NZ$20 - $30

John Varney, New Zealand

Large tinplate, friction drive toy Cadillac by Bandai, Japan, c1960, 10cm long.

$365 - $405

Beehive Old Wares & Collectables, VIC

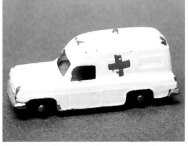

Metal 'Funho' Holden ambulance, New Zealand, c1960, 3cm wide, 9cm long.

NZ$24 - $34

Colonial Heritage Antiques Ltd, New Zealand

'Trax' FJ Holden utility, limited edition, individually numbered certificate, from only 1500 produced, features the Trax 10th anniversary 1980–1990, Hong Kong, c1990, 3.5cm high, 10cm long.

$115 - $135

Lucilles Interesting Collectables, NSW

Plastic model of a Vauxhall Velox with electric motor 1/18 scale, manufactured by Victory Industries (Surrey) Ltd. with original box, England, c1950, 26cm long.

$205 - $245

Terry & Noi, VIC

Boxed tin car, 1963 'Chevrolet Impala' convertible, Japan, c1963, 20cm long.

$380 - $420

Kings Park Antiques & Collectables, QLD

Mercedes Benz 'Bump 'n Go' battery operated model car, Japan, c1960, 26cm long.

$230 - $270

Antique Toy World, VIC

Clockwork tin, 1902 Mercedes Simplex Anno, made by Schuco, Germany, c1960, 20cm long.

$375 - $415

Traffic Developments Pty Ltd, VIC

Battery operated 'Shaking Classic Car' with its original box.

$105 - $125

Jan James, NSW

Tinplate double decker bus, made in Japan by ATD, Advertising Goodyear, Esso, Dunlop and Mobil gas, Japan, c1950, 16.5cm high, 9cm wide, 30cm long.

$185 - $205

Northside Secondhand Furniture, QLD

'Mamod' steam tractor, complete with burner, England, c1950, 17cm high, 12cm wide, 25cm long.

$330 - $370

ShopAtNortham, WA

'American Circus' truck in tin, by Exelo, with its original box, Japan, c1958, 24cm long.

$1195 - $1395

Traffic Developments Pty Ltd, VIC

'Fun Ho' tin toy tip truck, New Zealand, c1950, 8.5cm wide, 25cm long.

NZ$115 - $135

Hubbers Emporium, New Zealand

Boxed missile launcher dated October 1975, Russia, 5cm high, 5cm wide, 9cm long.

NZ$20 - $30

Ikon Antiques, New Zealand

Large Lesney 'Massey Harris' toy tractor, England, c1954, 21cm long.

$950 - $1050

Antique Toy World, VIC

Friction powered, tinplate 'Giant Crane Truck' by Nomura, with original box, Japan, c1965, 29cm high, 32cm long.

$275 $315

Antique Toy World, VIC

Red tin toy 'Farm Tractor', c1950, 10cm high, 14cm wide.

$25 - $35

Dr Russell's Emporium, WA

Tin plate toy tractor with rubber tyres, c1950, 16cm high, 16cm wide, 30cm long.

$85 - $105

Bob & Dot's Antiques & Old Wares, NSW

'Fun Ho' tin toy tractor with a disk plow and a front end loader, New Zealand, c1950, 13cm wide, 34cm long.

NZ$190 - $210

Hubbers Emporium, New Zealand

TOYS

Pluto the Dog, by Walt Disney Productions, United States, c1960, 20cm high.

$35 - $45
Retro Relics, VIC

Walt Disney Classic Collections from the 'Pinocchio 60th Anniversary' of 'Jiminy Cricket', Thailand, c2000, 10cm long.

$205 - $245
Chapel Street Bazaar, VIC

Plush character of 'Junior' the elephant, from the Disney film 'The Jungle Book' manufactured by Steiff, Germany, c1965, 15cm high, 15cm long.

$65 - $85
Chapel Street Bazaar, VIC

Mickey Mouse water bottle camera, China, c1990, 9cm high, 14cm wide.

$7 - $17
Chapel Street Bazaar, VIC

Disney 'Lady' figure, China, c1995, 9cm high.

$25 - $35
Chapel Street Bazaar, VIC

Donald Duck shampoo bottle, Japan, c1960, 24cm high.

$30 - $40
Castlemaine, VIC

Children's lamp featuring Disney's Louie (one of Donald Duck's nephews) with its original lamp, Japan, c1960, 50cm high.

$65 - $85
The Mill Markets, VIC

Boxed 'Mickey Mouse Handcar' set, by Wells o' London, England, c1955.

$2350 - $2550
Adornments, QLD

'Donald Duck' tin lunch box, made in Richmond, Victoria, Australia, c1955, 15cm high, 22cm wide, 14cm deep.

$155 - $175
Ace Antiques & Collectables, VIC

Boxed 'Mickey the Magician' battery operated toy made by Linemar toys. The hat lifts to reveal a chicken, drops, then lifts again and the chicken disappears, Japan, c1950, 24cm high, 13.5cm wide, 17cm long.

NZ$3900 - $4100
Bulls Antiques & Collectables, New Zealand

'Mickey Mouse Club' flag, c1950, 77cm long.

$110 - $130
How Bazaar, VIC

Star Wars 'Luke Skywalker' action figure in its original outfit, made by Kenner, China, c1978, 30cm high.

$115 - $135

Chapel Street Bazaar, VIC

Star Wars 'Princess Leia' doll in its original outfit, manufactured by Kenner, China, c1978, 30cm high.

$70 - $90

Chapel Street Bazaar, VIC

Star Wars 'Han Solo' action figure in its original outfit, manufactured by Kenner, Hong Kong, c1978, 30cm high.

$115 - $135

Chapel Street Bazaar, VIC

Star Wars 'Chewbacca' twelve inch collection action figure, from the original 1977 toy line and film, China, 30cm high.

$65 - $85

Chapel Street Bazaar, VIC

Large figure of 'C3PO', Hong Kong, c1978, 32cm high, 14cm wide.

$60 - $80

Obsidian Antiques, NSW

Star Wars 'Snowtrooper' from the 'Empire Strikes Back', manufactured by Hasbro, China, c1990, 30cm high.

$45 - $65

Chapel Street Bazaar, VIC

Star Wars 'At-At', second release, c1981.

$430 - $470

The Toy Collector, SA

Star Wars 'Millennium Falcon' playset vehicle, made by Galoob, China, c1994, 20cm long.

$115 - $135

Chapel Street Bazaar, VIC

Boxed 'Fambaa' with Shield Generator and Gungan warrior from Star Wars, Episode One, c2001.

$275 - $315

The Toy Collector, SA

Star Wars boxed figurine of 'C-3PO', manufactured by Hasbro Plastic, China, c1996, 30cm high.

$40 - $50

Chapel Street Bazaar, VIC

Star Wars 'Death Star Trooper' action figure in its original box, manufactured by Hasbro, China, c1996, 30cm high.

$65 - $85

Chapel Street Bazaar, VIC

Star Wars 'Ponda Baba' action figure in its original box, manufactured by Hasbro, China, c1990, 30cm high.

$40 - $50

Chapel Street Bazaar, VIC

Star Wars 'Barquin Dan' action figure in its original box, manufactured by Hasbro, China, c1990, 30cm high.

$75 - $95

Chapel Street Bazaar, VIC

TOYS

Japanese tin toy 'Batmobile', with a plastic batman driving, Japan, c1960, 23cm long.

$420 - $460

506070, NSW

Boxed model kit of the 'Bat Plane' from the Batman TV series, made by Polar Lights, China, c2002, 35cm long.

$20 - $30

Chapel Street Bazaar, VIC

Boxed 'Batmobile' by Corgi Toys, England, c1966, 12cm long.

$500 - $600

Traffic Developments Pty Ltd, VIC

Solid resin figurine of the 1920's cartoon character, 'Betty Boop' and her dog, China, c2004, 20cm wide.

$100 - $120

Chapel Street Bazaar, VIC

Plastic 'Batman' mask, United States, c1970, 29cm high, 22cm wide.

$115 - $135

Fat Helen's, VIC

Plastic 'Wacky Wobbler' bobblehead figurine of 'Betty Boop' in a cowgirl outfit, manufactured by Funko, China, c2000, 17cm high.

$20 - $30

Chapel Street Bazaar, VIC

Solid resin figurine of the 1920's cartoon character 'Betty Boop' reclining in a bath tub, China, c2004, 12cm high, 17cm long.

$85 - $105

Chapel Street Bazaar, VIC

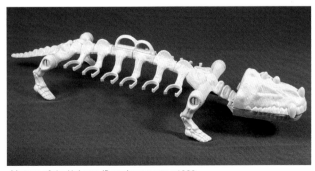

Masters of the Universe 'Bones' carry case, c1980.

$45 - $65

The Toy Collector, SA

Masters of the Universe 'Snake Face' with shield and snake staff, action figure, c1980.

$20 - $30

The Toy Collector, SA

Masters of the Universe 'Zoar', c1980.

$20 - $30

The Toy Collector, SA

Ceramic figurine of Garfield playing tennis, United States, c1981, 11cm high, 8cm long, 6cm deep.

$15 - $25   **Burly Babs Collectables/ Retro Relics, VIC**

Noddy 'Fuzzy Felt' toy in its original box, England, c1959, 28.5cm long, 17.5cm deep.

$65 - $85   **Decorama, VIC**

Celluloid toy of 'Popeye' with wind-up boxing action and head extension, Japan, 13cm high.

$230 - $270   **Collectable Creations, QLD**

Rainbow Brite Sprites from the popular 1980's cartoon, with soft bodies and hard faces, made by Mattel 1983 Hallmark Cards Inc. Priced per item, Korea (South), 28cm high, 26cm long.

$10 - $20   **The Toy Collector, SA**

Rainbow Brite Sprites from the popular 1980's cartoon, with soft bodies and hard faces, made by Mattel 1983 Hallmark Cards Inc. Priced per item, Korea (South), 28cm high, 26cm long.

$10 - $20   **The Toy Collector, SA**

Plush soft toy, 'Rainbow Brite's dog', with a soft plastic face, c1980, 25cm high, 26cm wide, 21cm long.

$20 - $30   **Fat Helen's, VIC**

'Twink', a plush leader sprite from the popular 80's cartoon 'Rainbow Brite', with white fur like body, vinyl/rubber face, felt stars and colourful material limbs, United States, c1983, 30cm high, 28cm wide, 10cm deep.

$10 - $20   **The Toy Collector, SA**

Sesame Street 'Big Bird' plastic camera, Thailand, c1988, 10cm high, 10cm wide.

$10 - $20   **Chapel Street Bazaar, VIC**

Dress Me Up 'Ernie' from Sesame Street by Tyco, China, c1995, 38cm high.

$30 - $40   **Chapel Street Bazaar, VIC**

Sesame Street 'Ernie' push button musical toy by Tyco, China, c1996, 17cm high.

$5 - $10   **Chapel Street Bazaar, VIC**

'Chicken Dance Elmo' from Sesame Street, by Fisher Price, China, c2001, 34cm high.

$30 - $40   **Chapel Street Bazaar, VIC**

'Sing and Snore Ernie' from Sesame Street, by Tyco, China, c1996, 50cm high.

$30 - $40

Chapel Street Bazaar, VIC

Sesame Street's 'Lets Pretend Elmo' by Fisher Price, China, c1999, 33cm high.

$30 - $40

Chapel Street Bazaar, VIC

Soft Plastic fire engine featuring the 'Cookie Monster' from Sesame Street, by Tyco, China, c1993, 9cm high, 24cm wide.

$7 - $17

Chapel Street Bazaar, VIC

Mr. Burns plastic Simpson's figure, China, c1995, 6cm high.

$5 - $13

Chapel Street Bazaar, VIC

Set of five Simpson family dolls in their original packaging, Burger King giveaways, China, c1990.

$135 - $155

Chapel Street Bazaar, VIC

Plastic Bart Simpson with a skateboard, China, c1995, 10cm high.

$5 - $15

Chapel Street Bazaar, VIC

Bart Simpson plastic figure as a little devil, China, c1996, 4cm high.

$5 - $13

Chapel Street Bazaar, VIC

Millhouse, a plastic Simpson's figure, China, c1998, 4cm high.

$5 - $13

Chapel Street Bazaar, VIC

Homer Simpson figure with a football, China, c1996, 9cm high.

$5 - $15

Chapel Street Bazaar, VIC

Boxed Smurf's 'Mushroom House', c1980.

$130 - $150

The Toy Collector, SA

Plastic Indian Smurf, China, c1970, 5cm high.

$10 - $20

Chapel Street Bazaar, VIC

Plastic drummer Smurf, China, c1970, 5cm high.

$7 - $17

Chapel Street Bazaar, VIC

Plastic Smurf with a pumpkin head, 'Halloween Smurf', European, c1970, 5cm high.

$55 - $75

Chapel Street Bazaar, VIC

Plastic Smurf with a skateboard, China, c1970, 5cm high.

$5 - $10

Chapel Street Bazaar, VIC

Plastic scholar Smurf, China, c1970, 5cm high.

$30 - $40

Chapel Street Bazaar, VIC

All plastic Smurf house, China, c1978, 12cm high, 8cm wide.

$20 - $30

Chapel Street Bazaar, VIC

Plastic sliding Smurf, China, c1970, 5cm long.

$5 - $10

Chapel Street Bazaar, VIC

Plastic Star Trek shuttle craft, manufactured by Playmates, China, c1989, 15cm high, 28cm long.

$50 - $70

Chapel Street Bazaar, VIC

Plastic model of the USS Enterprise, from the Star Trek Next Generation series, China, c1994, 8.5cm wide, 12cm long.

$5 - $10

Vintage Replacement Parts, NSW

Matchbox Thunderbirds 'Tracey Island', boxed, complete, China, c1990, 35cm high, 50cm long, 22cm deep.

$165 - $185

Cat's Cradle Comics, VIC

Matchbox 'Thunderbird Two', boxed, complete, China, c1990, 35cm wide, 45cm long, 15cm deep.

$165 - $185

Cat's Cradle Comics, VIC

Transformer 'Optimus Prime', c1984.

$190 - $210

The Toy Collector, SA

Viewmaster 'Heidi' slides, Australia, 10cm high, 10cm wide.

$7 - $17

Chapel Street Bazaar, VIC

TOYS

Viewmaster 'Superman' slides, Australia, 10cm high, 10cm wide.

$20 - $30

Chapel Street Bazaar, VIC

'Give-A-Show' Hannah Barbera projector, complete with slides and original box, England, c1960.

$70 - $90

Cat's Cradle Comics, VIC

Pepe Le Pew jug, hand painted in Australia, c1994, 22.5cm high.

$85 - $105

Marge's Antiques & Collectables, NSW

Hard solid rubber Gizmo figure from the Gremlins movie, Warner Bros. 1984 LCN Toys Ltd, China, 5.5cm high, 5cm wide, 2cm deep.

$5 - $15

The Toy Collector, SA

Hard rubber 'E.T' figures, featuring a child like E.T from the popular Steven Spielberg movie, made in 1988 by Applause, China, 6.5cm high, 5cm wide, 3cm deep.

$15 - $25

The Toy Collector, SA

'Archie Andrews' ventriloquist doll. (Archie Andrews was an English cartoon character, of the 1940's and 1950's), England, c1960, 35cm high.

$115 - $135

Chapel Street Bazaar, VIC

Evil scientist figure in a wheelchair, from Tim Burton's 'Nightmare Before Christmas', China, c1994, 11cm high, 5.5cm wide.

$75 - $95

Chapel Street Bazaar, VIC

'Lock, Stock & Barrel' figures from Tim Burton's 'Nightmare Before Christmas' movie, China, c1994, 7cm high, 4cm wide.

$45 - $65

Chapel Street Bazaar, VIC

'ALF' hand puppet, c1987, 20cm high.

$20 - $30

The Toy Collector, SA

Boxed 'Chitty Chitty Bang Bang' car by Corgi Toys in 1968, England, 15cm long.

$645 - $745

Traffic Developments Pty Ltd, VIC

'Mars Attacks' boxed 'Supreme Martian Ambassador' figure, China, c1996, 32cm high, 22cm wide.

$135 - $155

Chapel Street Bazaar, VIC

An early Davey Crockett pistol and knife pack, United States, c1956, 33cm long.

$165 - $185

P. & N. Johnson, NSW

Boxed action figure of 'Fonzie', from the TV series 'Happy Days', made by Figures Toy Company, India, c2004, 25cm high, 18cm wide.

$20 - $30

Chapel Street Bazaar, VIC

Aeronica 15 AC model aeroplane with 44cc engine, Australia, c1990, 34cm wide, 270cm long.

$2400 - $2600

How Bazaar,
VIC

DC3 toy plane, cast in lead, Australia, c1960, 17cm wide, 13cm long.

$40 - $50

Rose Cottage Antiques,
ACT

Pitch pine rocking horse, Australia, c1950, 80cm high, 80cm long.

$115 - $135

Antiques As Well,
VIC

'Heavenly Hearse' plastic model kit, unassembled and in its original box, United States, c1970.

$40 - $50

Atomic Pop,
SA

Tinplate friction driven toy space ship with two large rotating fans, Japan, c1955, 22cm long.

$230 - $270

Terry & Noi,
VIC

Plastic house guards by Timpo, England, c1970.

$330 - $370

Traffic Developments Pty Ltd,
VIC

Plastic model of a Pan-Am Boeing 747 Jumbo Jet, battery operated, in original box, Japan, c1970, 30cm wide, 32cm long.

$140 - $160

Antique Toy World,
VIC

'Cyclops' wooden rocking kangaroo, Australia, c1970, 60cm high, 80cm wide.

$85 - $105

Newport Temple Antiques,
VIC

Boxed 'Orbitory Satellite Space Spinner', tin spinning top, patented in 1969, New Zealand, 12cm high, 12cm diam.

NZ$110 - $130

Right Up My Alley,
New Zealand

TOYS

Tri-ang clockwork train and track, England, c1950, 10cm long.

$40 - $60

The Mill Markets, VIC

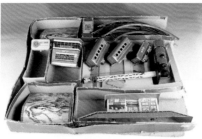

Mettoy key wind train set, in original box with accessories, England, c1950.

$230 - $270

Antiques & Collectables On Moorabool, VIC

Early 1960's Mettoy passenger train set number 'S366' clockwork, in its original box, England, c1960, 36cm high, 30cm wide, 6cm deep.

$510 - $610

Wisma Antik, WA

Boxed battery operated tin toy 'Jumbo the Bubble Blowing Elephant', with its original box, Japan, c1950, 20cm high, 20cm wide.

$45 - $55

Newport Temple Antiques, VIC

'Charley Weaver' battery powered bartender with its original box, Japan, c1962, 32cm high.

$140 - $160

The Mill Markets, VIC

Boxed 'Happy Clown' novelty camera, uses 110 cartridge film, China, c1995, 10cm high, 10cm wide.

$10 - $20

Chapel Street Bazaar, VIC

Boxed battery operated 'Chimp with Xylophone', Hong Kong, c1960, 16cm wide, 33cm long.

$45 - $55

Newport Temple Antiques, VIC

Plastic toy camera, Thailand, c1990, 8cm high, 12cm wide.

$5 - $13

Chapel Street Bazaar, VIC

Original 'Care Bears' cloud roller with 'Hard Cheer Bear', the rainbow circle rotating when rolled along the ground, complete with hard to find stickers, Taiwan, c1980.

$40 - $60

The Toy Collector, SA

Britains Guard figures, United Kingdom, c1970.

$4 - $10

Canberra Cards & Collectables, ACT

'Super Time-o-Matic' toy washing machine made by 'Modern Toys', Japan, 16cm high, 10cm wide.

$30 - $40

Newport Temple Antiques, VIC

Four piece household appliance toy/doll set, including a kitchen sink, fridge, kitchen range and a washing machine, Australia, c1950, 11cm high, 7cm wide, 7cm long.

$90 - $110

Tyabb Hay Shed, VIC

Daiya friction powered toy food mixer, in its original box, Japan, c1950, 14cm high, 4cm wide, 14cm long.

$35 - $45

Antique General Store, NSW

Friction powered Bar-B-Q set in its original box, Japan, c1950, 16cm high.

$65 - $85

Antiques & Collectables On Moorabool, VIC

Boomeroo toy cash register, Australia, c1960, 19cm high, 17cm wide.

$165 - $185

The Mill Markets, VIC

National Darts Co. toy croquet game, boxed, Australia, 14cm wide, 56cm long, 4cm deep.

$85 - $105

Jamberoo Antiques, NSW

Atari 'Yars' Revenge' game cartridge, Taiwan, c1981, 8cm wide, 9.5cm long.

$5 - $10

Chapel Street Bazaar, VIC

Atari game cartridge of 'Asteroids', Taiwan, c1981, 8cm wide, 9.5cm long.

$5 - $10

Chapel Street Bazaar, VIC

Atari game cartridge of 'Missile Command', Taiwan, c1981, 8cm wide, 9.5cm long.

$5 - $10

Chapel Street Bazaar, VIC

Atari game cartridge of 'Combat', Taiwan, c1980, 8cm wide, 9.5cm long.

$5 - $15

Chapel Street Bazaar, VIC

Atari game cartridge of 'Defender', Taiwan, c1981, 8cm wide, 9.5cm long.

$5 - $10

Chapel Street Bazaar, VIC

Tin toy gun, stamped 'Spaceman, Made in England', c1950, 22.5cm long.

$165 - $185

Decorama, VIC

Atomic tin 'Ray Gun', Japan, c1970, 16.5cm long.

$20 - $30

Antique Toy World, VIC

Plastic original Garfield 'I Want You' brooch, c1978, 4cm high, 4cm wide.

$5 - $10

Fat Helen's, VIC

Rubber 'Phantom' ring, a mail away with a coupon from the back corner of a 'Phantom' comic, Australia, c1959, 2cm high, 2.5cm wide, 2.5cm deep.

$40 - $50

P. & N. Johnson, NSW

Timber model of a Melbourne tram, Australia, c1950, 19cm high, 15cm wide, 55cm long.

$205 - $245

Coliseum Antiques Centre, NSW

Hover rally tin and plastic toy car, with a game wheel on top, Japan, c1980, 15cm long.

$35 - $45

Maryborough Station Antique Emporium, VIC

Boxed '18 inch Iteary Howitzer' by Britains, England, c1962, 18cm long.

$330 - $370

Traffic Developments Pty Ltd, VIC

Toy 'Shell' garage, Australia, c1960, 20cm high, 59cm wide, 59cm long.

$55 - $75

Step Back Antiques, VIC

'Massey Ferguson 780 Special' harvester, made by Lesney, England, c1960, 4cm high, 4cm wide, 7cm long.

$35 - $55

Woodside Bazaar, SA

Webb's toy mower based on an actual model, with an 8 inch cutting width, England, c1950, 53cm high, 28cm wide.

$405 - $445

Stumpy Gully Antiques, VIC

'Rotate-O-Matic Super Robot', complete with original box, Japan, c1970.

$225 - $265

Mockingbird Lane Antiques, NSW

'Scooter the Talking Robot', plastic with remote control action and audio produced by 'Vision', China, c1980, 67cm high.

$175 - $195

Terry & Noi, VIC

'Surfa Sam' skateboard, Australia, c1970, 63cm high, 15cm wide.

$265 - $305

Ace Antiques & Collectables, VIC

'Mettype Junior' tin toy typewriter, Australia, c1950, 5cm high, 17cm wide, 28cm long.

$65 - $85

Antique General Store, NSW

Strawberry Shortcake carded figure, 'Apricot with Hopsalot', c1980.

$20 - $30

The Toy Collector, SA

'Lemon Meringue picking a flower', carded Strawberryland figure by Kenner, c1980.

$20 - $30

The Toy Collector, SA

Carded Strawberry Shortcake 'Raspberry Tart', c1981.

$20 - $30

The Toy Collector, SA

Children's Tea set in its original box, Germany, c1950.

$75 - $95

Antique Toy World, VIC

Carded Strawberry Shortcake 'Lemon Meringe with a Bouquet', c1981.

$20 - $30

The Toy Collector, SA

Childs tea set in original box, consisting of four cups and saucers, teapot, milk jug and sugar bowl, England, c1950.

$110 - $130

Debbie Pech, VIC

Toy auto trolley by Ingap, boxed, Italy, c1950, 18cm long.

$330 - $370

Antique Toy World, VIC

Tin toy merry-go-round, Germany, c1950.

$170 - $190

The Junk Company, VIC

Tin toy kaleidoscope, Australia, c1950, 20cm high, 5cm diam.

$35 - $45 **Step Back Antiques, VIC**

Tin toy bartender, battery operated, with eyes that roll while pouring a drink into a glass, Japan, c1960, 25cm high, 10cm wide.

$140 - $160 **Chapel Street Bazaar, VIC**

Bizarre goat puppet with fleece body over wood, the month opens and shuts by pulling a string, 42cm high.

$75 - $95 **Patinations, NSW**

Child's tin drum with wooden drum sticks, Australia, c1950, 7cm high, 18cm diam.

$40 - $60 **Step Back Antiques, VIC**

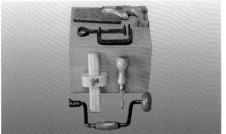

Juvenile tool chest by Superior, marked on the box 'No 477' and including small wood and metal tools, England, c1955, 14cm high, 18cm wide, 13cm deep.

$115 - $135 **J. R. & S.G. Isaac-Cole, NSW**

Keyper's toy lady bird, c1980.

$20 - $30 **The Toy Collector, SA**

Keyper's toy rabbit, c1980.

$20 - $30 **The Toy Collector, SA**

Tin toy cash register, made by Boomaroo toys, Australia, 19cm high, 17cm wide.

$275 - $315 **Colonial Antiques & Tea House, WA**

'Sing A Song Of Sixpence Humming Top' made by Chad Vallet, England, c1950, 26cm high, 18cm diam.

$40 - $50 **Colonial Antiques & Tea House, WA**

Keyper's toy snail.

$20 - $30 **The Toy Collector, SA**

Boxed children's 'Microscope Lab', Japan, c1980, 30cm high.

$20 - $30 **The Mill Markets, VIC**

Unopened set of 'Barbie' Viewmaster slides, c1980, 10cm high, 10cm wide.

$20 - $30

Chapel Street Bazaar, VIC

Black and white Bakelite Viewmaster, United States, c1950, 10cm high, 11cm long.

$110 - $130

Chapel Street Bazaar, VIC

Boxed rubber squeaky cat toy by Netta, Australia, c1960, 23cm high, 21cm wide.

$65 - $85

Chapel Street Bazaar, VIC

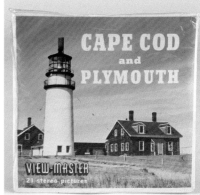

Viewmaster slides, 'Cape Cod and Plymouth', Australia, 10cm high, 10cm wide.

$7 - $17

Chapel Street Bazaar, VIC

Shoe shine bear, Japan, c1960, 25cm high.

$185 - $205

Jan James, NSW

Monkey squeeze toy, England, c1960, 25cm high.

$80 - $100

Tarlo & Graham, VIC

Child's wooden carpentry set in a case with six tools, Poland, c1950, 18cm wide, 25cm long.

$75 - $95

Bob & Dot's Antiques & Old Wares, NSW

Detailed cardboard model of the 'Imperial Hotel', Australia, c1950, 36cm high, 38cm wide, 38cm long.

$1100 - $1300

Antique Curiosity Shop, QLD

'Little Joiner' child's woodwork set, England, c1950, 20cm high, 33cm wide, 10cm deep.

$95 - $115

Antiques & More At 24, SA

Decorated coolamon from northern western Australia, label attached, artist Bob Bindurri, Australia, 18cm wide, 43cm long.

$500 - $600 **Budawang Tribal Art, ACT**

Boab nut, decoratedby a north western Australian aboriginal and depicting a dingo in the landscape, 9cm wide, 24cm long.

$70 - $90 **Budawang Tribal Art, ACT**

Andamooka rock sculpture signed by Milda Dobrota, with naive painting amongst opal imbedded in the rock in spectacular coloursof milky opal, blue, mauve and translucent green, Australia, c1994, 35cm high.

$2400 - $2600 **Seagull Antiques, VIC**

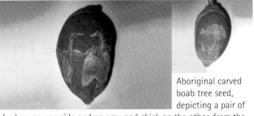

Aboriginal carved boab tree seed, depicting a pair of brolgas on one side and an emu and chick on the other, from the Kimberly area of North West Australia, c1950, 18cm long, 9cm diam.

$185 - $205 **Mockingbird Lane Antiques, NSW**

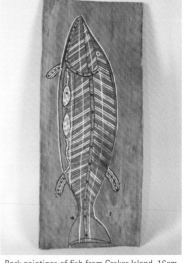

Bark paintings of fish from Croker Island, 16cm wide, 38cm long.

$375 - $415 **Budawang Tribal Art, ACT**

'Soakage water of Kirrimalunya', painted in 2005 with synthetic polymer on linen by George Ward Tjungurayi (1945-). Region: central Australia, country: north of Kiwurrkura, Western Australia, language: Pintubi. This painting shows the claypans of the water soakage area of Kirrimalunya in the country of the artist's father, to the north of Kiwurrkura. There was water in this area and it was used by the Tingari men as they travelled through the area, headed to Kaakuratinja (Lake McDonald) where Tingari rituals were held. The lines in the painting are the sand dunes and the shaped areas are water soakages. From Kintore and surrounding areas, Kiwirrkura, Lake Mackay, Karkun, WalaWala, Kilpiny, he started painting in 1976. He is married to Nangawarra Ward and they now live in WA at Warakuna. He paints stores about Tingari, Kuniya at Karrilwarra. He was awarded the Wynne Prize 2004, AGNSW, Australia, 18.3cm high, 31.2cm wide.

$63000 - $68000 **Lauraine Diggins Fine Art, VIC**

Original watercolour by Maurice Namatjira, Hermannsburg School, Australia, c1960, 43.5cm high, 61cm wide.

$1900 - $2100 **Etching House, NSW**

Keith Namatjira, son of Albert Namatjira, watercolour on paper signed lower left frame, matted and under glass, Australia, c1960, 24cm high, 35cm wide.

$940 - $1040 **Lucilles Interesting Collectables, NSW**

'Wing-Viga Country' painted in 1989 with ochre and binder on canvas by Rover Thomas (1926-1998). Region East Kimberley, Western Australia. Community: Warmun (Turkey Creek). Language: Kukatja/Wangajungka. This painting is, at its surface level, a topographical view of a specific landscape. In the characteristic colour coding devised by Thomas to contrast different features, the flow and outlines of the landscape are captured in their elemental parts and reduced to a series of sparse, colour volumes, Australia, 100cm high, 80cm wide.

$98000 - $103000 **Lauraine Diggins Fine Art, VIC**

Aboriginal bark, finely detailed cross hatching with food motifs on this bark painting from the Northern Territory, Australia, c1970, 95cm high, 42cm wide.

$540 - $640 **The New Farm Antique Centre, QLD**

Hardwood boomerang with traditional engraving, Australia, c1950, 7cm wide, 22.5cm long.

$110 - $130   **Antiques, Goods & Chattels, VIC**

Central Australian mulga wood boomerang with a red pigmented surface, c1960, 77cm long.

$110 - $130   **Rose Cottage Antiques, ACT**

Central desert decorated boomerang, collected in Alice Springs 1973, Australia, 7cm wide, 80cm long.

$330 - $370   **Budawang Tribal Art, ACT**

Male figure with a tail, in natural white and ochre paint, from the Sepik River province, New Guinea, 86cm high.

$245 - $285   **Karlia Rose Garden Antiques & Collectables, VIC**

Navajo Indian silver natural turquoise cuff, United States, c1960, 8cm high.

$330 - $370   **Rose Cottage Antiques, ACT**

Carved hardwood mask, decorated with ochre, from the coastal/lower Sepik River, New Guinea, c1970, 46cm long.

$110 - $130   **Rose Cottage Antiques, ACT**

Carved hardwood mask, decorated with pigments, from the lower Sepik River, New Guinea, c1970, 52.5cm long.

$85 - $105   **Rose Cottage Antiques, ACT**

Female figure with white and ochre paint and a red glass skirt, from the Sepik River province, New Guinea, 98cm high.

$245 - $285   **Karlia Rose Garden Antiques & Collectables, VIC**

Carved wooden tribal mask, New Guinea, c1960, 70cm high.

$200 - $240   **Tarlo & Graham, VIC**

Lifelike matching carved heads, male and female, New Guinea, 50cm high, 20cm wide.

NZ$750 - $850   **Colonial Antiques, New Zealand**

CONTRIBUTING DEALER'S INDEX

ACT

B'artchi
The Burley Griffin Antique Centre
Cnr Mundaring & Wentworth Ave
Kingston ACT 2604
T: 02 6293 2507
M: 0411 481 394
E: sales@work.netspeed.com.au

Budawang Tribal Art
The Burley Griffin Antique Centre
Crn Mundaring & Wentworth Ave
Kingston ACT 2604
T: 02 6293 2507
M: 0411 481 394
E: budawang@lightningpl.net.au

Cabinet of Discoveries
By Appointment, ACT
T: 02 6247 6337
E: info@oldmapsandprints.com

Canberra Antiques Centre
37 Townsville St
Fyshwick ACT 2669
T: 02 6262 3737
F: 02 6292 3170
E: ellavale@webone.com.au

Canberra Cards & Collectables
25 Centaurus St
Giralang ACT 2617
M: 0421 083 884

Fyshwick Antique Centre
84 Gladstone Street, Fyshwick ACT 2609
T: 02 6280 4541
F: 02 6239 1025
M: 0422 641 332
E: facantiques@optusnet.com.au

Nana's Pearls
Canberra Antiques Centre
37 Townsville St
Fyshwick ACT 2669
T: 02 6251 8008
F: 02 6251 8008
M: 0419 616 689
E: denisebird@bigblue.net.au

Needlewitch
Canberra Antiques Centre
37 Townsville Street
Fyshwick ACT 2609
T: 02 6162 3737
F: 02 6292 3170
M: 0414 453 825
E: needlewitch@ihug.com.au
http://stores.ebay.com.au/needlewitch

OK WOW
Shop 1, Canberra Antiques Centre
37 Townsville Street
Fyshwick ACT 2609
M: 0402 078 683

Out of the Ark
Canberra Antique Centre
37 Townsville Street
Fyshwick ACT 2609
T: 02 6292 1535
M: 0407 159 873
E: brucedan@bigpond.net.au

Ritzy Bits - ACT
PO Box 7099
Kaleen ACT 2617
T: 02 6241 3908
F: 02 6253 8429
M: 0418 623 007
E: ritzybits@homemail.com.au

Rose Cottage Antiques
Burley Griffin Antiques Centre
Cnr Wentworth and Mundarring Drives,
Kingston ACT 2604
T: 02 6293 2507
M: 0411 481 394
E: budwang@lightingpl.net.au

Selkirk Antiques & Restorations
29 Summerland Circuit
Kambah ACT 2902
T: 02 6231 5244
F: 02 6231 3656
M: 0418 631 445
E: selkant@iimetro.com.au

The Burley Griffin Antique Centre
Cnr Mundaring & Wentworth Ave
Kingston ACT 2604
T: 02 6293 2507

The Hall Attic
6 Victoria Street, Hall ACT 2618
T: 02 6230 9377
M: 0418 162 830

Upwell Antiques
Canberra Antiques Centre
37 Townsville St
Fyshwick ACT 2609
T: 02 6232 6255
F: 02 6232 6256
E: upwell.antiques@bigpond.com

Vintage Living
Unit 3/6 Weedon Close
Belconnen ACT 2617
T: 02 6253 2105
M: 0412 160 166
E: rosemac@homemail.com.au

NSW

506070
308 Trafalgar Street
Annandale NSW 2038
T: 02 9566 1430
M: 0413 764 101
E: mike@506070.com.au
www.506070.com.au

Abbott's Antiques
1/14 Eastern Rd
Turramurra NSW 2074
T: 02 9449 8889
F: 02 9144 1691
E: antiques@tech2u.com.au
www.abbottsantiques.com.au

Accent on Gifts
Shop 16 Crowne Plaza
Terrigal NSW 2260
T: 02 4385 1997
E: adecarne@bigpond.net.au

Alan McRae
By Appointment, NSW
T: 02 6332 1622
F: 02 6332 4430
E: amcrae@isp.com.au

Alan's Collectables
Shop 3, William Street Plaza
Gosford NSW 2250
T: 02 4324 6884
F: 02 4324 6884
M: 0408 546 073
E: alatique@bigpond.net.au

Antiquariat Fine Books
The Penders
Wingecarribee Street
Bowral NSW 2576
T: 02 4861 2199
F: 02 4861 2899
E: books@antiquariat.com.au
www.antiquariat.com.au

Antique General Store
Cnr Powderworks & Warraba Roads
North Narrabeen NSW 2101
T: 02 9913 7636
M: 0410 531 108

Antiques & Collectables – Hamilton
60 Beaumont Street
Hamilton NSW 2303
T: 02 4969 3003

Antiques On Consignment
117 Old Hume Hwy
Braemar NSW 2575
T: 02 4872 2844
F: 02 4872 3592
M: 0416 251 946
E: lydie@antiquesonconsignment.com.au
www.antiquesonconsignment.com.au

Architectural Décor Australia
812-820 Parramatta Road
Lewisham NSW 2049
T: 02 9560 2211
F: 02 9560 1311
M: 0419 417 721
E: tonyhealy@pacific.net.au
www.architecturaldecor.com.au

Auld & Grey 20th Century Antiques
Shop 12, The Centenary Centre
29 Centenary Road
Newcastle NSW 2300
T: 02 4926 4547
M: 0402 087 571

Austiques Antiques & Collectables
Shop 26, Antique Department Store
62 Parramatta Road
Glebe NSW 2037
T: 02 9692 8611
M: 0412 245 715
E: julie@austiques.com.au
www.austiques.com.au

Australian Antiquarian Book Centre
119 York Street
Sydney NSW 2000
T: 02 9261 1123
E: sales@aabc.com.au
www.aabc.com.au

Avoca Beach Antiques
173-175 Avoca Drive
Avoca Beach NSW 2251
T: 02 4381 0288
F: 02 4382 1149

Barry McKay
By Appointment, NSW
T: 02 9522 9239

Bob & Dot's Antiques & Old Wares
394 George St
Windsor NSW 2756
T: 02 4577 4055

Bowhows
PO Box 7332
Bondi Beach NSW 2026
M: 0433 556 440

Brae-mar Antiques
Shop 50, Southern Antique Centre
243-245 Princess Highway
Kogarah NSW 2217
T: 9553 7843
M: 0408 610 112

Bygone Beautys
20-22 Grose Street
Leura NSW 2780
T: 02 4784 3117
F: 02 4784 3078
M: 0412 478 431
E: info@bygonebeautys.com.au
www.bygonebeautys.com.au

Camperdown Mews
212-220 Parramatta Road
Camperdown NSW 2050
T: 02 9550 554
F: 02 9550 4990
E: themews@webmail.com.au

Celamation
5 Stapleton Street
Unanderra NSW 2526
T: 02 4271 3207
M: 0434 901 080
E: celamation@yahoo.com.au
http://au.geocities.com/celamation

Centuries Past
Sydney Antique Centre
531 South Dowling Street
Surry Hills NSW 2010
T: 02 9528 6161
M: 0419 219 236
E: kstratton@bigpond.net.au
www.centuriespast.com.au

Chilton's Antiques & Jewellery
579 The Kingsway
Miranda NSW 2228
T: 02 9524 0360
F: 02 9525 6625
M: 0416 082 278
E: chiltonsmiranda@bigpond.com.au

Christine McKenna
By Appointment, NSW
T: 02 9632 7878
E: c_mckenna50@hotmail.com

Claringbold's Fine Jewellery, Antiques & Gifts
117 Queen Street
Berry NSW 2535
T: 02 4464 2440
F: 02 4464 2512
M: 0418 642 448
E: ourjohnny@hotmail.com

Classic Vintage
Mittagong Antiques Centre
85-87 Main Street
Mittagong NSW 2575
T: 02 4872 3198
F: 02 4872 3216
M: 0411 851 298
E: mittagongantiques@bigpond.com

Classic Vintage
Shop 32 Mittagong Antiques Centre
85-87 Main Street
Mittagong NSW 2575
T: 02 4872 3198
F: 02 4872 3216
M: 0411 851 298
E: mittagongantiques@bigpond.com

Cobweb Collectables
'Cobwebs'
161 Great Western Highway
Mount Victoria NSW 2786
T: 02 4787 1212
E: alexis@hermes.net.au

Coliseum Antiques Centre
118 Maitland Road
Mayfield NSW 2304
T: 02 4967 2088
F: 02 4967 2428
E: coliseum@iinet.net.au
www.antiques-art.com.au

Collector's Cottage
Shop 7, The Centenary Centre
29 Centenary Road
Newcastle NSW 2300
T: 02 4926 4547

Dannykay Antiques
2/26 Bent Street
St Marys NSW 2760
T: 02 9673 6536
F: 02 9864 1039
E: kaydanny@optusnet.com.au

Doug Up On Bourke
901 Bourke Street
Waterloo NSW 2017
T: 02 9690 0962
F: 02 9690 0962
M: 0425 237 391

East West Collectables
Shop 85, Sydney Antique Centre
531 South Dowling Street
Surry Hills NSW 2010
T: 02 9361 3244
M: 0417 654 873

Eliza Jane Antiques
34c Taylor Street
Annandale NSW 2038
T: 02 9518 6168
M: 0416 167 151

Etching House
Shop 22, Sydney Antique Centre
531 South Dowling Street
Surry Hills NSW 2010
M: 0413 007 054
E: rolf@etchinghouse.com.au
www.etchinghouse.com.au

Galeria del Centro
78 Pudman Street
Boorowa NSW 2586
T: 02 6385 1109
E: glcent@yol.net.au

Gallery Narcisse
By Appointment, NSW
T: 0410 963 411
M: 0419 220 056
E: narcisse@fl.net.au

Gallery Savah
20 Glenmore Road
Paddington NSW 2021
T: 02 9360 9979
F: 02 9331 6993
E: savah@savah.com.au
www.savah.com.au

Global Transport Collectables Pty/Ltd
By Appointment, NSW
M: 0414 513 903
E: info@gtrans.com.au

Grafton Galleries
1/15 Boundary Street
Rushcutters Bay NSW 2011
T: 02 9361 3567
M: 0417 200 441
E: grafton_galleries@bigpond.com

Green Gables Collectables
Shop 3/124 Station Street
Blackheath NSW 2785
T: 02 9997 2879

Gumleaf Antiques
Shop 10, The Centenary Centre
29 Centenary Road
Newcastle NSW 2300
T: 02 4926 454/

Gumnut Antiques & Old Wares
296 The Entrance Road
Long Jetty NSW 2261
T: 02 4334 4444
F: 02 4334 4444
M: 0428 257 725
E: gumnutantiques@westnet.com.au

Habitat Antiques
101 Newcastle Rd
(New England Hwy)
East Maitland NSW 2323
T: 02 4934 3434
M: 0401 311 323

Heartland Antiques & Art
321 High Street
Maitland NSW 2320
T: 02 4933 9923
M: 0414 012 608

Home Again
121 Midson Road
Epping NSW 2121
T: 02 9876 3322
www.homeagain.com.au

Hunters & Collectors Antiques
681 Military Road
Mosman NSW 2088
T: 02 9968 3099
M: 0414 449 366
E: hacantiques@optusnet.com.au
www.huntersandcollectorsantiques.com

InPlace Antiques & Homewares
Shop 23, Sydney Antique Centre
531 South Dowling St
Surry Hills NSW 2010
F: 9345 0321
M: 0419 490 785
E: inplaceantiques@optusnet.com.au

Isadora's Antiques
Shop2/53a Manning Street
Taree NSW 2430
T: 02 6551 8333
F: 02 6551 8433
M: 0416 078 737
E: isadoras@bigpond.net.au

Island & Continent Coins & Stamps
PO Box 151
Belfield NSW 2191
M: 0413 319 150
E: avella@aapt.net.au

J. R. & S.G. Isaac-Cole
106 Manns Road
Narara NSW 2250
T: 02 4324 7287
E: james_workshop@bigpond.com

Jamberoo Antiques
10 Allowrie Street
Jamberoo NSW 2533
T: 02 4236 0865
M: 0417 436 223
E: jamberooantiques@ozemail.com.au
www.jamberooantiques.com.au

Jan James
Shop 215 Sydney Antique Centre
531 Sth Dowling St
Surry Hills NSW 2010
M: 0414 800 332

Janda Antiques
Southern Antique Centre
243-245 Princess Highway
Kogarah NSW 2517
T: 02 9553 7843

Josef Lebovic Gallery
34 Paddington Street
(Cnr Cascade Street)
Paddington NSW 2021
T: 02 9332 1840
F: 02 9331 7431
M: 0411 755 887
E: josef@joseflebovicgallery.com
www.joseflebovicgallery.com

Julie Sandry
By Appointment, NSW
M: 0418 484 608

Kollectik Pty Ltd
152 Falcon Street
Crows Nest NSW 2065
T: 02 9954 5345
M: 0402 577 272
E: kollectik@iinet.net.au

L.A. Design
26 Queen St
Woollahra NSW 2025
T: 02 9326 2888
F: 9326 2554
M: 0418 265 876
E: ladecdesigns@yahoo.com.au

Lesley's Treasures
Shop 3, The Centenary Centre
29 Centenary Road
Newcastle NSW 2300
T: 02 4926 4547
M: 0411 426 498

Love Vintage
By Appointment, NSW
T: 02 6628 6688
E: janel@lovevintage.com.au
www.lovevintage.com.au

Lucilles Interesting Collectables
22 Kable Street, Windsor NSW 2756
T: 02 4577 2797
M: 0404 882 518
E: dpe97417@bigpond.net.au
www.lucillesinterestingcollectables.com

Manfred Schoen
By Appointment, NSW
T: 02 9754 1647
M: 0429 002 900

Marge's Antiques & Collectables
Philip Cross Antiques
548 Old Northern Road
Dural NSW 2158
T: 02 9452 5084
M: 0411 881 714

Margo Richards Antiques
Shop 27 Nurses Walk
The Rocks NSW 2000
T: 02 9252 2855
F: 02 9660 0401

Mark's Book Barn
Unit 37/17-21 Henderson Street
Turrella NSW 2205
T: 02 9558 1829
M: 0417 065 089

Master Clockmakers
Rear - 31 Mitchell Street
Camden NSW 2570
T: 02 4655 8361
F: 02 4655 6628
M: 0416 288 445
E: amarkeri@bigpond.net.au

Max Rout
By Appointment, NSW
M: 0409 769 210

McLeod's Antiques
378 South Dowling Street
Paddington NSW 2021
T: 02 9361 0602
M: 02 9488 9414 (AH)

Mittagong Antiques Centre
85-87 Main Street
Mittagong NSW 2575
T: 02 4872 3198
F: 02 4872 3216
E: mittagongantiques@bigpond.com

Mockingbird Lane Antiques
12 Bate Street, Central Tilba NSW 2546
T: 02 4473 7226
F: 02 4473 7226
E: mockingbirdlane@bigpond.com
www.tilba.com.au

model-cars.com.au
Suite 132/243 Pyrmont Street
Pyrmont NSW 2009
T: 02 9571 6522
M: 0418 226 155
E: sumotee@yahoo.com.au

Modelcraft Miniatures
105 Chelmsford Street
Newtown NSW 2042
T: 02 9516 5921
M: 02 8504 1580
E: anthonywhanna@hotmail.com

Monetarium
111 Princes Highway
Kogarah NSW 2217
T: 02 9588 7111
F: 02 9588 6111
E: info@monetarium.com.au
www.monetarium.com.au

Morrison Antiques & Collectables
55 Carey Street
Tumut NSW 2720
T: 02 6947 1246
M: 0408 965 336
E: ronmorrison@yahoo.com

Myriad Art
Shop 44 Antiques & Collectables - Hamilton NSW
60 Beaumont Street
Hamilton NSW 2303
T: 02 4969 3003

Nicki's Collection
By Appointment, NSW
T: 02 9319 0181
M: 0403 551 360

Northumberland Antiques & Restorations
271 (Lot 88) Scenic Highway
Terrigal NSW 2260
T: 02 4384 6464
F: 02 4384 6464
M: 0417 232 893
E: info@ccantiques.com.au
www.ccantiques.com.au

Obsidian Antiques
Shop11, The Antique Department Store
62 Parramatta Road
Glebe NSW 2037
T: 02 9692 8611

Old Bank Corner Collectables
117 Albury Street (Hume Highway)
Holbrook NSW 2644
T: 02 6036 2560
F: 02 6036 2560
M: 0429 190 848
E: obcc@bigpond.net.au

Old World Antiques (NSW)
57 Evan Street
Sans Souci NSW 2219
T: 02 9529 7782

P. & N. Johnson
Shop 75, Southern Antique Centre
245 Princess Highway
Kogarah NSW 2212
T: 02 4625 7383

Parramatta Antique Centre
78 Pitt St
Parramatta NSW 2150
T: 02 9633 3426
M: 0412 400 611

Pastimes Antiques
Camperdown Mews
212 Parramatta Road
Camperdown NSW 2050
T: 02 9550 5554
M: 0408 210 905
E: barbil@ozemail.com.au
www.antique-art.com.au

Patinations
Shop 13, The Centenary Centre
29 Centenary Rd
Newcastle NSW 2300
T: 02 4926 4547
E: centenaryantiques@hunterlink.net.au
www.centenarycentre.com.au

Patrick Colwell
Shop 80, Sydney Antique Centre
531 South Dowling Street
Surry Hills NSW 2010
T: 9361 3244
F: 9332 2691
M: 0429 002 225

Philip Cross Antiques
548 Old Northern Road
Round Corner Dural NSW 2158
T: 02 9651 4138
M: 0411 881 714
E: pcrossantiques@optusnet.com.au

Phoenix Persian Gallery
St Ives Shopping Village
Shop 48, Memorial Level
St Ives NSW 2073
T: 02 9449 7222
F: 02 9450 1480
M: 0419 010 412
E: bryanstoneham@hotmail.com

Pitt Trading
274 Rocky Point Road
Ramsgate NSW 2217
T: 02 9529 3038
F: 02 9583 1066
E: info@pitt-trading.com.au
www.pitt-trading.com.au

Pittwater Philatelic Service
Shop 18/331-335 Barrenjoey Rd
Newport NSW 2106
T: 02 9979 1561
F: 02 9979 1577
M: 0412 904 295
E: pittwaterstamps@ozemail.com.au
www.ozemail.com.au/~pittwaterstamps/

Pymble Antiques - Linen & Retro
1003 Pacific Highway
Pymble NSW 2073
T: 02 9983 1340

Qian Long Antiques
Shop 88, Sydney Antique Centre
531 South Dowling Street
Surry Hills NSW 2010
T: 9380 8889
F: 9591 7278
M: 0416 088 933
E: qian_long_antiques@yahoo.com.au

Reflections Antiques
Shop 79, Sydney Antique Centre
531 South Dowling Street
Surry Hills NSW 2010
T: 02 9360 6628
M: 0418 827 779

Retro Antiques
Sydney Antique Centre
531 South Dowling Street
Surry Hills NSW 2010
T: 02 9664 2427
M: 0410 445 717
E: phil@retroantiques.com.au
www.retroantiques.com.au

River Emporium
81 River Street/Pacific Hwy
Woodburn NSW 2472
T: 02 6682 2255
F: 02 6682 2255
M: 0412 394 315
E: riveremporium@optusnet.com.au

Rosebud Antiques
By Appointment, NSW
T: 02 9223 2222
M: 0403 075 793
E: marie@jackmanconsulting.com

Serendipity Antiques - Newcastle
The Centenary Centre
29 Centenary Rd
Newcastle NSW 2300
T: 02 4952 6310
M: 0408 611 266

Settlers Store Antiques
131 Mortimer Street
Mudgee NSW 2850
T: 02 6372 3612
F: 02 6372 3513
M: 0412 672 913
E: antiques@settlersstore.com.au
www.settlersstore.com.au

Sew Yesterday
By Appointment, NSW
T: 02 4754 5395
E: liz@optusnet.net.com

Shaws Antiques
649 Boxers Creek Road
Goulburn NSW 2580
T: 02 4829 8100
F: 02 4829 8100
E: antiques@goulburn.net.au

Sherrill Grainger
Shop 9, Antiques & Collectables - Hamilton
60 Beaumont Street
Hamilton NSW 2303
T: 02 4984 2476
M: 0438 088 319
E: gringojg@virtual.net.au

Showcase Antiques
By Appointment, NSW
T: 02 9328 9545
M: 0401 976 741
awblinco@bigpond.com.au

Southern Antique Centre
243-245 Princes Highway
Kogarah NSW 2217
T: 02 9553 7843
F: 02 9553 7845
M: 0410 436 933
E: southernantiques@bigpond.com
www.southernantiques.com.au

Sweet Slumber Antiques & Collectables
76 Belgrave Street
Kempsey NSW 2440
T: 6562 1196

Sydney Antique Centre
531 South Dowling Street
Surry Hills NSW 2010
T: 02 9361 3244
F: 02 9332 2691
www.sydneyantcent.com.au

Terrace Collectables
26 Collins Street
Kiama NSW 2533
T: 02 4232 1147
M: 0409 898 474

The Bizarre Bazaar
14 Scarba Street
Coffs Harbour NSW 2450
T: 6651 1202

The Glass Stopper
59 The Kingsway
Kingsgrove NSW 2208
T: 02 9150 8305
F: 02 9150 0666
M: 0407 922 291
E: glassstopper@bigpond.com.au

The Antique Department Store
62 Parramatta Road
Glebe NSW 2307
T: 02 9692 8611

The Centenary Centre
29 Centenary Road
Newcastle NSW 2300
T: 02 4389 1922

The Nostalgia Factory
2/162 Moss Vale Road
Kangaroo Valley NSW 2577
T: 02 4465 1022
F: 02 4465 1233
M: 0413 084 605
E: nostalgiafactory@bigpond.com
0414 425 445

The Old Lolly Factory
144 Parry Street
Newcastle West NSW 2302
T: 02 4969 1649
F: 02 4959 2666
E: ajandaj@hunterlink.net.au

Thompsons Country Collectables
11 New Street (Rear 265 George St)
Windsor NSW 2756
T: 02 4577 2381
E: dandyprat@hotmail.com

Towers Antiques & Collectables
539 King Street
South Newtown NSW 2042
T: 02 9519 6574
F: 02 9799 4691
M: 0432 069 809
E: towersantiques@optusnet.com.au
www.towersantiques.com.au

Treats & Treasures
114 Cowabbie Street
Coolamon NSW 2701
T: 02 6927 3422
M: 0428 694 448
E: grahame@treatsandtreasures.com.au
www.treatsandtreasures.com.au

Trevor Wilkin Banknotes
PO Box 182
Cammeray NSW 2062
T: 02 9438 5040
F: 02 9438 5040
E: trevorsnotes@bigpond.com
www.polymernotes.com

True Blue Antiques
Shop 3, Southern Antique Centre
245 Princes Hwy
Kogarah NSW 2217
T: 02 4228 7059
F: 02 4272 7055
M: 0407 418 128
E: marj-goodwin@bigpond.com

Twice Around
Rear 107 Glenroi Avenue
Orange NSW 2800
T: 02 6362 0322
F: 02 9361 3570
M: 0416 277 490
E: info@twicearound.com.au
www.twicearound.com.au

Vampt
268 Cleveland Street
Surry Hills NSW 2010
T: 02 9699 1089
F: 02 9699 1856
M: 0414 806 549
E: info@vamptretrondeco.com
www.vamptretrondeco.com

Victor Harbour Antiques - Mittagong
Mittagong Antique Centre
Shop 68, 85-87 Main St
Mittagong NSW 2575
T: 02 7872 3198
F: 02 4872 3216
E: mittagongantiques@bigpond.com

Vintage Replacement Parts
80 Frances Street
Lidcombe NSW 2141
M: 0404 106 100

Vintage Times
Shop 32, Sydney Antique Centre
531 South Dowling Street
Surry Hills NSW 2010
M: 0413 703 780
www.vintagetimes.com.au

Wenlen Antiques
Shop 13 Antique Department Store
62 Parramatta Road
Glebe NSW 2037
T: 02 9692 8611
M: 0413 021 270
E: wenlen@optusnet.com.au

Whimsical Notions
293 Great Western Highway
Warrimoo NSW 2774
T: 02 4753 7700
F: 02 4753 7700
M: 0411 332 537
E: whimsical1@bigpond.com.au
www.local.com.au/whimsical

Woollahra Decorative Arts Gallery
228 Oxford St
Bondi Junction NSW 2022
T: 02 9389 8388
F: 02 9389 8399
M: 0414 338 363
E: amathest@ihug.com.au
www.nouveaudeco.com.au

Woollahra Times Art Gallery
2 Moncur Street
Woollahra NSW 2025
T: 02 9363 5616
F: 02 9363 2080
E: fellia@felliamelas-timesart.com
www.felliamelas-timesart.com

QUEENSLAND

Adornments
141 Latrobe Terrace
Paddington QLD 4064
T: 07 3369 2033
F: 07 3369 7839
M: 0412 527 159

Angel Cottage
127 Long Road (Gallery Walk)
Eagle Heights
Tamborine Mountain QLD 4271
T: 07 5545 0322
F: 07 5545 0322
M: 0414 732 000
E: angelajbowen@bigpond.com

Antipodes Antiques
Shop 9, Paddington Antique Centre
167 Latrobe Terrace
Paddington QLD 4064
T: 07 3369 1863
F: 07 3368 1502
M: 0412 451 369
E: antipodesa@optushome.com.au

Antique Curiosity Shop
5 Musgrave Street
North Rockhampton QLD 4701
T: 07 4922 3288
F: 07 4922 3288
M: 0407 692 946
E: houseofpenny@cqnet.com.au

Antiques at Redbank
34 Brisbane Road
Redbank QLD 4301
T: 07 3288 1711
M: 0400 140 652
E: antsred@bigpond.net.au

Atomic Boom
128 Days Rd
Grange QLD 4051
T: 07 3856 3229
M: 0423 173 484
E: atomic.boom@ozemail.com.au
http://stores.ebay.com.au/atomic-boom

Baxter's Antiques
2 Lombank Street
Archerfield QLD 4108
T: 07 3216 6146
M: 0418 192 188
E: feona@baxtesantiques.com.au
www.baxtersantiques.com.au

Bob Butler's Sentimental Journey
5 Michel St
Lowood QLD 4311
T: 07 5426 3399
F: 07 5426 3399
M: 0407 579 804

Bower Bird Art & Antiques
PO Box 230
Mt Molloy QLD 4871
T: 07 4094 2006

Brisbane Antiques Pty Ltd
23 Crosby Road
Albion QLD 4010
T: 07 3262 1444
F: 07 3262 1994
M: 0410 012 440
E: graham@brisbaneantiques.com.au
www.brisbaneantiques.com.au

Brisbane Vintage Watches
Brisbane Arcade
Shop 20-21 Gallery Level
160 Queen Street
Brisbane QLD 4000
T: 07 3210 6722
F: 07 3210 6766
M: 0407 676 838
E: sales@brisbanevintagewatches.com
www.brisbanevintagewatches.com

Chelsea Antiques & Decorative Art Centre P/L
20 Hudson Road
Albion QLD 4010
T: 07 3862 1768
F: 07 3862 1748
M: 0417 630 706
E: chelseaantiques@bigpond.com

Collectable Creations
339 Ruthven Street
Toowoomba QLD 4350
T: 07 4632 0546

Collector's Corner
540 Logan Road
Greenslopes QLD 4120
T: 07 3397 2947
F: 07 3397 7845
E: rmuller1@bigpond.net.au
www.collectorscornerantiques.com.au

Colonial Collectables
9 Logan Road
Woolloongabba QLD 4102
T: 07 3855 2490
M: 0431 403 897
E: colonialcollectables@msn.com

Discovery Corner
812 Sandgate Road
Clayfield QLD 4011
T: 07 3862 2155
F: 07 3862 1344
M: 0402 339 643

Eilisha's Shoppe
109 James Street
New Farm QLD 4005
T: 07 3358 1448
M: 0423 830 515

Flaxton Barn
445 Flaxton Drive
Flaxton QLD 4560
T: 07 5445 7321
F: 07 5445 7866

George Magasic Antiques & Collectables
Shop 3, Noosa Cinema Centre
29 Sunshine Beach Rd
Noosa Junction QLD 4567
T: 07 5447 4519
F: 07 5447 4519
M: 0408 690 771

H.O.W Gifts & Collectables
95 The Esplanade
Mooloolaba QLD 4557
T: 07 5478 3200
F: 07 5478 3233
M: 0414 240 624
E: howgifts@bigpond.net.au

Helen's On The Bay
By Appointment, QLD
T: 07 5529 4225
M: 0416 085 287
E: helensridge@optusnet.com.au

Journey to the Past Antiques & Collectables
490 Ruthven Street
Toowoomba QLD 4350
T: 07 4638 1199
F: AH 07 4635 0336
M: 0418 238 354
E: journeytopast@bigpond.com

Laidley Old Wares
149 Patrick St
Laidley QLD 4341
T: 07 5465 1214
E: laidleyoldwares@bigpond.com

Lancaster's Toowoomba Antique Centre
3 Railway St
Toowoomba QLD 4350
T: 07 4632 1830
M: 0403 372 054

Noeline's Collectables
Sanctuary Cove Antique Gallery
Masthead Way
SANCTUARY COVE QLD 4212
T: 07 5537 4584
F: 07 5537 4587
M: 0412 244 488
E: noeline@hotkey.net.au

Northside Secondhand Furniture
76 Loudon Street
Sandgate QLD 4017
T: 07 3269 3121
F: OR 07 3269 4490
M: 0403 339 618
E: dmwheildon@aol.com

Now & Then Antiques & Collectables
Shop 21 Southside Antique Centre
484 Ipswich Road
Annerley QLD 4103
T: 07 3287 3905
F: 07 3847 1719
M: 0417 745 599

Olsens Antiques
Behind the National Bank
Bundaberg CBD QLD 4670
T: 07 4152 5933
F: 07 4152 5933
M: 0407 556 301
E: pikekathy@hotmail.com

Paddington Antique Centre Pty Ltd
167 Latrobe Terrace
Cnr Collingwood Street
Paddington QLD 4064
T: 07 3369 8088
F: 07 3368 2171
E: info@pac.antiques.net.au
www.pac.antiques.net.au

Palliaer Antiques
770 Ipswich Road
Annerley QLD 4103
T: 07 3892 6993
F: 07 3892 3193
M: 0409 489 297
E: morgansmontage@hotmail.com

Possum's Treasures
25628 New England Hwy
Applethorpe
Via Stanthorpe QLD 4380
T: 07 4683 2223
F: 07 4603 2226

Relic
28a Horan Street
West End QLD 4104
T: 07 3255 2744
M: 0417 726 336
E: glen@relic.com.au
www.relic.com.au

Rockaway Records
249 Waterworks Road
Ashgrove QLD 4060
T: 07 3366 9555
F: 07 3366 9777
E: sales@rockaway.com.au
www.rockaway.com.au

Roger Hose Antiques
37 Logan Road
Woolloongabba QLD 4102
T: 07 3391 0440
F: 07 3391 3566
M: 0418 871 300
E: antiques@gabbavillage.com
www.gabbavillage.com/antiques/

Roundabout Antiques
Old Bank Building
at the Roundabout
Bunya Highway
Wondai QLD 4606
T: 07 4169 0111
F: 07 4168 5882
M: 0417 714 105
E: sales@roundaboutantiques.com.au
www.roundaboutantiques.com.au

Sherwood Bazaar
526 Oxley Road
Sherwood QLD 4075
T: 07 3379 7548
F: 07 3379 7548
M: 0419 737 810
E: sbazaar@ozemail.com.au
www.sherwoodbazaar.com

Southside Antiques Centre
484 Ipswich Road
Annerley QLD 4103
T: 07 3892 1299
M: 0417 702 950
E: ssac100@primusonline.com.au

Sue Ellen Gallery
Shop 133 Marina Mirage
Sea World Drive
Main Beach QLD 4217
T: 07 5532 2282
F: 07 5532 2282
E: enquiries@sueellengallery.com.au
www.sueellengallery.com.au

The Best Antiques & Collectables
Shop 6, City Centre Arcade
142 Bourbong St
Bundaberg QLD 4670
T: 07 4154 1333
F: ABN 91 689 797 708
M: 0414 676 024

The New Farm Antique Centre
85 Commercial Road
Newstead QLD 4006
T: 07 3852 2352
F: 07 3252 9295
M: 0419 786 967
E: newfarmantiques@optusnet.com.au

The Silky Oak Shop
31 Logan Road
Woolloongabba QLD 4102
T: 07 3891 3911
F: 07 3891 3511
M: 0413 657 999
E: lendit@bigpond.net.au
www.thesilkyoakshop.com

The Time Machine
101 Currie St
Nambour QLD 4560
T: 07 5441 2647

Tiffany Dodd Antique & 20th Century Furniture
Shop 31, Paddington Antique Centre
167 La Trobe Terrace
Paddington QLD
T: 07 3876 8117
M: 0414 693 738
www.tiffanydodd.com.au

Titles & Treasures
2/272 Lillian Avenue
Salisbury QLD 4107
T: 07 3216 6995
M: 0407 585 590
E: reilly.john@bigpond.com.au

Toowoomba Antiques Gallery
100 Margaret Street
Toowoomba QLD 4350
T: 07 4639 4989
F: 07 4638 5355
M: 0419 653 434
E: toowoomba.antiques@bigpond.com

Turn O' The Century
377 Oxley Road
Sherwood QLD 4075
T: 07 3379 7311
F: 07 3379 1660
M: 0419 706 875
E: totc@bigpond.net.au

Yande Meannjin Antiques
Shop 13, Paddington Antique Centre
167 Latrobe Terrace
Paddington QLD 4064
T: 07 3886 6037
F: 07 3886 6037
M: 0419 704 714
E: yande@iinet.net.au

SOUTH AUSTRALIA

All In Good Time Antiques
12a High Street
Strathalbyn SA 5255
T: 08 8536 4449
F: 08 8536 4449
M: 0408 832 757
E: aigt@bigpond.net.au

Antiques & More At 24
24 Murray St
Angaston SA 5353
T: 08 8564 2310
F: 8562 4720
M: 0417 847 372
E: am24@bigpond.net.au

Antiques Restorations of Unley
167 Unley Raod
Unley SA 5061
T: 08 8272 5680
F: 08 8272 5680

At The Toss of A Coin
2/219 Unley Road
Malvern SA 5061
T: 08 8373 0170

Atomic Pop
68 Payneham Road
Stepney SA 5069
T: 08 8363 6997
E: atomic-pop@hotmail.com

Bowerbird Antiques & Collectables
32 High Street
Strathalbyn SA 5255
T: 08 8536 3646
M: 0421 360 700

Clarence Park Bazaar
306 Goodwood Rd
Clarence Park SA 5034
T: 08 8271 7155
M: 0413 011 633
E: julie.cpbazaar@optusnet.com.au

Codger's Collectables
By Appointment, SA
M: 0415 999 350

Cool & Collected
161 Magill Road
Stepney SA 5069
T: 08 8362 5196

Danish Vintage Modern
148 Magill Rd
Norwood SA 5067
T: 08 8363 7086
E: info@danishvintagemodern.com
www.danishvintagemodern.com.au

Gaslight Collectables And Old Books
20 Market Square
Burra SA 5417
T: 08 8892 3004
F: 08 8892 3003
E: deeton@bigpond.com

Glenelg Antique Centre
6 Sussex Street
Glenelg SA 5045
T: 08 8376 0450

Half Moon Antiques & Interiors
93 Prospect Road, Prospect SA 5082
T: 08 8342 0777
F: 08 8344 4542
M: 0421 125 777

Kings Park Antiques & Collectables
325a Goodwood Road
Kings Park SA 5034
T: 08 8172 0566
F: 08 8276 2539

Lava Signs
By Appointment, SA
T: 08 8263 7779
F: AH 08 8263 5138

Mac's Collectables
PO Box 52
St Agnes SA 5097
T: 08 8263 7779 (Don)
F: 08 8263 7779
M: 0402 356 010 (Sue)
E: mac151@internode.on.net

Malvern Antique Centre
299 Unley Road
Malvern SA 5061
T: 08 8373 1499
F: 08 8373 1499

McKays Mart
99 Unley Road
Unley SA 5061
T: 08 8271 2477

Mid Century Modern
129 Magill Road
Stepney SA 5069
T: 08 8363 3413
F: 08 8362 1027
M: 0438 837 356
E: pjs@bigpond.net.au
www.midcenturymodern.com.au

Old World Antiques
133 Magill Rd
Stepney SA 5069
T: 08 8362 0166
F: 08 8272 9548
E: eamonp@tpg.com.au

Pedlars Antique Market
205 Magill Road
Maylands SA 5069
T: 08 8363 0087
F: 08 8363 0087
E: pedlars@bigpond.net.au

Pendulum Antiques
Mannum Road
Inglewood SA 5133
T: 08 8380 5414
F: 08 8380 5223
M: 0417 879 868
E: pendulumant@yahoo.com.au

Philicia Antiques & Collectables
317 Goodwood Road
Kings Park SA 5034
T: 08 8357 8177
F: 08 8357 8177
M: 0409 695 234
E: philicia@tpg.com.au
www.philicia.tpg.com.au/home.html

Principal Antiques
34 Margaret Street, Mt Gambier SA 5290
T: 08 8725 4660
F: 08 8725 4660
M: 0409 673 934
E: pfairchild@datafast.net.au
www.principalantiques.com

Rare Old Times Antiques & Collectables
453 Brighton Road
Brighton SA 5048
T: 08 8358 4288
F: 08 8358 4288
E: rareoldtimes@ihug.com.au

Rock N Rustic
187 Magill Road
Maylands SA 5034
T: 08 8363 3446
M: 0408 810 840

Squatters Antiques & Restorations
94 Thomas Street
Murray Bridge SA 5253
T: 08 8532 5087
M: 0418 800 031
E: michelegros@bigpond.com
www.squattersantiques.com

The Gizmo
187a Magill Road
Maylands SA 5069
T: 08 8363 3446
F: 0408 810 840 (P)
M: 0424 640 096 (D)

The House of Oojah
PO Box 48
Highgate SA 5063
T: 08 8276 8538
M: 0418 840 156
E: oojah.capivvy@gmail.com
www.thehouseofoojah.com

The Toy Collector
Ingle Farm Shopping Centre
Cnr Wakleys & Montague Road
Ingle Farm SA 5098
T: 08 8395 4567
F: 08 8395 4567
M: 0411 700 777
E: toys@thetoycollector.com.au
www.thetoycollector.com.au

Willunga Antiques
17 High St
Willunga SA 5172
T: 08 8556 7302
M: 0416 088 556
E: info@willungaantiques.com.au
www.willungaantiques.com.au

Woodside Bazaar
43 Onkaparinga Valley Hwy
Woodside SA 5244
T: 08 8389 7772
M: 0401 854 753
E: acaldhouse@adam.com.au

TASMANIA

Ancanthe Antiques
First Floor 102 Elizabeth Street
Hobart TAS 7000
T: 03 6236 9026
M: 0400 103 316
E: hcollect@bigpond.net.au

Archers Antiques
Sorell Antiques Centre
15 Somerville Street
Sorell TAS 7172
T: 03 6265 2246
F: 03 6265 2246
M: 0417 084 685
E: archersantiques@hotmail.com

Bathurst Street Antique Centre
128 Bathurst Street
Hobart TAS 7000
T: 03 6236 9422
M: 0407 812 423
E: bathurstantiques@iprimus.com.au

Eclectica
1567 Channel Highway
Margate TAS 7054
T: 03 6267 2545
F: 03 6267 2545
M: 0417 361 547

How Bazaar
122 St John Street
Launceston TAS 7250
T: 03 6331 4163
M: 0438 081 233
E: cco94705@bigpond.net.au

Kookaburra Antiques
113 Hampden Road
Battery Point TAS 7004
T: 03 6223 1019

Leven Antiques - Tasmania
23 King Edward Street
Ulverstone TAS 7315
T: 03 6425 5226
F: 03 6425 7316
M: 0419 509 730
E: cbroadfi@iinet.net.au
www.levenantiques.com

Louisa's Antiques
16 Albert Road
Moonah TAS 7009
T: 03 6278 3219
F: 03 6278 3408 AH
M: 0418 345 101

Merry's Jewels & Collectables
The Margate Train
1567 Channel Highway
Margate TAS 7054
T: 03 6227 1138
F: 03 6227 1468
M: 0417 832 551
E: merryjc@bigbond.net.au

Sorrell Antiques Centre
15 Somerville Street
Sorrell TAS 7172
T: 03 6265 2246
F: 03 6265 2246

The Evandale Tinker
10-B Russell Street
Evandale TAS 7212
T: 03 6391 8544 or
F: 03 6391 8192
M: 0419 331 821
E: evandale_tinker@yahoo.com.au
stores.ebay.com.au/evandaletinker

Warwick Oakman Antiques
62 Sandy Bay Road
Battery Point TAS 7004
T: 03 6224 9904
F: 03 6224 9904
M: 0439 990 854
E: woakman@bigpond.com

VICTORIA

369 Antiques
369 Lygon Street
Brunswick VIC 3056
M: 0402 271 836

Abra Card Abra Roycroft
680 High Street
East Kew VIC 3102
T: 03 9859 4215
F: 03 9589 4215

Ace Antiques & Collectables
555 Queensberry Street
North Melbourne VIC 3051
T: 03 9328 1710
M: 0412 883 112
E: aceantiques@bigpond.com

Ainsley Antiques
2120 Ballan Road
Anakie VIC 3221
T: 03 5284 1371
E: ainsleyball@hotmail.com

Alexa's Treasures
46 Sturt St
Ballarat VIC 3350
T: 03 5333 7377
M: 0427 337 378
E: alexastreasures@yahoo.com

Alltime Antiques & Bairnsdale Clocks
704 Princes Highway
Bairnsdale VIC 3875
T: 03 5152 6962
F: 03 5153 0756
E: info@bairnsdaleclocks.com.au
www.bairnsdaleclocks.com.au

Antique Décor
899 High St
Armadale VIC 3143
T: 03 9509 7322
F: 03 9509 6992
M: 0418 312 829
E: gk@mira.net

Antique Effects
108-110 Urquhart Street
Ballarat VIC 3350
T: 03 5331 3119
F: 03 5331 2063
M: 0418 508 011
E: info@antiqueeffects.com.au
www.antiqueeffects.com.au

Antique Revivals
94 Burgundy St
Heidelberg VIC 3081
T: 03 9440 7055
M: 0425 865 387

Antique Toy World
15 Cookson Street
Camberwell VIC 3124
T: 03 9882 9997
M: 0419 513 290

Antiques & Collectables Centre - Ballarat
9 Humffray Street North
Ballarat VIC 3350
T: 03 5331 7996
F: 03 5331 7996

Antiques & Collectables On Moorabool
200 Moorabool St
Geelong VIC 3220
T: 03 5221 3553
F: 03 5221 3320
M: 0408 303 768

Antiques As Well
94 Burgundy St
Heidelberg VIC 3084
T: 03 9458 2556
M: 0402 038 355

Antiques, Goods & Chattels
22-26 Main Road
Ballarat VIC 3350
T: 03 5334 3799
M: 0428 521 714

Armadale Antique Centre
1147 High Street
Armadale VIC 3143
T: 03 9822 7788
F: 03 9822 4499
M: 0412 732 590

Around The Grounds Football Memorabilia
By Appointment, VIC
T: 0412 291 577
M: 0412 792 236
E: sales@atgfootball.com
www.atgfootball.com

b bold - 20th Century Furniture & Effects
187 Elgin Street
Carlton VIC 3053
T: 03 9349 1166
www.antique-art.com.au/b-bold.htm

Barry Sherman Galleries
535 High Street
Prahran, Melbourne VIC 3181
T: 03 9521 5858
F: 03 9521 5858
M: 0418 534 849
E: barrysherman@optusnet.com.au
www.barryshermangalleries.com.au

Beehive Old Wares & Collectables
72 Main Street
Maldon VIC 3463
T: 03 5475 1154
F: AH: 03 5475 1300
M: 0403 316 606
E: bhive@bmail.com.au
www.maldon.com.au

Bill Millar
By Appointment, VIC
T: 03 5243 2783

Born Frugal
420 Church Street
Richmond VIC 3121
T: 03 9428 5889
M: 0409 979 865

Branxholme Mobile Books
By Appointment, VIC
T: 03 5578 6328

Burly Babs Collectables/Retro Relics
53 Humffray Street North
Ballarat VIC 3350
T: 03 5331 6236
F: 0419 586 882
M: 0408 329 131

C. V. Jones Antiques & Art Gallery
14 Armstrong Street North
Ballarat VIC 3350
T: 03 5331 1472 & FX
F: 0417 108 508 Ross
M: 0417 506 981 Craig
E: cvjones@netconnect.com.au
www.cvjones.com.au

Calmar Trading
By Appointment, VIC
T: 03 9435 5187
M: 0412 336 086
E: pruscuklic@labyrinth.net.au

Camberwell Antique Centre
25-29 Cookson Street
Camberwell VIC 3124
T: 03 9882 2028
F: 03 9882 2028
M: 0418 586 764

Capocchi
941-951 High Street
Armadale VIC 3143
T: 03 9822 3700
F: 03 9822 4315
E: info@capocchi.com.au
www.capocchi.com.au

Cardtastic Collectables
449 North Road
Ormond VIC 3204
T: 03 9578 5363
E: cardtastic@cardtastic.com.au
www.cardtastic.com.au

Carnegie Collectables
742 North Road
Ormond VIC 3204
T: 03 9597 9147
F: 03 9578 7225
M: 0402 154 054
E: sportmem@optusnet.com.au

Casey Antiques
Shop 4, The Arcade
48 High Street
Berwick VIC 3806
T: 03 9769 9788
M: 0404 089 231

Castlemaine
71 Forest Street
Castlemaine VIC 3450
T: 03 5470 6968

Catanach's Jewellers Pty. Ltd.
1212 High St
Armadale VIC 3143
T: 03 9509 0311
E: jewels@catanachs.com.au
www.catanachs.com.au

Cat's Cradle Comics
36 Sydney Road
Coburg VIC 3058
T: 03 9386 8885
M: 0425 776 158

Cedar Lodge Antiques
169-175 West Fyans St
Newtown, Geelong VIC 3220
T: 03 5221 3348
F: 03 5221 3348
M: 0418 520 024
E: cedarl@pipeline.com.au
www.pipeline.com.au/users/cedarl

Chapel Street Bazaar
217-233 Chapel Street
Prahran VIC 3181
T: 03 9529 1727
F: 03 9521 3174
M: 03 9510 9841
E: chapbaz@yahoo.com.au

Cherished Memories
95 Albert Street
Creswick VIC 3363
T: 03 5345 1392
F: 03 9379 5879
M: 0400 580 429

Circa Vintage Clothing
Shop 1/102 Gertrude Street
Fitzroy VIC 3065
T: 03 9419 8899
F: 03 9415 6765
E: enquiries@circa-vintage.com
www.circa-vintage.com

Colman Antique Clocks
1421 Malvern Road
Malvern VIC 3144
T: 03 9824 8244
F: 03 9824 4230
M: 0402 084 074
E: michaelcolman@optusnet,.com.au
www.colmanantiqueclocks.biz

Comics R Us
Level 1/220 Bourke Street
Melbourne VIC 3000
T: 03 9663 8666
E: comicsrus@bigpond.com

Curve
158 Gertrude St
Fitzroy VIC 3065
M: 0438 744 009

Debbie Pech
By Appointment, VIC
T: 03 5572 4129
M: 0419 116 988

Decades of Fashion
13 Main Road
Ballarat VIC 3350
T: 03 5332 2222
M: 0401 364 953
www.decadesoffashion.com.au

Decodence Collectables
By Appointment, VIC
M: 0411 141 075

Decorama
PO Box 482
Emerald VIC 3782
T: 03 5968 4531
E: mikesdecorama@yahoo.com.au

Dejanvou Antiques & Bric a Brac
By Appointment, VIC
M: 0421 042 223

Den of Antiquities
25a Bell Street
Yarra Glen VIC 3775
T: 03 9730 2111
F: 03 9730 2111
M: 0413 454 966

Design Dilemas
Shop 5/17 Irwell Street
St Kilda VIC 3181
M: 0425 718 736

Eagle Antiques
'Nandi'
680 Mountt Macedon Road
Mount Macedon VIC 3441
T: 03 5426 1561
F: 03 5426 2462
E: aten@hotkey.net.au
www.eagleantiques.com.au

Eaglemont Antiques and Interiors
67 Silverdale Road
Eaglemont VIC 3084
T: 03 9497 7195
M: 0408 530 259
E: dawnldavis@msn.com.au

Edward VIII Antiques
1519 Frankston / Flinders Road
Tyabb VIC 3913
T: 03 5977 3699

Elizabeth Holloway Prints
5 Glenferrie St
North Caulfield VIC 3161
T: 03 9509 1344
M: 0413 995 663
E: elizhol@netspace.net.au

Fat Helen's
78 Chapel Street
Windsor VIC 3181
T: 03 9510 2244 or
F: 0409 510 224
M: 0419 541 902
E: fathelens@optusnet.com.au
www.fathelens.com

Ferntree Gully Watch & Clock Company
117-119 Station Street
Ferntree Gully VIC 3156
T: 03 9758 7740
www.ftgwatch.com.au

Flashback
79 High Street
Northcote VIC 3070
T: 03 9482 1899
M: 0421 345 322
E: vinfab@alphalink.com.au
www.vintagefabric.com.au

Forever Amber @ The Tyabb Grainstore
Tyabb Grain Store
Opposite Tyabb Railway Station
Mornington Tyabb Road
Tyabb VIC 3913
T: 03 5977 3042
F: 03 5977 3420
M: 0407 141 700
E: tyabbgrainstor@pacific.net.au

Found Objects
Shop 6-7 Irwell Street
St Kilda VIC 3182
M: 0414 855 564

Furniture Revisited
209 Sydney Road
Brunswick VIC 3056
T: 03 9387 1867

Galerie Montmartre
PO Box 392
Clifton Hill VIC 3068
T: 03 9486 8686
F: 03 9486 8687
M: 0439 899 811
E: posters@galmont.com.au
www.galmont.com.au

Gardenvale Collectables
165 Martin Street
Gardenvale VIC 3186
T: 03 9596 0211

Geoffrey Hatty
296-298 Malvern Road
Prahran VIC 3181
T: 03 9510 1277
E: tcd@bigpond.net.au

Go Figure Collectables
Shop 3/116-120 Glenferrie Road
Malvern VIC 3144
T: 03 9576 2213
M: 0416 163 018
E: jeffx@gofigurecollectables.com.au
www.gofigurecollectables.com.au

Gorgeous
85a Chapel Street
Windsor VIC 3181
T: 03 9521 4227
M: 0416 399 403

Graham & Nancy Miller
By Appointment, VIC
T: 03 9578 1975

Granny's Market Pty Ltd
1098 High St
Armadale VIC 3143
T: 03 9509 1314
F: 03 9576 1646
M: 0408 995 867
E: rosies@bluep.com

Great Dane Furniture
116 Commercial Road
Prahran VIC 3181
T: 03 9510 6111
F: 03 570 6222
E: anita@greatdanefurniture.com
www.greatdanefurniture.com

Hamilton Street Antiques
181-183 Sunshine Road
Tottenham VIC 3012
T: 03 9314 9559
F: 03 9314 9559
M: 0407 056 960
E: hamant@ozemail.com.au
www.oddspot.com.au

Heather Bell Antiques
107 View Street
Bendigo VIC 3550
T: 03 5443 3192
F: 03 5441 3049
M: 0428 395 887

Hermitage Antiques - Geelong Wintergarden
51 McKillop Street
Geelong VIC 3220
T: 03 5222 3193
F: 03 5222 2240
M: 0409 658 738
E: metzger@hermitageantiques.com.au
www.hermitageantiques.com.au

High on Music
109 High Street
Kangaroo Flat (Bendigo) VIC 3555
T: 03 5447 2441
M: 0403 742 285
E: highonmusic@aapt.net.au
www.highonmusic.com

How Bazaar
310 Melbourne Rd
North Geelong VIC 3215
T: 03 5278 5453
F: 0418 510 977 Peter
M: 0437 420 725
E: howbazaar@aapt.net.au

Hurnall's Antiques & Decorative Arts
691 High Street
East Prahran VIC 3181
T: 03 9510 3754
F: 03 9510 3754
M: 0407 831 424
E: marvinhurnall@yahoo.com.au

I.S. Wright
1st Floor, 208 Sturt Street
Ballarat VIC 3350
T: 03 5332 3856
F: 03 5331 6426
E: ausnumis@netconnect.com.au
www.iswright.com.au

Ian's Cards
By Appointment, VIC
T: 03 9555 1673

Image Objex
By Appointment, VIC
T: 03 9406 6544
E: info@thesecondhandshop.com.au
www.thesecondhandshop.com.au

Imogene Antique & Contemporary Jewellery
Roy's Antiques
410 Queens Pde
Fitzroy North VIC 3068
T: 03 9569 5391
F: 03 9569 5395
M: 0412 195 964
E: imogene@imogene.com.au
www.imogene.com.au

Industria
202 Gertrude Street
Fitzroy VIC 3065
T: 03 9417 1117
F: 03 5983 2749
M: 0419 842 198
E: maxwatts@optusnet.com.au

Ivanhoe Collectibles Corner
231 Upper Heidelberg Rd
Ivanhoe VIC 3079
T: 03 9497 1935

Jack Maas
Tyabb Packing House Antiques
14 Mornington & Tyabb Rodds
Tyabb VIC 3914
T: 03 5978 8332
E: info@tyabbpackinghouseantiques.com.au
www.tyabbpackinghouseantiques.com.au

Jack Ross Antiques
Shop 20, Tyabb Packing House
1A & 18A Mornington & Tyabb Roads
Tyabb VIC 3913
T: 03 5977 4414
F: 03 5977 3216

Jan Johannesen
18 Hopgood Place
Barwon Heads VIC 3227
T: 03 5254 1184
M: 0402 159 983

Jeremy's Australiana
By Appointment, VIC
T: 03 5941 8884
M: 0438 197 193
E: jeremysdifferentstrokes@hotmail.com

Kaleidoscope Antiques
943 High Street
Armadale VIC 3143
T: 03 9824 8302
F: 03 9822 4315
M: 0418 300 482
E: antiquescentre@bigpond.com
www.antiquescentreonline.com

Karlia Rose Garden Antiques & Collectables
500 Portarlington Rd
Moolap, Geelong VIC 3221
T: 03 5250 1380
F: 03 5250 1380
M: 0416 285 099

Kenny's Antiques
53-55 Pakington Street
Geelong West VIC 3215
T: 03 5278 6110
M: 0409 960 041

Kilbarron Antiques and Collectables
PO Box 5068 Laburnum
Blackburn VIC 3130
T: 03 9878 1321/8
F: 03 9878 1328
M: 0417 392 110
E: kilbarro@bigpond.net.au
www.kilbarron.com.au

Kingston Antiques
379 St Georges Road
North Fitzroy VIC 3068
T: 03 9481 1307

Lauraine Diggins Fine Art
5 Malakoff Street
North Caulfield VIC 3161
T: 03 9509 9855
F: 03 9509 4549
E: ausart@diggins.com.au
www.diggins.com.au

Le Contraste
83 Chapel Street
Windsor VIC 3181
T: 03 9529 6911
M: 0439 732 006
E: contrast@bigpond.net.au

Licorice Pie Records
249A High Street
Prahran VIC 3181
T: 03 9510 4600
M: 0438 003 990
E: david@licoricepie.com

Lydiard Furniture & Antiques
205 Lydiard Street North
Ballarat VIC 3350
T: 03 5332 6841
M: 0427 348 917

M J Durand
PO Box 531
Templestowe VIC 3106
M: 0400 873 128

Malvern Antique Market
1008 High Street
Armadale VIC 3143
T: 03 9509 6337
F: 03 9572 2901
M: 0418 144 299
E: malvernantiquemarket@hotmail.com

Marsteen Collectables
By Appointment, VIC
T: 03 5229 6402
F: 03 5224 2008

Martin of Melbourne - Fine Jewels
529 High Street
East Prahran VIC 3181
T: 03 9533 6155
F: 03 9533 6199
E: info@martinofmelbourne.com.au
www.martinofmelbourne.com.au

Mary Titchener Antique Jewels
35 Toorak Road
South Yarra VIC 3141
T: 03 9867 4100
F: 03 9867 4100
E: marytitchener@bigpond.com

Maryborough Station Antique Emporium
Railway Station
Maryborough VIC 3465
T: 03 5461 4683
F: 03 5460 4988
E: stantique@iinet.net.au
www.stationantiques.com

Melbourne Vintage Pens
Armadale Antique Centre
1147 High Street
Armadale VIC 3143
T: 03 9891 6315
F: 03 9855 9671
M: 0419 382 547
E: pford@vintagepens.com.au
www.vintagepens.com.au

Memorabilia on Parade
Cnr Alexandra Pde & Wellington St
Clifton Hill VIC 3068
T: 03 9481 3342
M: 0414 659 759
E: camdoyle@alphalink.com.au

Mentone Beach Antiques Centre
68 Beach Road
Mentone VIC 3194
T: 03 9583 3422
M: 0414 166 914
E: frenchheri@froggy.com.au

Miguel Meirelles Antiques
1379 Malvern Road
Malvern VIC 3144
T: 03 9822 6886
F: 03 9822 6825
M: 0419 009 890
ww.meirelles.com.au

Mondo Trasho
387 Johnston Street
Abbotsford VIC 3067
T: 03 9486 9595
M: 0438 528 022
E: contact@mondotrasho.com.au
www.mondotrasho.com.au

Moustache Vintage Clothing
124 Gertrude St
Fitzroy VIC 3065
T: 03 9417 7637
M: 0401 353 268
E: agerngross@hotmail.com
www.moustachevintage.com.au

Mt Dandenong Antique Centre
1552 Mt Dandenong Tourist Road
Olinda VIC 3788
T: 03 9751 1138
F: 03 9751 2037
M: 0425 730 124
E: mdac@alphalink.com.au

Neville Beechey Antiques
208-210 Murray Street
Colac Vic 3250
T: 03 5231 5738
F: 03 5231 6238
M: 0418 523 538
E: antiquesand furniture@mail.com

Newlyn Antiques & Cottage Garden Nursery
2851 Midland Highway
Newlyn VIC 3364
T: 03 5345 7458
E: newlynantiques@netconnect.com.au

Newport Temple Antiques
405 Melbourne Road
Newport VIC 3015
T: 03 9391 3381
www.newporttempleantiques.com

Nextonix
162-164 Gertrude Street
Fitzroy VIC 3065
T: 03 9417 1296
M: 0410 251 934

Patti K Temporary Interiors
By Appointment, VIC
M: 0407 658 608
E: pattikinteriors@hotmail.com

Pearl Rose
By Appointment, VIC
T: 03 9585 6567
M: 0428 394 249
E: pearlrose@bigpond.com

Peter French Antiques
376 Hampton Street
Hampton VIC 3188
T: 03 9598 8343
M: 0419 134 051

Plasma
92 High Street
Prahran VIC 3181
T: 03 9525 1271
F: 03 9525 1271
M: 0414 339 001
E: dean@plasmafurniture.com.au
www.plasmafurniture.com.au

Prestige Philately
PO Box 126
Belgrave VIC 3160
T: 03 9754 7666
F: 03 9754 7677
E: info@prestigephilately.com
www.prestigephilately.com

Prism Original Lighting
By Appointment, VIC
T: 03 9885 8762
M: 0417 332 435
E: cturner@bigpond.net.au

Quality Records
263 Glenferrie Road
Malvern VIC 3144
T: 03 9500 9902
F: 03 9500 9902
www.qualityrecords.com.au

Rare Memorabilia Gallery
23 Cookson Street
Camberwell VIC 3124
T: 03 9882 0882
www.rareonline.net

Rathdowne Antiques
310 Rathdowne Street
Carlton North VIC 3054
T: 03 9347 1906
M: 0431 626 454

Regent Secondhand
692 High Street
Regent VIC 3073
T: 03 9471 1818
M: 0411 255 776

Resurrection Radio
203 High Street
Ashburton VIC 3147
T: 03 9813 8731
F: 03 9813 8145
E: resradio@ozemail.com.au
www.resurrectionradio.com.au

Retro Active
307 High Street
Northcote VIC 3070
T: 03 9489 4566
M: 0411 096 367
E: retroactive1@optusnet.com.au
www.antique-art.com.au/gallery/dealers/retroact

Retro Relics
53 Humffray Street North
Ballarat VIC 3350
T: 03 5331 6236
M: 0408 329 131

Robyn's Nest
By Appointment, VIC
M: 0417 241 772

Roy's Antiques Pty Ltd
410 Queens Parade
North Fitzroy VIC 3068
T: 03 9489 8467
F: 03 9489 8467
E: mail@roys-antiques.com.au
www.roys-antiques.com.au

Ruth Howlett Collectables
44 Brooke Street
Smythesdale VIC 3351
T: 03 5342 8186

Rutherford Fine Jewellery & Antique Silver
182 Collins St
Melbourne VIC 3000
T: 03 9650 7878
F: 03 9654 1832
E: info@rutherford.com.au
www.rutherford.com.au

Savers
330 Sydney Road
Brunswick VIC 3056
T: 03 9381 2393
F: 03 9381 2595

Scheherazade Antiques
PO Box 2340
Templestowe Heights VIC 3107
T: 03 9850 5623
M: 0408 583 515
E: scherant@optusnet.com.au

Seagull Antiques
By Appointment, VIC
T: 03 5254 1044
F: 03 5254 1044
M: 0402 352 489
E: robopage@yahoo.com.au

Seams Old Emporium
Argyle House
75 High Street
Maldon VIC 3463
T: 03 5468 7226
F: 03 5468 7229
M: 0408 380 524
E: gladrags@bigpond.com.au
www.gladrags.com.au

Seanic Antiques
419 Melbourne Road
Newport VIC 3015
T: 03 9391 6134
F: 03 9391 6134
M: 0418 326 455
E: seanicantiques@ozemail.com.au
www.antique-art.com.au/seanic.htm

Serendipity - Preston
497 Plenty Road
Preston VIC 3072
T: 03 9471 1430
F: 03 9471 1430
M: 0411 599 448
E: serentipity.ctore@optusnet.com

Shag
130 Chapel Street
Windsor VIC 3181
T: 03 9510 8817

Shappere
64 Chapel Street
Windsor VIC 3183
T: 03 9533 2006
F: 03 9882 8548
M: 0409 237 073
E: shappere@yahoo.com.au

Step Back Antiques
103 Burwood Road, Hawthorn VIC 3122
T: 03 9815 0635
F: 03 9645 7300
M: 0418 334 475

Stumpy Gully Antiques
1546 Frankston/Flinders Road
Tyabb VIC 3913
T: 03 5977 4169

Tarlo & Graham
60 Chapel Street
Windsor VIC 3181
T: 03 9521 2221
M: 0419 560 007
E: targra@bigpond.net.au

Terry & Noi
By Appointment, VIC
T: 03 9471 0404
M: 0421 568 692

The Botanic Ark
147 Copelands Road
Warragul VIC 3820
T: 03 5623 5268

The Bottom Drawer Antique Centre
545 Mornington Tyabb Road
Moorooduc VIC 3933
T: 03 5978 8677
E: sales@thebottomdrawer.com.au
www.thebottomdrawer.com.au

The Colonial Attic Antiques
145 Hudson Road
Spotswood Vic 3015
T: 03 9399 1142
M: 0425 759 379
E: colonialantiques@fastmail.fm

The Junk Company
583 Elizabeth Street
Melbourne VIC 3000
T: 03 9328 8121
M: 0417 032 829
E: thejunkcompany@hotmail.com
www.thejunkcompany.com

The Mill Markets
3 Mackey Street
North Geelong VIC 3215
T: 03 5278 9989
F: 03 5278 9929
E: iballis@ozemail.com.au
www.millmarkets.com.au

The Restorers Barn
129-133 Mostyn Street
Castlemaine VIC 3450
T: 03 5470 5669
M: 0407 879 270
E: shop@restorersbarn.com.au
www.restorersbarn.com.au

The Rustic Rose
38 Victoria Road
Loch Vic 3945
T: 03 5659 4445
M: 0407 594 445
E: therusticrose@dcsi.net.au

The Wool Exchange Geelong
44 Corio Street
Geelong VIC 3550
T: 03 5278 9989

Three Quarters 20th C Furnishings
128 Gertrude Street
Fitzroy VIC 3065
T: 03 9419 7736
F: 03 9372 9755
M: 0431 207 329
E: geeway@alphalink.com.au

Tongue & Groove
84 Smith St, Collingwood VIC 3066
T: 03 9416 0349
F: 03 9416 0549
M: 0409 161 454
E: info@tongueandgroove.com.au
www.tongueandgrove.com.au

Traffic Developments Pty Ltd
11 Regent St
Prahran VIC 3181
T: 03 9521 2522
F: 03 9521 2944
E: traffic@bigpond.net.au

Transference Antiques & Decor
465 Hampton Street
Hampton VIC 3188
T: 03 9597 0471
F: 03 9521 6741
M: 0408 059 947
E: transference@primus.com.au
www.transferencepl.com.au

Trinkets & Treasures
PO Box 590
Northcote VIC 3070
T: 03 9481 1941
F: 03 9481 1941
M: 0438 207 680
E: grantlb@bigpond.net.au

Tyabb Grainstore
14 Mornington Tyabb Road
Tyabb VIC 3913
T: 03 5977 3042
E: tyabbgrainstor@pacific.net

Tyabb Hay Shed
14A Mornington/Tyabb Road
Tyabb VIC 3913
T: 03 5977 3533
M: 0419 572 768

Tyabb Packing House
14A Mornington Tyabb Road
Tyabb VIC 3913
T: 03 5977 4414
F: 03 5977 3216
www.tyabbpackinghouse.com.au

Unique & Antique
PO Box 453
Hastings VIC 3915
F: 03 9766 4394
M: 0415 322 464
E: kyltyler1@optusnet.com.au

Vintage Posters Only
1158 High Street
Armadale VIC 3143
T: 03 9509 4562
F: 03 9509 4562
M: 0419 588 423
www.vintageposters.com.au

Virtanen Antiques
933 High Street
Armadale VIC 3143
T: 03 9822 7879
F: 03 9822 9097
M: 0412 125 173
E: sharen.virtanen@bigpond.com
www.virtanen-antiques.com

Wendy Morrison Antiques
Tyabb Packing House Antiques
14 Mornington Tyabb Road
Tyabb VIC 3914
T: 03 5977 4414
F: 03 5977 3216
E: info@tyabbpackinghouseantiques.com.au
www.tyabbpackinghouseantiques.com.au

Western District Antique Centre
64 Thompson Street
Hamilton VIC 3300
T: 03 5572 2516

Womango
47 Chapel Street
Windsor VIC 3181
T: 03 9533 6650
M: 0410 750 310

Wooden Pew Antiques
16 Mornington - Tyabb Road, Tyabb VIC 3913
T: 03 5977 4666
E: sales@woodenpew.com.au
www.woodenpew.com.au

Yanda Aboriginal Art Melbourne
731-735 High Street
Armadale VIC 3143
T: 03 9576 1813
F: 03 9576 1913
M: 0412 740 477
E: kit@yandaaboriginalart.com
www.yandaaboriginalart.com

Yarra Valley Antique Centre
8 Bell Street
Yarra Glen VIC 3775
T: 03 9730 1911
M: 0407 689 609

WESTERN AUSTRALIA

Antiques & Heirlooms
Shop 43 London Court
Hay St
Perth WA 6000
T: 08 9325 4242
F: 08 9244 3657
M: 0408 095 123
E: kuper@hotlinks.net.au

Ardeco Antiques & Collectables
84 Hampton Rd
Fremantle WA 6160
T: 08 9433 1015
F: 08 9331 6900
M: 0412 356 966

Carillon Antiques
Shop 39a Carillon City
Hay Street
Perth WA 6000
T: 08 9322 3838
F: 08 9244 3657
M: 0408 095 123
E: kuper@hotlinks.net.au

Colonial Antiques & Tea House
258 South Terrace
Cnr Silver Street
South Fremantle WA 6162
T: 08 9336 1288
F: 08 9331 6900
M: 0412 356 966
E: colonialantiques@iinet.net.au

Deco Down Under
24 Parade Street
Albany WA 6330
T: 08 9842 1974
F: 08 9842 9545
M: 0417 928 210
E: walters@decodownunder.com
www.decodownunder.com

Dr Russell's Emporium
476 Beaufort Street
Mt Lawley, Highgate WA 6003
T: 08 9328 8857
M: 0409 105 270
E: drrussellsemp@hotmail.com

Esmerelda's Curios
PO Box 47
Darlington WA 6070
M: 0419 464 245
E: esmerelda@ozemail.com.au

frhapsody
PO Box 118
Inglewood WA 6932
T: 08 9370 2056
E: frhapsody@upnaway.com
stores.ebay.com.au/frhapsody

Goodwood House Antiques
84-88 Goodwood Parade
Burswood WA 6100
T: 08 9361 6368
F: 08 9470 5364
E: goodwood@iinet.net.au
www.goodwoodhouseantiques.net.au

Hollywood Antiques
13 Hampden Road
Nedlands WA 6009
T: 08 6389 2559
F: 08 9386 3957
M: 0414 242 659

John Burridge Military Antiques
91 Shenton Road
Swanbourne WA 6010
T: 08 9384 1218
F: 08 9385 2611
E: john@jbma.com.au
www.jbma.com.au

Military Antiques Warehouse
21 Tulloch Way
Canning Vale WA 6155
M: 0400 078 937
www.militaryantiqueswarehouse.com.au

Perth Antiques
126 Murray St
Perth WA 6014
T: 08 9325 7700
F: 08 9325 7700

Shenton Park Antiques
197 Onslow Road
Shenton Park WA 6008
T: 08 9382 3180
F: 08 9382 4159
M: 0404 088 945

ShopAtNortham
PO Box 214
Mt Hawthorn WA 6915
T: 08 9622 1318
F: 08 9472 5288
M: 0419 985 746 Richard
E: info@shopatnortham.com.au

Steven Sher Antiques
Stall 30 Fremantle Markets
South Terrace
Fremantle WA 6160
T: 08 9433 5441
M: 0414 413 258
E: stevensher@iinet.net.au
www.trocadero.com/hensteeth/

The Rare Coin Company
12 Sanford Road
Albany WA 6330
T: 08 9842 50221800 641
F: 08 9842 1702
E: coindeal@bigpond.com
www.rarfecoin.com.au

Timeless Treasures
222 Scarborough Beach Road
Mount Hawthorn WA 6016
T: 08 9443 8244

Trinity Antiques
Shop 205 Trinity Arcade
72 St George's Terrace
Perth WA 6000
T: 08 9321 8321
F: 08 9321 6545

Willi - The Clockman
2 Bridgwood Road
Lesmurdie WA 6076
T: 08 9291 7736
M: 0429 335 007

Wisma Antik
44 Kathleen Street
Trigg WA 6029
T: 08 9447 3276
F: 08 9447 3276
M: 0422 272 278
E: antiques@wisma.com.au
www.wisma.com.au

New Zealand

Albany Hill Cottage
310 Main Highway
Albany 17RD3 New Zealand
T: 09 415 9619
F: 09 415 9609
M: 0274 941 116
www.albanyantiquesnz.com

Alexandra Antiques
Tirau Antique Centre
7 Hillcrest Steet
Tirau New Zealand
T: 07 871 9625
M: 021 152 0925
E: tony.hodgson@xtra.co.nz

Amour Antiques & Collectables
By Appointment, New Zealand
T: 09 525 5567
M: 021 270 4353

Anthea's Antiques Ltd
333 Remuera Rd
Remuera, Auckland New Zealand
T: 64 9 520 1092
F: 64 9 524 7695

Anticus Antiques
8 Cass Street
Russell, Bay of Islands New Zealand 255
T: 09 403 8000
F: 09 403 8000
M: 0256 161 498
E: anticus@slingshot.co.nz
www.anticusantiques.com

Antiques & Curiosities
Shop 4, 176 Great South Road
Remuera, Auckland New Zealand
T: 09 524 2344
F: 09 524 2346
M: 0274 842 122
E: fenellas@xtra.co.nz

Antiques & Decorator Items
PO Box 22010
Christchurch New Zealand
T: 03 374 2180
M: 021 5858 72

Antiques in Thames
638 Pollen Street
Thames New Zealand
T: 07 868 7541
F: 07 868 9288
www.antiquesthames.co.nz

Antiques On Victoria
89a Victoria Street
Cambridge New Zealand 2351
T: 07 823 4501
F: 07 823 4501
M: 0212 118 754

Ascot Collectables
704 Tay St
Invercargill New Zealand
T: 03 217 4276

Auburn Antiques
83 Great South Road
Remuera New Zealand
T: 09 520 1962

Bakelite Belle.com
By Appointment, New Zealand
T: 07 828 4626
E: www.bakelitebelle.com

Banks Peninsula Antiques
Private Bag 2001
Akaroa New Zealand 8161
T: 03 304 7172
M: 0274 372 178
E: erik.russell@xtra.co.nz

Best Antiques & Collectables
By Appointment, New Zealand
T: 03 389 4099
M: 0274 382 273
E: torea@netaccess.co.nz

Bonham's
630 Victoria Street
Hamilton New Zealand
T: 07 839 4953
F: 07 838 0080
M: 025 315 345
E: karen@antiques-nz.co.nz
www.bonhams.co.nz

Bulls Antiques & Collectables
High Street
Bulls New Zealand 0
T: 06 322 1518
F: 06 322 1518
M: 0274 428 499
E: bullsant@xtra.co.nz

Camelot Antiques
PO Box 268
Huntly, Waikato New Zealand
T: 07 828 9914
F: 07 828 9679
M: 0274 933 102
E: alan@huntly.net.nz
www.huntly.net.nz

Casa Manana Antiques & Collectables
5B Casabella
307 Barton Street
Hamilton New Zealand
T: 07 839 1440
F: 07 839 1871
E: casamanana@xtra.co.nz

Collectamania
118 Great South Road
Ohaupo, Waikato New Zealand 3803
T: 07 823 8225
M: 027 211 9446
E: janedaly@xtra.co.nz

Colonial Antiques
By Appointment, New Zealand
T: 07 544 3457
M: 027 497 6963

Colonial Heritage Antiques Ltd
Central Court 40 Duke Street, Cambridge New Zealand
T: 07 827 4211
F: 07 827 4024
M: 021 996 919
E: sheldrick@colonialheritage.co.nz

Country Antiques
489 Manukau Road
Epsom, Auckland New Zealand
T: 09 630 5252
F: 09 630 5252
M: 025 851 617
E: grovers@xtra.co.nz

Country Charm Antiques
State Highway 2
Clareville, Carterton New Zealand
T: 06 379 7929
F: 06 379 7930
M: 0274 456 409
E: cameron@wise.net.nz
www.country-charm.co.nz

Deans Antiques
378 Princes St
Dunedin New Zealand 9016
T: 03 470 1964
M: 021 033 2232
E: deansantiques@hotmail.com

Decollectables
72 Charlemont St
Ranfurly New Zealand
T: 03 444 9010
F: A/H 03 444 9196
M: 027 221 1692
E: ejmc@actrix.co.nz
www.ruralartdeco.co.nz

Diane Akers
By Appointment, New Zealand
T: 09 443 1797
M: 021 609 399
E: finechinadi@ihug.co.nz

Fendalton Antiques
203 Fendalton Rd
Fendalton, Christchurch New Zealand
T: 03 351 7460

Gales Antiques
385 Princes St
Dunedin New Zealand
T: 03 477 6023
F: 03 477 8828
E: hello@gales.co.nz
www.gales.co.nz

Glenis Parker
By Appointment, New Zealand
T: 09 445 2206
F: 096 445 2243
M: 027 482 6730
E: parkerx4@ihug.co,nz

Gregory's of Greerton
143 Greerton Road
Tauranga New Zealand
T: 07 578 9696

Hubbers Emporium
68 Dee St
Invercargill New Zealand
T: 03 218 8737
F: 03 230 4643
E: hubberantiques@xtra.co.nz

Ikon Antiques
462 Colombo Street
Sydenham, Christchurch New Zealand
T: 03 366 9330
M: 027 220 7844
E: ikonantiques@xtra.co.nz

In Vogue Costumes & Collectables
40 Rosemont Road
Waihi, Waikato New Zealand 3041
T: 07 863 9366
M: 0211 465 525
E: invogue@clear.net.nz
www.invogue.co.nz

John Varney
By Appointment, New Zealand
T: 09 299 8356
M: 021 654 800

Kelmscott House Antiques
Tirau Antique Centre
7 Hillcrest Street
Tirau New Zealand
T: 07 8719 819
M: 0211 390 377
E: apps@xtra.co.nz

Lord Ponsonby Antiques
84-86 Ponsonby Road
Cnr Williamson Avenue
Auckland New Zealand
T: 09 376 6463
F: 09 376 6463

Maison Jolie
By Appointment, New Zealand
T: 09 520 3858
E: maisonjolie@paradise.net.nz

Maxine's Collectibles
180 Shakespeare St
Cambridge New Zealand
T: 02 7478 9877
F: 02 7827 7111
E: maxine.robertson@xtra.co.nz

Memory Lane
356 Tinakori Road
Thorndow, Wellington New Zealand
T: 04 499 2666
E: memory.lane@paradise.net.nz

Middle Earth Antiques
227 Manchester St
Christchurch New Zealand
T: 03 366 7825
F: 03 377 6667
M: 027 563 4120
E: robynne.b@xtra.co.nz

Moa Extinct Stuff
Right Up My Alley
Volcom Lane
Raglan New Zealand 2051
T: 07 825 7004
F: 07 825 7000
M: 0272 899 381
E: ruma1@xtra.co.nz
www.ruma.co.nz

Mr Pickwicks
240 Colombo Street Beckenham
Christchurch New Zealand
T: 03 337 5776
F: 03 337 5780
E: mrpickwicks@paradise.net.nz
www.mtpickwicks.co.nz

Old & Past Antiques & Collectables
20 Westminster St
St Albans, Christchurch New Zealand
T: 043 355 0590

Oxford Court Antiques Centre
'Top of The Hill'
1 Hillcrest Street
Tirau New Zealand
T: 07 883 1720
F: 07 833 1721
E: oxfordcourt@msn.com

Peachgrove Antiques
24 Peachgrove Road
Hamilton New Zealand
T: 07 856 9976
M: 025 987 029
E: peach.grove@xtra.co.nz

Pleasant Place Antiques
By Appointment, New Zealand
T: 07 377 1137
M: 0274 418 480
E: mau.john@xtra.co.nz

Queens Gardens Antique Centre
16 Queens Gardens
Dunedin New Zealand
T: 03 474 0222
E: r.a.proctpr@xtra.co.nz
www.antiquesatqueensgardens.co.nz

Right Up My Alley
Volcom Lane
Raglan New Zealand 2051
T: 07 825 7004
F: 07 825 7000
E: ruma1@xtra.co.nz
www.ruma.co.nz

Shand's Emposium
88 Hereford Street
Christchurch New Zealand
T: 03 366 5442
M: 021 499 015
E: lindonw@paradise.net.nz

Strangely Familiar
348a Tinakori Road
Thorndon, Wellington New Zealand
T: 04 472 3400
F: 04 472 3400
M: 0274 504 090
E: rodney.dormer@xtra.co.nz

Sue Todd Antiques Collectables
401 Princes St
Dunedin New Zealand
T: 03 477 7547
M: 027 314 1717
sue-todd-dolls.co.nz

The Curiosity Shoppe
5 Charlemont Street East
Ranfurly
Central Otago New Zealand
T: 03 444 9015
F: 03 444 9757
E: johnandmarieeagles@xtra.co.nz

The Modern Miss
141 High St
Dunedin New Zealand
T: 03 479 0031
M: 0211 186 740
E: violetfaigan@yahoo.co.nz

The Wooden Rose
Old Post Office
143 Williams St
Kaiapoi, Christchurch New Zealand
T: 03 327 2071

Tinakori Antiques
291A Tinakori Road
Wellington New Zealand
T: 04 472 7043
F: 04 472 7043
E: jfyson@paradise.net.nz

Tirau Antique Centre
7 Hillcrest Street
Turau New Zealand
T: 07 871 9625

Trevor & Pam Plumbly
74 Princess Street
Dunedin New Zealand
T: 03 477 0574
M: 021 448 200
E: books@trevorplumbly.co.nz
www.trevorplumbly.co.nz

Waterfords of Mangaweka Village
By Appointment, New Zealand
T: 06 382 5886

INDEX